Postmodernism and Its Critics

Postmodernism and Its Critics

John McGowan

CORNELL UNIVERSITY PRESS

Ithaca and London

First published 1991 by Cornell University Press.

International Standard Book Number 0-8014-2494-1 (cloth)
International Standard Book Number 0-8014-9738-8 (paper)
Library of Congress Catalog Card Number 90-55758

Printed in the United States of America

*Librarians: Library of Congress cataloging information
appears on the last page of the book.*

⊗The paper in this book meets the minimum requirements of
the American National Standard for Information Sciences—Permanence
of Paper for Printed Library Materials, ANSI Z39.48-1984.

7-16-92

*In memory of my
ever-generous father*

Contents

Preface   ix

1   Toward a Definition of Postmodernism   1

     Modernity and Romanticism 3
     Postmodernism 12

2   Postmodernism's Precursors   31

     Kant: Modernity and Liberal Humanism 31
     Hegel and the Relational Rule of the Dialectic 43
     Marx: Power versus Freedom 61
     Nietzsche: Ironist Theory and Negative Freedom 70

3   The Problem of Freedom in Postmodern Theory   89

     Derrida and the Possibility of the Other 89
     Foucault and the Ethos of Permanent Critique 121
     The Literary Left: Jameson, Eagleton, Said 145
     Postmodern Pragmatism 180

4   Positive Freedom and the Recovery of the Political   211

     Toward a Postliberal Democracy 212
     Recognition 217
     Semiautonomy Again 223

Social Norms and the Social Whole 230
Social Reproduction in the Context of Legitimacy 237
Social and Individual Identity 242
Negative Freedom, Theory, and Modernity 248
Power 252
Positive Freedom and the Recovery of the Political 262
What's an Intellectual to Do? 274

Works Cited   281

Index   291

Preface

Everyone begins the discussion of postmodernism by asking what the word could possibly mean. This book attempts to answer that question by examining the term's use to designate a specific form of cultural critique that has become increasingly conspicuous in the academy since about 1975. This critique is resolutely antifoundationalist—eschewing all appeals to ontological or epistemological or ethical absolutes—while also proclaiming itself resolutely radical in its commitment to the transformation of the existing Western social order. The four most prominent variants of postmodern theory are poststructuralism, the new Marxism, neopragmatism, and feminism. Prudence and cowardice have led me to attempt an account of only the first three in this (already long enough) book; the body (significant image) of feminist work is so vast and the phrasing of its concerns different enough from, although obviously related to, the issues I pursue that I deemed it foolhardy to try to fit that work into the general schema offered here. That choice became doubly prudent once I had decided that I could discuss the other three discourses only if I considered their relation to four nineteenth-century German forefathers: Kant, Hegel, Marx, and Nietzsche. Needless to say, the crucial intellectual ancestors of feminism are hardly this German quartet; the story of feminism's rewriting of its own traditions to adopt its current postmodern stances would be quite different.

What this book offers, then, is an attempt to characterize poststructuralism (represented here by Jacques Derrida and Michel Foucault), contemporary Marxism (Fredric Jameson, Terry Eagleton, and Edward Said), and neopragmatism (Jean-François Lyotard and Richard Rorty) in a way that highlights why, despite their many differences, they all deserve to be called postmodern. I may appear to be putting the cart before the horse. One of the reasons that *postmodernism* has been so slippery a term is that we don't know whether it names the kind of theorizing now rampant in the academy, the kind of architecture now cluttering our downtowns, and the kind of novels being written by Salman Rushdie, Gabriel García Márquez, and Angela Carter, or whether it names the social and historical matrix within which and because of which these particular cultural phenemona flourish. My title suggests that there is something called *postmodernism* and there are writers who are critical of that something, but in fact general usage now calls those very writers postmodern, as if they were identical with the cultural form they hope to oppose. I cannot claim to undo this Gordian knot. I leave pretty much unexamined the issue of whether some larger social change explains the appearance of new strategies for intellectual work and focus instead on the new strategies themselves. I do not know whether we have entered an age sufficiently different from earlier historical periods to justify a brand new name, but I am confident that contemporary intellectuals' attitudes toward their work and their understanding of how that work might potentially serve to maintain or transform society has changed. The oppositional strategies of the first part of the twentieth century no longer seem effective to contemporary radicals. Much has been made of postmodern theory's negative side—its aggressive dissolution of all certainties and its suspicious relation to the verities of humanism and the Western philosophical tradition—while its positive side—the attempt to forge effective strategies for intervention in the social—has attracted less attention. I attempt to focus on that positive side here and have posed the issue in terms of freedom: What kinds of freedom are possible in the contemporary West, and what can intellectuals do to achieve the kinds of freedom they profess to desire?

Postmodern theory, I argue, is driven by the simultaneous fear that a monolithic social order shapes contemporary life and hope that a strategy for preserving pluralism (difference) can be found. My fundamental polemical point (which shapes the story I tell about how and why postmodern theorists come to take the positions they do) is that the association of freedom with difference is too flimsy a notion on which to build a just society. We need a stronger, more positive version of freedom—one that includes norms to which citizens, institutions, and practices are responsive—if we want to achieve the effects of freedom and pluralism that postmodern theorists desire. My critique of postmodern criticism is obviously indebted to Jürgen Habermas, and in certain ways this book is another entrant in the continuing debate between Habermas and the poststructuralists, a debate in which Habermas's *The Philosophical Discourse of Modernity* is the key text. Like Habermas, I am interested in teasing out those places in postmodern theory where it relies on more positive notions of freedom and of norms and of social agreement than it is willing to acknowledge openly.

I am, however, much more willing than Habermas to accept the postmoderns' repudiation of universals, their abandonment of appeals to reason, and their insistence that modernist strategies are ineffective at best and counterproductive at worst. I am also much more interested in thinking through what selfhood could possibly mean once we grant the cogency of postmodern accounts of the subject's constitution by social orders and codes. For these reasons, I end this book by outlining at some length a model of the social that is neither postmodernist nor Habermasian—although indebted to both sides in the current debate. I believe my account of the subject's immersion in a social whole that is differentiated into semiautonomous spheres offers a better way to think about the conditions of political action and about how to protect and promote the pluralistic democracy that every contemporary critic—whether liberal, poststructuralist, leftist, or feminist—presents as an ideal. I hesitate in today's highly charged polemical atmosphere to name the writers to whom my model is indebted, lest some readers find such a list reason to stop reading right here, but my debt to the work of Hegel, Charles Taylor, Charles Altieri, Chantal Mouffe, Pierre Bourdieu, Peter Dews, Anthony Giddens, C. B. Macpherson, and Samuel Bowles and Herbert Gintis will become obvious soon enough to those who push ahead.

This book owes its existence to the National Endowment for the Humanities fellowship that gave me the time to write it. An earlier, unpaid leave from the Eastman School of Music of the University of Rochester allowed me to do much of the background reading that made my grant year so productive. The administration and my colleagues at Eastman—especially Jon Baldo, Doug Dempster, Tom Donnan, Ruth Gross, Hans Kellner, Aimée Israel-Pelletier, and David Roberts—have provided the kind of congenial intellectual community that many of us entered academic life in hopes of finding. I was also blessed while writing this book with simultaneous membership in the academic community of Hobart and William Smith Colleges. Scott Brophy, Randi Davenport, José DeVinck, Susan Henking, Martin Kelly, Dunbar Moodie, Lee Quinby, and Linda Robertson provided me at various times with everything from a roof over my head to use of computers to engaging intellectual debate (especially about Foucault, my section on whom owes much to our reading group) during my year in Geneva. For general support and encouragement, I thank Reid Barbour, Robert Boyers, Daniel Hayes, and my family.

Earlier stumblings toward the overview of postmodernism presented in Chapter 1 were given as papers at the 1986 MLA convention and at conferences on postmodernism at Hofstra University and Syracuse University, where I benefited from the interest and comments of my auditors. I have also retained a sentence or two from my first published thoughts on this topic; my thanks to Willard Spiegelman and Betsey McDougall of *Southwest Review* for their hospitality to that essay. The book itself incorporates revisions suggested by three anonymous readers for Cornell University Press and by John Kucich (greater love than this no man hath, to read a six-hundred-page manuscript for a friend). Charles Altieri requires my special thanks, both because he has so faithfully supported my work since I was a graduate student at Buffalo and because his own work has had such a formative influence on my own thinking; I always somewhat dread rereading any of Charlie's writings, since I inevitably find out that what I thought I had discovered last week, I had actually read in his work five years ago and had come only recently to understand and assimilate.

What many will deem the mindless optimism of this book's outlook can be blamed entirely on Jane and Kiernan.

JOHN MCGOWAN

Rochester, New York

Postmodernism and Its Critics

I

Toward a Definition of Postmodernism

Postmodernism refers to a distinct shift in the way that humanistic intellectuals (Alvin Gouldner's useful, if inelegant, phrase) view the relation of their cultural work to society at large.[1] The various themes, postures, and stylistic hallmarks of postmodernism can, I believe, be traced to a heightened anxiety about what impact intellectuals have on a world that appears increasingly inimical to the values promoted in the arts and in intellectual work. Of course, humanistic intellectuals since the time of the romantics have thought of themselves as distanced from and in opposition to the prevailing mores of commercial society, and have envisioned various schemes for that society's transformation. Postmodernism marks a particular despair about the possible success of these schemes along with a far-reaching search for new strategies of intervention in the dominant order. I believe that postmodernism can best be defined as a particular, if admittedly diminished, version of romantic dreams of transformation—hardly the middle age that poets in their youth would have chosen, but a despondency that is fitting all the same.

The scheme of this particular book is quite simple. The first chapter describes the general cultural problematic within which I think it is fruitful to consider the work of contemporary artists and intellectuals. Chapter 2 offers readings of Kant, Hegel, Marx, and Nietzsche that highlight their influence on postmodern writers and the relevance of their texts to the polemical position about intellectual work that I am trying to promote. Chapter 3

[1]Gouldner (1982b 4).

provides a detailed discussion of Jacques Derrida, Michel Foucault, the literary left (Fredric Jameson, Terry Eagleton, and Edward W. Said), and the neopragmatists (Jean-François Lyotard and Richard Rorty). I take these writers as representing crucial variants of postmodernism, and I attempt to indicate what they hold in common (that is, why it makes sense to think of them all as postmodern) and to suggest that they all remain tied to a notion of negative freedom that is unprofitably close to the modernist goal of autonomy. (Jameson is the exception in this regard.) Finally, I propose an alternative model of social action, one that I think is more faithful to the holistic assumptions found everywhere in postmodern thought, assumptions that appear forgotten when the postmodern writers I discuss begin to consider possible strategies of opposition to the status quo. Having the courage of these holistic models, I suggest, would lead to a much more satisfying set of strategies for intellectual work and its relation to the formation of a desirable social order. I encapsulate these strategies under the rubric of *positive freedom* and argue that the approach to positive freedom must be through a position that takes seriously the issue of legitimating intellectual work and social arrangements and authority. The refusal to distinguish between legitimate and illegitimate action goes hand in hand with dreams of an escape into negative freedom.

We can begin this rather long journey by identifying humanistic intellectuals as workers in the realm of culture, as (in Peter L. Berger's phrase) "occupied in the production and distribution of symbolic knowledge" (1986 67). The term *culture* is, of course, a notoriously vague one, used both to designate the social milieu in its entirety and to designate only that portion of social activity that manifests itself in the arts, in games, in festivities, and in other activities apart from the strictly economic, political, or technical/scientific. Raymond Williams attempts to demonstrate the "convergence" of these two common uses of the term by describing "culture as the *signifying system* through which necessarily (though among other means) a social order is communicated, reproduced, experienced, and explored" (1981 13). The parenthetical "among other means" suggests that society's course is hardly shaped completely by its "signifying practices," although Williams does insist that "a distinctive 'signifying system' is . . . essentially involved in *all* forms of social activity." The maintenance or transformation of, coupled with reflection upon, society's signifying patterns has traditionally been the stuff of artistic and intellectual endeavors. This fundamental orientation has become both more important and more problematic over the past two hundred years because artists and intellectuals have increasingly insisted on the centrality of culture's signifying systems to social life as a whole, while at the same time calling attention to or promoting cultural significations that the development of modern economic, political, and technical practices ignores or destroys. Thus artists and intellectuals often find themselves in the position of coming close to claiming the absolute constitutive power of signification while also bemoaning the fact that modern society marginalizes the cultural.

My use of the term *intellectuals* is meant to encompass both the artists and the critics/teachers/theorists who work in the cultural domain, because I believe they share a similar outlook and feel defensive about their activities in similar ways. Once I move beyond the generalities of this first chapter to consider more particular positions in current debates, however, I confine myself to the work of contemporary intellectuals who explicitly address issues of social theory. The institutional sites, respective traditions, and distinctive media within which artists and intellectuals work all serve to differentiate these two groups from each other. But it is no coincidence that the impetus for the postmodern reflection on social theory has come from intellectuals who, in many cases, have received their academic training in criticism of the arts. The emphasis on signifying practices within contemporary intellectual discourse is what justifies the conviction that artists, critics of the arts, and intellectuals—these last described by Cornelius Castoriadis as "those who, by their use of speech and through their explicit formulation of general ideas, have been able or are now able to attempt to have an influence on how their society evolves and on the course of history" (1988 163)—are involved in trying to work through similar issues about the relation of their particular activities to society as a whole.

MODERNITY AND ROMANTICISM

The humanistic intellectuals' social position can be understood only within the context of modernity itself, where modernity is understood as the condition in which society must legitimate itself by its own self-generated principles, without appeal to external verities, deities, authorities, or traditions. (Throughout this book, I am careful to use the term *modernity* to designate this need for self-legitimacy in the Western world during the past two to three hundred years, while reserving the term *modernism* to designate the artistic movement that stretches from, roughly, 1890 to 1945.) In Jürgen Habermas's description, "modernity can and will no longer borrow the criteria by which it takes its orientation from the models supplied by another epoch; *it has to create its normativity out of itself.* Modernity sees itself cast back upon itself without any possibility of escape" (1987a 7).

The causes for and the exact date of the emergence of modernity have been the subject of much discussion, which I here sidestep by asking for my readers' consent that almost all of the factors I am about to list were in place by 1800. From Marx's description of the transition from feudalism to capitalism through T. S. Eliot's notion of a "dissociation of sensibility" to Foucault's various versions (in *Madness and Civilization, The Order of Things,* and *Discipline and Punish*) of the great transformation into modernity, a general consensus about the occurrence of some drastic change has emerged, no matter how we continue to argue details and dates. The challenge to Catholicism by the various Protestant sects, the challenge to Eurocentrism in the discovery of radically different societies in other parts of the globe, the challenge to religion manifested in both new scientific discoveries and new economic practices, the challenge to monarchy/oligarchy in the rise of popular, democratic agitation, and the challenge to traditional patterns of social integration in changing modes of production and distribution and the growth of towns and cities all combine over a three-hundred-year period (1500–1800) to transform Europe. By the end of this period, the West has recognized, in the face of diversity and change, that it is thrown back upon itself to ground, legitimate, and make significant its own practices. Society, in Viconian fashion, is understood as the realm of human making. *Autonomy* names the new conviction that society must forge its own practices and grounds apart from any external determinants or influences.

Autonomy, however, proves an unpredictable guide, both in theory and in practice, and tracing its vicissitudes occupies much of my attention in this book. In the first place, autonomy is a major plank of humanism, with its insistence that humans can produce their lives and their social world on their own. For this reason, much postmodern work, with its antihumanist slant, has been at pains both to deny the possibility of achieving autonomy and to indicate autonomy's pernicious consequences. Second, much (perhaps everything) depends on where within the social order one locates autonomy. If, in Hegelian fashion, autonomy rests with the social order or Reason as a totality, then the actions of particular components (including individuals) within that social order will be tied to that totality. Liberalism, at the other extreme, preaches an autonomy of the individual, understood as free only when she chooses her own ends and methods for achieving those ends. In between these two extremes, we can locate the Kantian attempt to distinguish autonomous spheres of pure reason, practical reason, and judgment, or Habermas's argument that various social "systems" (particularly, the economic, the legal/administrative, and the aesthetic) within modernity separate themselves out from the social whole (the "lifeworld" that serves as the

horizon of common social interactions). These spheres develop autonomously according to their own traditions, logics, and procedures, with little
interference from other systems or from the practices of the lifeworld.[2] From
this last point of view, the battles within modernity often become struggles
among these various almost completely autonomous spheres for dominance
within the society as a whole. Artists and humanist intellectuals, working
within the aesthetic system, protest against what they deem the excessive
control of social life by either the economic or the legal/administrative
systems.

The almost simultaneous birth of romanticism with modernity can thus be
explained as a response to the social fragmentation that the new emphasis on
autonomy causes. In the simplest terms, romanticism can be characterized as
the attempt to recreate the ethical totality of society through a revitalized
mythology conveyed to the people in poetry and the other arts.[3] It would be
wrong, however, to locate romantic artists and intellectuals as the simple foes
of autonomous individuality or autonomous spheres of social activity. The
romantics, like all the other inhabitants of modernity, recognize autonomy as
liberating, and it is the variations of their responses to and attempts to use
autonomy that differentiate the various periods and movements within the
two-hundred-year history of romanticism. Postmodernism, as one phase in
that history, represents a new set of attitudes toward autonomy.

The first romantics attempted to reconstruct a social totality. Blake abhors
reason whereas Hegel enshrines it, yet both are striving to overcome what
they see as modernity's resistance to unity. These early romantics introduce
the theme of "the excluded"—a theme that, along with autonomy, has dominated artists' and humanist intellectuals' relation to society ever since. By "the
excluded" I mean those elements of human life that appear to romantic
intellectuals as insufficiently acknowledged in the societies that they inhabit.

---

[2]Chapter 6 of the second volume of *The Theory of Communicative Action* (1987c) is devoted to
"the uncoupling of system and lifeworld." Habermas describes the lifeworld as "a social a priori,"
the "vast and incalculable web of presuppositions" (1987c 131) that members of a speech
community must take for granted if they are to be able to speak to one another at all. "The
lifeworld is constitutive for mutual understanding *as such*" (1987c 126). Pierre Bourdieu's notion
of the "habitus" as the set of taken-for-granted dispositions that underlie communal life places
the same emphasis as Habermas's concept of the lifeworld on the necessity of the common
experience of an unquestioned manner of being-in-the-world at the basis of social life. "The
homogeneity of habitus is what—within the limits of the groups of agents possessing the schemes
(of production and interpretation) implied in their production—causes practices and works to be
immediately intelligible and foreseeable, and hence taken for granted. . . . 'Communication of
consciousness' [i.e., individuated, differentiated utterances] presupposes community of 'uncon-
sciouses' (i.e., of linguistic and cultural competences)" (1977 80). The notions of lifeworld and
habitus underwrite the holistic social vision I offer in this book.
[3]I am paraphrasing Habermas (1987a 88–89) here.

Lear in the storm discovers the things he has taken too little care of. The romantic artist, everywhere and continually, makes this discovery; he denounces society's indifference to and ignorance of the very values, ideas, desires, and aspirations that the artist deems important. The early romantics usually called such ignored entities "natural" and accused society of repressing an awareness of the natural, and hence real, bases of existence. Subsequent writers, culminating with the postmodern aversion to naturalist appeals, have often focused instead on society's willful ignorance of conditions or elements of existence (for example, poverty) that society's own arrangements and functioning have caused. Because artistic activity itself figures prominently among the entities that modern society is accused of slighting, romanticism can look like special pleading, but the artists have also consistently championed other endangered species. Put baldly, art since 1800 has shared a romantic ethos that manifests itself in the protest against a commercial/technocratic culture that excludes considerations beyond the cash nexus and atomistic physics from its calculus of human behavior, its use of the term *real*, and its legitimation of social organization. Whether by expanding the terms *reason* and *reality*, as Hegel does, or by insisting on the reality and significance of the irrational, as Blake does, or by indicating by-products of the cash nexus that classical liberal economic theory does not acknowledge, romantic artists and intellectuals try to bring back onto the stage of awareness entities that modernity neglects. We might rephrase this accusation as the fear that the economic sphere, developing now in the almost complete autonomy that modernity confers upon it, has come either to dominate the social whole or, even worse, to be understood as constituting in itself the social whole. Romanticism protests against this hegemony of the economic by presenting an alternative vision of the totality, a vision that it insists is more inclusive. We can identify two dominant strains within romanticism: the spiritualist strain, which favors changes in consciousness, perception, and values as the road to the desired totality, and the realist strain, which adopts more directly political and worldly methods of change. The common tendency to call the spiritualists "romantic" should not blind us to the deeper affinities between realism and romanticism; realism is recognizably a subset of the crucial romantic desire to use art to transform modernity.

Paradoxically, the romantic artist claims an autonomy for his own activities that weakens the very insistence on totality that is his starting point—a paradox that reaches its fullest development in modernism. Working within the contested field of the social, the artist feels the need to insist that his artistic vision is not answerable to the values promoted by other claimants to cultural authority. This understandable withdrawal from competing value systems can isolate the artist and jeopardize the success of his attempt to win society over to his view. By jettisoning his connection to orthodox religion or to bourgeois common sense (practical interests), the artist helps create the establishment of art as a relatively autonomous activity that Habermas describes. (The artist only helps; he is far from solely responsible, since utilitarian theories like Bentham's are actively involved in circumscribing art's proper sphere of action and influence. Thus autonomy is partly chosen and partly imposed, an ambiguity crucial to all aesthetic activity over the past two hundred years.) Practically, autonomy severs the artist from audiences attached to orthodox religion or to classical political economy; the artist as nonproductive, amoral bohemian is born. Theoretically, the artist takes up his appointed place in a now-fragmented social order whose very fragmentation his holistic vision was meant to contest. The spheres of religion, science, and bourgeois economics continue to unfold just as the artistic tradition does, with the possibility of mediating among all these traditions the site of political struggle (when one sphere attempts to dominate over the others) or of indifference (when members of a sphere pursue their own activities and ignore the activities of other spheres).

The complexity of modernism stems from its containing both the spiritualistic, religious impulses of high romanticism and the scientific, rationalistic impulses of realism while at the same time bringing to center stage the issue of art's autonomy. Modernism can never decide if it wants to occupy the fully secular and political world of modernity that realism attempts to master or if it wants to escape into some separate aesthetic realm that is more free and more pure than the world of ordinary human making. Realist novelists such as George Eliot and Zola still understood themselves as involved in the mundane political making of the world; they represented values not endorsed everywhere in that political world, but they did not view themselves as hopelessly alienated from it. Flaubert's contempt for the bourgeoisie and the later Tolstoy's retreat into moral absolutism more fully foreshadow the modernist dynamic. Modernism, in various times and at various places, rehearses all of the complaints, both of high romanticism and of realism, against modernity's commercial culture. It is impossible to tell which comes first in the heightened antibourgeois rhetoric of modernism: the total rejection of bourgeois values or the conviction that commercial culture completely ignores what artists have to say. Like all romantic artists, the modernists harbor hopes of transforming the world of modernity, but with much less belief than nineteenth-century artists/intellectuals that such acts of transformation are within their power. Modernism, in fact, offers no distinctive transformative vision of its own; instead, different modernists recycle different versions of high romanticism's synthetic visions or realism's radical political utopias. What is distinctive about modernism is its strategies of engagement with the enemy, its opting for an endless battle with the Philistines or for a complete separation from them. Doubtful whether victory can ever be won, the modernist either defiantly struggles without hope or (more usually) retreats to a barricaded world of art where he or she can work in peace and associate only with those of similar views.

The cornerstone of the modernist defiance of the dominant culture is the insistence on art's autonomy. Answerable to nothing, with no prescribed or proscribed subjects or forms, modernist art proclaims a heady freedom from traditions, from social environment, from reality itself. Yet throughout its dizzying experiments, modernism remains haunted by the scarcely repressed fear that the negative liberty it annexes to itself carries with it an inescapable impotence. Constructed oppositionally, as the negation of everything bourgeois, modernist freedom can dream whole new worlds (Joyce on the artist as God) within art but has, by virtue of its autonomy, no established route by which to make its dreams effective in the world beyond art. Postmodern art and thought have been particularly hard on the characteristic modernist strategy of retreat, arguing that this move ensured the very impotence that modernism wanted to avoid.

The modernists' embrace of autonomy reflects their obsession with purity, with their attempt to construct a realm untainted by the pettiness, brutality, compromises, and hypocrisy of bourgeois life. The modernists, we might say, choose to make themselves the "excluded" in the belief that freedom and purity are only available to those who step outside the ever-growing domain of commercial culture. To be excluded becomes a badge of honor now that the social whole is so repugnant, and the artist now devotes as much, if not more, time to the effort to remain excluded (to avoid being coopted) as she does to imagining a social whole organized on some radically different principle than enlightened pursuit of self-interest.[4] Of course the psychological costs of such exclusion are high, and postmodernism will question the inevitable self-delusions and hypocrisies that deliberately chosen postures of alienation

---

[4]The last great defender of the modernist faith is William Gass. His essay "The Death of the Author" (1985) is an elegant plea for the self-sufficiency of the text against all the interpretive strategies that would dissolve it into larger contexts. His more recent "Vicissitudes of the Avant-Garde" (1988), subtitled "In Search of a Worthy 'No,'" is as poignant a statement of the modernists' hope to achieve a noble exteriority to crass commercial culture as one is ever likely to find. Not surprisingly, given modernism's history, Gass can only conclude that the avant-garde's integrity "might be defended still, if painters refused to show, composers and poets to publish, and every dance were danced in the dark. That would be a worthy 'no.' But it will never be uttered" (1988 70).

entail. Oscar Wilde's declaration that useful things are vulgar and that only the utterly useless thing can be artistic or beautiful reverberates throughout modernist attempts to create abstract (or "pure") works that do not refer to anything but themselves and that will remain immune to any circulation within a utilitarian culture.[5]

The modernist retreat into art makes sense as a transformative strategy only if we accept that the hypothetical alternative visions forged in the unimpeded space of autonomy can eventually be brought back into the ordinary lifeworld.[6] Even in its most ethereal and self-enclosed forms, modernist art rarely abandons its revolutionary intentions. The notion of an apolitical modernism that pursues the high road of an indifferent, disinterested contemplation of ambiguous, paradoxical truths or that is devoted to the pure exploration of its forms' possibilities is a fabrication of the American domestication of modernism in its university curricula, a domestication encoded by the New Criticism in literary studies and by Clement Greenberg in art history.[7] Abstract painters such as Kandinsky and Mondrian did not believe that their work was about nothing or only about itself (i.e., only about the problems of painting in some Greenbergian sense); they believed that their work embodied spiritualist and imaginative alternatives to commercial, secular modern life. These artists thought that they were preserving and forging alternatives and that in some unforeseeable future the world would be transformed through the experience of artists and the influence they had on their audiences. It is, however, fairly typical that, far from seeing their goal of transformation as a concrete political task undertaken in a world people continually make in their negotiations/conflicts with one another, the modernists only relied on some vague, apocalyptic change postponed to some future date and usually imagined as a miraculous change in the orders of perception and consciousness. The process of such change would be analogy;

[5]Wilde's "Decay of Lying" and Ortega's *The Dehumanization of Art* provide two classic statements of the modernists' yearning for purity and of their resistance to all arguments about art's ethical or social responsibility or about art's determination by historical, social, and psychological factors. Wilde tries to construct an account of the transcendent genius to fortify his account of the transcendent work of art. Ortega is more skeptical about the possibility of dehumanizing art, but faithfully records the attempt to accomplish it.

[6]The classic leftist statement that artistic autonomy fosters conditions under which alternatives to the existing culture can be formed is Herbert Marcuse's "Affirmative Character of Culture" (1968). For a description of Adorno's similarly motivated defense of modernism's quest for autonomy, see Jay (1984 chap. 4). Richard Wolin (1985) offers an interesting contemporary defense of autonomy that juxtaposes Marcuse's and Adorno's position to the portrait of the avant-garde found in Peter Bürger (1984).

[7]Newman (1985 15–39) is good on the topic of modernism's domestication in America. For a recent reiteration of all the old chestnuts by which academic modernism sought to insulate the work of art from any connection to the grubby passions of politics, see Donoghue (1989).

the alternatives portrayed in the autonomous artwork would be recognized as applicable, by transfer, to the actual lived world. Even such an aestheticist as Wilde believed that the beautiful, useless thing would eventually have an impact on life, since life imitates art.

Not all modernist artists were content with completely vague strategies of transformation, and they attempted to further institutional changes more directly. This fact has led to some confusion lately, especially in the growing acceptance of Peter Bürger's division of modernism into the haughty elite who practiced an esoteric, hermetic art and the various avant-gardes who took a more openly confrontational course.[8] The reputed difference is that the modernist elite (among them Eliot, Mondrian, Matisse, Le Corbusier, and Schönberg) exalted art as the closest the secular world could come to the sacred, while surrealism, dadaism, and the other avant-garde movements questioned art's integrity and value, thus submitting it to the same critique that repudiates the bourgeois ethos as a whole. In such writers as Rosalind Krauss and Andreas Huyssen the avant-garde thus becomes the precursor of postmodernism, if not actually the first example of postmodernism.[9] Bürger contends that the avant-garde failed in its efforts to deconstruct the institution of art, however, and I believe that it is better to reserve the term *postmodernism* for the repudiation of both high modernism's and the avant-garde's failed strategies, especially when we recall that the strategies of these two supposedly different camps are remarkably similar. Both exhibit a penchant for formal experimentation, a desire to *épater le bourgeois*, and the belief that changes in perception and consciousness could drastically alter prevailing social forms. For all their attention to Nietzsche and Freud and their flirtation with Marxism, the avant-gardes remained almost as relentlessly idealistic as modernism proper. Transformation from above—via spiritual, ethical, and intellectual constructs—rather than materialist transformation from below (via the proletariat or the id) characterizes both modernism and the avantgardes, which is one reason why recent writers have begun to associate the artistic avant-garde with the Leninist avant-garde. In both cases, the potentially anarchic forces down below in the mob or the psyche are carefully

[8]See Bürger (1984) and the introductory essay to Bürger's text by Jochen Schulte-Sasse, who faults Renato Poggioli's "tendency to equate modernism and the avant-garde," a tendency that Schulte-Sasse claims "typifies the Anglo-American tradition" (1984 xiv).

[9]Krauss argues that Picasso's collages, "by setting up discourse in place of presence," turn from "modernism's search for perceptual plenitude and unimpeachable self-presence" and thus bring us to "the threshold of a postmodernist art" (1985 38). Huyssen, acknowledging his debt to Bürger, sees "the historical avantgarde" as having "aimed, unsuccessfully, at freeing [modernist] art from its aestheticist ghetto and reintegrating art and life" (1986 60), an aim he sees carried forward by postmodernism, albeit in different ways.

controlled and directed from above. On the whole, modernists, whether avant-garde or not, work to ensure the primacy of the will, since they believe that only the integrity of the willful, autonomous self can afford them an escape from the general cultural condition that they abhor. Alone in the wasteland, threatened by the madness of being overwhelmed by society's decay and his own isolation, the poet can still assert that "these fragments I have shored against my ruin." This heroic maintenance of the self and its ability to create the artwork that represents and encapsulates its will stands as the quintessential modernist gesture when all hope of having any impact on the culture at large has been lost.

Surrealism offers the one crucial exception to these generalizations. Its interest in automatic writing and in Freudian theory leads it to attack the integrity of the self, and its use of collage leads it, less frequently, to question the integrity of the artwork. Despite Breton's and other surrealists' self-proclaimed communism, surrealism's true political outlook is anarchistic, with a resultant taste for fragmentary, theatrical confrontation instead of extended social critique or disciplined political conspiracy. The failure of surrealism as a transformational strategy resided, finally, not in its isolation from everyday capitalist culture, but in its unexpected perfect consonance with that culture. By 1936 Man Ray was a much sought-after and highly paid fashion photographer, and it has become a commonplace that surrealistic techniques of fragmentation and unexpected juxtaposition fetishize objects in a way that stimulates consumerist desires. Postmodern advocates of heterogeneity (against the perceived monotony of commercial culture) must eschew surrealistic, anarchistic strategies for generating plurality because they have proved supportive of, not oppositional to, the rule of the commodity.[10]

To differentiate between the forms heroic willfulness took in modernism proper and in the avant-gardes is to attempt, after the fact, to find some essential difference that explains modernism's apparent equal affinity with the radical right and the radical left. But the explanation for modernism's indeterminate political content does not lie in the formal strategies characteristic of the different modernist artists or movements. Rather, spiritualist romanticism offers a tradition of a conservative (Tory Radical) critique of capitalism that focuses on communal bonds and nationalistic identity, while realism offers a tradition of radical, leftist critique.[11] That Anglo-American and German

---

[10]The complicity of modernism with consumer capitalism is a favorite postmodern theme, found in writers as diverse as Graff (1979), Newman (1985), and Foster (1985). See McGowan (1987) for an extended discussion of this issue.

[11]See McGowan (1990) for a description of the Tory Radical tradition and its postmodern manifestations.

modernism follows the conservative path reflects the relative strength of high romanticism (especially in poetry) in these national literatures, while the French avant-garde's predominant leftism continues the realist strand in its painting and literature and the revolutionary memories of 1789, 1848, and 1870. There are, of course, exceptions to these national generalizations. It is noteworthy that one such exception, Bertolt Brecht, was very much concerned with articulating his relationship to realism and in preserving it as an appropriate term for his work,[12] while a similar allegiance to realist traditions is characteristic of American novelists in the thirties.

Modernist art, then, is poised between dreams of purity/autonomy and dreams of transforming the world in which the modernist artist finds herself. This particular constellation—which, whatever its other characteristics, proved remarkably fertile for artists—might have enjoyed a longer life if the dream of purity had not also been taken up in certain Western societies. The urge to purity in the social world, linked with a high romantic vision of a unified national community, finds echoes in the various forms of totalitarianism and ethnic intolerance that arise in the aftermath of World War I, and manifests itself most completely and most terribly in Hitler's racial theories (and murders). The long list of modern writers who lent their voices to rightist dreams of social transformation suggests that purity, as an ideal, may have more to do with the right than with the left. Certainly, postmodern celebrations of heterogeneity have much to do with the trauma of modernism's long flirtation, and in some cases even direct involvement, with fascism. The spirited defense of artistic autonomy by Adorno and Marcuse, however, should dispel any notion that goals of separation and integrity for the artwork are ipso facto rightist or leftist, just as twentieth-century history proves that neither side has a monopoly on totalitarianism or purges that aim to "purify" society. Certain strategies adopted by modernist writers in their attempt to repudiate bourgeois culture find their way into the political programs followed by twentieth-century social movements and/or states that also find bourgeois values (for whatever reason) unacceptable.

POSTMODERNISM

Postmodernism revives the early romantic vision of a unified world, but experienced this time as a frightful reality, recalling Goethe's warning to take

---

[12]See Brecht (1964 107–15) for his attempt to appropriate the epithet "realistic" for his own work.

care what we dream of in youth, since we will receive it in middle age. The Western world has achieved what the high romantics wished for: a monolithic world in which everything is subsumed under a universal principle. But this monolith is capitalism itself, utterly triumphant in the West and almost completely triumphant (through economic imperialism) throughout the rest of the world. Within this monolith, willful modernist self-exclusion, the claim to stand outside, is only a delusion; the postmodernist insists that everything is included, that nothing can achieve the autonomy or distance in which the modernists found their last defense against all-encompassing capitalism.

Postmodernism thus turns the traditional romantic fears about modernity on their head. The problem addressed by the pioneers of sociology (Edmund Burke, Alexis de Tocqueville, Auguste Comte, Emile Durkheim)—and by nineteenth-century writers ranging from Coleridge and Dostoyevsky on the right to John Stuart Mill, George Eliot, and Matthew Arnold in the center to Tolstoy and William Morris on the left—is how, in the absence of the foundational truths and values that modernity spurns, can any principle of social solidarity be found? Fragmentation, subjectivism, anarchy, perpetual conflict, and anomie seemed the inevitable consequence of the breakdown of religious and philosophical certitude. While conservative intellectuals worked to shore up society's foundations and radical intellectuals considered attacks on foundational beliefs in themselves effective political action, capitalism blithely went its own way, indifferent to conservative and radical theorizing alike. What the modernists' efforts to escape the dominant culture implicitly indicated, and what postmodernism makes absolutely explicit, is the belated recognition that the result of modernity's abandonment of foundational principles has been increased unanimity, an increased intolerance (perhaps fostered by insecurity about legitimating principles) of differences within the social whole, and the general hardening of the social arteries that calls forth such images as Weber's "iron cage," Adorno's "administered society," and Levi-Strauss's "monoculture."[13] Consent to capitalist society (and, perhaps, to any society), it now appears, is not a matter of belief at all—or not, at least, belief in foundational, traditional truths. Work in ordinary language philosophy inspired by Wittgenstein, the ethnomethodological studies of Harold Garfinkel, the notions of lifeworld found in phenomenological sociology and of habitus in the work of Pierre Bourdieu, all suggest that acceptance of a social order has more to do with the daily experience of its solidity, of its ability

---

[13]On the development of bureaucracy into an "iron cage" in Weber, see Giddens (1971 232–42); for Adorno's notion of an "administered world," see Jay (1984 38). Lévi-Strauss (1974 41) laments that "mankind has opted for monoculture."

to provide a framework for action that functions without being obtrusive or having to be questioned. Capitalism has shown itself remarkably indifferent to both the destruction or retention of fundamental (religious, metaphysical, or even ideological) truths and the beliefs dependent upon them. Capitalism's continued existence in any particular society rests more crucially with its establishment of what Adorno calls "the fungibility of all services and people" (1978 128) than on the presence or absence of religious or philosophical certitudes.

While the cumulative effect of capitalism has certainly been the destruction of traditional communities and traditional forms of social integration, capitalism is not necessarily hostile to such entitites. Rather, capitalism separates the economic from both the public (political) realm in which social unity is forged and from the private (familial or communal) realm from which agents' motivations are primarily derived. The economic sphere is dependent—in ways liberal economics has consistently refused to admit—on both the political and private spheres, but the legitimation of the economic has rested almost entirely on its institutional stability and its ability to deliver the goods, to increase the wealth of the nation. Social consent to capitalism in the West rarely has much to do with its adherence to, protection of, or (alternatively) destruction of foundational truths. Capitalism's legitimacy rests instead on three considerations: its provision of a functioning framework within which daily economic activity takes place; its effective production of goods and wealth; and its nondisruption of certain key liberties and institutional procedures that characterize democratic politics in the West. The Marxist might contend that my list merely concedes to capitalism the ability to set the political agenda within its domain, and that only an appeal to fundamental principles can upset capitalism's established power. My contrary position is that a truly democratic politics must work within terms that have some possibility of appealing to a broad public, and for this reason the consideration of capitalism's troubled and perhaps even necessarily antithetical relationship with democratic principles already widely accepted will prove the most fruitful course to follow.

This disagreement about appropriate strategies forms the polemical center of this book. I take it as axiomatic that postmodernism rejects any reliance on critique's inherent liberating powers, devoting itself instead to developing new aesthetic, textual, and political strategies to combat or undermine the monolith. Much of this work has focused on introducing, protecting, or finding an institutional home for any and all differences that might work to disturb the seemingly placid unanimity of the current Western order. Always implicit—and often enough explicit—in these efforts is a commitment to democracy and its concomitant values of egalitarianism and pluralism. For reasons I will discuss shortly, the postmodern critique of the Western monolith is linked to critiques of reason, of humanism, of imperialism, and of patriarchy that carry forward the attempt to shake off foundational principles that is characteristic of modernity as a whole. Instead of emphasizing the battle between foundationalist and antifoundationalist thought that continues to grab most of the attention, I attempt in this book to focus on the alternative strategies for social action that postmodernism proposes as appropriate responses to foundationalism's demise and as adequate protections against the static social orders that have arisen in foundationalism's stead. Not only do I believe that foundational truths are not essential for capitalism's maintenance, but also I contend that fragmentation of the capitalist monolith cannot be effectively achieved by an anarchistic celebration of difference wherever it appears. Such a strategy merely replays, on slightly different terrain, the modernist delusion that some particulars can escape the general operating principles of the social context. I insist throughout the book that postmodernism's holistic theories of how societies operate (accounts that justify the postmodern deconstruction of the self, the unified text, and other pretensions to the integral identity of particulars) must rule out any mere reliance on unrecuperated particulars as the antidote to capitalist order. The habits of modernism and of the liberal association of freedom with the negative liberty of autonomy are hard to shake off, however, and postmodernist writers persistently adopt strategies of resistance that their own theories of the social would deem inappropriate.

In contrast to anarchistic heterogeneity, I argue that only political and ethical principles always already inherent in the society can serve as curbs on the rule of fungibility and as safeguards of pluralism within society. This argument takes the Hegelian form of insisting that significant individual differences are possible and can be preserved only within a social whole that *recognizes* such differences and contains norms and institutions empowered to protect them. Freedom, then, is only possible within the terms of membership in a society; these terms, however, are not foundational but are produced by society itself. This affirmation of inclusion by positive freedom stands in stark contrast to the valorization of exclusion, of otherness, and of distance in negative freedom, a valorization found everywhere in postmodernism, marking its strange affinity with traditional liberalism. The attempt to construct an alternative social whole, based on different principles of inclusion and organization, to capitalism (which has filled the vacuum left by the liberal denial of social wholes) is a quintessentially political endeavor, and I devote my attention to those elements in the writers I discuss that are politically, as opposed to philosophically or epistemologically, relevant. My acceptance of the general outlines of postmodernism's epistemological attack on foundational philosophy (an attack that hardly adds much to Nietzsche's full-scale assault and is only the latest of modernity's efforts to slip the shackles of the past and of truth) and of its related attacks on humanism, Western rationalism, and autonomy will be clear throughout this book. What I contest throughout is postmodernism's vision of where we should go from here, once we consider these long-waged battles as won. Like Habermas, I believe that the task then becomes the society we wish to construct in the absence of external, nonhuman foundational principles; the task modernity hands to social actors remains unfinished.[14] Too much postmodernist thought chooses to continue its anarchistic demonstrations against the existing order, demonstrations that appear intended more to prove the agent's independence and purity than to address seriously the transformation of that order or the agent's own involvement in and/or complicity with it. Of course, postmodern thought offers strong reasons for despairing over the possibility that social agents can ever attain such control over their destinies, and a more optimistic vision of our political capabilities must attempt to come to terms with postmodern descriptions of society's and social power's production of agents who serve the needs of the existing order.

Postmodernism begins from the fear expressed by Fredric Jameson that we are witnessing "the apotheosis of capitalism" (1984b 77), the "prodigious expansion of capital into hitherto uncommodified areas" (1984b 78) since World War II. Late capitalism constitutes the totalized terrain of contemporary life; the name of the despised totality is different in other postmodern texts, but the specter of patriarchy, or Western metaphysics, or disciplinary power, or some other dominant social form haunts the postmodern imagination. This fear of a distopic totality is sometimes even embraced, partly in the heroic spirit characteristic of Nietzsche's and Freud's determination to face the worst truths without flinching, partly as a weapon to use against the hopes for autonomy found in modernist and avant-garde work, partly as a refutation of the liberal insistence that capitalism is not only compatible with, but actually productive of, pluralism. Thus the theoretical establishment of the monolith's existence is often a necessary first step in postmodern work, although the desire to transform that monolith into a truly pluralistic society surfaces everywhere as the primary postmodern goal. Cornel West's version of that goal is fairly typical (as is his misreading of Hegel as the theoretical enemy of pluralism):

[14]See Habermas (1983).

I do not have any Hegelian nostalgia for undifferentiated unities now or in the future. We are in a world of differences forever. . . . I cannot envision, within the logics of the modern West, with its legacy of slavery, societies that do not have racial differences. Consequently, our social emancipatory visions and projects have to acknowledge the irreducibility of racial differences but fight against a translation of such differences into hierarchical social relations and symbolic orders. So we will not get beyond the play of differences and binary oppositions. The question is how we arrest the political and economic translation of such differences into hierarchical relations. (1988 30)

Postmodernism's overt political goal is the disruption of this hierarchical totality, a disruption to be enacted by empowering the suppressed differential components within that totality.

In keeping with their primary concern with cultural issues, postmodern artists and intellectuals focus not on the economic practices and institutions of late capitalism, but on late capitalism's colonization of culture's signifying patterns and on late capitalism's affinity to certain traditions in Western thought. Horkheimer and Adorno's analysis of the "culture industry" in *Dialectic of Enlightenment* introduces the notion that the language of advertising and popular culture debases words "as substantial vehicles of meaning" and makes them "signs devoid of quality" (1972 164).[15] "Terms themselves become impenetrable," acting as labels (brand names) attached to things and with no further resonance. These terms provide no space for reflection on the thing's significance; they serve as "a defense against the true kind of relationship" (1972 165) between social agents and the objects they use and consume in daily life. This unthinking acceptance of the things that consumer capitalism provides "links advertising with the totalitarian watchword," which induces a similar passive acceptance in the populace. Various theorists have picked up on Horkheimer and Adorno's argument and have developed ways of describing late capitalism's deformation of the signifying order.

Perhaps the most influential of these writers for postmodern thought has been Jean Baudrillard. In Baudrillard's work, capitalism achieves its apotheosis when it moves from its nineteenth-century organization of production to its twentieth-century "perfect manipulation of social representation" (1983b 128). Marxists who still analyze the modes of production and look forward to their seizure by the working class have missed the crucial transition from capitalism's appropriative control over the final result (product) of labor to

[15]The publication history of *Dialectic of Enlightenment* explains its delayed influence; first published in German in New York in 1944, the book was not published in Germany until 1969 and not translated into English until 1972.

late capitalism's control over the initial models or images that govern social actors' activities, including production but also encompassing all kinds of other activities that productivist capitalism never sought to control. "Practically and historically, this signified the substitution of social control by the *end* . . . for social control by anticipation, simulation, and programming. . . . Instead of a process which is finalized according to its ideal development, we generalize from a *model*" (1983b 111). These models exist separate from any signified; we might say that they exist prior to the objects that will subsequently be produced, desired, bought, or consumed according to the model's heuristic. The referent is secondary at best, but more accurately conceived as completely absent, since the sign or model governs any apprehension of the actual thing. "It was capital which was the first to feed throughout its history on the destruction of every referential, of every human goal, which shattered every ideal distinction between true and false, good and evil, in order to establish a radical law of equivalence and exchange, the iron law of its power" (1983b 43). The law of exchange is fundamentally symbolic, not economic. Capitalism installs the sign system of the simulacra (images divorced from all content or referent) in order to secure itself from any unpleasant surprises, from the production of any new social demands or new forms of social life. Thus the needs of the social reproduction of the same come to dominate over the earlier capitalist emphasis on production. Baudrillard characterizes postmodern social life as organized around simulation, "a set of signs dedicated exclusively to their recurrence as signs, and no longer to their 'real goal' at all" (1983b 41). Capitalism's restructuring of society's sign systems thus justifies postmodern artists' and intellectuals' concentration on linguistic, aesthetic, and textual issues; Baudrillard's work makes the case that capitalist power is most fully operative on just these cultural terrains and must be contested there. The challenge this view poses to more traditional ways of viewing political engagement is obvious.

Dialectic of Enlightenment is also a founding text for another key feature of postmodernism: the linking of capitalist social order to the distinctive features of the Western intellectual tradition. Horkheimer and Adorno identify the "inescapable compulsion to social domination of nature" (1972 34) as the essential feature of Western reason. This compulsion for domination is "the vehicle of progress and regression at the same time" (1972 35), because to gain control over the natural environment necessitates mechanisms of control over the individual's wayward impulses (Freudian instincts for Horkheimer and Adorno) and over the populace (through the hierarchical organization of labor and the political imposition of order). Each gain in domination over nature is won only at the price of increasing "fixation of the instincts by means of heavier repression" (1972 35) and increasing "organization and administration" (1972 36) of society. Horkheimer and Adorno trace this dialectic of simultaneous progress and regression all the way back to the *Odyssey*; the culture industry represents only the latest form of social control.

Postmodernism's development of this theme focuses particularly on attacking various versions of autonomy and integrity. The West's characteristic strategy for gaining control, postmodernists often insist, has been to establish a powerful agent by repressing, excluding, or distancing any considerations that would vitiate the agent's single-mindedness. Such a strategy entails not only the control of internal ambivalence and conflict, but also the establishment of the agent's goals as superior to the different goals of other social actors, as above the requirement to take them into account. Western reason's fundamental attachment to the law of noncontradiction can thus be seen as based on the instrumental utility of that principle in the attempt to assert control. The repression of contradiction both within the self and within the social body favors integrity and unanimity over difference and multiplicity. The boundaries that traditional reason draws between the integral, noncontradictory thing and its others are now seen as a process of excluding contents that were included in a more complete, if also more chaotic, whole before reason began its divisive work. Postmodernists often proclaim their allegiance to this more inclusive whole, one that avoids the hierarchical differentiations and exclusions that mark the more ordered and less complete, integral wholes created by reason. (The similarity to Blake should be obvious, and there are times when Derrida and Deleuze, in particular, claim that the heterogeneous whole to which they contrast reason's homogeneous orders exists prior to, is more primordial than, reason's constructs.[16] This urge toward totality, coupled with an equal urge to avoid a structured, hierarchical whole, explains poststructuralism's simultaneous fear of and fascination with Hegel.)

Since reason's divisive strategies are taken as its means toward achieving domination, postmodernism attacks any number of traditional differentiations, including those between literary and other types of discourse, between high and low, between artist and critic, and between signified and signifier. In each case, the goal is to unsettle a privilege that accrues to one side of the pair

---

[16]Dews (1987 11–34) provides a powerful interpretation of Derrida that focuses on the consequences of "an essential *logical priority* of nonidentity over identity" (27) in Derrida's thought. In Deleuze and Guattari's *Anti-Oedipus* (1983) the fragmented, multitudinous body of schizophrenia is taken as primary; identity is only a later construct imposed upon that multiplicity, an understanding of the relation of identity to dispersion that contrasts with Lacan's account. See Dews (1987 168) for a discussion of this point.

and that can be maintained only by a logic of separation. The autonomy of high art or of literature, their being uncontaminated by elements of popular culture or other discourses, justifies their place on the top of a hierarchy. Feminism is so intimately linked to postmodernism because it pursues a similar strategy of showing that the hierarchical pair masculine/feminine depends on the social construction of the two terms as polar opposites where the very status of masculinity is dependent on the forceful (and pathological) assertion of its purity, of its not incorporating any of the traits labeled "feminine." High art's relation to low art can be understood as tied to a similar enforcement of difference.[17] Against the modernist obsession with purity, now interpreted as part and parcel of the fundamental flaw of Western reason, we find postmodernism's celebration of heterogeneity.

Postmodern thought demonstrates that purity and autonomy are illusions when it indicates, by strategies of reading that have become lumped together under the term *deconstruction*, that texts (and we can add here "selves," "institutions," and "societies") always contain the very elements that they most wish to deny possessing. Nothing can be excluded, although we often (and perhaps inevitably) want to exclude things. The intellectual target here is the tradition of humanism, with its emphasis on the construction (or, more passively, the discovery) of a unified individual identity that assures the self's power to act autonomously. (Humanism's construction of the self is obviously akin to reason's construction of integrated wholes; Odysseus's mastery of his instincts in Horkheimer and Adorno's account can be taken as the humanist moment of reason.) Postmodernism views the humanist self as a social/historical construct that is harmful in two ways: because it denies the fact that the self is socially constructed, thus promoting the anarchic liberal individualism first described by Adam Smith; and because the very act of constructing such a self (an act that humanism tries to deny even occurs) necessitates the repression of heterogeneous elements—the feminine and the nonutilitarian, to name two—that would threaten the self's sense of unity.

Postmodernism carries this last claim over into the realm of politics when it understands Western cultures as constructing their self-images as societies (nation-states) on a similar basis. The suppression of women and of minority groups within the society and of non-European races wherever they were encountered must be read as the outcome of the West's obsession with identity, singleness, and purity, with its belief that only unified, homogeneous entities (be they selves or states) can act effectively. Postmodernism finds in

[17]See Andreas Huyssen's superb essay "Mass Culture as Woman: Modernism's Other" (1986 44–62).

the modernist drive for autonomy another version of Western reason's obsession with integrity and insists that this obsession has drastic political consequences, in both the oppression of women and minorities and in the establishment of hierarchical orders that must threaten the egalitarian distribution of power (as capacity to engage in and influence the social processes of decision making) espoused by democracy. Only by abandoning this traditional form of reason and by accepting the fact of heterogeneity could a different politics, a different understanding of how societies are constituted and what they could strive to achieve, be reached.

There remain considerable difficulties in outlining what a practical politics of heterogeneity would look like, not to mention how we might begin to put such a politics into practice. Much of this book may appear to be a lengthy and churlish complaint that the repeated gestures in this direction by many postmodernist writers rarely move beyond vague recommendations that generally appear hopeless the moment one begins to think seriously about fleshing them out. With all the emphasis on deconstruction and on the postmodern attack on foundationalism, however, it is crucial to emphasize that postmodernism's importance and vitality stem from its having a positive as well as a negative component. Postmodernism is not merely an attack on modernist notions of autonomy or, more globally, on Western traditions of humanism and rationality as they have spawned late capitalism; it is also the attempt to rethink politics and social life on the basis of these attacks, an undertaking to which I hope this book makes a contribution. As Richard Rorty puts it, once we place the traditional orientations of Western reason behind us, we can "substitute Freedom for Truth as the goal of thinking and of social progress" (1989b xiii).

A quick summary of the definition I have offered thus far of postmodernism will make apparent an inconsistency that reverberates throughout the texts I discuss in this book. I argue that postmodernism understands contemporary capitalism as an all-inclusive order from which nothing and no one can escape, and that this successful appropriation of everything by late capitalism can be attributed to its annexation of culture's signifying processes to its own needs of self-maintenance and self-reproduction. Thus capitalism itself proves the all-embracing social totality for which the early romantics yearned, albeit a repressive totality in place of the utopian totality Hegel or Blake imagined. I have also suggested, however, that postmodernism retains the traditional romantic critique that a capitalist social order is not inclusive enough, a critique that now takes the form of contrasting reason's ordered wholes with the larger wholes of heterogeneity. The postmodernist insists that the social totality within which we live is a *constructed* whole that gains unity only through a process of exclusion. This is not my confusion, I think, but a confusion inherent in postmodern thought itself, one that manifests itself most crucially in the deep ambivalence toward totality found in that thought. Postmodernism would be merely anarchistic (and it certainly reveals a continual urge to drift in that direction) if it understood heterogeneity as incompatible with totality, as just a random collection of particulars. But postmodern writers usually retain, if only slightly, the sense that hetero-geneous particulars rest their claim on our attention (on our *recognition*, in the Hegelian sense of the term) because they are parts of the whole. In other words, we could not expect the now-excluded elements that threaten the text's, or the self's, or the society's asserted integrity to pose a true threat unless those elements actually were understood, within an expanded view of the whole, as necessary parts (or members) of that text, that self, or that society. The truly external may pose a threat by aggression; but it is only the internal that threatens integrity by claims upon our (ethical, emotional, politi-cal, or scholarly) attention.

Postmodernism favors internal models of transformation, relying on a return of the unsuccessfully repressed, of the outsider or marginalized who was formerly (originally) an insider. This preference does not mean that postmodernism always relinquishes the dream of the existing order having to confront a truly exotic other that "it cannot absorb without losing its own identity and wholly transforming itself." But this search for an external savior is, from my perspective, the modernist remnant in many postmodern texts—texts that, for the most part, adopt the holistic principle "that all contact with otherness is also at one and the same time of necessity a return upon ourselves."[18] The others we are most likely to encounter are those to whom we are related—by ties of denial, if by nothing else. For this reason, the characteristic postmodern genre is pastiche or parody, the recycling of already recognized cultural signs in altered contexts. Postmodern art's claims to novelty stem not from wholly new imaginative constructs or from assertions of independent thought, but from the rearrangement of the relations within which particulars stand to one another in a constructed order. That pastiche is much more closely related to metonymy than metaphor is clear; less often noticed is how close deconstructive readings are to pastiche, to the reassem-bling of the parts of a text or of an author's oeuvre to highlight themes, obsessions, or tendencies a more traditional, more "straight," reading would barely register.

Postmodernism's ambivalence about wholes carries over into a radical

[18]The passages quoted are from Jameson (1988b 117 and 119).

questioning of the very utility and justification of social theory. It does not help clarity in these matters that the term *theory* has become enshrined in academic literary circles as the name for those forms of thought that reject all the aims of traditional theorizing. Gayatri Chakravorty Spivak tells us that "critical theory in my part of the academic establishment (Lacan, Derrida, Foucault, the late Barthes) sees the text as that area of the discourse of the human sciences—in the United States called the humanities—in which the *problem* of the discourse of the human sciences is made available. Whereas in other kinds of discourse there is a move toward the final truth of a situation, literature, even within this argument, displays that the truth of a human situation *is* the itinerary of not being able to find it" (1988 77). Spivak's description of *theory* in literary circles makes clear its oppositional character (hence her qualifying term "critical") as well as its paradoxical tendency to make a truth claim about our inability to discover the truth.

I will try hard not to harp on this epistemological inconsistency in this book. The inconsistency is rampant (pointing it out has become a favorite academic exercise) and is best understood as a practically inevitable consequence of modernity. We moderns spin our truths out of our own bowels (to paraphrase Yeats), and the conviction that this is so engages modernity in its endless polemic against truth claims that deny their human origin; but this polemic has no force if the fundamental insistence that humans make rather than find truth is not accepted as an unalterable truth. Broadly conceived, postmodern theory (what Richard Rorty calls "ironist theory"[19]) sets itself against the traditional theoretical aspiration to uncover essential and necessary truths that are not contingent upon the temporal and the human, and, in my view more important, also claims to repudiate general explanatory schemas, even when such schemas are contingent rather than necessary. Rorty, Derrida, and other postmodern writers take philosophy to represent traditional theory at its most persistent, hubristic, and formidable. When it becomes a question of a new, alternative, postmodern philosophy, "metaphysics" or what Rorty calls "the Plato to Kant canon" (1989b 97) names the traditional form, while "pragmatism," "deconstruction," and "historicism" are among the names for this new, nontraditional philosophy.[20]

As I have already suggested, I think we are chasing a red herrring when we

[19]See Rorty (1989b chap. 4).

[20]The best overview of contemporary philosophy's abandonment of traditional epistemological foundationalism and the various alternatives antifoundational thought proposes can be found in Bernstein (1983); the collection of essays edited by Baynes, Bohman, and McCarthy (1987) gathers representative samples of the work of almost every important antifoundationalist philosopher.

take antifoundationalism as the essential feature of postmodernism. We will do much better to conceive of postmodernism as only a distinctive response to the lack of foundations that has faced the West (at least) since the dawn of modernity. And what is distinctive about that response, I contend, is the belated recognition that the loss of foundations leads neither to chaos nor to liberation (which can be names for the same thing), but to social orders that appear as invulnerable to change as any divinely sanctioned reality. Phrased positively, postmodernism is the attempt to legitimate knowledge claims and the moral/political bases for action, not on the basis of indubitable truths, but on the basis of human practices within established communities. The recognition of such communities' stability means that the worry that such a foundation is not strong enough is absurd; our constant worry should be that this communal foundation is too strong. We must attempt continually, in Roberto Mangabeira Unger's words, to "maximiz[e] the corrigibility of social institutions" (1986 52).

Postmodern theory's professed suspicion of generalizations is directed against these entrenched social orders that it hopes to shake from their torpor. The notion that Western reason suppresses differences in constructing identities leads to a compensating emphasis on particulars. The covering laws and explanations of more traditional theory are subjected to a critique that is as much ethical as epistemological. But it is not the least of postmodern theory's internal contradictions that it must resort to grand generalizations itself in order to characterize the tradition(s) it wishes to upend. The recent proliferation of all-embracing totalities such as Western metaphysics, pastoral power, partriarchy, humanism, and the dominant culture has led Quentin Skinner to see our age as marked by "the return of grand theory." Writers such as Derrida and Foucault, Skinner says "have given reasons for repudiating the activity of theorising, [but] they have of course been engaged in theorising at the same time" (1985a 12). While attempting to avoid totality in its own positions, postmodern theory persistently ascribes monolithic totality to its opponent.

The first moment in ironist thory is devoted, almost inevitably, to convincing the reader that these monoliths the writer wishes to oppose do exist. After all, the urgent need to gain a true heterogeneity will hardly be felt by those who accept the liberal democracies' portrait of themselves as the guardians of an achieved pluralism. The new social theory proves that the monolith exists by showing that all particulars, no matter how independent they seem, are actually subsumed by the whole. In this respect, Derrida's revelation of Western metaphysics' grounding distinctions in every text, Jameson's arguments for the encroachment of late capitalism everywhere, and Catharine MacKinnon's description of patriarchy's omnipresence are all similar. Postmodernists continually argue that the distinctions we make, distinctions that identify one thing as different from another and subject to different constraints, cannot be understood as stemming from the distinct essences possessed by the things themselves, but as differences produced by a relational totality. This holistic moment in postmodern thought explains its continued reliance on Hegelian and Marxist models of interpretation. But this identification of the existing totality contrasts strongly with the announced animosity to totality, so that the adoption of a holistic, systemic hermeneutic is paired (none too easily) with a rejection of holistic (Hegelian or Marxist) solutions. Postmodern texts thus often begin their work by making deeper the very hole out of which they hope to climb. I suggest that a better solution would be to have the courage of our holism, to find within totality the possibility of freedom and of legitimate political action.

Postmodernism is thus distinguished from modernism by the belief that artistic autonomy is neither possible nor desirable. Postmodernism questions the efficacy of strategies of transformation associated with autonomy, declaring that modernism inexorably reaches a dead end. The modernist hope and belief that intellectuals can occupy a space outside capitalist society is not only illusionary but also artistically and politically sterile. The purity of the alienated artist forecloses his access to the energies and disputes that are lived within the culture, while also severing his connection to any audience beyond the purlieu of the artistic elite. The modernist places himself high and dry. Mass or popular culture inevitably springs up to fill the vacuum created by the elitist artists' divorce from a wide audience. By following the path of its own aesthetic revolution and its fetishistically precious values, modern art distances itself from any social group large enough, central enough, or powerful enough to effect a social revolution. Postmodernism must entirely rethink the relation of intellectuals to the rest of society. A model of engagement must replace the model of alienaiton, and my argument for positive as opposed to negative freedom is meant to point in that direction.

The denial of autonomy provides the best framework for explaining postmodernism's privileging of representation over abstraction, of historical, contextualized explanations over appeals to the thing's nature, and its persistent interest in questions of narrative. Jonathan Arac, in my view correctly, has argued that the association of postmodernism with an attack on representation results from a misreading of the early Derrida—a misreading that, in my terms, can be characterized as assimilating Derrida to a familiar modernist position.[21] What Derrida's early work argued was that representation could not be anchored, its truth could not be guaranteed, by reference to some

[21]See Arac (1986b xx–xxviii).

thing-in-itself to which it corresponded. Derrida showed that that thing-in-itself was always absent and thus could not be called in as a witness to the representation's validity. This absence, however, does not mean that Derrida thought of the representation (the signifier) either as now utterly discredited (a mere fiction) or as floating free in some utopian space of freedom.[22] The notion of a free, abstract signifier is modernist through and through, and utterly at odds with Derrida's notion of the signifier's being embedded within a system of signifiers, of traces. Derrida attacks correspondence theories not because they enthrall the signifier to the signified but because they liberate the signifier from its constitutive relation to other signifiers within the totality of the differential system of signs. The point becomes that representation, that signifiers, are all that we have; the order of signifiers cannot be abandoned in favor of some direct relation to things-in-themselves. As Arac puts it, "the inescapability of representation is Derrida's deconstructive point against the metaphysical fantasy of pure presence" (1986b xxiv). Postmodernist thought everywhere pulls signifiers back within determinant systemic relations, as opposed to modernism's effort to free the signifier from all determinants. To declare all representations "fictions," thus freeing them from responsibility to things-in-themselves, is liberating only when the signifier itself is then treated as a thing-in-itself and not as a differential element in a signifying system. The subsumption of signifiers back into a system of meaning is a fundamental postmodern tactic found in both its art and its criticism.

Postmodern historicism is also best seen as a variant of the attack on autonomy. Where Derrida and de Man (as heirs of structuralism) tend to see relational systems, the historicists see social and historical contexts. In both

---

[22]The persistent association of Derrida with indeterminacy and the notion of "freeplay" is the result of "Structure, Sign, and Play" (1970) being the first Derridean essay widely available in English translation *and* the fact that where the French version of that essay has "*jeu*" (1967 427), the English version published in *The Structuralist Controversy* (1970 264) unaccountably says "freeplay." (The translator of *Writing and Difference*, Alan Bass, removes "freeplay" in favor of just "play" without mentioning this change, only telling us that "most of the translation" of "Structure, Sign, and Play" in his volume comes from the earlier translation [1978 xx].) Derrida has recently commented on this whole contretemps in a way that makes his current opinion (at least) very clear: "I never spoke of 'complete freeplay or undecidability.' I am certain that the 'American critics of [my] work' can find nothing in my texts which corresponds to that. . . . This notion of 'freeplay' is an inadequate translation of the lexical network connected to the word *jeu*, which I used in my first texts, but sparingly and in a highly defined manner" (1988a 115–16). Derrida then goes on to explain play's "supplementary complication" (1988a 117) of "the order of the calculable" (1988a 116), thus placing play in a relationship to traditional thought that both circumscribes the range of play's possibility and unsettles "classical and binary logic" (1988a 117). See Norris (1987 21–27 and 138–41) for a spirited refutation of the notion that Derrida's work in any way justifies a belief in indeterminacy or in inevitable misreadings unaccountable to the interpreted text.

cases, the individual thing no longer retains an intrinsic meaning or even firm boundaries of individuality. Instead, the fluidities of the larger whole can alter the identity of the thing, which is now recognized as a product of (as constituted by) the context as a whole. The achievement of freedom for particulars within such a view becomes problematic; the new historicism often suggests a historical determinism akin to Marx's. The interpretive vistas opened up by a relational or historicist view are practically endless. The relevant whole to which particulars should be related can be constituted and reconstituted through a series of dialectical maneuvers. But whether historicism can survive with no notion of the whole is a trickier issue. Hegel, though unwanted, keeps returning in postmodern theory because the claims about determinate relations and the constitution of things and selves by context or system can be made good only by pointing to some whole or identifying some context that does the constituting.

A similar problem assails the resurgence of interest in narrative that marks postmodernism. Lyotard's dramatic identification of postmodernism with skepticism about the *grands récits* that characterize the legitimating narratives of liberal progress or Marxist liberation sits uneasily with the new historicists' inclination to "tell stories" in place of giving arguments.[23] Historicist relational accounts are nonstructuralist insofar as they replace system with narratives that gather together particulars as causes of, influences on, dependent upon, or transformed by one another. Postmodern theorists of narrative, such as Hayden White, aim to demonstrate that narratives are man-made according to preexisting cultural patterns rather than some simple relation of facts or the discovery of a temporal pattern that organically emerges from the historical events. Yet as with totalities, postmodernism finds itself constrained to resort to narrative even while it strives to disrupt it. Genealogy, *petits récits*, and the attempt to construct what Walter Benjamin called "a history of the losers" are all ways of attempting to preserve a historicist account of particulars' meanings while also stressing the contingency of those meanings. The trouble with Hegelian *grand récit*, like Hegelian totality, is that it is too fixed. While denying the possibility of self-sufficiency, as Hegel does, postmodern theory

[23]Rorty tells us that the loss of foundational truths and of "rational grounds" (1985c) that accompanies ironist theory entails adopting the "strategy of using narrative where argument fails" (1985c 135). Convincing someone, or at least keeping the conversation going, is best attempted by "telling stories: stories about why we talk as we do and how we might avoid continuing to talk that way. When you find yourself at an argumentative impasse, baffled by your opponent's refusal to stop asking questions which you think you really should not have to answer, you can always shift the ground by raising questions about the vocabulary he or she is using. . . . You can use historical narratives to show why the issue previously discussed is moot and why it needs to be reformulated in terms which are, alas, not yet available" (1985c 135).

works to imagine totalities and narratives more fluid, more open to chance, and more tolerant of heterogeneity than Hegel's universalizing Reason.

Finally, we should recognize how fully the ideal of an egalitarian, pluralistic democratic order informs most postmodern work. Stanley Aronowitz describes postmodern politics as taking place "in the gap between the promises of modern democratic society" and the "subversion" of those promises by actual social arrangements and state actions (1987 108). But Aronowitz complains that "radical democracy as a political stance" exists only as "*an ethical a priori*" in postmodernism, because these thinkers refuse to see democratic demands as produced by "the struggles over class formation," struggles grounded in "the idea that social forces are situated in a determinate relation to the means of material production" (1987 104).

Postmodern theory's rejection of a Marxist *grand récit* or of any appeal to natural, universal rights to explain the appeal of radical democracy cannot, however, be mitigated by an optimistic and willful assertion of democracy as a self-created (or, more aptly, socially created) ideal. Such an assertion smacks too much of modernity's heedless *hubris,* its humanistic belief in its own powers. Thus postmodernism finds itself between a rock and a hard place, unable to ground democracy by appeal to external, nonhuman principles, but unwilling to accept humanly generated principles as legitimate norms rather than further instances of arrangements imposed by power. The result, in Jean Franco's phrase, is that postmodernism becomes associated with "the withdrawal from moral action" (1987 61). Unable either to ground or to construct an ethics within the terms of its critiques of foundationalism and of dominating, humanistic reason, postmodern politics is often reduced to the ironic, anarchistic effort to transform the existing order by means of play, *jouissance,* or other textual strategies that Franco spurns as aestheticist.

Claims and counterclaims about postmodernism's political content and consequences abound. Suffice it to say, for now, that postmodern discourse in the 1980 has been, to a large extent, a despairing discourse about the failure of the anarchistic, spontaneous politics and arts of the 1960s. The looming monolith of postmodern theory serves to explain why free play and *jouissance* did not bring the house down and why we are, at best, in for what Raymond Williams calls "the long revolution." Derrida's elaborate models of recuperation and Foucault's tortured dialectics of complicity fit postmodernism's mood better than any heady proclamation that a new day is approaching.

What I do want to stress about postmodernism's politics is that, whatever form it takes (whether aestheticist, textual, or tied to local, community action or to the new social movements), an underlying commitment to democracy reveals itself. Faith in traditional leftist visions of a revolutionary avant-garde, of a dictatorship of the proletariat, and of a scientifically managed technological Utopia has all but vanished, to be replaced by decentered, pluralistic visions of untroubled local diversity. I argue in my closing chapter that only some notion of semiautonomy—in which localities are still answerable to a holistic democratic norm—could underwrite such a decentered politics. More transcendentally, I argue throughout this book that a recognition of a humanly created norm of democracy as fundamental to Western political life is the only way to enable legitimate political action and ensure freedom. Ironist theory's refusal of this recognition gets it into continual difficulties, as I hope Chapter 3 makes clear.

The claim that a democratic norm operates within postmodern discourse carries weight only if these theorists (and others who do not explicitly adopt the norm) can be shown to rely upon it implicitly in their work. Certain prevalent postmodern themes do indicate an implicit ethic of democratic egalitarianism. The generalized attack on hierarchies provides one instance, while the distaste for the elitism of the high/low art distinction offers a specific example of postmodernism's affinity with populism. In a critic such as Charles Jencks, populism becomes associated with the local community's input into the design decisions concerning public buildings and space, as opposed to the arrogance of the magisterial modernist architect.[24]

More generally, postmodern populism is associated with what I think of as "cultural recidivism." Against the universalized, international canons of modernist taste or the generalized truths of liberal or communist ideology, postmodernism cherishes the particularized *habitus* of smaller groups. From fundamentalists in America to Catholic dissidents in Poland to fans of Barry Manilow everywhere, such groups have proved remarkably resistant to the efforts of various elites to educate them out of their prejudices and into acceptance of the prevailing views of value, goodness, and taste. That the new right in this country, rather than liberals or leftists, has been more successful in using cultural recidivism to its political advantage indicates not a built-in conservatism in populism but the continued attachment of liberals and leftists to the international, educated sensibility of urbane modernism. The 1988 Jesse Jackson campaign demonstrated what a leftist populism would look like and, not surprisingly, the rhetoric and supporters of the Rainbow Coalition made the Democratic party elite nervous in ways remarkably similar to the

---

[24]Jencks associates postmodernism with "architects who wanted to get over the Modernist impasse, or failure to communicate with their users," and believes that postmodern work must deal with a "primary dualism" between "elitism and populism" or, in other words, between the specialized discourse and tradition of the field and "the tastes and goals [of] . . . the various publics that inhabit and use" a building (1984 6).

nervousness caused among Republican leaders by Pat Robertson's campaign. Such writers as Leslie Fiedler (1982) and Herbert Gans (1974) have recognized the link between a commitment to democracy and the populist ability not only to let "taste cultures" (as Gans calls them) be, but also to recognize in them a crucial safeguard against tyranny. Insofar as it sheds the modernist urge to reeducate all provincials by using a strictly limited canon of "the best that has been thought and said," postmodernism encourages faithfulness to the cultural world from which individuals spring. This encouragement coincides with the resurgence of such allegiances throughout the world in a "politics of identity" that bases its resistance to the totalizing orders of late capitalism or state socialism on the defense of its existing beliefs, tastes, and patterns of life.

The ethic of democracy connects with postmodernism's attack on autonomy wherever postmodernism's holistic premises make it realize that the protection of local diversity can only be ensured within a social whole that provides for certain basic civil liberties. This social whole, furthermore, can only provide those liberties where all members of the society are politically equal. Such a holistic outlook denies that the modernist artist can achieve an autonomous freedom irrespective of the freedoms that can be achieved by her fellow citizens. The characteristic isolation of the modernist artist, her inability to find a wide audience, is one price she pays for her failure to link her own quest for freedom to that of society as a whole. The theorists I discuss suffer, I believe, from a similar failure. Their refusal to formulate democratic norms explicitly and to connect those norms to their holistic interpretation of contemporary social reality severely limits their ability to describe or engage in positive political action. Instead, ironist theory's fear of normative assertions renders it incapable both of defining legitimate political action and of explaining what social end its own intellectual work serves. In this book I aim to consider how such a normative assertion could be possible in the face of postmodernism's doubts, thus enabling a quite different description of political action and intellectual endeavor.

2

Postmodernism's Precursors

Borges has taught us that the great writer, like Kafka, creates his own precursors. As both a belated and an academic discourse postmodernism has been particularly obsessed with rewriting the intellectual tradition. The accounts of Kant, Hegel, Marx, and Nietzsche below are shamelessly selective as I attempt to show what postmodernism derives from these nineteenth-century writers and to introduce certain themes from their work that I develop more fully in my final chapter.

KANT: MODERNITY AND LIBERAL HUMANISM

Hilary Putnam distinguishes between two philosophical perspectives: an "externalist perspective," which believes that "the world consists of some fixed totality of mind-independent objects," and an "internalist perspective," which holds that "*what objects does the world consist of?* is a question that it only makes sense to ask *within* a theory or description" (1981 49). For the externalist, "truth involves some sort of correspondence relation between words or thought-signs and external things and sets of things"; for the internalist, "'truth' . . . is some sort of (idealized) rational acceptability—some sort of ideal coherence of our beliefs with each other and with our experiences *as those experiences are themselves represented in our belief system*—and not correspondence with mind-independent or discourse independent 'states of affairs'" (1981 49–50). Not surprisingly, Putnam takes Kant as the starting point for philosophy of the internalist sort. "Before Kant it is perhaps impossible to find *any* philosopher who did *not* have a correspondence theory of truth" (1981 56). "Kant is best read as proposing for the first time what I have called the 'internalist' or 'internal realist' view of truth" (1981 60). I trust that my readers will recognize how nicely Putnam's internalist fits the description of modernity from which I have been working. The internalist perspective is fully, almost aggressively, humanistic, insisting that our notions of truth and of the real are the products of human systems of thought, belief, or discourse. In my discussion of Kant I emphasize how this humanistic modernity is connected in his work to a liberalism that stresses autonomy and limits.

Kant's work presents the reader with an odd mixture of hubris and timidity. His continual strategy is to circumscribe carefully the subject he is discussing, refusing to make claims beyond the delimited topic. But these scrupulously observed limitations are also the source of his strength. A sphere's autonomy is constructed by this delineation of its bounds, and the resulting isolation of the subject to be considered allows its fundamental operating principles to be examined in their entirety. Kant calls this attention to the internal "laws" or "conditions" of a subject "critique," and announces that "our age is, in especial degree, the age of criticism, and to criticism everything must submit" (1965 9). This turn of thought upon itself to discover its own grounds not only serves as the opening move of Kant's philosophy, but establishes the "critical" (in this strictly Kantian sense) bias of almost all theorizing in the human sciences ever since. Criticism aims to uncover the very conditions under which humans can experience and can think. Criticism, for Kant, is thus "transcendental," which means that it identifies the necessary and a priori conditions under which experiences or thoughts are even possible. Within modernity's internalist perspective, transcendental philosophy can be understood as the investigation of the ways in which humans set about constructing their world and their truths.

Since postmodern writers often deny the very possibility of transcendental thought, it is worth considering the sources of Kant's confidence in what his critical philosophy reveals. First and foremost is his faith in reason. For Kant reason is always and everywhere the same. His profoundly ahistorical view means that the investigation of reason as experienced now will yield a transcendental knowledge applicable to all places and at all times. In addition, the internalist view isolates reason from all external contingencies, thus providing a pure focus on the universal. Of course, Kant does distinguish between "pure reason," which designates the laws of thinking and of our apprehension of the empirical world, from "practical reason," which is the application of the rational categorical imperative to the contingent experiences of individual life in order to make moral decisions, and from "aesthetic judgment," which involves not just the apprehension of objects that pure reason makes possible but also the decisions about whether those objects are beautiful or not, pleasing or not. Thus reason is divided into three spheres for Kant, but he does not expect the principles of its operation in each sphere to change from culture to culture or from one historical period to another. Transcendental philosophy can identify, within each sphere, the principles under which reason *always* operates.

Surprisingly, Kant feels no particular need to justify the self-reflective capacities of critical philosophy, its ability to uncover the underlying principles of reason's operation. He simply assumes reason's transparency to itself.

> To search in our common knowledge for the concepts which do not rest upon particular experience and yet occur in all knowledge from experience, of which they as it were constitute the mere form of connection, presupposes neither greater reflection nor deeper insight than to detect in a language the rules of the actual use of words generally and thus to collect elements for a grammar (in fact both researches are very nearly related), even though we are not able to give a reason why each language has just this and no other formal constitution, and still less why any precise number of such formal determinations in general, neither more nor less, can be found in it. (1950 70)

The status of transcendental theory as metalanguage does not trouble Kant, and he does not feel the need to develop any special interpretive practice for uncovering fundamental principles or to justify at length the very possibility of such uncovering. (He does differentiate among the various types of "deductions" that he practices to discover the a priori conditions, but he does little to substantiate the deductions' possibility or accuracy.) For Kant each and every possessor of reason is equally capable of this reflexive feat; only with Hegel, as we shall see, does the notion appear that some special form of interpretation is necessary to understand Reason's principles, and that notion almost inevitably introduces certain groups of interpreters who have privileged and superior insight.

The passage just quoted also indicates that Kant's ahistoricism relieves him from all curiosity about why reason takes the form it does. The heroic view of modernity stresses that if humans make the world, then they have the power to make it as they see fit. But Kant, while fully claiming reason as the human and as only human, does not view reason as malleable; rather, reason is the distinctive characteristic of the human, that which must be present a priori in all humans, and it is present in every one of them in exactly the same way. To describe reason, then, is only to describe what *must* be, and Kant says that philosophy should not, *pace* Leibniz, be concerned with trying to explain how it is that reason exists in this particular form.

Since reason is already at work before critical philosophy describes it, Kant locates the usefulness of his work not in anything it enables us to do but in its delineation of the limits of our capabilities. A critique's "utility . . . ought properly to be only negative, not to extend, but to clarify our reason, and keep it free from errors—which is already a very great gain" (1965 59). We can best understand Kant's position here by referring to his strong support of religious tolerance. While reason will inevitably lead all who employ it properly to the same conclusions, one of those crucial conclusions is that large areas of human concern actually lie outside reason's purlieu. In such cases, the only rational response is to respect different preferences, since no legitimate grounds exist for asserting the superiority of one preference to another. We might rephrase this point to say that the rational in Kant designates what all humans hold in common, but that he also recognizes realms apart from the rational that allow for (explain) singularity and difference. One of the crucial functions of transcendental philosophy is to delineate between the rational and these other realms so that we know what we share as rational human beings and where we can expect there to be differences that we should tolerate. It is worth noting that this tolerance itself is rational in Kant's terms; it is only what is tolerated that is apart from reason. This point is crucial because it justifies setting up tolerance as a universal imperative, an attitude all must hold in common.

The recognition of realms beyond critical philosophy's ken is intimately connected to issues of freedom in Kant. In his famous phrase: "I have therefore found it necessary to deny *knowledge*, in order to make room for *faith*" (1965 29). The negative moment of criticism, its discovery of reason's limits, opens the space of freedom, of individual difference. Kant himself does not embrace irrationalism as a consequence of this move in his thought, but he does open the way to locating freedom in the territory of reason's other. Since reason is identified with what is universally necessary, freedom becomes identified with the possibilities of individuality that exist apart from the realms where reason holds sway.

I want to go very slowly here, both because the notion of freedom just adumbrated is built upon a number of assumptions that must be questioned and because Kant himself holds two not very compatible images of freedom. We might characterize the basic tension in Kant's understanding of freedom as that between individual autonomy and universality. Kant's insistence on individual autonomy—on what he calls the "transcendental ego"—follows from his assertion of reason's autonomy from (and priority to) the empirical and from his assumption that reason is always fully present in each human being. The human's experience of the world is only possible when the whole of reason (the a priori categories) is brought to bear upon the empirical manifold. Hence any particular individual must possess these categories before having any experience. The "transcendental ego" names this possession. Kant's universalist insistence that reason must underlie all experience yields an ontological belief in the priority of the individual to any shaping context. Furthermore, since unity is one of the Kantian categories, he insists that the self unifies its various experiences as all sharing the characteristic of happening to or belonging to its self. Thus, as Michael Sandel describes Kant's position, "the subject is the something 'back there,' antecedent to any particular experience, that unifies our diverse perceptions and holds them together in a single consciousness" (1982 8).

So far there is no strain between individual autonomy and universality, since each individual merely possesses the reason necessary to have experience, hence the reason possessed by all in exactly the same form. So long as Kant emphasizes the individual's connection to reason, he presents a version of freedom that stresses similarity, not difference. He argues that "my external and rightful *freedom* should be defined as a warrant to obey no external laws except those to which I have been able to give my own consent" (1970 99). The exercise of this autonomy, however, yields no conflicts or significant differences, because the autonomous individual will consent only to what is reasonable, and all autonomous individuals will, in freely following the dictates of the practical reason they find within themselves, come to the same conclusion. "A human being [is] a being subjected by his own reason to certain duties. . . . If we violate [the idea of duty], even without considering the disadvantages which might result, we feel the consequences directly, and appear despicable and culpable in our own eyes" (1970 72). Freedom can be exercised only as the affirmation of our own reason; the attempt to flee reason's dictates would make us less than human and thus "despicable in our own eyes." The famous categorical imperative, which is the end result of practical reason's operation, captures perfectly this independent arrival of each individual at universality: "I am never to act in any way other than *so I could want my maxim also to become a general law*" (1949 150). At this point Kant does not seem very far from Hegel, since reason underwrites for both a guarantee of universality that brings all individuals under the rule of one whole. And like Hegel, Kant is deeply committed to showing that the world he inhabits right now is the world that autonomous reason creates; there is no gap between what the reasonable individual in his freedom conceives and the world to which he is asked to give his consent.

Since Kant, unlike Hegel, recognizes the existence of realms separate from reason, however, individual autonomy can also lead to difference in Kant's work. The crux here is Kant's insistence that questions of consequences are utterly irrelevant to the moral considerations of practical reason. Kant's thinking here is profoundly antiutilitarian; he radically disassociates the moral quality of an action from either its intended or its actual consequences. The good an agent hopes to do, the happiness the agent strives to achieve, or the unintended good an action brings about have nothing to do with the rational determination of whether the planned action is moral, that is, if it is an action I could will that all other human beings perform. Kant wants to isolate moral decisions, which are made prior to acting, from questions of consequences, questions that must remain unanswered until some time after the action has been performed. The unpredictability of consequences renders utilitarian moral calculations inevitably fallible; to base a moral decision about how to act now on an uncertain guess about the action's consequences in the future removes morality from the solid ground upon which Kant hopes to place it. But the insistence that consequences are unknowable also serves Kant's need to identify what he calls the "empirical" as separate from the deterministic laws of reason; transcendental philosophy identifies the rational categories by which we must perceive the world, by which we must make moral decisions, and by which we must judge aesthetic qualities, but transcendental philosophy does not identify any a priori forms that can determine in advance the contingent appearances of the empirical (or their order of appearance). The insusceptibility of consequences to rational calculation introduces a break in a purely deterministic world view that Kant further exploits by identifying the whole realm of ends as the space of freedom. Morality, the law, duty, and hence reason are all separated in Kant from the personal decision of what end I shall pursue and what means I choose for its pursuit. The autonomous individual is completely on her own when it comes to choosing what she wishes to do in order to aim for happiness; the inability of anyone to say for certain what actions will yield happiness justifies this freedom. "Men have different views on the empirical end of happiness and what it consists of, so that as far as happiness is concerned, their will cannot be brought under any common principle nor thus under any external law harmonising with the freedom of everyone" (1970 73–74).

The political position that follows from this freedom concerning "the empirical end of happiness" is now commonly known as "deontological liberalism." Michael Sandel describes this position as the conviction that "society, being comprised of a plurality of persons, each with his own aims, interests, and conceptions of the good, is best arranged when it is governed by principles that do not *themselves* presuppose any particular conception of the good; what justifies these regulative principles above all is not that they maximize the social welfare or otherwise promote the good, but rather that they conform to the concept of *right*, a moral category given prior to the good and independent of it" (1982 1). In Kant, *right*'s independence stems from its being determined by practical reason, and he describes the embodiment of right in the laws of a commonwealth as existing in tension with the negative freedom of each autonomous individual's determination of his own ends without external interference. *"Right* is the restriction of each individual's freedom so that it harmonises with the freedom of everyone else (in so far as this is possible within the terms of a general law). And *public right* is the distinctive quality of the *external laws* that make this constant harmony possible. Since every restriction of freedom through the arbitrary will of another party is termed *coercion*, it follows that a civil constitution is a relationship among *free* men who are subject to coercive laws" (1970 73). The restriction on individual freedom embodied in *right* is rational insofar as it places individual actions under the rule of the categorical imperative. But Kant also call the commonwealth an "arbitrary will," because the end of social harmony and the means toward its achievement ("the *external laws*") can be seen as products not of reason but of an arbitrary choice of an end and of the means that may or may not (given the uncertainty of consequences) further that end.

Kant's identification of a tension between social laws and freedom resurfaces in most discussions of "negative freedom." In his famous essay "Two Concepts of Liberty," Isaiah Berlin offers a deceptively simple definition of freedom: "By being free . . . I mean not being interfered with by others. The wider the area of non-interference the wider my freedom" (1969 123). We only confuse the issue, Berlin insists, if we try to define freedom in ways that take into account the constitutive constraints the social context places on individual action. Versions of positive freedom, which link the very possibility of action to the social forms within which the individual is embedded, may have "begun as a doctrine of freedom," but have "turned into a doctrine of authority and, at times, of oppression" (1969 xliv); accounts of positive freedom are guilty "of the confusion . . . of identifying freedom with its conditions" (1969 lviii).

Having proscribed any reference to the enabling social context, however, Berlin must admit that negative liberty presents an ideal that can never be fully achieved. "I do not wish to say that individual freedom is, even in the most liberal societies, the sole, or even the dominant, criterion of social action" (1969 169). Rather, we must realize that we live in a world of competing ends and values of which negative liberty is only one, and there will necessarily be cases where that freedom will be restricted in the name of other goods. "Ends collide; . . . one cannot have everything. Whence it follows that the very concept of an ideal life, a life in which nothing of value need ever be lost or sacrificed, in which all rational (or virtuous or legitimate) wishes must be capable of being truly satisfied—this classical vision is not merely utopian, but incoherent. The need to choose, to sacrifice some ultimate values to others, turns out to be a permanent characteristic of the human predicament" (1969 li).

Apart from any doubts we might entertain about this metaphysical assertion about the "permanent human condition," we should note that Berlin's rejection of the "utopian" here echoes Hegel's argument that proponents of negative freedom pursue an abstract vision that could never possibly be realized.[1] If freedom is defined as the absence of all limitations, then freedom can never be realized, and the political theorist will be hard pressed to legitimate any social limits on such freedom.[2] Berlin's final position is that, given the plurality of possibly desirable ends, our best safeguard is to grant as much individual freedom of choice as possible, while accepting that the perpetual problem of liberalism is how to achieve "a maximum degree of noninterference compatible with the minimum demands of social life" (1969 161). The advantage of this position for Berlin is that it calls a spade a spade, as in Kant's decription of "right" as "coercive." Berlin praises Hobbes for at least being "candid: he did not pretend that a sovereign does not enslave: he justified this slavery, but at least did not have the effrontery to call it freedom" (1969 164).

Like all liberal thinkers who assume an original state of individual autonomy, Kant must explain how these individuals ever came to submit to "coercive laws." He fully recognizes that the original submission—the agreement of all to be subject to the law—requires unanimity, an expression of a "general will" that includes everyone. And the model for this original agreement is, of course, the social contract. But Kant can only endorse the reality of the contract as a useful idea, not something that could have ever happened. The condition of unanimity is too stringent to have ever been met in actuality. "We need by no means assume that this contract . . . based on a coalition of

---

[1]See Hegel (1967a 22), a portion of which I quote below, page 55.

[2]Ronald Dworkin has persistently attempted to dissociate liberalism from an attachment to negative liberty on the grounds that the notion has "caused more confusion than it has cured" because it can be translated into a practical political imperative only "by so watering down the idea of a right that the right to liberty is something hardly worth having at all" (1978 268). For Dworkin, liberalism must be founded on the twin pillars of rights and equality, both of which are seriously compromised by attachment to a stringent notion of noninterference with the individual. This is not the place for a full discussion of Dworkin's work, but I find him the contemporary liberal thinker most attuned to the problems with classical liberal thought that concern me in this book, and I find his concern with issues of social norms and of legitimation congenial.

wills of all private individuals in a nation to form a common, public will for the purposes of rightful legislation, actually exists as a *fact*, for it cannot possibly be so. . . . It is in fact merely an *idea* of reason, which nonetheless has undoubted practical reality; for it can oblige every legislator to frame his laws in such a way that they could have been produced by the united will of a whole nation, and to regard each subject, in so far as he can claim citizenship, as if he had consented within the general will" (1970 79).

Kant's version of right (of the legitimate restriction of individual freedom by the commonwealth) as based not on an actual contract but on the *idea* of a contract has curious consequences. The legislator is not answerable to the contract or to the people, in Kant's view, but only to "the idea of reason." Kant describes how the legislator determines the legitimacy of any planned legislation: "If the law is such that a whole people could not *possibly* agree to it . . . it is unjust; but if it is at least *possible* that a people could agree to it, it is our duty to consider the law as just, even if the people is at present in such a position or attitude of mind that it would probably refuse its consent if it were consulted" (1970 79). It is the idea of justice that provides the criterion, never the actual granting of consent by the governed. Thus it follows that the people have no right of resistance to the legislator's decisions. "For so long as it is not self-contradictory to say that an entire people could agree to such a law, however painful it might seem, then the law is in harmony with right. But if a public law is beyond reproach with respect to right, it carries with it the authority to coerce those to whom it applies, and conversely, it forbids them to resist the will of the legislator by violent means" (1970 80–81). This formulation might seem to open the door for legitimate protest on the ground that a law is not beyond reproach; but Kant squelches that notion by telling us that no court of appeal exists for settling a dispute between the legislator and others about whether a law fits the criterion, so the people must submit because they have given the legislator the authority to make the decisions about which laws are rightful.

Kant thus insulates right from any actual expression of the general or democratic will. Right is an absolute standard, the idea of what would be compatible with a general will if such a will were ever possible in fact. (Right, we might say, is a kind of thought experiment.) Right is rational, nonempirical, autonomous, universal, coercive, and public. It is contrasted to freedom, the state of being unrestricted, which is nonrational, empirical, individuated, and private. The only characteristic shared by right and freedom is autonomy: right is autonomous in respect to the people's will; freedom is autonomous to any social bond to others or to any social influence on the formation of desires. Right and freedom meet only on the limited space of the public, a space in which the individual cedes to the rightful restrictions of his freedom within a commonwealth. The meeting ground is the rational; the individual can freely consent to coercive laws that fit the rational form of being acceptable to all and applicable to all.

Kant believes that he can mitigate the potential conflict between right and individual freedom by insisting that right only applies within the realm of the rational and by expecting that the rational element in each individual will freely align itself with the right. Thus the public becomes rationality's sphere, while the private remains the nonrational sphere of freedom. The goal in Kant's politics, as in his transcendental philosophy, is to carefully circumscribe the sphere of the rational in order to leave as large a space as possible for freedom. Here we have the essence of the concept of negative freedom, which can be formulated as the conviction that freedom is possessed apart from, not in conjunction with, the public (as embodied in the state, or in society, or in social bonds). The liberal proponent of negative freedom pitches his political philosophy toward the limitation of society's or the state's right to make demands on the individual, trying to find the perfect minimal amount of restriction that will prevent the war of all against all without introducing any superfluous constraints.

Clearly, the ideal of negative freedom presupposes an autonomous individual who can shape desires and courses of action apart from any social context. The holism of postmodern thought radically questions that such an individual—the self-directed humanist subject—can ever exist. At the other extreme, the liberal is not willing to accept the fully anarchist proposition that selves—or perhaps even some fragmentary, atomistic impulses or desires prior to any conception of a unified self—are radically incommensurable, and thus have no way of relating to one another. Liberalism invariably offers some version of the public/private split, where the public designates the grounds for communal life and the private indicates the grounds for individuality. The drawing of the boundaries between the public and the private spheres, needless to say, is crucial, since it designates what activities come within the sphere of the political, that is, of the legitimate jurisdiction of the social body as a whole. Within postmodern thought, the liberal attempt to retain both a public and a private sphere, both a rational social harmony and an empirical pursuit of individual happiness (to use Kant's terms), often appears like wanting to have your cake and eat it too. It is hard to see how the claims of both spheres can be maintained. Marxist-inspired social theories push toward the dominance of the public over the private encapsulated in the belief that "all is political," while anarchist theories (either rightist versions of extreme individualism or leftist versions of polymorphous heterogeneity) identify all sources of public authority as oppresssive and undesirable.

Kant reconciles universality and individual autonomy by giving each its separate sphere *and* by locating both universal reason and individual difference within the self. And in that wonderful sleight of hand that underlies bourgeois humanism, the priority of individual difference is guaranteed under the sign of universality. The individual is sacred—always an end and never a means, in Kant's famous formula—by virtue of what she holds in common with all other individuals: rational faculties and autonomy. Similarity, not difference, is what leads Kant to value the individual and to envision a public sphere built on these elements of similarity but charged with protecting (or at least not interfering with) the experiences of difference. Legitimacy in Kant must always be tied to reason, to what is held in common by all humans; the careful circumscription of reason ensures that legitimate authority will be restricted so that it never restrains freedom but creates that social world in which the possibility of individual freedom is maximized only because each citizen "accord[s] to others the same rights as he enjoys himself" (1970 74).

In Kant's work, then, a self-consciousness about the "internal" production of truth that characterizes modernity generates a search for underlying conditions of the production's possibility, a search that Kant calls "critique" and that we can recognize as essentially constitutive of what we now call "theory." The movement of philosophy's focus from the external facts of the universe to the internal processes of thought necessarily leads theory to "transcendental" subject matter, to the introduction of concepts and contents that are not directly observable and will not ordinarily be part of subjects' reports on their own behavior. Some kind of rational deduction from observed actions to a statement of the a priori grounds for those actions will be necessary. In addition, Kantian theory will only concern itself with the universal, with those experiences and their grounds that are common to all humans. The particular is distanced from theory's notice or its interference.

Insofar as he posits a unified, coherent individual who is constituted prior to all experience as a necessary precondition of experience, and insofar as he insists on the universality of reason and its sole legitimacy in the arbitration of disputes, the conclusions Kant reaches in his own theoretical deductions are recognizably bourgeois. He believes that appeals to reason and reason alone will settle all disputes, either by rendering a clear principle to which all will subscribe or, more often, by indicating clearly what lies beyond reason's appeal as an element of individual freedom that must be reasonably tolerated. His whole enterprise is resolutely humanist, from its initial Copernican turn from the objective world to his continual use of philosophy to erect and protect a realm of human freedom. Thus at its very inception the new kind of critical philosophy or theory that accords with modernity is linked to a humanist conception of an autonomous human subject and to a liberal politics determined to limit severely the social realm's ability to interfere with that autonomous subject.

Postmodern writers inevitably find themselves continually at odds with Kant. Ironist theory wants to repudiate the bias toward the universal that Kant built into theory and wishes to argue that, whatever Kant's good intentions toward difference, the effect of designating universal conditions of rationality that define the essentially human is to exclude various differences as, by definition, nonhuman. In addition, postmodern theory has at times questioned the serene Kantian confidence in the powers of reflection by adopting the more troubling view that we are least likely to understand our own motives and conditions of existence.[3] Finally, postmodernism, with its suspicion of autonomy, has questioned the barriers that Kant erects between the different spheres of the public and the private, and of pure reason, practical reason, and aesthetic judgment.[4] At its most extreme, postmodernism would like to move away from the certainties that Kant's transcendental deduction provides, abandoning the claim to uncover necessities in favor of projecting us into the differential play of practices, meanings, and options that it portrays as the terrain of human endeavor.

To scuttle the Kantian version of theory, however, has proved none too easy. For one thing, ironist theory retains Kant's bias toward the human, his exclusive interest in the world humans make and inhabit. For another, the description of our condition as one of insertion within networks (or systems) of differential play is hard put to avoid transcendental claims in the process of arguing that such *is* our condition. The play itself might not require any transcendental knowledge, but to describe the play usually does. (And Kant, of course, never claims that apprehension of objects requires knowledge of the categories; theory for Kant reveals necessities that operate whether we know of them or not.) Postmodern theory is suspicious of all identifications of necessary conditions, worrying that these discovered necessities are merely

---

[3]Foucault's assertion, in *The Archaeology of Knowledge*, that "it is not possible for us to describe our own archive, since it is from within these rules that we speak" (1972 130) offers but one instance of the widespread notion that it is easier to decipher the determinants of others' behavior than the determinants of one's own.

[4]Deleuze's lack of patience with Kant is shared by many postmodern writers, although not by Lyotard. For Deleuze, Kant "seems to have confused the positivity of critique with a humble recognition of the rights of the criticised. There has never been a more conciliatory or respectful total critique. The opposition between project and results . . . is easily explained. Kant merely pushed a very old conception of critique to the limit, a conception which saw critique as a force which should be brought to bear on all claims to knowledge and truth, but not on knowledge and truth themselves; a force which should be brought to bear on all claims to morality, but not on morality itself. Thus total critique turns into the politics of compromise: even before the battle the spheres of influence have already been shared out" (1983 89).

used to close down certain possibilities, to attempt to control from above the proliferation of differences, of oppositions, and of unforeseen novelties. But it is very difficult to describe the conditions that allow for differences and novelties themselves without relying on transcendental claims about this or that being *the* way that humans interact in the world. In fact, to make my own transcendental claim about a necessary condition of theoretical thought, I believe that once the processes of meaning formation or social interaction are discussed, the identification of enabling conditions for certain types of human behavior cannot be avoided, no matter how hard the writer tries.

Most troubling for me is Kant's resolute ahistoricism. While it may turn out that we want to identify some transcendental conditions as everywhere applicable, I think that we would do better to begin by trying to describe the conditions that foster the experiences of humans in particular cultures and at particular times. Whether a historicist transcendentalism is a complete contradiction in terms, so utterly foreign to Kant's thought as to be inconceivable, is of course a matter of debate. Hegel's work suggests that a historicist theory can still aspire to identify fundamental conditions within a circumscribed time and place, while also suggesting that such an outlook radically questions Kantian assumptions about reason's autonomy from the empirical and the individual's autonomy from the social.

HEGEL AND THE RELATIONAL RULE OF THE DIALECTIC

The postmodern insistence on cultural and historical differences has made Hegel's work of crucial importance once more. But that emphasis ensures that postmodernism's Hegel is shorn of all the ontological claims about the rationality of the real that allow him to adopt eventually a universalism that makes Kant's look pale by comparison. We are left with a Hegel who is the philosopher of change and becoming. Crucially, Hegelian change takes place within a holistic, relational system; the identity of particulars and the dynamic processes to which they are submitted are functions of their differential relations to other elements in the system. When Hegel's teleology of Spirit's movement toward self-consciousness is dropped as well as his ontology, the Hegelian whole strikingly resembles the relational wholes found in Saussure's structuralism and Derrida's poststructuralism.

Kant asks how it is possible that the world appears to us (is experienced by us) in a certain way. His question is not interpretive insofar as he assumes that appearances as experienced are unproblematic once we figure out how there can be any experience at all. His acceptance of appearances' simplicity is in keeping with his calm assumption that reason is transparent to itself and that the autonomy of reason (both pure and practical) is never seriously threatened. Hegel challenges this Kantian universe by portraying a reason that is divided within itself. Without doing too much injustice to the two philosophers, we might say that Kant's dualism allows him to present two spheres—human experience and things-in-themselves—utterly separate from one another (except in the moment of "intuition") but completely unified within themselves, whereas Hegel's monism commits him to a single sphere—the rational real that is Spirit—is nonetheless riven by internal divisions. His presentation of a fragmented, pluralistic monolith indicates why Hegel is so important to postmodernism.

The fact of difference leads Hegel to ask, in a way Kant never does, the question of meaning. The way things appear to us does not necessarily allow us to grasp their meaning. Appearances are always only partial. Only an interpretation that reveals their relation to the whole correctly identifies their significance. With Hegel, modern philosophy is introduced to a metaphysics of the whole and to issues of interpretation. (Of course, the Judeo-Christian tradition provides a long history of concern with interpretive questions, but modern philosophy from Descartes to Kant, in both the rationalist and the empiricist traditions, did not think that the central problems of epistemology were problems of interpreting meaning.) Hegel attempts to make interpretation theoretically rigorous; he does so by portraying the meaning of any particular as constituted by its position within a whole order and its relation to other particulars within that whole. Thus meaning is systematic in Hegel, or "logical," to use his term. "Concepts [in Hegel] acquire their meaning, their determinateness, from their logic, from their behavior *vis-à-vis* other concepts. The logic of a concept is therefore not external to its determinateness but instead internal to it, constitutive of it."[5]

Autonomy for Hegel can only equal meaninglessness; the particular only exists as a particular and gains significance within the whole, and the movement of the dialectic is toward the whole that includes absolutely everything. The human sciences are deeply influenced by Hegel insofar as they take interpretive issues (how humans construe, construct, and are constrained by the meanings the world has for them) as their subject matter and, more recently in structuralism and poststructuralism, insofar as they look to systematic wholes as constitutive of the meaning of particulars.

Interpretation is crucial to Hegel because the multiplicity evident in human

[5]Pinkard (1985 88).

history does not immediately reveal that history's essential unity. Like Kant, Hegel begins with the fact of human experience, but in Hegel's case that means the facts of historical change and of human blindness to the workings of absolute Spirit. Blindness raises the question of why human beings fail to recognize that, essentially, they are of the same nature as the realities that they confront as other than themselves. Since, ontologically, subject and object are the same, why does the world appear dualistic or multiple to human observers? Hegel's answer, of course, is that Spirit is alienated from itself and that history must be read as the long detour toward the eventual reconciliation of Spirit to its multiple manifestations. This narrative, implausible to twentieth-century readers, would be of little contemporary interest if not tied to Hegel's presentation of the logic of contradiction and to the hermeneutical strategies he develops to interpret various historical moments in relation to the alienated, but still determinate, whole.

The logic of contradiction becomes preeminent in Hegel because Spirit cannot think itself, cannot have any awareness of its own existence and identity, unless it confronts another that stands over against it, defining its limits by negation. The subject does not take on existence until it encounters an object. Hence, contradiction on the most basic level involves a contestation of the subject's ubiquity (of its being all that is) that defines the subject's boundaries and its difference from objects (or others) that occupy the world with it. "Everything that exists stands in correlation, and this correlation is the veritable nature of every existence. The existent thing in this way has no being of its own, but only in something else" (1975 191). The existential confrontation with an other establishes the thing's boundaries, its specificity. But this existential situation must yield to logical contradiction, which for Hegel captures the true state of affairs: that the subject both is and is not the object that it confronts, in the first instance, as its utter negation.

The historical narrative of Spirit's progress relates the slow coming to terms with and learning how to think this second (logical) contradiction. This process unfolds by way of the dialectic. "We are aware that everything finite, instead of being stable and ultimate, is rather changeable and transient; and this is exactly what we mean by that Dialectic of the finite, by which the finite, as implicitly other than what it is, is forced beyond its immediate or natural being to turn suddenly into its opposite" (1975 118). Such "sudden turns" occur when the existing confrontation of the subject with its negation is *aufhebung* (often translated as "overcome") by the positing of a new subject that better expresses the unity of the previously confrontational pair. "The Speculative Stage, or stage of Positive Reason, apprehends the unity of terms (propositions) in their opposition—the affirmative, which is involved in their disintegration and transition" (1975 119). For Hegel, the confrontation of any subject with any object always defines the boundaries of each, but we can find a third term that encompasses both the subject and the object in a way that captures their essential unity (within diversity) with each other. Hegel cheerfully recognizes that his speculative stage "means very much the same as what, in special connexion with religious experience and doctrines, used to be called Mysticism" (1975 121). He only insists that we recognize that he has made the insights of Mysticism now totally accessible to reason: "The reason-world may be equally styled mystical—not however because thought cannot both reach and comprehend it."

Within history, change is explained by the fact that successive contradictions before the dialectic reaches the final stage of absolute Spirit's complete recognition of itself are inherently unstable, because they are not the complete truth. Each contradiction must yield to the new subject that provides a better understanding of the essential unity that the dialectic will ultimately reveal. "Contradiction is the very moving principle of the world: and it is ridiculous to say that contradiction is unthinkable. The only thing correct in that statement is that contradiction is not the end of the matter, but cancels itself" (1975 174). But change in Hegel is not contingent; each contradiction necessarily yields to one, and only one, new subject, because only one subject logically subsumes the two earlier, confrontational terms. Once a certain contradiction generates a dialectical series, the successive moves are locked into place; no variations are possible.

But, crucially, the perception of that necessity is only possible within an interpretive framework that recognizes Spirit's quest. History witnesses multiple misinterpretations of its own meaning; necessity overwhelms contingency only at the moment when the correct interpretation is reached. And since each historical moment can only interpret itself and the past in the terms provided by the point the dialectic has reached at that moment, the achievement of a correct interpretation is itself a necessary development. In fact, that moment (logically) can only be reached when Spirit finally recognizes itself for what it is.

As we might expect, contemporary theory is not very interested in Hegel's vision of correct interpretation, but his notion of incorrect interpretation has been immensely important. We might best grasp just why by considering Hegel's overall attitude toward incompletion. Misinterpretation, on any level, can always be described in Hegel as mistakenly taking as whole (or complete or self-sufficient) an entity that cannot be understood unless placed in relation to something else. Within the dialectic, this mistake breaks down into two distinct moments: the case in which a subject sees itself as self-sufficient and the case in which a dialectical pair—subject and negation—does not recognize its need to be subsumed within a new subject. For Hegel, the subject's blindness of either sort is completely necessary; my use of the term *recognition* suggests that somehow the subject sees its mistake and then corrects it, but in fact the movement of the dialectic is completely divorced from human will. The dialectic proceeds by logical necessity and the subject's blindness is also logically necessary. (Hegel identifies this blindness as "understanding," which "sticks to fixity of characters and their distinctness from one another: every such limited abstract it treats as having a subsistence and being of its own" [1975 113]. Understanding is overcome by dialectics, but understanding is a necessary phase of thought, not an error that is to be avoided altogether.)

This account of human blindness within history has at least four important consequences. First, it places the impetus of change on the assumption that contradictions are unstable and must, in fact, dissolve into new conditions. The transferral of the properties of logic into history has, of course, particularly bedeviled Marxist theories of change; twentieth-century pessimism from Nietzsche on can often be located in the counterassertion that the contradictions in human life, while productive of suffering, also prove remarkably durable.

Second, the Hegelian position necessarily represents a severe diminution of the optimistic humanism we found in Kant. We have to be careful here because, in his own quirky way, Hegel is a more vehement humanist than Kant. Hegel very much accepts modernity's founding assertion that humans occupy a world of their own making, whose basic principles are immanent to the species. By making both humans and reality isomorphically rational, Hegel achieves a radical immanence. Spirit is not transcendent because Spirit is the very essence of humans, and eventually (in Hegel's philosophy), a knowledge of Spirit is as available to humankind as a knowledge of the Kantian categories. This moment of pure transparency, however, comes only at the end of a long history during which humans in fact do not know the truth about their essence or the true foundations of their actions, and during which those actions have consequences that are the product not of human intention but of "the cunning of reason." No matter that Spirit is finally revealed as immanent to humans; for most of history, it acts as radically transcendent to them, an inaccessible controlling force that renders human decisions and control negligible. Autonomy and freedom are achieved in Hegel only at the end of the dialectical narrative. And since postmodern theorists influenced by Hegel reject the very notion that the dialectic is leading to some kind of ultimate resolution, they are more likely to adopt Hegel's implicit antihumanistic undermining of human control and comprehension rather than his eventual restoration of humanism. Hegel provides ways of talking about forces in history that escape human control and human cognizance.

Third, Hegel's account of history's unfolding uses Spirit, an immanent principle unknown to the humans within which it dwells, in ways roughly parallel to twentieth-century notions of the unconscious. The important point here is not to note how similar Hegel and Freud are, but to recognize that the procedures and claims of interpretation alter drastically once we posit that agents are not conscious of their own motivations. Interpretive theory must now justify claims that would not meet with the agents' consent, an undertaking that almost always involves privileging the observers' account over the agents'. Hegel understands the meaning of Roman history far better than the Romans ever could. Some version of the interpreter's privilege, built on some version of information unavailable to the agent, crops up in almost every human science that follows the interpretive turn taken by Hegel. The justification of that privilege has become increasingly difficult as postmodern theorists attempt to evade the ontological claims on which Hegel rests his case. Hegel claims his interpretations are correct because he is uniquely situated at the moment and place where such a correct interpretation is possible. Postmodern theory almost never makes such a bold claim for its own interpretive privilege, yet it also refuses to grant full authority to agents' self-understanding.

Fourth, and finally, Hegelian interpretation always depends on establishing the relation of parts to an all encompassing whole. His understanding of any particular's meaning assumes that in and of itself it carries no meaning; it becomes significant only by virtue of its participation in totality. We see here the beginning of an antisubstantialist bias that is carried on in structuralist and poststructuralist thought, the insistence that *relations* create meaning. And we see here the impetus toward totalizing, monolithic visions that accompanies such a bias. If things gain meaning only in relation to other things within a systematic whole, the dynamic of interpretation is toward the recognition of ever larger wholes that place ever larger numbers of particulars in relation to one another.

I suggested in Chapter 1 that such an enterprise—the inclusion of everything within an all-encompassing whole—is characteristic of romanticism, while the recognition of how everything is included within the monolith that is contemporary society characterizes the nightmare vision of postmodernism. Crucially, Hegel believes that particulars can remain blind to the totality of constituting relations, which his philosophy finally uncovers. Postmodernism often shares this sense that particulars are blind to the facts of the monolith.

Thus one important strain in postmodern thought is to reveal the monolith that "ideology" (or other forms of mystification) has obscured, but this project exists in conspicuous tension with postmodernism's other goal: to remain faithful to and protect the experience of heterogeneity. Like Hegel, postmodernism often finds itself struggling to find a way to articulate differences within a monist order, often relying on Hegelian images of a whole divided against itself. What postmodernism lacks, of course, is Hegel's faith that the unifying principle, Spirit itself, is exactly what best ensures particularity. In postmodern thought the unifying principle is what destroys plurality—which is another way of saying that while postmodern writers are deeply attracted to and influenced by Hegel's interpretive dialectics, they are repulsed by his politics.

Those postmodern philosophers who follow the Hegelian as opposed to the Kantian path reject Hegel's ontological and/or teleological visions of an eventual reconciliation of Spirit with the objective order and with man in his rational essence. Instead, postmodern Hegelianism adopts a covert ontology that posits meaning as constituted by a relational totality, while stressing the internal divisions (contradictions) within that totality. Contradiction is adopted as the inevitable, necessary status of thought and of being-in-the-(social)-world. Thus postmodern theory pictures us as permanently immersed in the intermediate stages of Hegel's historical narrative, a position that brings Hegel's latent antihumanism and assertions of agents' ignorance to the forefront.

The prevalence of the logic of contradiction in postmodern thought is perhaps so obvious as to escape notice. Certainly, the continental propensity to accept contradictions explains much of the oft-commented-upon failure for a dialogue to develop between continental and Anglo-American philosophy. Marxism, structuralism, poststructuralism, and other derivatives of Hegelianism (including psychoanalysis) all render visible contradictions that are somehow both immanent and hard to discern. Marx and Freud still retain (in the notions of a communist society and in the cure) some hope for eventual overcoming of contradiction, but structuralism and poststructuralism find in contradiction (binary oppositions or the antinomies revealed by a deconstructive reading) both beginning and end. The contradiction generates texts and actions and the interpreter's revelation of contradiction brings his task to an end. These theorists believe contradiction is inevitable because they adopt the Hegelian notion that thought necessarily expands until it meets its negation. We might say that thought, like Napoleon or Hitler, will annex all territories to itself until it meets a resistance it cannot overcome, its definitive negation. Hegel's Spirit finally annexes everything, but contemporary theory retains a hope that no thought or totality has Spirit's power. (In its darkest moments, postmodernism accords such power to capitalism, which has led Stuart Hall to characterize postmodern politics as the desperate search to see if there is discernible somewhere some faint kick against the machine.) Somewhere out there a contradiction can be found that suggests capitalism's limits, that can serve as the starting point for resistance, for the reestablishment of distance, difference, dialogue, of the two-dimensional as opposed to the one-dimensional. The insistence that all thought will meet an other that it cannot completely subdue is at once covert ontology and political hope.

Postmodernism's ontology rests on its claims that the contradictions uncovered by its interpretations *really* exist, although hidden to the agent/ author, who always wants to present his text as the successful achievement of unified, coherent thinking. The interpreter can reveal the inevitable limits to unity and success, embodied in contradictions the author cannot face consciously. We can see that the kind of necessity recovered in this location of contradiction at the foundation of all thought comes very close to a Kantian revelation of the necessary conditions of thought itself. But apart from sharing an ultimate transcendent claim, the differences between neo-Kantian and neo-Hegelian thought are far more important than the similarities. Kantian philosophy aims to reconstruct what makes thought (and experience) coherent; Hegelianism shorn of eventual reconciliation demonstrates thought's continual incoherence. Ironist theory understands thought as nontransparent to itself (although neo-Kantians continually point out that this insistence contradicts the postmodern theorists' own clarity about the nature of thought and its nontransparency), inevitably entangled in contradiction, and situated within a systematic whole that establishes thought's possibility but also generates the divisions and contradictions characteristic of thought.

When we turn to Hegel's politics we begin to see why ironist theory must reject Hegel's explicit ontology of reconciliation to the rationality of the real as embodied in Spirit. In keeping with his emphasis on the way that totalities confer meaning on particulars, Hegel's vision of society is directed against all forms of liberal individualism and of negative liberty. For Hegel, the individual can have no identity and no purpose apart from the social order within which he exists, and thus a freedom that is defined as autonomy from the social order would be completely vacuous. An individual thus freed would have no self that could act on this freedom. The liberal belief in sovereign individuals who preexist society, which is only formed as a later date through a "contract" among the individuals, reverses the actual causal sequence. The individual is always born into a social order (is situated within a family) and only develops a sense of self in relation to others who define his or her limits and, crucially, who extend their acknowledgment or "recognition" of the individual's selfhood. If every particular gains its identity through its confrontation with and/or relation to another, then the Hegelian notion of "recognition" indicates that for conscious selves the crucial confrontation is with another conscious self. "Self-consciousness," the awareness of one's self as a bounded, defined entity, "exists in itself and for itself, in that, and by the fact that it exists for another self-consciousness; that is to say, it *is* only by being acknowledged or 'recognized'" (1967b 229). I take the concept of recognition to imply not only that identity is conferred upon the self by others, but also that this conferral cannot be evaded. Action is by selves because selves are the social form that consciousness takes. Freedom cannot entail an escape from society, for even if such an escape were possible it would hardly be desirable because it would obliterate the very agent who was to gain freedom.

Which is not to say that gaining a self is an unmixed blessing. Hegel presents a "positive" form of freedom, in which the individual discovers and fulfills her complete potential within the framework offered by the social order. In its most chilling form, this freedom consists in the perfect reconciliation of self with society, where the self wills for itself what society asks of it. Of course, Hegel's ontology ensures that such a reconciliation is not a forced subjection of self to society, since both are essentially the same. Self and society alike find their true essence when they conform to the fundamental reality of Spirit. "Freedom is nothing but the recognition and adoption of such universal substantial objects as Right and Law, and the production of a reality that is accordant with them—the State" (1956 59). The perfectly rational self and the perfectly rational state could never come into conflict, and the state's laws would provide the environment in which the self would be liberated into the fullest realization of its essence.

This prior definition of purpose is what troubles most subsequent readers of Hegel. (The other troubling point is his willingness so easily to identify the State with embodied Reason and his seeming lack of criteria for determining in what instances the State is corrupt, does not truly represent Spirit.) If, as so often seems to be the case, individuals manifest a great variety of purposes and experience themselves as in conflict with social forms and other individuals, what justifies the identification of a universal and preexisting standard to which all must conform? Hegel's answer that the standard of rationality already exists and is immanent in humans appears a newer version of Plato's vision of a forgotten knowledge that all possess and that once recalled will foster political unity; Hegel's version of this Platonic notion appears to generate a political vision every bit as tyrannical as Plato's. Conflict will only exist during the time when the principle of rationality is imperfectly understood.

Once again, Hegel's vision is technically humanist (since the rationality he aims to uncover is all our own), but practically antihumanist insofar as a standard not available to humans (at a given moment in history) defines society's and individuals' proper goals. Contemporary political visions almost all reject Hegel's notion of a predetermined purpose, insisting instead that freedom must involve the human creation of purposes not yet forged. Where that freedom rests with each individual, we have deontological, liberal negative liberty. Where, following Rousseau, that freedom rests with society as a collective body, we have a version of "positive freedom" that insists on the openness of the future, on the boundless possibilities of human creativity.

Postmodern thought runs into what I consider its deepest problems at just this point—and I devote the next chapter to a full discussion of this issue. But let me anticipate the argument by suggesting postmodernism's troubled relation to Hegelian politics. With the exception of Richard Rorty, the writers I discuss are prepared to accept the Hegelian denial of negative liberty on the ground that it makes no sense to accord the individual an autonomous existence. Individuals cannot have purposes apart from the social relations that constitute them; thus negative liberty must be an illusion and devoid of content. Postmodernism's stress on contradiction as opposed to reconciliation, however, leads it to look for something that exists in resistance to society and the state. Furthermore, postmodernism's implicit or explicit political commitment to changing the existing order of capitalist society also makes a search for resistant entities necessary. Thus postmodern theory has a built-in tendency to celebrate the resistant, while at the same time holding to a relational view of how entities are constituted that fails to explain how the resistant can even exist. In addition, postmodernism's hostility to self (which it associates with bourgeois humanism) means that it must locate resistance somewhere other than in individuals. The prevalent reverence for resistance (or opposition) indicates a hope for some kind of (even if limited) distance from society, and the political ideal of distance has always found its expression in notions of negative liberty. The end result is an uneasy combination of a Hegelian (holistic) analysis of present conditions with an anarchistic politics that is very close to the liberalism postmodern writers claim to despise.

The version of positive freedom that can be derived from Hegel is founded on the holistic premise that the individual is not self-sufficient and can only be understood in relation to the social. Albrecht Wellmer provides a good overview of this position. His summary is explicitly derived from the work of Hegel and Charles Taylor:

If . . . human individuals are essentially *social* individuals, if, in their very individuality, they are constituted and, as it were, permeated by the culture, traditions, and institutions of the society to which they belong, then their freedom as well must have a social character. Even as *individual* freedom this freedom must have a *communal* character, or at least an essentially communal aspect, expressing and manifesting itself in the way in which the individual participates in and contributes to the communal practices of his society. The originary locus of freedom, then, would not be the isolated individual, but a society that is the medium of individuation through socialization; freedom would have to be thought of as ultimately residing in the structures, institutions, practices, and traditions of a larger social whole. But since this larger social whole is what it is only through being kept alive, "reproduced," and interpreted by the individuals who are part of it, individual and "public" freedom now become inextricably intertwined. (1989 228–29)

My contention is that postmodern thought accepts the premises of the social production of individuals that Wellmer outlines here, but it cannot find a way to describe social "structures, institutions, practices, and traditions" as anything but oppressive, as never productive of freedom. Postmodernism remains stuck on its identification of communities with tyranny.[6] The terms of individual life within the whole provides one central issue in Hegel's *Philosophy of Right*, a book that I attempt to recast in contemporary terms in my closing chapter. At stake is describing the minimal terms of connection between selves and social groups that allows them to "recognize" others' claims to participation in the society's political and material life.

We can highlight this distinction between positive and negative freedom by considering the difference between Hegelian and Kierkegaardian irony. Hegel distinguished between a subjectivist irony that merely distances the self from the world it inhabits and an irony that recognizes how, in this world, "the highest is existent in a limited and finite shape" (1967a 101n.). Hegelian irony is an interpretive move that goes beyond the "finite shape," the particular, to recognize its positioning within the larger set of relations that give it meaning. This type of irony is what Kenneth Burke has in mind when he identifies irony as the trope best suited to dialectical thought because it always indicates the provisional nature of any statement or temporary resting place.[7] Such irony,

---

[6]See Young (1990) for a typical postmodernist insistence that ideals of community "generate exclusions" that conflict with the desirable "openness to unassimilated otherness" which characterizes "a politics of difference" (1990 301). Yet when she turns to describing the "norm for the unoppressive city" (1990 301) that could underwrite the politics of difference, Young unwittingly, but I think inevitably, begins from the fact that even large, anonymous modern cities retain "a continuing sense of national or ethnic identity with millions of other people" (1990 317).

[7]Burke writes: "Irony arises when one tries, by the interaction of terms upon one another, to produce a *development* which uses all the terms. Hence, from the standpoint of this total form . . .

which Burke associates with "humility," keeps looking over its shoulder, expecting the moment or particular to be subsumed into a fuller context or into a new relational system. The key to Hegelian irony is that, like the dialectic, it is dynamic and moves through the experience of particularity to the conscious recognition of the particular thing's constitution by the whole. Heglian irony is not a complete repudiation of the current form, but an awareness that that form is only provisional and partial.

Kierkegaardian irony performs just the opposite task: it preserves the inviolability of the self by refusing the self's investment in the imperfect (from both Hegel's and Kierkegaard's perspective) world in which humans find themselves. (The particular imperfections I would stress are communal, intersubjective institutions such as language, marriage, the state, and the like.) Kierkegaardian irony is essentially spatial and static, since it rests on dividing the self (or part of the self) from its social context and maintaining its distance.[8] It is worth noting that, for Kierkegaard himself, the subjective or Socratic irony that he describes in *The Concept of Irony* is not a final resting place, but a stage to be overcome. In fact, Kierkegaard criticizes Socrates in exactly the terms Hegel uses to criticize negative freedom. "The infinite yet negative freedom" (1971 192) that Socrates finds in irony serves to create the self as a bounded, separate entitity, but Socrates' inability to move beyond the negative moment of self-definition means that "he was incapable of contracting any real relation to the existent" (1971 203). "Socrates appears as one who stands poised ready to leap into something, yet at every moment instead of leaping into this 'other,' he leaps aside and back into himself" (1971 192). Socrates' negative refusal of all relations to things apart from the self is contrasted by Kierkegaard to the position of the Christian who "knows himself to be in a real relationship to his God" (1971 202n.).

I shall have several occasions to return to this distinction between a dynamic Hegelian irony oriented toward a temporal, dialectical overcoming of the partial or fragmentary and a spatial Kierkegaardian irony, because a static

---

none of the participating 'sub-perspectives' can be treated as either precisely right or precisely wrong. They are all voices, or personalities, or positions, integrally affecting one another. When the dialectic is properly formed, they are the number of characters needed to produce the total development" (1969 512).

[8]In his very influential essay "The Rhetoric of Temporality," Paul de Man uses a spatial, subjectivist concept of irony (which he derives from Baudelaire, with a nod toward Kierkegaard) to deconstruct the claim of certain romantic writers to use the symbol to effect a union between disparate entities (such as the sacred and the profane in Coleridge's theory of the symbol). We should recognize that de Man stacks the deck by failing to recognize Hegelian irony as another possible version of romantic irony, a version that would, in turn, undermine de Man's correlation of irony with spatial juxtaposition, metonymy (as opposed to metaphor and its unities), and distance. De Man's insistence that "it is a historical fact that irony becomes increasingly conscious of itself in the course of demonstrating the impossibility of our being historical" (1983 211) is completely inimical to Hegel's or Kenneth Burke's understanding of irony.

denial of dialectical progress reverberates throughout postmodern thought. In addition, the persistent ideal of negative freedom makes a subjectivist irony continually attractive. In Kierkegaard the ironist stands aloof because he refuses to allow any appearance to stand for or represent a subjective truth that he feels exceeds any possible representative. A similar distrust of all representation as compromised can be found in many postmodern writers. A continual irony negates the partiality of each expression, always reminding us that words are, in de Man's phrase, blind and insightful at the same time. Kierkegaardian irony's perpetual negativity evades any tie to such untrustworthy representatives. Irony "negates the phenomenal, not in order to posit anything by means of this negation, but negates the phenomenal altogether. It flees back into itself instead of going out of itself, it is not in the phenomenon but seeks to deceive by means of the phenomenon, the phenomenon is not in order to manifest essence but to conceal essence" (1971 235n.).

The use of the single term *irony* by both Hegel and Kierkegaard is justified by their common repudiation of complete identification with the here and now as an adequate expression of meaning, truth, or what is finally desired. But this refusal can reflect either a commitment to a future in which the present will stand transformed into a closer approximation of what is sought or a commitment to a purity of self that would be sullied by any involvement in this imperfect world. Hegel is adamant that the negative freedom imagined in subjectivist irony is a fantasy that evades the necessary involvement of all selves in particular sets of determinate relationships. We can, in Hegel's view, be attuned to the hope and necessity of those determinate relationships' transformation and thus view them ironically, but we cannot be disengaged from them entirely. Hegel is scathing in his contempt for what he deems an "abstract" image of a free-floating self and what he sees as that image's disturbing consequences. Such abstraction leads to the

> flight from every content as from a restriction. . . . This is the freedom of the void which rises to a passion and takes shape in the world; while still remaining theoretical, it takes shape in religion as the Hindu fanaticism of pure contemplation, but when it turns to actual practice, it takes shape in religion and politics alike as the fanaticism of destruction—the destruction of the whole subsisting social order. . . . Only in destroying something does this negative will possess the feeling of itself as existent. Of course it imagines that it is willing some positive state of affairs, such as universal equality or universal religious life, but in fact it does not will that this shall be positively actualized, and for this reason: such actuality leads at once to some sort of order, to a particularization of organizations and individuals alike; while it is precisely out of the annihilation of particularity and objective characterization that the self-consciousness of this negative freedom proceeds. Consequently, what negative freedom intends to will can never be anything in itself but an abstract idea. (1967a 22)

The failure of the proponents of negative freedom to will the societal and institutional means of their political visions stems from the fact that such actualizations within a determinate social context must always appear to them as entailing limitations on the negative freedom that they cherish. Negative freedom is, in Hegel's view, condemned to eternal negation.

Hegel also criticizes the version of positive freedom espoused by Rousseau, a version Hegel calls "absolute freedom." Hegel believes that the attempt to put "absolute freedom" into practice must result in tyranny and even political terror. His argument amounts to a complete denial that revolutions are possible. From where will revolutions derive the content of their new social order? Hegel asks. The identities, self-understandings, and allegiances of citizens are necessarily wrapped up in the social order in which they grew up. Only realities immanent to them (i.e., the principle of rationality or, more concretely, the experienced contradictions of current social forms) can shift those allegiances in any lasting way. We see here how committed the dialectic is to continuous, as opposed to abrupt, change. In ignoring the (relative) validity of current social forms and the prescriptions enforced by the preexistent standards of rationality and morality, the Rousseauian revolutionary assumes his "absolute freedom" to remake the world. But in disregarding these constraints, the revolutionary also disregards the fact that his vision cannot possibly emanate from the collective, even while he insists that the legitimacy of political actions is dependent on their being products of the "general will." The revolutionary must encounter some resistance from some members of society because he refuses to recognize either the fact or the validity of their identification with current social forms. Consensus can only be reached by overriding or exterminating those groups that oppose the revolutionary's vision.

Hegel's argument here is that only a full appreciation of pre-existing constraints on what we can actually achieve politically allows for change that does not destroy the very fabric of society. And only such changes, which grow out of existing allegiances, will last. We can recognize here once again how the logic of the dialectic overwhelms any actual human intentions. Hegel must argue that the changes actually wrought by the French Revolution are the changes possible at that stage in history given the constraints that he theoretically describes. Thus Robespierre and the rest did not achieve their conscious aims, but their actions did foster the dialectic's movement to its next stage. There is no "absolute freedom" of the kind to which Rousseau and some versions of Marxism aspire—the ability to forge an entirely new social order. Instead, there is only what Charles Taylor calls a "situated freedom," which is not negative because the individual's identity is only achieved within the social situation in which she lives and is not absolute because the situation limits the possibilities for constructive and successful action.[9]

The problem Hegel's notion of "situated freedom" articulates can be stated as the experiential fact that everywhere humans are found, some kind of social order is always already in place. These orders exhibit a collective coherence that is hard to explain theoretically or historically. The myth of the social contract and Rousseau's notion of the lawgiver provide accounts of the origins of society, but such myths are misleading if they suggest that any individual anywhere has ever found herself existing apart from society. And such origin stories do not explain the identification of individuals with their societies or the persistence of societies over time. Hegelian theory, the notion of situated freedom, does not answer why human life must take this social form but simply provides a theoretical description of how individual identity and desire are shaped within the constraints of social order. Sociology has followed Hegel's lead here, focusing on uncovering the particular determinant influence given societies have on their individual members. Or to put it slightly differently, the necessary conditions for individual thought and action that sociology highlights are social conditions rather than universal, rational ones of a Kantian sort. This emphasis on social conditions has become increasingly important in the other human sciences—anthropology, history, philosophy, literary studies, and even psychology—over the past forty years. The anthropological theory of culture, Wittgenstein's notion of "forms of life," Bourdieu's notion of "habitus," and Habermas's attempt to reveal the implicit social contract that underlies communication all share a propensity to locate within communal life elements of a preexisting order that constrains possible individual behavior.

Radical thinkers have routinely denounced such theories of social determinants as conservative because those theories place limits on the possibility of change. Marcuse's attack on ordinary language philosophy in *One-Dimensional Man* (1966) is but one example. More recently, Roberto Mangabeira Unger has launched a full-scale attack on what he calls the "false necessity" that characterizes most social and political theory. Such theories, Unger claims, see "in the constraints on social invention the reality that makes possible general and historical explanations" (1987 145). Certainly, Unger's warning against prematurely closing down our options by defining large areas of impossibility is crucial, but only an anarchy akin to Feyerabend's proclamation that "the only rule is that there are no rules" can achieve a complete break

---

[9]See Taylor (1979 100–169). My description of Hegel's views on absolute freedom is deeply indebted to Taylor's account, while the stress on positive freedom throughout this book follows a path that Taylor's work on Hegel and his subsequent work on identity lays out.

from the Hegelian identification of contextual determinants. Postmodern writers on the whole resist that anarchistic break when analyzing current social forms, partly because they still believe that the identification of social determinants is a crucial element of any politically useful knowledge (the lingering allegiance to critique in postmodern thought), partly because their continued attachment to relational models of explanation makes them suspicious of claims about the autonomous freedom to forge novel purposes and visions. Those engaged in political conflicts are related to one another historically and within the given social field on which the conflict is waged; the delineation of that field and the limits it imposes on possible action can be enabling as well as stultifying. An emphasis on how context enables action follows from a recognition of positive freedom's account of the capacities that social embeddedness produces, as contrasted to negative freedom's focus on the constraints that result from immersion in the social.

We should also note that the contemporary versions of preexistent determinants are not committed (except in Habermas's case) to the "rationality" of the identified constraints; and none of these contemporary thinkers would insist that the constraints are universal. Setting these important differences aside for the moment, however, the Hegelian conviction that immanent, preexisting, and not necessarily (or even often) conscious social frameworks shape individual behavior has resurfaced dramatically in contemporary social theory, with the important consequence that the debate between liberal negative liberty and radical versions of absolute freedom are now complicated by the other kind of positive freedom espoused by Hegel. Liberal negative freedom posits an autonomous self that can form its own purposes and act on its own to achieve them; radical absolute freedom posits an autonomous society that can collectively form its own purposes and act to achieve them. Hegelian positive or "situated" freedom is more constrained. It presents both individuals and society as shaping their identities and their purposes in relation to others and to the past, and it understands the capacity for successful action as limited by what the existing conditions make possible. This stress on contextual constraints may make the term *freedom* seem the wrong one to use. But the other half of the argument is that the self in isolation would have no capacity to act at all; the self's (or a society's) ability to have an identity, purposes, and the wherewithal to act upon them are products of its relation to a concrete situation. This capacity to act, and to act purposively with some chance of successful accomplishment of one's purposes, justifies using the term *freedom*.

My attempt in Chapter 4 to use this Hegelian positive freedom as part of a postliberal democratic vision must mitigate Hegel's monism in two respects.

While accepting that selves and purposes are forged in and constituted by social settings, I will try to evade the Hegelian focus on *one* purpose—Spirit's coming to self-consciousness—to which all selves must finally be aligned. The recognition (in the full, Hegelian, sense of the term) of a multiplicity of purposes within the social whole is crucial to a democratic ideal. Moreover, the substitution of society for the state as the locus of the whole is necessary if a more pluralistic, differentiated model of the total context is desired. Different webs of relations throughout society must be recognized as constitutive of selves and purposes; pluralism wants to avoid the absolute subordination of any particular context or sphere of relations to one overriding sphere, the State. I will adapt Althusser's notion of semiautonomy in order to differentiate various spheres while also maintaining that the concept of the social whole still retains some sense and some value.

But even in this pursuit of a more supple holism that respects the concerns expressed by pluralism, Hegel can serve as a guide. The stereotyped notion of Hegel's wish for "undifferentiated wholes" or Prussian absolutism is roughly equivalent to the "vulgar Marxist" view that the economic absolutely determines everything; both positions find some support in Hegel's or in Marx's work, but there is also much to suggest that neither writer ever held so simplistic or unappealing a view.[10] Hegel was concerned with retaining differentiation—both of individuals and of the spheres of family and civil society—within the social totality.[11]

Although freedom for Hegel consists in the alignment of self and State, he does not aim for some kind of mystical dissolution of the self into the State. Rather, he thinks of citizens and of the social order as a totality as different articulations of the same Spirit, thus preserving their difference from one another. "The essence of the modern state is that the universal be bound up with the complete freedom of its particular members and with private well-being, that thus the interests of family and civil society must concentrate themselves on the State, although the universal end cannot be advanced without the personal knowledge and will of its particular members, whose own rights must be maintained. Thus the universal must be furthered, but subjectivity on the other hand must attain its full and living development. It is only when both these moments subsist in their strength that the state can be

[10]I am referring again to Cornel West's comment (quoted in Chapter 1) about the "Hegelian nostalgia for undifferentiated unities" (1988 30). The willfully blind complaint that a Marxist society entails a boring sameness offers a different version of the same misunderstanding.

[11]For a sympathetic account of Hegel's attempt to ensure individual freedom within his vision of the rational State, see Wellmer (1989). This same essay provides a brilliant summary of the claims of negative and positive theories of freedom within contemporary political and philosophical debates.

regarded as articulated and genuinely organized" (1967a 280). Hegel opposed the "general will" in part because it fails to allow for differentiation in
the social places occupied by individuals. "Where civil society, and with it the
State, exists, there arise the several estates in their difference: for the universal substance, as vital, *exists* only so far as it organically *particularizes* itself"
(1974 277). Hegel believed that the division of labor is both necessary and
rational (as well as practically efficient) and insisted that social unity is
enhanced by the diversity of its component parts.

We enter here both into that vexing philosophical problem known as the
One and the Many and into political debates (particularly crucial for postmodernism) concerning the significance of difference. Contemporary radical
theory, in particular, appears transfixed before the issues raised here, wanting
to follow Marx's condemnation of the division of labor (his desire for a society
in which all belong to one class) and to find a way to preserve (celebrate)
differences in a modern world that appears more homogeneous each hour.
Such theorists would no doubt endorse Hegel's insistence that "liberty is only
deep when it is differentiated in all its fullness and these differences manifested in existence" (1974 290). An insistence on differences combats the
monolith, but a hard-to-abandon allegiance to equal rights (univeralist, liberal, and bourgeois though they be) makes contemporaries want to ensure
that such differences never place anyone in a social position of advantage or
disadvantage (i.e., that the differences not make any political, economic, or
social difference). Hegel's notion of articulated differences within the social
totality aims to reconcile a notion of the collective with a recognition (that key
Hegelian term) of individuality, a reconciliation also sought by much postmodern theory, particularly feminist and leftist theory. (Admittedly, we cannot
simply equate the postmodern acceptance of the "irreducibility of differences"—in Cornel West's phrase [1988 26]—with an insistence on the
integrity of individuals. Much postmodernism tries both to preserve difference and to deny individuality. I am not convinced, however, that such an
attempt can succeed, if only because the enjoyment of difference and of
freedom is almost always sought for some self or selves.) Hegel's claim to have
successfully protected subjectivity within the universality represented by the
State is not very credible unless we find the freedom he offers to individuals
satisfying. It is an indication of how deep-seated our liberal, humanist heritage is that a freedom that aligns the self with the social order satisfies very
few contemporaries, even while the holistic and relational theoretical vision
that justifies such a concept of freedom appears especially compelling.

In sum, Hegel's theory rests on an ontology that provides a necessity and a
telos to human history and, by an ingenious sleight of hand, makes that

necessity and telos completely immanent to men and women (i.e., fully humanist), even though humans often—usually—are unconscious of the fact. In rejecting Hegel's rationalist ontology, contemporary theory often adopts a covert ontology from Hegel in the form of a universalist account of how thought works by confronting its negation. This postmodern theory can retain assertions of necessity by identifying the inevitability of contradictions, regardless of whether the theorist believes that such contradictions can eventually be overcome (in some dialectical sequence) or not. We can recognize that uncovering the conditions of thought returns us to Kantian (transcendent and internalist) grounds, where theory describes only the necessary conditions of thought and not reality itself. But this somewhat deontologized version of Hegel differs greatly from Kant in its description of thought's conditions, in its insistence that thought's formative contradictions will change over time (thus repudiating Kantian universalism), in its doubts about the transparency of reason to itself, and in its consequent emphasis on the necessity of interpretation. Hegel's politics offer a critique of liberal and radical positions that raises disturbing questions about the limitations of both while also limiting political creativity in ways that can look tyrannical. His political theorizing uncovers preexisting constraints to action that greatly limit our political options. As a result, Hegel's political views have been less explicitly acknowledged as influences by postmodern thought. Yet we can recognize that the questions he raises—particularly about the nature and limits of freedom—continue to figure largely in attempts to delineate the (necessary?) conditions of political action. Since radical political theories and postmodern theory have adopted so much of Hegel's way of theorizing about human action and totalizing contexts, it is not surprising that their political meditations keep returning to Hegelian terrain that they would probably for the most part prefer to avoid. Thus it is also not surprising to find Hegel already concerned with the preservation of multiplicity within totality, a topic that constitutes the most crucial political issue in much contemporary thought.

MARX: POWER VERSUS FREEDOM

Marx's version of Hegelian holism resonates throughout postmodern thought. Peter Berger chastises Marxism for being "prone to what logicians call the fallacy of *pars pro toto*, taking the part for a whole" (1986 30). Marx replaces Spirit with the economic (the material production of material necessities) and interprets all social relations and institutions in terms of their expression of the

economic. Of course, twentieth-century Western Marxism repudiates any
simple version of economic determinism, which it castigates as "vulgar Marxism." But we should recognize that monolithic descriptions of contemporary
society in postmodern thought owe a large debt to Marx's insistence that
society is all of a piece. The substitution by the Frankfurt School or by
Baudrillard of cultural processes of reproduction for material relations of
production does not alter the basic predilection for understanding particulars
as resulting from and functioning as parts of a unified set of activities. On the
other hand, the efforts of contemporary Marxists to combat vulgar Marxism
while retaining some effective form of holism makes them the most subtle
theoreticians of that supple holism at which I also aim, and my debt to them is
evident throughout this work.[12]

More important than Marx's turning of Hegelian idealism on its head (a
move that Western Marxism does much to annul) is Marx's identification of
the whole as a product of power. Hegel questions neither the legitimacy of the
whole nor its desirability. Marx declares that the whole—prior to the achievement of communism—is illegitimate because it always functions to the benefit of one class. The truth (the reality) of history is class conflict, so that any
whole that encompasses more than one class can only be stable if the dominant class keeps the other classes in subjection. The classless, or one-class,
society of communism will be a whole devoid of domination, but all the
wholes that history has known are internally divided. They remain wholes
since the various members (classes) within them are completely defined by
their relation to one another in the given social configuration, but they are
inherently unstable because the contradictions that foster class conflict impel
changes in the total organization of material production and the social relations that form around that production. Thus Marx, like Hegel, introduces a
whole that has a history that is propelled by the overcoming of contradictions
and is internally divided in different ways at different historical stages. The
existing whole (of capitalism) is something to be contested for Marx; the
reality of class conflict indicates differences that combat the reality of the false
wholes of power.

I use the word *reality* deliberately, since Marxist interpretations depend on
an ontology that asserts both that membership in a particular class shapes
one's interests, beliefs, and practices and that the meaning of any particular is
constituted by its relation to the social conditions in which it is produced.

---

[12]See McGowan (1989) for a fuller account of my understanding of the strengths and
weaknesses of contemporary Marxism. The title essay of Jay (1988) provides a wonderful
overview of contemporary Marxism, especially its attempts to slide out from under the totalized,
deterministic visions of an orthodox materialism.

Thus, in the *Grundrisse*, Marx writes: "The more deeply we go back into history, the more does the individual, and hence also the producing individual, appear as dependent, as belonging to a greater whole. . . . The human being is in the most literal sense a political animal, not merely a gregarious animal, but an animal which can individuate itself only in the midst of society."[13] Even if we historicize Marx (avoiding, for example, his tendency to take capitalism as everywhere following the same course of logical development), his fundamental (transcendent) model of the primacy of the social cannot be evaded. In *The German Ideology*, Marx and Engels enjoin us to keep firmly in view "individuals, not as they may appear in their own or other people's imaginations, but as they *really* are; i.e., as they operate, produce materially, and hence as they work under definite material limits, presuppositions and conditions independent of their will" (1970 46–47). This subjection of individuals to "conditions independent of their will" justifies the antihumanist reading of Marx found in the work of Louis Althusser. "Life is not determined by consciousness," Marx and Engels insist, "but consciousness by life" (1970 47). Particular circumstances vary but the universal fact of such determination remains.

The Marxist notion of power adds that the life that determines consciousness is not the product of some neutral or benign force like Hegel's Spirit but rather of some part of society, some particular class, that shapes life to its own interests over and against those of other classes. Marxism calls into question the serene Hegelian conviction that the human force that makes history in modernity is a single, in-dwelling spirit that all humans possess and share. "For Hegel," Althusser writes, "the principle unifying and determining the social totality is not such and such a 'sphere' of society but a principle which has no privileged place or body in society, for the simple reason that it resides in all places and all bodies" (1970 204n.). By contrast, "the unity discussed by Marxism is *the unity of the complexity itself*. . . . The mode of organization and articulation of the complexity is precisely what constitutes its unity. It is to claim that *the complex whole has the unity of a structure articulated in dominance*" (1970 202). The Marxist social whole is forged (produced) by a dominant group.

Different groups in Marx possess different purposes because they occupy different positions within the prevailing social relations. He does not, however, see social reality as the product of an intermingling of these different groups' projects but retains a fairly uncomplicated view of a holistic power. He sees one class as pretty much entirely getting its own way and imposing the

[13]Quoted from Tucker (1978 222–23).

social life that serves its needs on society's other groups. And Marx's own criticism of the societies power has created is that they are too partial (in all senses of the word); the true whole will be the society in which every member equally enjoys the benefits of society's material production. But such partiality (the sign of which is class conflict) does not mean that these imperfect wholes fail to function as the determining system in their particular historical moment. They effectively govern each particular's meaning; their organization of productions and its relations is complete, even if fraught with conflicts that make the successful maintenance of the current arrangements by power always in doubt.

Marx's own universalism appears in his judgment of existing wholes as partial and hence illegitimate. Marxist teleology depends on the image of a nonpartial, nonconflicted whole—and this image provides the absolute, all-or-nothing criterion that leads doctrinaire Marxists to condemn liberal democracies as no more legitimate than military dictatorships, and a lot more insidious. As we could expect, postmodern Marxists often try to abandon Marx's teleological vision and its concomitant notion of legitimacy. Instead, these postmodern writers simply affirm the right of each social group to its own interests, an affirmation based partly on the epistemological grounds that disinterested behavior or knowledge is impossible and partly on the political grounds that groups can only preserve their difference and resist oppression if they aggressively promote their interests. Abandoning Marxist teleology, then, means accepting that social conflict is perpetual, just as abandoning Hegelian teleology entails accepting the ubiquity of contradiction. This position involves the complete repudiation of any notion of legitimate social authority or political agenda. All power and all goals are the products of interest, with no claims on others who do not share those interests.

One further variant of Marx's thoughts on power—the notion of ideology—has been particularly influential in postmodern thought. Although Marx himself rarely uses the word *ideology* or discusses the concept after the early text of *The German Ideology* (written by Marx and Engels in 1845–46 but not published during either man's lifetime), the notion has become central to many twentieth-century versions of Marxism. Very simply, *ideology* can be defined in two ways, with each definition highlighting one of the two factors in Marx's confusing and contradictory use of the term. Definition 1 takes ideology as the ideas or beliefs possessed by any group by virtue of its social position. This definition simply posits the determination of consciousness by one's place in the relations of material production; and since everyone has such a determinate place, everyone would possess or produce an ideology. Definition 2 takes ideology as the conscious (or superstructural or idealistic or cultural) legitimation of the prevailing social arrangements, a legitimation whose most salient feature is its denial of the facts of social conflict that reveal those arrangements' partiality. For Marx and Engels, the "German ideology" is work that denies partiality by denying that material production and its relations are the core of social arrangements; rather, the ideologists locate unity elsewhere, in a national spirit or culture or patriotism, because a good, hard look at material conditions would make the lack of unity obvious. Any and every claim to have achieved social unity does well to take this Marxist skepticism into account.

These two definitions of ideology would not conflict if ideology in the second sense was limited to the dominant class. But Marx waffles on the question of what ideas (or ideological vision) we might expect a given individual, as a member of a class, to hold. He sometimes takes the straightforward position that one's class position determines one's ideas; we can predict that the bourgeoisie and the proletariat will conflict on the ideological as well as the economic plane. At other times, however, Marx proposes what has been called "the dominant ideology thesis," which holds that the ruling class is able to impose its own ideological views on society as a whole.[14] "The ideas of the ruling class are in every epoch the ruling ideas, i.e., the class which is the ruling *material* force of society, is at the same time its ruling *intellectual* force. The class which has the means of material production at its disposal, has control at the same time over the means of mental production, so that thereby, generally speaking, the ideas of those who lack the means of production are subject to it" (1970 64). This statement greatly extends the range of the ruling class's power: Not only do the other classes live within social arrangements formed by the dominant class, but their very apprehension of those arrangements, the ways they think about themselves and their social position, are seen as given to them by the dominant class.

Steven Lukes has usefully distinguished three "dimensions" of power. In the first, "to exercise power is to prevail over the contrary preferences of others" (1986 9); in the second power also includes "controlling the agenda," that is, determining what issues will ever get staged as matters to be contested or decided. The third dimension "incorporates power of the first two kinds, but also allows that power may operate to shape and modify desires and beliefs in a manner contrary to people's interests" (1986a 10). Marx shows little interest in Lukes's second dimension, but his notion of "ruling ideas"

---

[14]Abercrombie, Hill, and Turner (1980) offer what I think is an absolutely correct and devastating attack on "the dominant ideology thesis," arguing that the constraints of the economic and social facts of life keep people going about their daily business, not some intellectual consent that has been manufactured by the ideological forces of the ruling class.

involves a jump from the first dimension to the third. This notion of an imposed ideology, which explains the "false consciousness" of a nonrevolutionary working class, has proved a useful way for twentieth-century Marxism to explain the proletariat's lack of enthusiasm for socialism. Of course, the existence of a dominant ideology also introduces a formidable obstacle to achieving any socialist future, since it makes power that more impregnable. One response to the notion of a dominant ideology has been Western Marxism's shift in interest to the cultural (rhetorical) terrain of combatting the dominant culture's representation of itself. I do not believe that such a shift has proved very useful, especially when combined with a belief that the masses' "false consciousness" must be corrected. I consider alternatives to the whole problematic of ideology in chapter 4.

The classic epistemological problem raised by Marx's theory of ideology is how he can account for his own immunity. If all ideas are motivated by economic interest or if all ideas carry the stamp of the ruling class's views, then how can Marx explain his own privileged access to real causes? This objection, (sometimes referred to as "Mannheim's paradox," since it was first formulated by Karl Mannheim) has troubled Marxists, especially those who are already uneasy with Marx's foundational claims. Alvin Gouldner, examining the concrete interests that Marxism serves, comes to the conclusion that Marxism is the ideology of the intellectuals, not of the proletariat. Gouldner sees Marxism as afflicted by a peculiar false consciousness of its own—the belief that a socialist society would benefit workers rather than the intellectuals who most follow Marx.[15] Postmodern Marxists have been less overtly hostile to the proponents of Marxism than Gouldner has, but they generally have adopted a similar claim that no privileged position can exist and that Marxism's own ideas should thus be fully acknowledged as "interested" and hence ideological in their own right. I pursue some of the consequences of this position in my discussion of Terry Eagleton in the next chapter.

For now I want only to suggest how close this postmodern Marxism can find itself to the Nietzschean notion of the will to power. Marx's teleology (his goal of the one-class society in which everyone's interests are the same and thus relations of domination no longer exist) and his ontology (his ability to reveal the real material conditions that explain—allow for a correct interpretation of—a group's ideology) provide him with concepts and ethical norms (goals) that are outside the play of power. Postmodern Marxism looks with suspicion upon these escape valves, with the result that contemporary

[15] I am summarizing here the complex, and compelling, argument made in Gouldner (1982b), a work that fully justifies Gouldner's description of himself as an "outlaw Marxist."

Marxism is both more and less holistic than Marx himself. More holistic insofar as the rule of power is everywhere; we are always *within* power relations, whereas Marx envisioned a place of knowledge apart from power and an eventual society in which power did not figure. Less holistic insofar as the whole of power is always characterized by conflict, and the very idea of a nonconflicted whole where everyone has the same interest is given up as both impossible and undesirable.

The alignment of postmodern Marxism with Nietzsche would be complete if the postmoderns simply affirmed the fact of perpetual conflict. Postmodern thought, however, while often adopting Nietzsche's enshrinement of power in the place of disinterested knowledge or of any action not motivated by the wish to dominate, usually retains the Marxist hope of diminishing (at least) the sway of power over social groups and social selves. For Nietzsche, freedom and power are joined, either with freedom understood as the utmost exercise of one's own will to power or (as I discuss below) with freedom connected to the affirmation of being dominated. But for Marx and most postmodern writers, freedom is still something that is contrasted to power and imagined as a release from power's constraints, not an exercise, or an acceptance, of power. And it is in asserting the primacy of the social that the Marxist finds a way to counter the Nietzschean portrait of endless conflict. Since power constructs and is subsequently embedded in the social relations that establish the terms of individual life in any given society, there remains the hope that certain social relations will afford greater freedom, will minimize domination. In other words, to return to Lukes's definition of power, certain social arrangements will reduce the chances that one social group will *consistently* "prevail over the contrary preferences of others," always be in the position to set the agenda, and be situated in a position that allows it "to modify" the desires and beliefs of others. The goal is not necessarily the cessation of all social conflict but the prevention of predetermined outcomes or premature resolutions. Nietzsche has little to say about how social conditions shape the play of power; Marxists are obsessed with social determinants, and they associate freedom with social arrangements that either prevent the play of power altogether (the traditional vision of communism) or with social arrangements that make the play as equal as possible for all participants. Thus while Marxists practice the Nietzschean hermeneutic of suspicion that reveals the fact of power behind practices pretending to something else, they also practice a second hermeneutic of suspicion meant to reveal the institutionalization of inequities that give certain groups an often irresistible advantage in social conflicts.

Because Marx believes that the individual's location within a set of social relations is inescapable, he is fully committed to a version of positive freedom. To live where power does not predetermine the outcome of conflicts or one's own determinate position in social relations is not to live outside society but to live within a society that is set up in such a way as to ensure the possibility of freedom. Social arrangements are certainly *the* primary locus of domination for Marx, but they are also the only possible place for the establishment of the conditions of freedom. The movement from necessity to freedom is completely within the social, is a movement of social transformation. "Only in community with others," Marx and Engels write, "has each individual the means of cultivating his gifts in all directions; only in community, therefore, is personal freedom possible" (1970 83). A Marxist politics must, at the least, consider the form community should take in order to promote the kinds of freedom we desire. The abrogation of that necessary act of imagination, the pursuit of freedom apart from a vision of the social context that underwrites its possibility, belongs to anarchist or liberal versions of a negative freedom that the individual enjoys prior to, apart from, or after the abolition of the social order. Nietzsche offers a particularly influential version of such negative freedom, and postmodern Marxism will never drift entirely into Nietzsche's camp so long as it keeps its sights on the primacy of the social.

The Marxist desire for freedom from domination is everywhere present in postmodern thought, even if only as an implicit norm that intellectuals find hard to justify and even harder to imagine achieving. Marx himself unfortunately proves little help in trying to consider how freedom might emerge from situations of dominance. In his most extremely deterministic moments, Marx portrays freedom's emergence as an inevitable future development of capitalism. Obviously, given capitalism's endurance, this Marxist version of history's movement toward socialism offers no hope. More useful, perhaps, is the notion that different groups within a society, by virtue of the different positions they occupy in the social whole, will have different aspirations and visions. If we emphasize this aspect of Marx, the hold of the dominant ideology will be mitigated, the opportunities for conflict and for alternative visions multiplied, the notion that a dominant social order also generates internal resistance introduced, and a theoretical explanation of novelty and change offered. Marx, read this way, appears close to presenting a view that is now associated with Foucault, namely that power itself produces the possibility of freedom and the terms within which freedom is enacted. The classic Marxist formulation of this relationship of power to freedom is the claim that the bourgeoisie creates the proletariat who will bring the realm of freedom. In other words, power inevitably creates social relations and social situations that afford certain strategic possibilities to the agents within those situations and relations. The options for these agents are certainly finite and context-dependent, but power can neither predict nor fix the limits of that range of options in advance. The space of freedom becomes what power has made possible (inadvertently or not) and cannot control. Each new social configuration (constructed by the ruling class) makes new actions possible, and the playing out of these possibilities by different agents in different positions leads to results that power could not have determined in advance and that, in some cases prove inimical to power's, to the dominant group's, interest.

This more optimistic view of power's relation to freedom articulated, it remains necessary to supplement this interpretation of Marx through Foucault with the Marx who is concerned with the concrete resolution of conflicts within particular societies. The trouble with the play of resistance at particular sites of confrontation with power is that Foucault often seems to locate freedom in the play and write as if we have achieved our goal when we have theoretically satisfied ourselves that "practices of freedom" are possible. What such an account misses is that something is usually at stake in confrontations and that we designate a dominant and a dominated partner in such relations on the basis of how the confrontation's resolution leaves one party relatively better off or more satisfied than the other. The portrait of productive power ignores how specific social arrangements bias possible outcomes from the start and what arrangements might work to mitigate such bias. Foucault focuses too exclusively on activity (the freedom to engage in confrontation) rather than on *what* agents hope to gain from such confrontations. From the standpoint of productive power, all social arrangements, apart from the limit case of total domination, are pretty much the same, affording various possibilities for freedom. Not much can be said about the relative superiority of any particular social configuration over any other.[16] But the Marxist notion of

[16]I discuss Foucault's notion of productive power more fully in the next chapter. His lack of interest in the specific institutional frameworks in which power confrontations take place is illustrated in the interview titled "Space, Knowledge, and Power" (1984 239–56): "I do not think that it is possible to say that one thing is of the order of 'liberation' and another is of the order of 'oppression.' . . . I do not think that there is anything that is functionally—by its very nature— absolutely liberating. Liberty is a *practice*. So there may, in fact, always be a certain number of projects whose aim is to modify some constraints, to loosen, or even to break them, but none of these projects can, simply by its nature, assure that people will have liberty automatically, that it will be established by the project itself. The liberty of men is never assured by the institutions and laws that are intended to guarantee them. This is why almost all of these laws and institutions are quite capable of being turned around. Not because they are ambiguous, but simply because 'liberty' is what must be exercised" (1984 245). My point is not that liberty can be guaranteed, or that liberty is not something that must be exercised, but that there is still a lot to be said about the differing possibilities for liberty being exercised in different social conditions. To claim that "almost all" laws and institutions leave some space for abuse does not necessarily mean we

positive freedom rests on the conviction that different social contexts can make all the difference between a condition of freedom and a condition of unfreedom. I think we need to hold on to that conviction. And as I argued in the preceding chapter, Marx's own refusal to consider the possible legitimacy of any social forms prior to the completely socialist society stands in the way of his taking full advantage of this sensitivity toward the difference that social contexts can make.

In sum, Marx is crucial because he shifts the creation of the world from Spirit to power and because he locates freedom in opposition to power. (Even if we see freedom as produced by power in Marx, that freedom is used to overthrow the power that produced it.) The postmodern refusal of Marx's teleological vision of a society without power can push Marxism toward Nietzsche, but the differentiation of freedom from power and the emphasis on social conditions prevents a full slide into a Nietzschean affirmation of the will to power. Postmodernism noticeably retains the Marxist desire to find a way to mitigate power's sway and the Marxist reliance on transformed social arrangements to achieve that mitigation. But Marx makes power so strong— especially in the dominant ideology thesis—that freedom's chances often appear dim. Marx has a tendency to see social conditions not as a dialectical product of conflicting forces but rather as the pure product of one force: the economic base or the ruling class. In this tendency to see a part as governing the structure of the whole, we find the origins of the stagnant, evil monolith that replaces both Hegel's benign totality and Marx's hopeful vision of communist society in so many postmodern texts.

NIETZSCHE: IRONIST THEORY AND NEGATIVE FREEDOM

Even if we grant that every "strong" writer remakes the work of his predecessors, the diversity of ways in which Nietzsche has been "misread" in our century is astonishing. The fragmentary, nonsystematic, and often downright contradictory thoughts presented in Nietzsche's aphoristic texts have helped to make his work all things to all people.

Poststructuralism's enchantment with Nietzsche takes a rather peculiar direction. The acceptance of Nietzsche's extreme skepticism about traditional philosophical concepts such as substance, truth, and reason grounds

---

cannot distinguish between laws that provide wider opportunities for inequity than others. The Marxist, I am arguing, will place more emphasis than Foucault does on the effect that different social arrangements can make on the possibility of *practicing* liberty.

ironist theory's robust assertions about the collapse of epistemology. That such assertions reintroduce a totalizing view suggests that poststructuralism wants to use Nietzsche's skeptical views but exhibits a strong ambivalence toward the extreme atomism that underlies those views. Nietzsche's atomism conflicts with the postmodern habit of linking all particulars to determinant contexts, or, more strongly stated, from poststructuralism's adherence to the Hegelian insistence (found in structuralism as well) that particulars have no significance in and of themselves but are constituted by their relationships within a whole. Nietzsche's atomism reenters postmodern theory, however, in its understanding of the politically desirable. Postmodernism inherits from Nietzsche an extreme version of negative freedom, the association of freedom with detachment from determinate wholes. As a result, contemporary critics are torn between their interpretive bias toward holistic, Hegelian explanations and their desire for an anarchistic, negative freedom. This conflict makes the freedom they desire appear impossible to achieve, a position that Nietzsche already foreshadows in his own insistence on the tragic character of life and the necessity of suffering.

Nietzsche's skepticism embraces both the externalist and the internalist perspectives that Hilary Putnam differentiates. His rejection of metaphysical realism is most succinctly stated in the assertion, "There are no facts, only interpretations,"[17] a phrase that has echoed throughout the work of the poststructuralists. If truth and knowledge depend on the exact correspondence of our representations (either mental images or words) with some actually existing state of affairs, then Nietzsche insists that truth and knowledge are impossible to achieve. "The world . . . has no meaning behind it, but countless meanings.—'Perspectivism.' It is our needs that interpret the world; our drives and their For and Against. Every drive is a kind of lust to rule; each one has its perspective that it would like to compel all the other drives to accept as a norm" (1968 267). No single state of affairs emerges as the true object of knowledge; instead, there are as many worlds as there are perspectives. Nietzsche makes it clear that his "perspectivism" does not amount to subjective relativism, because the self is never a single perspective but composed of the multiplicity of its "drives." (Of course, Nietzsche's denial of the self's reality is not consistently maintained throughout his work; in several crucial instances, he writes as if the self is the most fundamental unit in his ontology.) The very notion of the "self" as referring meaningfully to some identifiable entity is an interpretation made from a certain perspective.

[17]See Danto (1980 76) and Nietzsche (1968 267).

If there is any grounding term in Nietzsche's epistemology, it is *drive* or *need*, which is why Nietzsche declares psychology "the queen of the sciences," "the road to the fundamental problems" (1973 36). Separate perspectives can be identified with separate drives or needs; but Nietzsche sees no reason to limit the endless proliferation of such drives or to claim that the hunger experienced today expresses itself and interprets the world in the same way the hunger experienced yesterday did. Our tendency to group various experiences together as similar falsifies the fact of multiplicity, even if the interpretation of similarity serves (as we would expect it must) some particular need. "The fictitious world of subject, substance, 'reason' etc., is needed—: there is in us a power to order, simplify, falsify, artificially distinguish. 'Truth' is the will to be master over the multiplicity of sensations:— to classify phenomena into definite categories" (1968 280). Of course, Nietzsche's perspectivism offers him no ground for his metaphysical assertion that *substance* and *subject* are "fictitious" terms, a limitation that he conveniently ignores time and again. More interesting to me than this blatant and oft-repeated self-contradiction is that Nietzsche's metaphysical claims are so often radically atomistic, insisting that we cannot legitimately group together individual momentary experiences or sensations.

Nietzsche's atomism is forefronted in "On Truth and Falsity in Their Ultramoral Sense," the early essay that has been such a key text for poststructuralism.[18] Nietzsche focuses here not on the proliferation of interpretations generated by needs but on language's unwarranted functioning to limit that proliferation. In Nietzsche's psychology of perception, the core experience is "a nerve stimulus . . . transformed into a percept! First metaphor! The percept is again copied into a sound! Second metaphor! And each time he leaps completely out of one sphere right into the midst of an entirely different one." We delude ourselves into thinking that this double translation (both of which utterly transform the thing-in-itself) somehow corresponds to some object. "When we talk about trees, colours, snow and flowers, we believe we know something about the things themselves, and yet we only possess metaphors of the things, and these metaphors do not in the least correspond to the original essentials" (1911 178). Ironist theory has found this essay congenial because it stresses the arbitrary character of linguistic signs while also suggesting that such signs are secondary representations, products of a double removal (neither one of which maintains any true correspondence) from the real.

[18]For a typical poststructuralist reading of this essay, see Miller (1985).

In Nietzsche's view, this double removal only prepares the way for a second introduction of the fictitious: the hardening of words into concepts that blind us to the differences among our atomistic experiences.

> Let us especially think about the formation of ideas. Every word becomes at once an idea not by having, as one might presume, to serve as a reminder for the original experience happening but once and absolutely individualised, to which experience such word owes its origin, no, but by having simultaneously to fit innumerable, more or less similar (which really means never equal, therefore unequal) cases. *Every idea originates through equating the unequal.* As certainly as no one leaf is exactly similar to any other, so certain is it that the idea "leaf" has been formed through an arbitrary omission of these individuated differences, through a forgetting of the differentiating qualities, and this idea now awakens the notion that in nature there is, besides the leaves, a something called *the* 'leaf,' perhaps a primal form according to which all leaves were woven. (1911 179)

Nietzsche, as in this case, often denies correspondence theories of truth on the ground that all conceptual and linguistic systems inevitably falsify the actual fact of endlessly different (we might say "incommensurate") experiences. A metaphysical statement about the nature of reality is used to refute *all* human accounts of that reality, because all accounts must rely on generalizing terms. Nietzsche approaches mysticism here, or at least a belief that the absolute particularity of each experience makes those experiences inexpressible in language.[19] "Truth is the kind of error without which a certain species of life could not live" (1968 272). One problem, of course, concerns the truth value of this definition of truth; the statement would suggest that Nietzsche's own claims can only be recognized as the kind of error that best suits his needs.[20] But it also seems clear that Nietzsche aspires to telling us some truths about how humans act in the world; that aspiration apparently dooms him to mysticism, since his version of language denies language the ability to state the truth. "We really ought to get free from the seduction of words" (1973 27), writes Nietzsche, as if we had anything else but words.

Nietzsche's hankering for some kind of pure knowledge or pure perception, apart from the structures of thought influenced by habit, grammar, and

---

[19]Danto writes: "Nietzsche's view of the world verges on a mystical, ineffable vision. . . . Yet if he was a mystic, it must be said of him that the motives which drove him had nothing to do with a union of himself with the object of his insight. . . . He was less interested in stating what was true than in telling what was false" (1980 97–98).

[20]Habermas (1987a chap. 4) devotes a lot of attention to the "performative contradiction" between Nietzsche's own truth claims and the dismantling of the notion of truth in Nietzsche's work.

tradition, points not only toward mysticism but also toward the fantasy of a private-language. Wittgenstein's private language argument sets out to prove that we cannot even be meaningfully said to have had an experience except within the structures of thought provided by the language into which we are born. Nietzsche's insistence on the given language's inadequacies leads him to dream of escape, while his notion of freedom leads him to associate such an escape with liberty. I think that poststructuralism often follows this Nie-tzschean path, identifying a linguistic or discursive context (which governs what "can be thought") that is also described in ways that make it appear inherently unsatisfactory: The writer, by way of implied negation, suggests an alternative that is never articulated because the described context has been presented as the necessary conditions of human practice. If we emphasize the necessity of these conditions, then writers such as Derrida and Foucault come to appear rather similar to Wittgenstein. If, however, we contrast the patent (if never explicit) complaint in Derrida and Foucault against these conditions with Wittgenstein's much calmer acceptance of the way things are, poststruc-turalism and ordinary language philosophy appear worlds apart. And insofar as there is a suggested call to action in poststructuralism, it is a call to actions that would disrupt or dismantle the status quo in the name of something different that, under present conditions, cannot be quite articulated.

Of course, self-contradictions within a text are inevitable from Nietzsche's point of view, and he makes no claim to being exempt. The inevitability of contradiction justifies Nietzsche's refutation of the "internalist" perspective's attempt to establish norms of rational acceptability based on coherence, simplicity, common sense, or other contextually accepted standards (rather than on objectivist grounds). Nietzsche—like any good deconstructive reader—can always show that no discourse ever successfully embodies the very features that according to the internalist rational thought must display; all discourses contradict themselves by violating the standards of acceptable argument and appeal that they establish. Writers are not able to exclude the types of assertions that their model of rationality insists must be repressed. For Nietzsche, the conditions of rational acceptability have been culturally produced and always stand in danger of imminent contradiction. "If the majority of men had not always considered the discipline of their minds—their 'rationality'—a matter of pride, an obligation, and a virtue . . humanity would have perished long ago. . . . Man's greatest labor so far has been to reach agreement about very many things and to submit to a *law of agreement*—regardless of whether these things are true or false. This is the discipline of the mind that mankind has received; but the contrary impulses are so powerful that at bottom we cannot speak of the future of mankind with much confidence" (1974 130–31).

The question usually posed at this point is, What does thought of this sort accomplish? What good comes of recognizing our endless repetition of a limited set of moves within a tightly defined game? In some places, Nietzsche adopts a completely passive, tragic outlook, finding the only possibility of affirmation in the dictum *amor fati*. At other times he denies that humans must persist in untruth and looks toward the *Übermensch*, who can energetically carry life forward without relying on the old illusions.

In a more limited sense, Nietzsche seems to argue that ironist theory does accomplish historical changes; the revelation of the illusory nature of certain traditional truths can explain the downfall of Christianity, for example, while the general recognition that all truth claims are now undermined ushers in the age of "nihilism." In Nietzsche's work "the will to truth becomes conscious of itself as a *problem*." And "as the will to truth thus gains self-consciousness— there can be no doubt of that—morality will gradually *perish* now: this is the great spectacle in a hundred acts reserved for the next two centuries in Europe" (1969 161). Nietzsche here asserts that the arguments and exhortations he presents will make some impact on his readers and that philosophy (leading to self-consciousness) actually influences history. But Nietzsche hardly holds these views consistently. His descriptions of historical change often emphasize randomness; his oft-stated contempt for consciousness denies thought's determination of behavior; his doctrine of eternal recurrence introduces a strong dose of fate into any causal schema; and his descriptions of the strong, noble man often suggest that his actions (and words) are not intended to influence anyone else. To complain that his thought does not do us any good, that it even does us harm by removing our grounds for action, is the essence of nihilism, and Nietzsche sets himself the task of indicating the way beyond nihilism toward an affirmation of the exhilarating terror of living in a world without foundational truths or purposes.

Nietzsche very often locates the aesthetic as the realm within which such an affirmative life could be led, but we should resist the notion that Nietzsche is rejoicing in some kind of unrestricted creative freedom achieved by humans no longer accountable to any standards beyond themselves.[21] For one thing,

---

[21]The account of Nietzsche I am offering has two primary goals: to counter the facile interpretation of Nietzsche as the prophet of self-creation and to highlight the tragic resonance of the Nietzschean concepts of affirmation and play adopted by Derrida and of genealogy and the will-to-power adopted by Foucault. Nehamas (1985) and Rorty (1989b) offer two recent versions of Nietzsche as the promoter of joyous self-creation. Nehamas writes: "As he [Nietzsche]

as we have already seen, much of Nietzsche's work would deny the existence
of a self that might enjoy that freedom; creativity would derive from drives
that are not controlled by an ego and that might very well conflict with one
another within a single organism. Furthermore, Nietzsche's vision of the
aesthetic always emphasizes its tragic character. All human affirmations in
Nietzsche—whether of creativity, freedom, strength, pleasure, or of life
itself—always discover a limiting counterforce. Energetic affirmation in
Nietzsche is always against an immovable negation of human desires. "The
contradiction at the heart of the world . . . the primordial contradiction . . .
concealed in things" is what tragedy reveals (1967 71).

Nietzsche contemptuously dismisses as "romanticism" the art that expresses its "dissatisfaction with reality" by attempting to escape into a fictional
world of its own creation (see 1968 445). The tragic, or classical (Nietzsche
uses the terms interchangeably), artist, in contrast, fully recognizes that
"there is only *one* world, and this is false, cruel, contradictory, seductive,
without meaning—a world thus constituted is the real world" (1968 451).
Tragic art actually "prefers questionable and terrifying things" to the "pretty
and dainty" version of reality offered by romantic art, because such a preference "is a symptom of strength" (1968 450). "The feeling of *power* applies the
judgment 'beautiful' even to things and conditions that the instinct of impotence could only find *hateful* and *ugly*." A world view that most fully negates all
human aspirations is sought out, affirmed, and labeled the most noble and the
most beautiful precisely because it offers the most extreme possibility for
demonstrating strength. In tragedy, "being is counted as *holy enough* to justify
even a monstrous amount of suffering. The tragic man affirms even the
harshest suffering: he is sufficiently strong, rich, and capable of deifying to do
so. The Christian denies even the happiest lot on earth: he is sufficiently
weak, poor, disinherited to suffer from life in whatever form he meets it. The

thought Goethe had done, he too created himself. His great innovation was to accomplish this
end by saying that to create oneself is the most important goal in life, by saying in effect that this
was just what he was doing. His passion for self-reference combines with his urge for self-
fashioning to make him the first modernist" (1985 233–34). Rorty tells us that Nietzsche "hoped
that once we realized that Plato's 'true world' was just a fable, we would seek consolation, at the
moment of death, not in having transcended the animal condition but in being that peculiar sort
of dying animal who, by describing himself in his own terms, had created himself. More exactly,
he would have created the only part of himself that mattered by constructing his own mind"
(1989b 27). Such a heroic view of Nietzsche must resolutely ignore all his attacks on the very
notion of the self, refuse to take seriously the interpretive location of all actions and willings
within genealogical sequences, and disregard the notion of the eternal return. All of which is not
meant to deny that part of Nietzsche dreams of the kind of free self-creation Nehamas and Rorty
find in his texts, but only to suggest that it is disingenuous to overlook the serious impediments
Nietzsche himself places in the way of self-creation.

god on the cross is a curse on life, a signpost to seek redemption from life; Dionysus cut to pieces is a *promise* of life: it will be eternally reborn and return again from destruction" (1968 543).

Nietzschean aestheticism combines the realist demystifier's vision of a harsh reality that most humans wish to avoid recognizing as the real with the defiant and powerful affirmation of that reality as the best possible world, or at least as a set of conditions about which the artist will not complain but will understand as a fully suitable stage for a joyous, if terrible, life. Nietzsche's work has done some good when it can lead us to this clear vision of the real, in the process dissolving older faiths and visions such as Christianity. Nietzschean rhetoric has done its task when it convinces us that the tragic aestheticist response to that clear vision is better than the nihilistic response. And like other aestheticisms, Nietzsche's denies that art could possibly transform the real; for Nietzsche, suffering is not something to alleviate or to end, but only an inevitable reality that we should affirm.

Such an account, however, makes Nietzsche much too existentialist (and hence humanist) with this focus on the human response to a meaningless world. If we return to the Nietzschean psychology of multiple drives and also introduce the Nietzschean concept of "genealogy," the possibility for some chosen response on the part of the individual begins to evaporate. If the interpretations that serve humans in place of facts are not in any meaningful sense chosen but are the products of uncontrollable forces, then the heroic pictures conjured up by Nietzsche's use of the terms "will," "noble," and "tragic" must be severely qualified.

"Genealogy" is especially important to postmodern readings of Nietzsche, because the term introduces the question of historical development and contextual determinism into Nietzsche's meditations about the willful individual. (Foucault, of course, is the poststructuralist who most explicitly revives the methodology of genealogy.) Nietzsche's description of the principles of genealogical investigation derides the belief that origins are definitive while also denying that a historical sequence makes any progress or is directed toward any determinate end. Changes are merely the transformations imposed by the temporarily more strong, while proffered explanations (what we nowadays call "ideologies") must be understood as "signs" that, correctly interpreted, point to the imposing power.

> The cause of the origin of a thing and its eventual utility, its actual employment and place in a system of purposes, lie worlds apart; whatever exists, having somehow come into being, is again and again reinterpreted to new ends, taken over, transformed, and redirected by some power superior to it; all events in the

organic world are a subduing, a *becoming master*, and all subduing and becoming
master involves a fresh interpretation, an adaptation through which any previous "meaning" and "purpose" are necessarily obscured or even obliter-
ated. . . .

But purposes and utilities are only *signs* that a will to power has become
master of something less powerful and imposed upon it the character of a
function; and the entire history of a "thing," an organ, a custom can in this way
be a continuous sign-chain of ever new interpretations and adaptations whose
causes do not even have to be related to one another but, on the contrary, in
some cases succeed and alternate with one another in a purely chance fashion.
The "evolution" of a thing, a custom, an organ is thus by no means its *progressus*
toward a goal, even less a logical *progressus* by the shortest route and with the
smallest expenditure of force—but a succession of more or less profound, more
or less mutually independent processes of subduing, plus the resistances they
encounter, the attempts of transformation for the purposes of defense and
reaction, and the result of successful counteractions. The form is fluid, but the
"meaning" is even more so. (1969 77–78)

On the one hand, this description introduces a radical contingency into
history; the prior meanings or uses of a thing or custom in no way determine
what future form it might take. The effects of power are discontinuous. On
the other hand, history's resistance to all attempts to understand its movement as logical, directed toward a telos, or tied to an origin emphasizes its
transcendence of all attempts to order or to control it other than in the
conflictual war of strengths that Nietzsche understands as history's creator.
Whether we interpret that war as humanist or antihumanist depends on
whether we take the will to power to be an essentially human attribute (one
that humans actively will in a moment of freedom) or an instinctual drive
whose particular forms are historically determined and whose aims are always
invariably modified by the resistances it meets. We can find passages in
Nietzsche to support both readings, which produce the existentialist Nietzsche and the poststructuralist Nietzsche. When Foucault radically divorces
power from any connection to self or intention, he can find support for this
move by reference to Nietzsche's work.

Genealogy, in this view, names the history of meaning's production, and the
self, as in any structuralist schema, must be understood as just one among the
other meaningful units that have been produced. Power produces history,
meaning, and selves, and there are no grounds for believing that humans
freely choose the forms that these productions take. The only possible significance that might be accorded to the term *freedom* would refer to the possible
moves within the given historical arrangement of forces and selves. Such an
understanding of freedom would come very close to Hegel's, but in Nietzsche
this acceptance of the law imposed upon the individual by the whole can only

be described as *amor fati*, as the defiant affirmation of suffering. This shift in the emotional tenor of freedom assures that Nietzsche and both his existentialist and poststructuralist followers will look for another version of freedom, a negative freedom of separation from the whole, even when they present theoretical arguments that tie the individual inexorably to the whole.

Genealogy also historicizes the conditions in which humans find themselves, thus raising the question of whether some times in history produce less suffering than others. Historical differences must be measurable by some criteria, yet Nietzsche's notion of the overman's duty to embrace suffering does not recognize different historical circumstances. Similarly, Nietzsche's denial of progress commits him to a stern agnosticism about the issue of whether some circumstances are better than others. Presumably, Nietzsche does delineate differences by considering how humans respond to suffering in one period (say the Christian era) as opposed to another (the time of nihilism), but despite the fact that his work strongly declares the Christian response contemptible, he grants himself no grounds for declaring any one response better than another. We find in Nietzsche, then, a deeply contradictory combination of the historicist and the existentialist; genealogy contends that historical conditions change radically, but the primal fact of suffering remains an existential constant throughout history. Thus the existentialists could ignore genealogy altogether and focus on the human response to the eternal existential facts, while Foucault can emphasize historical change but still take the operations of power as inevitable in every era and as never taking a form more desirable (less pernicious) at one time than at another. The will to power is everywhere present; it simply manifests itself differently at different times.

Both truth (claims to knowledge) and values (all moralities) collapse into the will to power. We declare something true or good when it serves our purposes; the true and the good are what we have found useful. Nietzsche at times seems to be approaching a pragmatist test for truth. "A morality, a mode of living tried and *proved* by long experience and testing, at length enters consciousness as a law, as *dominating*. . . . Exactly the same thing could have happened with the categories of reason: they could have prevailed, after much groping and fumbling, through their relative utility. . . . From then on, they counted as a priori, as beyond experience, as irrefutable. And yet perhaps they represent nothing more than the expediency of a certain race and species— their utility alone is their 'truth'" (1968 277–78). Nietzsche's emphasis on outcomes rather than on origins or justifying grounds (evidence, consistency, or what have you) allows him to turn Kantian morality on its head. Kant tried to insulate all questions of value from the actual consequences of a decision; Nietzsche insists that all actions, positions, values, and claims should be judged entirely on the basis of their consequences. This Nietzschean habit reflects, of course, a complete skepticism about finding grounds for evaluating knowledge and moral claims apart from their effects.

But Nietzsche does not hold this pragmatic view consistently. Often he speaks as if the will to power is only motivated by the sheer instinctual desire to dominate. Power is its own end. "Every animal—therefore *la bête philosophe*, too—instinctively strives for an optimum of favorable conditions under which it can expend all its strength and achieve its maximal feeling of power" (1969 107). Power is not for anything; rather, everything else is for power. Nietzsche's version of the hermeneutics of suspicion uncovers the power drives that generate all phenomenon—both human and inhuman.

> Granted that nothing is "given" as real except our world of desires and passions, that we can rise or sink to no other "reality" than the reality of our drives—for thinking is only the relationship of these drives to one another—is it not permitted to make the experiment and ask the question whether this which is given does not *suffice* for an understanding even of this so-called mechanical (or "material") world? . . . Granted finally that one succeeded in explaining our entire instinctual life as the development and ramification of *one* basic form of will—as will to power, as is *my* theory—; granted that one could trace all organic functions back to this will to power and could also find in it the solution to the problem of procreation and nourishment—they are *one* problem—one would have acquired the right to define *all* efficient force unequivocally as: *will to power*. The world seen from within, the world described and defined according to its "intelligible character"—it would be "will to power" and nothing else. (1973 48–49)

Despite the provisional nature of the assertion here, Nietzsche's thought often moves toward just such a radical reduction.

Gilles Deleuze condemns the notion that power is its own end in Nietzsche, expressing scorn for those who read Nietzsche "as if power were the ultimate aim of the will and also its essential motive" (1983 80). Both Deleuze's interpretation of the will to power and that interpretation's consequences provide a good indication of the poststructuralist use of Nietzsche. (Cornel West calls Deleuze's *Nietzsche and Philosophy*, with "its provocative and often persuasive attack on Hegel and dialectics from a Nietzschean viewpoint," the "originary text of poststructuralism" [1988 28].) For Deleuze, the will to power cannot be seeking for power, because such a search implies the situation presented in Hegel as the dialectic of the master and slave. Power necessarily involves a relation to others in which the master's power is *recognized* by those over whom he has that power; recognition necessarily requires representation, a capturing of power within a code that allows it to be signified and hence recognized. And, for Deleuze, tying the will to power to an established code for representing power necessarily domesticates it. "When we make power an object of representation we necessarily make it dependent upon the factor according to which a thing is represented or not, recognised or not. Now, only values which are already current, only accepted values, give criteria of recognition this way" (1983 81). The will to power aims for the "*creation* of new values" (1983 82), not for dominance over others or over the material world.

What is crucial in Deleuze's reading of the will to power is the emphasis that such creation can only occur outside of any established social order or any preexisting representational system; new values can only be created in solitude. Thus the will to power can be understood only within a celebration of difference. "The question which Nietzsche constantly repeats, 'what does a will want, what does this one or that one want?,' must not be understood as the search for a goal, a motive or an object for this will. What a will wants is to affirm its difference. In its essential relation with the 'other' a will makes its difference an object of affirmation. 'The pleasure of knowing oneself different,' the enjoyment of difference; this is the new, aggressive and elevated conceptual element that [Nietzsche] substitutes for the heavy notion of the dialectic" (1983 9).[22] Where Hegel reconciles differences in the moment of *Aufhebung*, Nietzsche wills and affirms difference. And "Nietzsche announces that willing *liberates*" (1983 84).

What Deleuze finds in Nietzsche, then, is an affirmation of difference that is connected to a distancing of self from social and representational systems. (Note that Deleuze here accepts without question the identification of the willing agent with the self, ignoring in this early text [published in France in 1962] Nietzsche's own intermittent deconstruction of the self. Later on, of course, Deleuze [in *Anti-Oedipus* most crucially] will deny the self's unity as an entity or agent, locating difference *within* as well as between the self and others.) The establishment of difference is associated with freedom and is contrasted to the oppressive consequences of the Hegelian dialectic's final revelation of identity. Where dialectic leads to unity, the will to power as affirmation of difference produces multiplicity. "The monism of the will to power is inseparable from a pluralist typology" (1983 86), by which Deleuze means that Nietzsche's reduction of everything to the will to power (hence the theory's "monism") has the effect of generating a multiplicity of types, since each will to power will realize itself differently.[23]

---

[22]The passages from Nietzsche that Deleuze quotes here can be found in *Beyond Good and Evil* (1973 260).

[23]The connection of Nietzsche's version of negative freedom to what I have been calling Kierkegaardian irony, as well as its connection to the fantasy of a private language, is made absolutely clear in Charles Altieri's excellent essay (1985) on *Ecce Homo*. Altieri is interested in

To associate differences with liberation points to an extreme version of negative liberty. But we must recognize that the celebration of negative liberty in Nietzsche's texts alternates with what we might call a transvalued version of Hegelian freedom. (I believe that poststructuralism preserves this same alternation.) On the side of Hegelian freedom in Nietzsche, we can gather the themes of affirmation, eternal return, tragedy, *amor fati*, suffering, and humans' essential impotence in the face of existence's conditions. When following through this line of thought, Nietzsche denies vehemently any notion of "free will," and even the will to power itself becomes, paradoxically, an assertion of strength that proves its strength by its ability to face honestly its impotence, to affirm the suffering that it cannot prevent.[24] Strength is not mastery of the world but the rejection of all illusions of mastery (such as religion, science, philosophy, or other cultural consolations). Within this schema, Nietzsche's atomism denies all unifying, organizational entities that might gather any strength to themselves; the self, the will, history itself are all fictions that attempt to organize what is, in fact, random multiplicity, ungovernable chaos.

To affirm difference within the most extreme version of Nietzschean atomism is simply to give oneself (except that to talk of the self in this context is self-contradictory) over to the multiplicity of impulses, drives, and experiences that defy all organization into a larger, coherent, or meaningful whole. The only whole that grants some sense to this multiplicity finds expression in the mysterious concept of the eternal return, which may mean that the whole of history has a determined form or may only mean that reconciliation to the chaos can be achieved only by willing its repetition. Freedom means to will that the world be the way that it is. When Nietzsche envisions reconciliation, it is not the Hegelian reconciliation of the self (or anything else) with the reality (Spirit) that it now knows to be essentially the same as itself. Rather, it is a reconciliation to a reality that is absolutely other to the human hopes we find expressed in philosophy, science, religion, and the various illusions that humans wish to be true. The reality to be affirmed is a Heraclitean world of random multiplicity that is seen as absolutely different in each successive moment, as well as absolutely different from the world men would create for themselves if they had the power of creation. Hegelian freedom in Nietzsche approaches masochism, the willful submission to a world that inflicts suf-

---

how the very desire for self-creation and the subsequent need to stage that self-creation for others undermine the claims of the self-creator to be utterly independent of social norms and social usages.

[24]Nietzsche (1973 29–33) refuses any simple notion of what it means to will something, arguing that the term "free will" misreads the arrangement of forces in the self and the agent's subjugation to his drives.

fering. That the submission is willful allows Nietzsche to identify it with strength—the only strength possible in our essential weakness.

But once again we must note that if we take Nietzsche's denial of the self seriously, then it becomes unclear who or what can be said "to will" except the will itself. And presumably the will cannot help but will, so the factor of choice—without which it is meaningless to talk of freedom—seemingly disappears. Of course, Nietzsche believes that different things can be willed; for example, the will can negate existence or it can affirm it. But these different willings only become relevant to freedom if we can think of some agent who chooses among the different possibilities. As a result, Nietzsche's deconstruction of the self appears to take for granted the existence of a self, since he imagines the consequences of that deconstruction to be the eventual affirmation of multiplicity, randomness, and so forth. Affirmation becomes a meaningless term if we do not imagine an agent who affirms; we cannot leave affirmation entirely up to an undirected will without denying all freedom. Atomism strictly pursued yields unfreedom, since it assures the absolute impotence of the self or any other agent that would aim to control will. Nietzsche's texts continually move toward this paradox of the atomism he adopts in order to gain a radical freedom actually serving to render the human impotent. At times, as we have seen, Nietzsche is willing to insist that this impotence is the fundamental fact of existence and to see the will to power as a compensatory drive. Humans encounter a random, fated world, and will itself is simply a matter of fate—some wills are affirmative and some negative by nature (one is born a "noble" or a "slave"), and they cannot be changed. Freedom is a meaningful concept in Nietzsche only insofar as he maintains a humanist notion of a self that makes willful choices; the antihumanist Nietzsche hands all power over to fate.

To complicate matters even further, we can identify a non-Hegelian freedom in Nietzsche, not the affirmation of an unalterable if monstrous Heraclitean world, but an ideal of freedom as escape from determinant orders. He looks forward to the appearance of "the *sovereign individual*, like only to himself, liberated again from morality of custom, autonomous and supramoral (for 'autonomous' and 'moral' are mutually exclusive)"; a man filled with "a consciousness of his own power and freedom" (1969 59). In his discussion of "the free spirit" in the second part of *Beyond Good and Evil* Nietzsche declares that "every superior human being will instinctively aspire after a secret citadel where he is *set free* from the crowd, the many, the majority, where, as its exception, he may forget the rule 'man' " (1973 39), and goes on to list all the possible alliances that the free spirit must resist: love, friendship, patriotism, pity, and knowledge (see 1973 52).

Paradoxically, the list ends by warning the free spirit not to become attached to its detachment or to its virtues (autonomy, strength, etc.), because such self-love in itself becomes an alliance that ties the self down, commits it to certain courses of action. Instead, "rich and noble souls [must] expend themselves prodigally, almost indifferently" (1973 52), the proof of their freedom residing in the very fact that their actions are not undertaken to achieve freedom or to become a certain kind of self, but are merely uncalculated expressions of the fullness of their natures.[25] And in his freedom the noble man takes upon himself the task of assigning values. "The noble type of man feels *himself* to be the determiner of values, he does not need to be approved of, he judges 'what harms me is harmful in itself,' he knows himself to be that which in general first accords honour to things, he *creates values*" (1973 176).

In Nietzsche's insistence that freedom entails autonomy, and his differentiation of noble morality from the herd instinct that accepts culturally given standards, we can recognize high modernism's goal of separating itself, in the name of purity and autonomy, from its surroundings. Nietzsche exhibits the contempt for the masses and the association of democracy with mediocrity that pervades much modernist discourse; he provides a discourse of radical disaffection with bourgeois, commercial society that is also vehemently anti-socialist, a combination to be found in many modernist writers as well as in fascism.[26] Nietzsche also speaks the modernist language of purity. "For solitude is with us a virtue: it is a sublime urge and inclination for cleanliness which divines that all contact between man and man—'in society'—must inevitably be unclean. All community makes somehow, somewhere, some-

[25]The insistence that the noble man's actions are gratuitous is necessary to separate them from the petty, self-conserving motives that characterize the herd and the bourgeois. The theme of expenditure that yields no return (no interest or profit) influences various modernist attempts to protect the artwork from becoming a commodity. The most important theorists of the unrecuperated, of an expenditure or a pleasure that exceeds any "return" on the investment, are Georges Bataille and Roland Barthes. But we should note that, in Nietzsche's case, the master's "indifference" must always be rigorously differentiated from "disinterestedness," the hallmark of Kantian morality and aesthetics. I am not convinced that Nietzsche everywhere successfully enforces this distinction; his concept of "nobility" continues to harbor the very old association of nobility with being above concerns for the self. This transcendence of self-regard need not be morally considered or motivated; in fact, moral motives (especially when tied to Christian ideas of salvation) still often suggest the hope of an eventual reward. Rather, the noble's disregard of self stems from a unwillingness to stoop to petty stratagems of self-advancement. But such a nobility inheres to Kantian art and Kantian morality also.

[26]See Nietzsche (1973 33, 43–44, and 106–7) for typical passages deriding socialism and democracy. Nietzsche's connection to fascism is problematic, but I think it foolish to deny that—no matter how the Nazis misappropriated certain Nietzschean themes—the work provides concepts that lend themselves to fascist ideology. It is not mere coincidence that the fascists fastened on Nietzsche's work rather than on Kant's, just as they celebrated Wagner's work more than Mozart's or Beethoven's.

time—'common'" (1973 195). The ability to endure separation is the very key to freedom, since it is our fear of solitude that acts as the strongest reason to heed the herd instinct.[27] To aim for social harmony and the reconciliation of competing interests (differences) is weakness in Nietzsche's view.

At this point, it might seem possible to associate Nietzsche's affirmative (i.e, Hegelian) freedom with his existential view of an unalterable world of suffering while connecting his negative freedom with his thoughts about historical, social forms. In this way we can explain the combination in Nietzsche, as in so many other modernists, of a radical critique of contemporary society with an overarching pessimism about the possibility of creating a better society. The strong individual must disentangle himself from a despicable bourgeois culture but only to encounter the real, existential, ennobling conflict with a tragic universe. Postmodernism, in this view, would deny to the moderns their exalted sense of having escaped local conflicts and determinants; indeed, postmodernism would chide the modernists for mistakenly believing that the conflicts in which they engaged were anything else but such local, contextualized, historical conflicts. There is no solitude and there is no realm of the existential; there are just the social circumstances in which we are all embedded. And if we take this tack, we would associate negative freedom with the moment in modernism that aspires to escape from bourgeois society while linking affirmative freedom with the moment in modernism that aspires to a tragic nobility embodied in the artist/hero who goes beyond society and convention to encounter the real itself. Postmodernism might then be understood as denying the possibility of negative freedom's escape while also resisting an affirmative freedom based on confronting the real. Instead, the postmodernist would contest the validity of both images by stressing how we are always already embedded in the social, always situated within preexisting orders of significance and response from which there is no escape. Any meaningful freedom would have to be defined within this context in which agents are situated.

This simple dichotomy between the modernist and postmodernist understanding of freedom does not work, however. The combined legacy of bourgeois liberalism and modernist autonomy is too strong; postmodernism, for all its criticism of its ancestors, still tends to imagine freedom (a freedom to which it can enthusiastically aspire) in terms of negative liberty. Positive freedom looks like tyranny since it involves accepting rules and regularities that are not self-created. Postmodern writers have again and again detailed these rules and regularities but have almost always identified them as *necessary*

---

[27]See Nietzsche (1974 114–15) for comments on the weakness shown by fear of solitude.

conditions that are experienced as oppressive. Postmodernism remains unable to make the leap over to declaring these contextual constraints as the conditions of freedom. The selves produced by power, culture, forms of life, or absent structures are seen as unfree, as positioned by forces exterior and alien to them. And while postmodernism has excelled in identifying those exterior forces, it has seldom called on the constituted selves to affirm those forces. Quite the contrary. Postmodernism almost invariably identifies the constitutive structures it unveils with oppression and looks desperately for ways to evade that oppression or to generate and protect liberating differences.

The neat notion that postmodernism undercuts the Nietzschean move out of society also breaks down when we consider the essentialist uses to which poststructuralism has put Nietzsche. Deleuze's work provides a good example. He does not present difference and multiplicity as socially created, and he affirms difference as liberating in and of itself, no matter what the circumstances. Difference is an ontological fact in Deleuze's work, which can be recognized in this case as an acceptance of Nietzsche's ontological atomism. (An adoption of difference as the fundamental nature of the real does not of course commit one to an individualism of a modernist or existentialist sort. In *Anti-Oedipus*, Deleuze and Guattari insist on the differential nature of the self itself. But we should recognize that they take the multitudinous self as originary; the self only achieves a spurious and oppressive unity later on. And they understand the reaffirmation of the self's multiplicity as a key move toward freedom.) Difference can only appear such a potent and desirable concept within a perspective that understands freedom negatively. And difference itself can only be understood negatively when some kind of step outside the Hegelian whole is imagined, because differences within the Hegelian whole are positive differences, recognized as positional articulations of the whole. In most postmodern interpretations, differences are only effects within a whole, effects that are recuperated when we explain how they were generated by that whole. Hence the atomistic emphasis on difference is only momentary, since interpretation leads back from the particulars to the systematic conditions of their production and significance. Even while adopting the Hegelian denial of atomism as its model of interpretation, poststructuralism adopts Nietzsche's atomism as its model for freedom.

Postmodernism finds in difference that principle of multiplicity, or irreducibility, that allows it to escape the totalizing visions it associates with necessity and unfreedom. What I want to emphasize is that this commitment to difference stems from a negative image of freedom. The need for the concept of difference often leads postmodern writers to abandon their usual reliance on historical contexts to declare difference a universal fact. Furthermore, postmodernism only half believes in the fact and efficacy of difference; it remains torn between its Hegelian and Nietzschean convictions, a fact dramatized by Deleuze's need to interpret Nietzsche entirely in terms of his rejection of Hegel. "There is no possible compromise between Hegel and Nietzsche" (1983 195).

Postmodernism can never entirely embrace the chaos of difference. It continually oscillates between its identification of the necessities to which that play is answerable and more pleasant visions of liberation. In Nietzsche's case that oscillation is revealed in his continual undermining of the possibility of autonomy as he reinscribes the will within the dynamics of a will to power to which all are instinctively bound; or as he genealogically explains the generation of the circumstances within which the will must operate; or as he describes the fated confrontation of will with a world that always frustrates it and causes suffering; or as he denies the very notion of self and of "free will" that would allow the will to power to be associated with freedom. Postmodernism's anarchistic moment gains its very intensity from its coexistence with continued holistic theorizing about necessary conditions of human action and thought. Its particular oscillation between the monolithic and the pluralistic appears determined by its susceptibility to the logic of totalizing, Hegelian explanations, even while it yearns for a multiplicity that it associates with freedom. Politically, this combination yields a desire for a pluralistic society within a social order that can universally guarantee certain rights, freedoms, and economic goods. The conjunction of these seemingly contradictory (or at least problematically reconcilable) perspectives is best explained by postmodernism's complete adherence to a vision of negative freedom (even if it often believes such freedom to be unattainable). Nietzsche's work discredits for twentieth-century humanistic intellectuals the versions of positive liberty found in Hegel and Marx. Of course, Nietzsche did not achieve this feat alone, but he offers a version of negative liberty radical enough to release the concept from its guilt of association with bourgeois liberalism and thus to allow its becoming an orthodoxy precisely among those intellectuals who understand themselves as engaged in a battle to the death with liberal capitalism. As is by now clear, I believe that only a recommitment to positive freedom can actually provide an effective platform for the kinds of political transformation that humanistic intellectuals profess to seek.

Nietzsche's legacy to postmodernist theory, then, is his deeply ambiguous atomism, which embodies a radical desire for freedom (understood negatively) and provides a powerfully skeptical ontology in his battle against the truth value of human representational schemes, discourses of knowledge, and moral systems. Atomism's ambiguity resides in the fact that, pursued to its logical end, it must also undermine Nietzsche's own truth claims and his own image of freedom. In the chaotic world of atomistic impulses, percepts, and experiences, all explanatory schemes must fail because random chaos is the only reality, and all freedom must be impossible because there can be no agent who directs or chooses the movements of will. Postmodern Nietzscheans, no more than Nietzsche himself, cannot hope to adhere to such an extreme atomism consistently; rather, they will repeat in their own way Nietzsche's movement between truth claims and the deconstruction of truth, between the aspiration toward negative freedom and the deconstruction of negative freedom's possibility. As a result, like Nietzsche, postmodern theory often finds itself in the position of affirming (and desiring) something that it also declares impossible to attain.

3

The Problem of Freedom
in Postmodern Theory

In this chapter I develop further the connections between the work of some key postmodern theorists and the issues I have highlighted in the history of critical philosophy since Kant. The tensions, even contradictions, that I find in these writers do not in my view invalidate their work. My goal is not to dismiss but to understand why, within the configuration of postmodernism, two (or more) incompatible things are desirable and what different strategies are involved in the effort to think these incompatibles together. I assume that the work of Derrida, Foucault, Rorty, Jameson, and the rest is so widely read and discussed precisely because it accurately reflects contemporary intellectuals' perplexities, not because it captures some widespread moral and/or intellectual failing.

DERRIDA AND THE POSSIBILITY OF THE OTHER

Derrida's work often announces itself as the attempt to deconstruct the Western metaphysics of identity, of the presence of the self to itself in consciousness. He argues that the philosophical tradition, at least from Plato on, has always privileged the concept of the same; the aim of philosophical thought has been to reveal the essential characteristics that two things hold in common. The discovery of such essences depends on a movement of consciousness (the Platonic or Hegelian dialectics are prime examples) through the experience of multiplicity to the recognition of the underlying unity. This movement depends on the suppression of differences in favor of similarities and on the ontological designation of similarities and essences as "more real" than apparent differences. As I have suggested already, poststructuralism, particularly in the work of Deleuze and Guattari, often appears to offer a counterontology in which heterogeneity, not homogeneity, is primary. Derrida at times offers his own version of this counterontology, but he has also been particularly sensitive to the possibility of simply creating a mirror image, by way of negation, of traditional philosophy, and has tried very hard to evade that fate by insisting that deconstruction is not a method and that *différance*, which opens up language and thought to a "play" that undermines the stability of identity, is not a concept, or an origin, or a metaphysical determinant of the forms that Being takes.

Derrida usually maintains that we cannot have access to something that is outside philosophy, its absolute other or absolute negation. Counterconcepts, he argues, quickly take on all the baggage of philosophical concepts and become the foundation of a new system, a new ontology with pretensions to accounting for the totality of what is. From the beginning, philosophy has been obsessed with its other, so it is foolhardy to think that a contemporary writer could discover some negation of philosophy that could stand outside it. "Philosophy has always insisted upon this: thinking its other. Its other: that which limits it, and from which it derives its essence, its definition, its production" (1982 x). Rather, Derrida wants deconstruction and *différance* and play to subvert and unsettle traditional forms of thought from within. "How to interpret—but here interpretation can no longer be a theory or discursive practice of philosophy—the strange and unique property of a discourse that organizes the *economy* of its representation, the law of its proper weave, such that *its* outside is never its *outside*, never surprises it, such that the logic of its heteronomy still reasons from within the vault of its autism?" (1982 xvi). Here we find the monolithic, Hegelian Derrida, who demonstrates how Western thought "infinitely reappropriate[s]" every other in a "process of its expropriation (Hegel again, always)" (1982 xv) that finds in its other (its negation) simply another occasion to move toward its final, all-inclusive unity. The plural, Nietzschean Derrida wants to find ways to keep that other from being reconciled to its opposite in the dialectical movement toward the same. The tortuous, roundabout difficulties of Derrida's work stem from the obstacles confronting a Nietzschean strategy. Philosophy's ability to appropriate everything that tries to set itself up as other to philosophy necessitates a continual suspicion about any claims to have broken from the monolith or even to have disrupted it to the extent of having altered its processes. Freedom in Derrida, then, is linked to a disengagement from philosophy's "law" and logic, but his work continually insists that such a disengagement, although deeply desired, is well-nigh impossible. Hence I find Derrida's thought marked everywhere by the tragic revelation of irresolvable contradictions, of *aporias*, that we also find in Nietzsche.

For Derrida, the fear of difference, of the other, is a crucial constitutive feature of all totalizing systems, while the addiction to totalization in thought is what he calls "Western metaphysics" or the "philosophy of the same." *Being, God*, the *Real*, and so forth (what Derrida calls the "transcendental signified," the ultimate substances to which all appearances refer) are the covering terms by which Western philosophy has included everything within the totalities constructed by thought. "Absolute fear would then be the first encounter of the other as *other*: as other than I and as other than itself. I can answer the threat of the other as other (than I) by transforming it into another (than itself), through altering it in my imagination, my fear, or my desire" (1976 277). Philosophy contemplates this other which it perceives as a threat and constantly works to bring it under control, often by denying the "reality" of otherness. Difference, both the difference between two things and the differences within what we normally construe as one thing, is relegated to the realm of "appearance," while an essential unity is designated "the real." "If it is true that 'Western philosophy most often has been an ontology' dominated since Socrates by a Reason which receives only what it gives itself, a Reason which does nothing but recall itself to itself, and if ontology is tautology and egology, then it has always *neutralized* the other, in every sense of the term" (1978 96). Herein lies what Derrida terms "the violence of metaphysics" (1978 79) and the implied ethical complaint against a Reason that not only dominates nature but justifies "the tyranny of the state as an anonymous and inhuman universality" (1978 97).

The ethics are only implied, however, since these assertions, along with the flat statement that "the only incarnated nonviolence . . . is respect for the other" (1978 96), are views ascribed to Emmanuel Levinas, only reported by Derrida. Of course, Levinas is important to Derrida precisely because he challenges radically the philosophy of the same, and the themes highlighted in the essay on Levinas—including the notion of philosophy's violent suppression of the other—run throughout Derrida's own work. Derrida's enterprise makes sense only if we have some reason to want to disrupt Western metaphysics. His most explicit statement of that reason locates the originary impulse of deconstruction in the "call" of the oft-abused other. "Deconstruction is, in itself, a positive response to an alterity which necessarily calls, summons, or motivates it. Deconstruction is therefore vocation—a response to a call. The other, as other than self, the other that opposes self-identity, is not something that can be detected and disclosed within a philosophical space and with the aid of a philosophical lamp. The other precedes philosophy and necessarily invokes and provokes the subject before any genuine questioning can begin" (1984 118). (Note the use of the words *necessarily* and *genuine* here, as well as the insistence that the other *precedes* philosophical discourse rather than being constituted by it.)

The problem Derrida's work raises is whether we can escape that philosophical discourse which cannot do justice (pun intended) to the other.[1] "The idea that we might be able to get outside of metaphysics has always struck me as naive," Derrida insists (1984 111), yet he also sees himself as having "attempted more and more systematically to find a non-site, or a non-philosophical site, from which to question philosophy. But the search for a non-philosophical site does not bespeak an anti-philosophical attitude. My central question is: from what site or non-site [*non-lieu*] can philosophy as such appear to itself as other than itself, so that it can interrogate and reflect upon itself in an original manner? Such a non-site or alterity would be radically irreducible to philosophy. But the problem is that such a non-site cannot be defined or situated by means of philosophical language" (1984 108). I want to explore the dimensions of this problem here, focusing on Derrida's attempt to use the nonconcept of *différance* to disrupt philosophy's serene self-identity. My account of the disruptive strategies appropriate to *différance* highlights Derrida's inconsistent pronouncements on the possibility of being outside of philosophy, his quasi-mystical gestures toward an other that retains an "irreducible alterity," and his continual return to tragic conclusions that portray the violence of metaphysics or the more mysterious violence of *différance* as inevitable.

The complexities of Derrida's emphasis on *différance* can be highlighted by considering Derrida's complex relation to Hegel. The philosophy of *Geist* represents, of course, a prime example of Western philosophy's emphasis on identity: within the Hegelian schema, nothing remains other or outside; everything is finally revealed as part of Spirit. Yet, as we have seen, Hegel does offer an intricately differentiated portrait of the real *prior* to the end of Spirit's

---

[1]The implicit norm of respect for difference, or otherness, must remain implicit in Derrida because all the institutional and social means for enforcing such a norm would inevitably partake of the processes of identity and of universality that Derrida associates with the violence of metaphysics. Thus I think that Derrida is also guilty of the "cryptonormativism" that Nancy Fraser (1981), Charles Taylor (1986), and Jürgen Habermas (1987a) have discussed in Foucault's work. Derrida, like Foucault, appeals to an implicit norm that his own procedures and position do not allow him to explicitly justify. I take this inability to legitimate social norms or institutions as a major defect of postmodern theory, as well as a symptom of its essential negativity.

alienation; furthermore, Hegel announces and tries to theorize the desirability of differentiation within unity in the political community. Hegel thus tolerates, even recommends, difference. What Hegel cannot tolerate is that which is completely other, that which, by existing outside the whole, has no relation at all to Spirit or to the other entities within the system. The movement of Spirit in Hegel is always relentlessly toward incorporation of all others. In large part, this move is understood by Hegel as a conceptual necessity; the very fact of difference could only be recognized in the relationship of difference established between one thing and the other. And once a relationship is established, we are halfway toward reconciliation, since the fact of relationship means that some mediating term between the two things has already been found. Hegel would not accept the notion of "incommensurable" difference found in Lyotard, a notion that (although given a different name) intrigues Derrida in the work of Levinas and Artaud. For Hegel, the very ability to assert a difference assumes a basis for measurement, hence a relationship.

Derrida, following Bataille, calls the Hegelian system a "restricted economy," by which he means a system in which nothing is ever lost or wasted. Everything is conserved, saved, invested; resources are only spent in order to make a profit, to gain a return. Nothing is ever simply expended, used up, utterly consumed. "Dialectics is the movement through which expenditure is reappropriated into presence—it is the economy of repetition. The economy of truth. Repetition *summarizes* negativity, gathers and maintains the past present as truth, as ideality. The truth is always that which can be repeated" (1978 246). The Hegelian *Aufhebung* represents a supreme instance of the philosophy of identity. In the dialectic, Hegel continually allows thought to confront its other, but just as continually he recovers that other into the same. What Derrida wants to insist is that this movement of incorporation necessarily suppresses what is most radically different in the other. "The blind spot of Hegelianism, *around* which can be organized the representation of meaning, is the *point* at which destruction, suppression, death and sacrifice constitute so irreversible an expenditure, so radical a negativity—here we would have to say an expenditure and a negativity *without reserve*—that they can no longer be determined as negativity in a process or a system" (1978 259). The *Aufhebung* puts negativity to work by reappropriating that part of it which can be useful to the system's progress as a whole; we might say that what is valuable in the other is squeezed out of it, while its worthless rind is thrown away. It is crucial for Derrida that we recognize that representation, the very functioning of our discursive system, is based on this appropriation of a part of the other coupled with the suppression of that part of the other which is most radically different. What can be repeated in representation is that part of the other which has now been subsumed, in the *Aufhebung*, into the system. "In discourse (the unity of process and system), negativity is always the underside and accomplice of positivity" (1978 259). In Hegel, we find "reawakened or revealed the most permanent philosophical determination of negativity." (1978 259). The threat of the truly other is neutralized by this moment of incorporation/suppression.

Derrida's portrayal of Western metaphysics does not emphasize any particularly significant historical development in its strategies and desires until the attacks on metaphysics begun by Nietzsche and Heidegger. True, Hegel is not Plato, but the philosophy of the same repeats its moves, even its tropes, with astonishing regularity. Thus the preface to *Margins of Philosophy*, titled "Tympan," can describe "philosophy's" aims and achievements as a whole, without bothering to distinguish among Aristotle, Spinoza, and Kant. Derrida's crucial premise is that philosophy continually works to bring the other inside its boundaries, where it can be controlled by being subordinated. Left outside, the excluded would remain too dangerous, would be free and independent. Instead, philosophy neutralizes its other (which it names, at various moments, writing, irrationalism, the feminine, figurative language, nature) by locating it within a system of asymmetric relationships that try to fix the other in a secondary position. "Now, in its mastery and its discourse on mastery . . . philosophical power always seems to combine *two kinds*. . . . These two types of appropriating mastery, hierarchy and envelopement, communicate with each other, according to complexities we shall define" (1982 xix–xx). Hierarchy, we might say, is only possible within the context of envelopment, since only that which has been brought under philosophy's aegis can be subjected to its law, to its assignation of value. And, given Derrida's reading of Hegel, we must recognize that philosophy here means the very foundation of representational discourse; the incorporation of something into language necessitates its submission to the economy of repetition and its subsumption under the name (or the concept) that represents it. (In "The Supplement of Copula: Philosophy before Linguistics," Derrida discusses this "law of reappropriation" in language by returning to consider Nietzsche's "On Truth and Falsity in Their Ultramoral Sense," with its insistence that the particular thing's distinctive differences are lost once the general terms of language are put into use.) Presumably only a nonrepresentational discourse would provide a different economy than that which Derrida associates with Western metaphysics.

Despite Derrida's apparent lack of interest in historical differences, we must recognize, in the context of this study, how much his portrait of metaphysics resembles various accounts of the postmodern condition, especially those of Jameson and Baudrillard.[2] What Derrida describes is an order that can appropriate everything to itself by making each thing take its place within a signifying system. Immersed in the differential system of signs, we lose any access to an otherness that might disrupt the system. One sign can be easily substituted for another not just because all signs are commensurate but also because all signs are recognized as representatives of the same in merely slightly different guise. Of course, to call this process of universal incorporation "commodification" rather than "the philosophy of the same" carries a somewhat different rhetorical charge, but the processes at work are fundamentally similar in each case: envelopment and hierarchy (the assigning of relative values), incorporation/suppression. And Derrida's proclivity toward the economic metaphor already suggests the complicity of philosophy with a bourgeois emphasis on work, investment, and the long-term return on savings. But if Derrida is right in portraying the Western omnivore as not merely the multinational capitalism of the twentieth century but the West's entire philosophical tradition, then the task facing those who wish to topple the monolith is that much more daunting. Derrida's work, in this way, repeats the sobering analysis of Adorno and Horkheimer's *The Dialectic of Enlightenment*, their insistence that the disease is not capitalism but Western reason itself.

In Derrida, then, a monolithic vision of our present condition yields to a monolithic vision of our whole historical tradition. I think this is a mistake generated by Derrida's failure to be sufficiently sensitive to his own historical moment. He never asks how it is that the critique of Western reason should begin with Nietzsche and Heidegger and take on such significance in our own day. In Heidegger (as in Adorno and Horkheimer) that critique is explicitly tied to a revulsion against modern society and the "calculative thinking" of "a distanced subjectivity that stands over and against objects, judging and manipulating them for its own chosen goals."[3] The motives for Nietzsche's attack are less explicit, but we would certainly have to take into account Nietzsche's hatred and fear of what he called "the herd" and what we now call "mass society." Particular historical developments in the West, then, call forth a particular rereading of the West's philosophical tradition, a rereading that offers a genealogy for current conditions by finding in reason almost from the

---

[2]Jameson (1984b 61–63) attempts to include "what is today called contemporary theory" (1984b 61) within his model of postmodernism, while also faulting poststructuralism for ignoring the "historicist" position that the "death of the subject" is characteristic of our specific cultural formation in favor of the ontological position that "such a subject never existed in the first place" (1984b 63).

[3]Kolb (1986 119–20). Chapters 7 through 9 of Kolb's work detail Heidegger's critique of modernity.

start (Adorno and Horkheimer locate the fall in the *Odyssey*, whereas Nie-tzsche and Heidegger more usually cast Socrates as the villain) the tendencies that have produced the present. My suggestion is that what these writers and Derrida find in the tradition is governed by their antagonism to the present, and furthermore, that their tendency to construct a monolithic tradition is more the product of the monolithic conditions of the postmodernity they inhabit than the actually monolithic nature of a tradition (spanning three thousand years) that has undergone various historical transformations.

We need to turn now to the strategies that Derrida devises to unsettle this monolith. In "The Ends of Man" Derrida writes that a "radical trembling [of metaphysical humanism can only come from the *outside*," and that "this trembling is played out in the violent relationship of the whole of the West to its other" (1982 134). The reference here seems to be to the challenge to the West that is embodied in the peoples of the Third World and in its own abused minorities. (At the beginning of the essay Derrida explicitly dates its composi-tion as April 1968, a month marked by strong protests against the Vietnam War and by the murder of Martin Luther King.) Perhaps, Derrida appears to suggest, only the West's true other, true outside, could disrupt its system of thought, a fear that haunts postmodern intellectuals with particular intensity, since it implies (at best) their own impotence against and (at worst) their complicity with the monolith they hope to combat. In any case, the audience Derrida addresses is a group of philosophers, and he must turn from this appeal to the "outside" to consider what those, including himself, who are "in" the West should do. "Taking into account these effects of the system, one has nothing, from the inside where 'we are,' but the choice between two strategies" (1982 135). The choice comes down to working from the inside or attempting to get outside, and it is typical of Derrida that he focuses on the considerable likelihood of failure if one adopts either course.[4] Here is how Derrida describes the alternatives:

> a. To attempt an exit and a deconstruction without changing terrain, by repeat-ing what is implicit in the founding concepts and the original problematic, by

[4]Rorty (1984 41–43) discusses this same passage in "The Ends of Man" and argues that it represents Derrida's "hope to move outside the tradition instead of being mired within it as Heidegger was" (1984 43). Rorty expresses both his skepticism about Derrida's monolithic portrayal of the tradition ("it is just not true that the sequence of texts which make up the canon of the ontotheological tradition has been imprisoned within a metaphorics which have remain unchanged since the Greeks" [1984 13]) and the notion that Derrida's "plural" style is anything new ("speaking several languages and writing several texts at once is just what all important, revolutionary, original thinkers have done" [1984 13]). Rorty is less interested than either Derrida or me in the issue of whether one is inside or outside, both because he is not so sure we can really define *one* inside and because, as my discussion of his work argues, he does not find that the ability of a self to speak in its own idiom poses any significant theoretical problem.

using against the edifice the instruments or stones available in the house, that is, equally, in language. Here, one risks ceaselessly confirming, consolidating, *relifting* [*relever*], at an always more certain depth, that which one allegedly deconstructs. The continuous process of making explicit, moving toward an opening, risks sinking into the autism of the closure.

b. To decide to change terrain, in a discontinuous and irruptive fashion, by brutally placing oneself outside, and by affirming an absolute break and difference. Without mentioning all the other forms of *trompe-l'oeil* perspective in which such a displacement can be caught, thereby inhabiting more naively and more strictly than ever the inside one declares one has deserted, *the simple practice of language ceaselessly reinstates the new terrain on the oldest ground* [my emphasis]. The effects of such a reinstatement or of such a blindness could be shown in numerous precise instances. (1982 135)

Despite this rather discouraging account of the difficulties facing either strategy, Derrida continues by claiming that "it goes without saying that these effects do not suffice to annul the necessity for a 'change of terrain.' It also goes without saying that the choice between these two forms of deconstruction cannot be simple and unique. A new writing must weave and interlace these two motifs of deconstruction. Which amounts to saying that one must speak several languages and produce several texts at once" (1982 135). And, as usual when he imagines a successful disruption of Western metaphysics, Derrida invokes the name of Nietzsche: "What we need, perhaps, as Nietzsche said, is a change of 'style'; and if there is style, Nietzsche reminded us, it must be *plural*."[5]

How does Derrida pursue each of these two strategies in his own work? I will begin with the "brutal" attempt to reach a "new terrain" outside, then turn to the internal strategies of disruption. In his essay on Artaud's "theater of cruelty," Derrida rather sympathetically portrays the attempt "to consume pure difference with pleasure" (1978 246). Such an "expenditure without reserve" disdains the repetitions of representation in favor of experiencing in the present "that which constitutes its irreplaceable and mortal presence, that within it which cannot be repeated." The word *mortal* comes into play here because the consumption of difference accepts that the present, once consumed, must be lost absolutely; only its death, its inaccessibility to return or repetition, affirms (protects) its difference. Artaud's aesthetic thus sets itself not only against Hegelian dialectics but against writing as well, since "writing is space itself and the possibility of repetition in general" (1978 247).

[5]Derrida has, of course, pursued this injunction to produce "plural" texts, most notably in *Glas* (1986), but also in "Tympan" (1982 ix–xxix). A consideration of how successful these attempts at play have been is impossible within the confines of this book, so I have followed Rodolphe Gasché's lead in limiting my discussion of Derrida to "the more philosophically discursive texts" (1986 4).

Despite his sympathy for Artaud's anti-Hegelianism, Derrida closes the essay by insisting that Artaud's project is impossible. (Derrida also argues that Artaud was fully aware of this impossibility.) Since "the theater of cruelty . . . is already within representation" (1978 248), even its desire for pure differ- ence is stated in terms that allow for that desire's recuperation. "What is tragic is not the impossibility but the necessity of repetition." The very concepts of the present, of difference, and of affirmation are "accompanied by [their] own representation" (1978 249), and could not be thought otherwise. Artaud "wanted to save the purity of a presence, without interior difference and without repetition"; he dreamed of an autonomous other that was completely and purely itself, existing in an isolation and an utter difference that left it untainted by relationship to anything else. Derrida denies the very possibility of this recognizably modernist dream. Even though he shares Artaud's deep disgust with the appropriative dialectics of the *Aufhebung*, Derrida finds that we cannot repudiate our whole conceptual and representational system. We cannot think pure difference or a pure other. (To do so, Derrida makes clear, requires the annihilation of time, its dissolution into utterly discrete moments of absolute consumption.) And this is "tragic" in the most classic sense of that term: a necessity to which we must submit although we wish for other conditions.

The crucial obstacle to a nontragic view is Derrida's insistence that the system of Western metaphysics is embedded within the very language we use. " 'Everyday language' is not innocent or neutral. It is the language of Western metaphysics, and it carries within it not only a considerable number of presuppositions of all types, but also presuppositions inseparable from meta- physics, which, although little attended to, are knotted into a system" (1981 19). Hence the statement in "The Ends of Man" that "the simple practice of language ceaselessly reinstates the new terrain on the oldest ground" (1982 135). "There is only one discourse," Derrida writes in the essay on Bataille, and "it is significative, and here one cannot get around Hegel" (1978 261). To use language is to rejoin Hegel's economy of repetition—and this is, paradox- ically, most true of those who are most fervently anti-Hegelian. "Levinas is very close to Hegel, much closer than he admits, and at the very moment when he is apparently opposed to Hegel in the most radical fashion. This is a situation he *must* [my emphasis] share with all anti-Hegelian thinkers" (1978 99). What attracts Derrida in Levinas is the earlier writer's insistence that the philosophical tradition has violently subdued the other. But Derrida also must remind us that Levinas's attempt to identify, to think, a radical other only repeats philosophy's obsession with the other, and that, since Levinas is constrained to use language, this new version of the other merely expands philosophy's ability to include a negativity hitherto beyond its ken. Thus anti-

Hegelians, in attempting to specify the Hegelian system cannot include, succeed only in colonizing what was previously aloof and so reinforce Hegelian holism. (Derrida suggests that Kierkegaard's work can be read this way.) The charge that Hegel provides a "restricted economy" always points toward a more inclusive "general economy," one that takes in the repressed other, the wasteful by-products, ignored by the dialectic. The result, in Derrida's terms, is a "Hegelianism without reserve" (1978 251), the ironic transformation of anti-Hegelianism into super-Hegelianism. The new terrain is removed to the oldest ground. And Derrida fully recognizes that this new version of a Hegelian holism continually surfaces in his own work, as he demonstrates again and again how marginal figures such as Artaud and Levinas are subject to the tradition.

If Western metaphysics and language are systems that imply one another, then the only true outside would be beyond language. Levinas is important because he tries to occupy such mystical terrain, pointing toward the experience of an other that cannot be captured in words. "What, then, is this encounter with the absolutely other? Neither representation, nor limitation, nor conceptual relation to the same. The ego and the other do not permit themselves to be dominated or made into totalities by a concept of relationship. And first of all because the concept (material of language), which is always *given to the other*, cannot encompass the other, cannot include the other" (1978 95). Derrida is deeply attracted to this notion of an other that *exceeds* all concepts, all words, and thus can be said to exist outside of thought. Yet he also remains firmly convinced of Western thought's continual ability to appropriate whatever other might appear on the horizon, just as he remains convinced that we live within language and cannot realistically hope to escape it. The essay on Levinas is a rhetorical disaster, surely the worst Derrida ever wrote: repetitive, returning again and again to worry the same issues from slightly different angles, yet at the same time schematic and scattered, constantly raising questions that it cannot pause to pursue. These rhetorical flaws reflect, I believe, Derrida's deep ambivalence about Levinas's work. He agrees with Levinas's challenge to the tradition and wants to be able to affirm Levinas's attempt to step outside of that tradition entirely. But he cannot quite bring himself to endorse the mysticism that a fully external strategy requires. We could render Derrida's dilemma here in traditional religious terms: he wants to believe (not in God, but in an unassimilated other), yet cannot quite bring himself to do so.[6]

---

[6]Handelman (1982) discusses Derrida's troubled relation to Levinas in order to identify the religious (Jewish) subtext of Derrida's thought; her reading describes Derrida's pursuit of what I would call a "negative mysticism," the identification of an other that will necessarily remain absent and out of reach.

Derrida explains that this radical other in Levinas makes language itself possible even while it remains outside language (see 1978 98). This dependence of language on an other it cannot represent is carried over almost without change into the essay *"Différance."* In order to elucidate the (non)concept *différance*, Derrida admits "that the detours, locutions, and syntax in which I will often have to take recourse will resemble those of negative theology, occasionally even to the point of being indistinguishable from negative theology" (1982 6). The difficulty of Derrida's position stems from the need to portray *différance* as that which makes all thought possible (puts thought into play), but is not itself to be thought. *"Différance* is not only irreducible to any ontological or theological—ontotheological—reappropriation, but as the very opening of the space in which ontotheology—philosophy—produces its system and its history, it includes ontotheology, inscribing it and exceeding it without return" (1982 6). Such excess, it seems, can only be guaranteed by placing *différance* outside philosophy and outside language. *"Différance* is neither a word nor a concept" (1982 7). In fact, insofar as Derrida's own essay has talked about *différance*, it has reduced *différance* to "a metaphysical name, and all the names that it receives in our language are still, as names, metaphysical" (1982 26). Apparently, then, there is a system of even wider inclusiveness than philosophy itself, the system of *différance* within which philosophy is inscribed. But we have no means of access to that wider system, that more general economy. *Différance* is outside philosophy and language, but the fact of its exteriority offers no possibility that we will ever get outside. ("We" as humans or "we" as Westerners who inherit a certain metaphysical tradition? Derrida offers no clues to help us answer this question.)

Our knowledge of *différance* always comes from within, from the effects it produces in our systems of thought and language. "'Older' than Being itself, such a *différance* has no name in our language. But we 'already know' that if it is unnamable, it is not provisionally so, not because our language has not yet found or received this *name*, or because we would have to seek it in another language, outside the finite system of our own. It is rather because there is no *name* for it at all, not even the name of essence or of Being, not even that of *'différance,'* which is not a name, which is not a pure nominal unity, and which unceasingly dissociates itself in a chain of differing and deferring substitutions" (1982 26). Unlike traditional transcendent categories such as God or the Platonic Good, *différance* does not call us to itself, but instead returns us to (pushes us back into) the very world of multiplicity (the unceasing dislocations of linguistic substitutions) from which traditional universals promised an escape. *Différance* allows (produces?) the endless "play" of "nominal effects" instead of foreclosing that play in the way traditional unifying terms ("transcendental signifieds") do. And Derrida proclaims that "we must *affirm* this, in the sense in which Nietzsche puts affirmation into play, in a certain laughter and a certain step of the dance" (1982 27). We might characterize Derrida's position here as "negative mysticism," akin to that which Danto ascribes to Nietzsche. *Différance* is completely other, but the goal is not to seek some union with that otherness but to affirm the endless play of difference that the completely other guarantees. And Derrida appears to believe that the refusal of union works to preserve human otherness, as if the distinctively human could only be preserved by this distance established between "the finite system of our own" (1982 26) and the wider, all-embracing system of *différance*.

Freedom can be identified with this distance insofar as we can affirm a play that we can neither guarantee nor control. (This is the freedom pursued by the internal strategy, of which more below.) But Derrida's thought very often stresses the impotence of those inside the system, so that his concept of affirmation comes to look very much like Nietzsche's *amor fati*. "The subject (in its identity with itself, or eventually in its consciousness of its identity with itself, its self-consciousness) is inscribed in language, is a 'function' of language, becomes a *speaking* subject only by making its speech conform—even in so-called 'creation,' or in so-called 'transgression'—to the system of the rules of language as a system of differences, or at very least by conforming to the general law of *différance*" (1982 15). The very terms of our existence as subjects are given to us by the system; it would be hard to identify theoretically anything but a Hegelian freedom here, a willed "conformity" (to use Derrida's word) between subject and law. Or, to anticipate Derrida's internal strategy, freedom will have to be reconceived as something that does not belong to subjects—a way of understanding freedom that breaks radically with any humanist understanding of the term.

This drastic reduction of the effectiveness and freedom of the subject within the system is coupled with the enormous power ascribed to *différance*, a power that stems from its being outside, its "absolute alterity" (1982 21). *Différance* is utterly unavailable to us, yet has an ability to disrupt the law that no subject possesses. "Not only is there no kingdom of *différance*, but *différance* instigates the subversion of every kingdom. Which makes it obviously threatening [to] and infallibly dreaded by everything within us that desires a kingdom" (1982 22). *Différance* looms as the ever-present (in its absence) troublesome stranger. Strictly speaking, *différance* is an absent other that is not external to the system but constitutive of it. The "absolute alterity" ascribed to *différance*, however, grants it the power to disrupt the very system that it also makes possible. Despite all his attempts elsewhere to insist that we stop dreaming of a pure other and recognize that disruption must take place within the structuring laws of thought, Derrida in this case retains the model of negative freedom, with its belief that only the entity that escapes determination by the general rules can act on (or play out) its own agenda and confront the system with an *other* model of experience. This appeal to a pure otherness repeats the modernist hope for autonomy, although with the crucial difference that Derrida never suggests that such autonomy is available to humans. In *"Différance,"* at least, Derrida believes that only that which escapes the general conditions by which thought is governed can successfully disrupt kingdoms. Which is why Derrida must go to such great lengths to insist (ensure) that *différance* is not a thing, not a concept, not a name. Only the completely other has the disruptive power we seek, and Derrida's own work has shown how difficult true alterity is to achieve. I am not particularly interested in whether *différance* falls back into metaphysics or not. What I want to stress is how some part of Derrida still associates freedom with complete disengagement, even though he must come close to mysticism to present such negative liberty as ever possible and though he must deny that human beings could ever accomplish this disengagement.

The possibilities open to human agents are more fully addressed in Derrida's consideration of possible disruptive strategies *within* the prevailing system of thought. The internal strategy searches out those elements within the system that are marginalized or kept under a tight rein as lowly elements in the hierarchy. The challenge posed by such others, once they are located, is directed toward the "alleged homogeneity," the "apparent unicity," the "imperial totality" of the philosophical "order" (1982 xvi). What deconstructive readings reveal is that the repression of these dangerous secondary terms, the violence of metaphysics, never fully succeeds. The other is only spatially and temporally dislocated, not completely annihilated. By searching that other out, deconstruction can unsettle the pose of consensus, of unruffled homogeneity, of completely lucid self-awareness of its unified identity that characterizes traditional Western thought. Derrida's work insists that Western reason is not transparent to itself, as it loves to believe, but actually founds itself on a constitutive blind spot: its willful refusal to "recognize" (in the Hegelian as well as the ordinary sense of this word) the others that it dominates. This dominated other (in a master-slave dialectic) is both within the system and invisible, and deconstruction can be usefully thought of as the return of the repressed.

Against the "work of the negative" in the "restricted economy" of the Hegelian system Derrida poses "play"—probably the most unambiguously positive term in all his work. "One could call *play* the absence of the transcendental signified as limitlessness of play, that is to say as the destruction of ontotheology and the metaphysics of presence" (1976 50). "The absence of the transcendental signified extends the domain and the play of signification infinitely" (1978 280). Play thus involves "the liberation of the signifier from its dependence or derivation with respect to the logos and the related concept of truth or the primary signified, in whatever sense that is understood" (1976 19).

The substitutions of one signifier for another are now no longer grounded and can no longer be called to a halt, or to an accounting. *Différance* (as opposed to a transcendental signified) puts the system in a motion that is endless (without a stopping point and without a telos). Play also means that the system as a whole has lost its power to govern; the totality of the system (its inclusion of everything) does not, understood this way, provide it with the means to totalitarianism. It cannot control the movement of the parts. "If totalization no longer has any meaning, it is not because the infiniteness of a field cannot be covered by a finite glance or a finite discourse, but because the nature of the field—that is, language and a finite language—excludes totalization. This field is in effect that of *play*, that is to say, a field of infinite substitutions only because it is finite, that is to say, because instead of being an inexhaustible field, as in the classical hypothesis, instead of being too large, there is something missing from it: a center which arrests and grounds the play of substitutions" (1978 289). In this exuberant passage, Derrida strives to find within our finitude the very possibility of play. Our inability to transcend the system of language means that the play of substitutions cannot be ended. The outside, the transcendental signified, to which philosophy has always pointed must be given up in favor of an affirmation of the finite system within which we dwell. And Derrida's formulation of the concept "play" in this instance appears to proclaim that we will find the finite system of language capable of producing "infinite substitutions" and "inexhaustible" novelties. The shattering of the old limiting concepts appears to open up a field of infinite possibilities.

Significantly enough, the term *freeplay*, which has been so identified with Derrida, derives from the first English translation of "Structure, Sign, and Play" and is not justified by the text of that essay as printed in *L'écriture et la différence*.[7] (In fact, *freedom* and its cognates are words found very seldom in Derrida's texts.) There is much to suggest that the play of substitutions in Derrida is never very free, can always be recuperated within a tradition.

[7]On the translation of "Structure, Sign, and Play," see above, Chapter 1, note 38.

There are various ways to describe the determinants of linguistic substitutions. Schemas of intertextuality and the history of tropes reveal how concepts and figures of speech are shaped in relation to earlier formulations; present utterances are deeply influenced by what has already been said. Or the interpreter can emphasize the institutional, social, economic, or psychological constraints that govern the path taken by signifiers. True, Derrida does talk of "the innocence of becoming" (1978 292) in "Structure, Sign, and Play," but for the most part his work reveals that the movement of signifiers is far from innocent and that play is about as free as the rather ironically named "free association" of a Freudian thought that uncovers the rigid overdetermination of even the most casual utterance.[8] Derrida much more usually wants "to remark upon the necessity proper to the structure of a discourse or a project" (1982 181) than to celebrate the possibility or achievement of freedom.

Furthermore, the concept of play in Derrida carries a strong connotation of one of the secondary meanings of the word: "a space in which something, as a part of mechanism, can move."[9] The play possible for a part in a machine takes place within a strictly defined space; when there is "too much play" in a part, it disrupts the machine. I think it is useful to think of Derrida, at least part of the time, as aiming toward unsettling the machine (the system) of philosophy by introducing just a bit too much play in some of its concepts, a strategy that involves not separating the concept from the system as a whole and also not opening up some huge, unlimited space in which the part can spin off aimlessly out of control. Instead, the play of the concept is limited by a Hegelian sense that it is always engaged with other concepts, and the subversion is based on reconfiguring, on bringing into question, the prevailing relationship. Derrida connects play in exactly this sense with freedom when pondering the possibilities opened up by academic philosophy. "Certain societies, when they accept the idea of having, for instance, philosophy departments—which is not the case with all societies—give themselves the possibility of thinking not only the essence of the university, but the essence of society. That's the place where thought can be free; that's what I call 'free-

---

[8]Lentricchia (1980) has been the reader of Derrida who has most fully emphasized the strong determinism within Derrida's notion of play: "Consciousness, the subject, the presence or absence of being, apparently forever dissolved as versions of the untouchable transcendental signified, now suddenly return as they all become situated as intertextual functions of semiological systems which do recognize the 'rights of history, productions, institutions' to coerce and constrain the shapes of free-playing discourse. Semiological systems based on the principle of difference 'have been produced' and the key questions become what and by whom: what discharges of power, under what networks of guidance, to what ends, and in what temporal and cultural loci have semiological systems been produced?" (1980 175).

[9]Random House Dictionary (1968 1018).

play.' Play, not in the sense of gambling or playing games, but what in French we call *jouer*, which means that the structure of the machine or the springs, are not so tight, so that you can just try to dislocate: that's what I meant by play" (1987 20). Here Derrida appears to connect freedom to reflection on "essences" in a very traditional manner.

His other recent discussion of play, in the "Afterword" to *Limited Inc.* (1988a), more fully captures the novelty of his usage and the reason "play" can be connected to *freedom* even though the term *freeplay* carries all the wrong connotations. "Without play in and among these questions, there would be no space for conflicts of force. The imposition of a meaning supposes a certain play or latitude in its determination. . . . Stabilization is relative, even if it is sometimes so great as to seem immutable and permanent. It is the momentary result of a whole history of relations of force. . . . In order for this history to have taken place, in its turbulence and in its stases, in order for hegemonies to have imposed themselves during a determinate period, there must have been a certain play in all these structures, hence a certain instability, or non-identity, nontransparency" (1988a 145). Derrida's argument here is that the very existence of attempts to fix meaning, of logical arguments for this or that being true, of laws that aim to delimit allowable behavior, indicates the *fact* of variations, of other possibilities that power ("a whole history of relations of force") tries to regulate. History's violences and its changes can only be explained by this play, by this absence of absolute determination. "Once again, that was possible only if a non-self-identity, a *différance* and a relative indeterminancy opened the space of this violent history" (1988a 145). Exploring the conditions of this "relative indeterminancy" does not lead to any simple-minded celebration (or belief in) indeterminancy. "What has always interested me . . . is not indeterminancy in itself, but the strictest possible determination of the figures of play, of oscillation, of undecidability, which is to say, of the *différantial* conditions of determinable history." What gets placed into play is never random, nor are the ways it can be played. But the introduction of play does unsettle the dominant order by supplementing or exceeding the determinations that order has tried to make stable and permanent. Plays points to other (suppressed or unacknowledged) possibilities; hence its link with freedom, with change, with opposition.

Derrida's favorite strategy along these lines is to take an oppositional pair between which a text (or a society) asks us to choose (which term is worth more or should be privileged or should be granted priority either logically or temporally) and to declare that the choice is "undecidable." In place of the hierarchical resolution of the contrast, a resolution that places one term above the other, the Derridean (non)solution places them in a tensional play with one another, an oscillation that is not resolved in favor of one or the other. *Play*, in this understanding of the term, still disrupts philosophy's constant reliance on establishing hierarchy, but this disruption neither is free nor comes from outside the terrain established by the relation of philosophy's basic terms. Concepts are still strictly determined by their relation to their opposites, but now the *aporia* of an unending tension replaces the resolution of tension in the Hegelian *"Aufhebung,* which . . . remains in control of the play, limiting it and elaborating it by giving it form and meaning" (1978 255). To let the play continue would be to let differences bloom and contradictions remain in tension, as opposed to the recuperation of the other into the same that is always imposed as the end (telos) of a traditional philosophy.

Play, then, might be characterized as what results from irresolvable contradictions; just as the distance from *différance* preserves the play of differences, so the inability to resolve these tensions generates an endless play of thought and language around various binary oppositions. Here we come to the point where Derrida is closest to establishing a counterontology. His description of history as the tension between the will to establish a determinate order and the pressure of the supplement, of the repressed, against that order delineates the transcendent conditions of human life. And often he argues that all thought will inevitably exhibit both impulses within itself. Every thought wills the resolution of oppositions (the achievement of unity and self-identity) *and* engages in a "supplementary play" that spins off from the inevitable failure to achieve that resolution. The philosophy of the same tries to suppress this second movement, but play is "always already there." Thus every single text can be deconstructed; it can be shown to move toward play, to move toward a dissolution of its proffered unities.[10] Derrida associates this inevitability of play (as the effect of *différance*) with writing as opposed to speech (logocentrism), with metaphor as opposed to the literal or the "proper," with the feminine as opposed to the masculine (phallologocentrism). Traditional philosophy has tried to evade the facts of difference and play embodied in writing, but such evasion must always fail because they are facts. Derrida's antitheory—which dissolves all the solutions and unities thought usually prides itself on—is still theoretical because he insists that the double movement both toward and away from resolution describes the *necessary* form

[10]Norris (1987) formulates this same point in a way that stresses (unintentionally) deconstruction's ahistoricity and its eternal repetition of the same. "For deconstruction is *always already* at work, even in those texts that would seem most expressly committed to a 'logocentric' order of assumptions. And conversely, as Derrida often repeats, it is impossible for a deconstructive reading to escape that ubiquitous system of ideas, impossible to leap outside it and land 'with both feet' on some alternative ground" (1987 57).

thought takes. Deconstruction thus provides "a lock opened to a double understanding no longer forming a single system" (1982 xxiv), and Derrida suggests that "it may be about this multiplicity that philosophy, being situated, inscribed, and included within it, has never been able to reason" (1982 xxvii). The inscription of philosophy within play gives the antisystem of play an ontological weight that permits Derrida's assertions about the nature of language, of thought, and of philosophy. "In interpreting negativity as labor, in betting for discourse, meaning, history, etc., Hegel has bet against play, against chance. He has blinded himself to the possibility of his own bet, to *the fact* [my emphasis] that the conscientious suspension of play . . . was itself a phase of play; and to *the fact* [my emphasis] that play *includes* the work of meaning or the meaning of work, and includes them not in terms of *knowledge*, but in terms of *inscription*: meaning is a *function* of play, is inscribed in a certain place in the configuration of a meaningless play" (1978 260). Thus play and its pluralism becomes the term that embraces more of reality (in good Hegelian fashion) than its counterpart: univocal philosophy. The antisystem of meaningless play appropriates philosophy as merely one of its components (or functions) and deconstruction works to undermine philosophy's pretensions to name the real as the same by naming the real as the different. Deconstruction makes pluralism manifest within the totality of *différance*.[11]

Derrida can avoid his own totalizing, hierarchical system, his own "Hegelianism without reserve" only if he refuses to privilege pluralism above unicity; only an endless double movement will maintain play and irresolution. I think that Derrida, like Nietzsche, tries to avoid ontology by taking the path of psychology. No matter what the facts are, the human animal, Derrida suggests, cannot lose its desire to achieve unity, identity, and mastery over otherness; deconstruction, like the Nietzschean critique of truth, is never going to end the discourse of the same, is never going to annihilate the strategies of representational discourse. "I have identified logocentrism and the metaphysics of presence as the exigent, powerful, systematic, and *irrepressible* [my emphasis] desire" to "place a reassuring end to the [play of]

[11]The notion that play or *différance* affords a more inclusive, more general, theory than that offered by traditional thought (the logic of noncontradiction) is suggested in the "Afterword" to *Limited Inc.*: "To this oppositional logic . . . I add a supplementary complication that calls for other concepts, for other thoughts beyond the concept and another form of 'general theory,' or rather another discourse, another 'logic' that accounts for the impossibility of concluding such a 'general theory.' This *other* discourse takes into account the conditions of this classical and binary logic, but no longer depends entirely upon it. If the proponents of binary opposition think that the 'ideal purity' to which they are obliged to appeal reveals itself to be 'illusory' . . . then they are obliged to account for this fact. They must transform concepts, construct a different 'logic,' a different 'general theory,' perhaps even a discourse that, *more powerful* than this logic, will be able to account for it and reinscribe its possibility. This is what I try to do" (1988a 117; my emphasis).

reference from sign to sign" by appealing to "the transcendental signified" (1976 49). In its most ontological moments, deconstruction might insist that the desires that underlie the philosophy of the same will always be frustrated because multiplicity is a fact. (Again, the similarity to Nietzsche is clear.) But if Derrida avoids such ontological claims, as he often succeeds in doing, then deconstruction can offer its disruption of unicity only as an attempt to play out other possibilities whose adoption might prove desirable. The criteria for making decisions about what is desirable, however, are conspicuously missing in Derrida's work.

Shorn of its ontological grounds, deconstruction quickly adopts a Nietzschean pessimism about its capability of changing human habits. If the play that deconstruction highlights has always already existed within texts, then deconstruction is resolutely *within* Western philosophy. The "irrepressible desire" at the foundation of Western metaphysics is confronted with another "exigency," that of *différance* and play; we could even say that, at some level or at some times, we also desire *différance*. At the very least, Nietzsche's and Derrida's texts exhibit such a desire, while deconstruction shows that *différance* is at work in all texts. The confrontation of philosophy and play, of these two desires, has already been in play for many long years. Thus there is no reason to claim that Derrida is introducing anything new to the game or any reason not to believe that thought will continue on as it has been. "Thus one could reconsider all the pairs of opposites on which philosophy is constructed and on which our discourse lives, *not in order to see opposition erase itself* but to see what indicates that each of the terms *must* appear as the *différance* of the other, or as the other different and deferred in the economy of the same. . . . And on the basis of this unfolding of the same as *différance*, we see announced the sameness of *différance* and repetition in the eternal return" (1982 17; my emphasis). The play never changes its form, as the mention of the "eternal return" insists. The only change, perhaps, is that now we can learn to "affirm" the play of differences rather than to try to suppress it.

Just what difference such a change in attitude would make is not clear. For some feminists, the shift means adopting a feminist mode of thought as opposed to a masculine one.[12] But Derrida, strictly understood, must resist such a recommendation, since he wants to avoid simply reversing hierarchies (placing the formerly repressed feminine in the ascendancy in a new order) in favor of permanently unsettling them. The distinction between masculine and feminine should be rendered undecidable, with an endless oscillation be-

[12]Luce Irigaray and Hélène Cixous are the most prominent proponents of a "l'écriture féminine" that opens up an entirely different order of thought and signification. For an excellent overview and appraisal of this direction in feminist theory, see Jones (1985).

tween the two as a result. (Which is not to say that Derrida himself never privileges play or never suggests apocalyptic transformations if we manage to learn how to play joyfully. But such pronouncements, although wellknown and often cited, finally pale in comparison with his more usual, if more mundane, meticulous diffidence, with its refusal of any hope of glorious reversals or refashionings of the tradition we inhabit.[13]) The internal strategy in Derrida, then, leads to a firmly antidialectical impasse of thesis and antithesis in an unresolvable, tensional play. The difficulty of maintaining such an impasse (our urge toward resolution) is indicated by Derrida's own slips into hierarchical privileging at various times, his assertions of the ontological priority of play or of *différance*. In fact, the very notion of oscillation suggests that thought (including Derrida's own) will continually swing between moments of construction (of identities) and moments of deconstruction (when "play" reigns for a while).[14]

Let me summarize the argument so far before looking at one last dichotomy in Derrida's thought. Derrida presents a monolithic vision of a Western philosophy that is ethically condemned for its violent suppression of difference, of others. His external strategy for disrupting that monolith looks for an other (non-Western peoples, the feminine?) who can radically challenge its organization and its forceful imposition of the same. His own (non)concept of *différance* is presented in ways meant to guarantee its irreducible alterity and thus presumably its power to disrupt kingdoms and its ability to remain independent. We have, however, no good access to *différance*; it functions as close to a mystical other in Derrida's work. More usually, Derrida suggests that the search for an independent other is useless, even though he appears to long for such an other himself at times. He proves himself comparable to Hegel in his mastery of the logic of recuperation, able to demonstrate again and again that disparate texts partake in the founding concepts and strategies of Western metaphysics. From this perspective, *différance* and play are understood as internal, necessary features of any discourse or any thought, albeit features that traditional philosophy has tried to deny or control. The internal strategy calls for us to affirm this play, this unrestricted economy, which, I

---

[13]In the interview with Richard Kearney, Derrida expresses his lack of hope as a regret: "Unfortunately, I do not feel inspired by any sort of hope which would permit me to presume that my work of deconstruction has a prophetic function" (1984 119).

[14]That the disruptive play introduced by deconstruction can only be momentary is necessitated by Derrida's insistence that "there is only one discourse" (1978 261). Therefore, deconstruction must be "that *in every discourse* which can open itself up to the absolute loss of sense . . . of unknowledge or of play, to the swoon from which it is reawakened by a throw of the dice" (1978 261). But Derrida rules out the possibility that "significative discourse" will not return after every irruption of play. (On this last point, see especially 1978 268.)

believe, qualifies as another example of the romantic effort to replace one whole (the philosophy of the same) with another, more inclusive whole.

What remains unclear is whether Derrida's version of the whole actually offers a freedom and a nonviolence that distinguish it from the oppressive philosophy of the same. Derrida has a strong tendency to assert the (tragic) inevitability of thought's eternal repetition of an oscillation between dialectics and their dissolution, identity and *différance*, in a kind of fated, unprogressive pas de deux. Even more confusingly, it is far from clear whether Derrida believes that any whole—either Western philosophy's or his own—can escape the necessity of violence. "I believe violence remains in fact (almost) ineradicable," Derrida writes (1988a 112), suggesting that our attempts to escape from the rule of violence, like our attempts to escape the discourse of representation and of Western metaphysics, must fail. I shall close my discussion by posing the tragic Derrida against the more positive attempt to find some hope in that "almost" he places in parentheses before the word "ineradicable."

Derrida offers few concrete reasons for hope. Like Foucault in the last years of his life, Derrida appears to have been stung by the charges that his work is at best apolitical and at worst politically disastrous. He has recently discussed explicitly the political implications of deconstruction, and he has virtually dropped the association of *différance* with an "economy of death," to be found in the early essays, in favor of more positive images of deconstruction. Yet Derrida remains unable to say how the insights of *différance* can be translated into a political program. Asked by Richard Kearney if "the theoretical radicality of deconstruction [can] be translated into a radical political praxis," Derrida replies: "I must confess that I have never succeeded in directly relating deconstruction to existing political codes or programmes. . . . The absence of an adequate political code to translate or incorporate the radical implications of deconstruction has given many the impression that deconstruction is opposed to politics, or is at best apolitical. But this impression only prevails because all of our political codes and terminologies still remain fundamentally metaphysical, regardless of whether they originate from the right or the left" (1984 119–20). Since an essay such as "The Politics of Friendship" suggests that the very conditions of the political are metaphysical, the possibility of a nonmetaphysical politics appear remote indeed. In the interim, Derrida attempts to "gesture in opposite directions at the same time: on the one hand to preserve a distance and suspicion with regard to the offical political codes governing reality; on the other, to intervene here and now in a practical and *engagé* manner whenever the necessity arises. This position of dual allegiance, in which I personally find myself, is one of perpetual uneasiness. I try where I can to act politically while recognizing that such action remains incommensurate with my intellectual project of deconstruction" (1984 120).

In the "Afterword" to *Limited Inc.*, Derrida uses the occasion of answering a set of questions from Gerald Graff to explain the intellectual project of deconstruction and its positive, political utility. Deconstruction, if not fully "nonviolent," is at least potentially "less violent" than other forms of thought. "And if, as I believe, violence remains in fact (almost) ineradicable, its analysis and the most refined, ingenious account of its conditions, will be the least violent gestures, perhaps even nonviolent, and in any case those which contribute most to transforming the legal-ethical-political rules: *in* the university and *outside* the university" (1988a 112). The fundamental argument is that deconstruction—Derridean interpretation—breaks open the philosophy of the same in such a way that its "other" is given more space. Deconstruction "does not suspend reference—to history, to the world, to reality, to being, and especially not to the other, since to say of history, of the world, of reality, that they always appear in an experience, hence in a movement of interpretation that contextualizes them according to a network of differences and hence of referral to the other, is surely to recall that alterity (difference) is irreducible" (1988a 137). The emphasis on difference, then, protects the other from the violence of becoming the same. Derrida's "concept of writing or of trace perturbs every logic of opposition, every dialectic" (1988a 137), and contests the stabilities of identity. "This is why (a) the finiteness of a context is never secured or simple, there is an indefinite opening of every context, an essential nontotalization; (b) whatever there can be of force or of irreducible violence in the attempt to 'fix the contexts of utterances,' or of anything else, can always communicate, by virtue of the erasure just mentioned, with a certain 'weakness,' even with an essential nonviolence. It is in this relationship, which is difficult to think through, that responsibilities jell, political responsibilities in particular."

"Essential nonviolence" here appears to be the ability to leave the other in peace, an other embodied in the "weakness" that force encounters and subdues, but that force remains troubled by even after the relation of domination is established. Political responsibility takes the form of disturbing every form that incorporates or recuperates the other, by describing the conditions of that incorporation or by introducing the counterlogic of *différance*. The affinity of this negative politics (rather like Adorno's "negative dialectics") to anarchism is clear.[15] Yet Derrida objects to the notion—which his work has been interpreted as putting forward—that the law is inevitably oppressive.

[15]In the interview with Kearney, Derrida accepts "responsible anarchy" as a somewhat adequate description of his position (1984 120–21).

"My intention was therefore not primarily to determine the law, the tribunal, or the police as political powers *repressive in themselves*. Moreover, I do not believe that they are that, purely and simply. . . . We need here to distinguish very carefully if we are not to succumb to the facile solutions and ideological consensus of the *doxai* of right or left. . . . Every police is not repressive, no more than the law in general, even in its negative, restrictive, or prohibitive prescriptions. A red light is not repressive" (1988a 132). And not only is the law not necessarily repressive, but there are situations in which the law is "a logical necessity" (1988a 133). "There is no society without police, even if one can always dream of forms of police that would be more sublime, less refined or less vulgar" (1988a 135). What is required is not the anarchistic denunciation of law but the "political evaluation" (1988a 132) of particular laws in their specific contexts.

I do not see how such "evaluation" is possible without some appeal to standards of legitimacy. If there are always a police and always some laws, then we need and want to be able to distinguish good (or less bad) laws from evil ones. And Derrida comes very close to accepting the need for a communally determined notion of legitimacy. His very phrasing of that acceptance, however, makes his impatience with the notion obvious. "There are analyses and formalizations proposed by Searle concerning certain rules, and sometimes concerning rules which constitute right, morality, and politics, and are accepted as such by a majority of persons in given communities, for example, ours. To this extent, if a repressive police, that is to say, one which violates these laws, commits abuses, then one can indeed 'invoke' these rules to contest police power, thus opposing to it, by virtue of good rules, the reference to a more just police. This I will readily grant you" (1988a 138–39). But Derrida does not linger on this point; he is much less interested in appeals to existing standards than to the notion of complete novelty. "The deconstruction of these 'assumptions,' and hence of these codes, if it also has a political dimension, is engaged in the writing (or if you prefer, in the future production) of a language and of a political practice that can no longer be comprehended, judged, deciphered by these codes" (1988a 139). A Hegelian "situated freedom," in which practice invokes existing norms, appeals less to Derrida than the absolute freedom of a practice that exceeds all current codes, which is why Thomas McCarthy complains that Derrida offers a "politics of the ineffable" (1989 146).

My argument is that Derrida does not avoid all reference to existing norms but justifies his visionary politics with the vague norm of nonviolence, even while he resists more specific norms of legitimacy as forged by particular societies. The communal bases for "political evaluation" and the very possibility of the social figure more prominently in Derrida's later work than in his earlier texts, but he still fights shy of everything that might limit the play of difference. He knows that we can never live pure difference or pure otherness, just as surely as he insists that the idealities of pure presence and of pure self-identity can never be maintained. But he holds on to some sense that the violence of the philosophy of the same explains the failure of pure difference to win its way, and the equation of pure difference's (impossible) victory with freedom lies just below the surface in many of his texts.

Derrida's proclivity for tragic impasse and for making global pronouncements surfaces once again in his 1988 essay/lecture "The Politics of Friendship."[16] This essay accepts the necessity of law as the very foundational condition of both politics and any human community. "Before even having taken responsibility for any given affirmation, we are already caught up in a kind of asymmetrical and heteronomical curvature of the social space, more precisely, in the relation to the Other prior to any organized *socius*, to any determined 'government,' to any 'law.' Please note: prior to any determined law, as either natural law or positive law, but not prior to any law in general. This heteronomical and asymmetrical curvature of a sort of originary sociality is a law, perhaps the very essence of the law" (1988c 633–34). To some extent, Derrida appears close to Habermas here, in this acceptance of an intersubjective bond as the precondition of all sociality. The social, even the law, is "always already" there before any experience of self or other, and there is even a "responsibility" in which the self is entangled by this prior law. But Derrida's position diverges from Habermas's in two crucial ways. First, while Derrida is willing to talk of this social bond as "law in general," he refuses to specify any forms that this law must take; a multiplicity of possibilities, apparently, lie open. Habermas—ill-advisedly in my opinion—takes just the opposite tack and attempts to identify fairly specific conditions that must apply (at least as counterfactual ideals) to any and all communicative exchanges. A contextual approach to understood conventions and conditions would avoid Habermas's universalism, while allowing more specificity than Derrida offers. Second, Derrida wants to insist that the intersubjective en-

---

16"The Politics of Friendship" was presented as lecture at least twice: at Cornell University in October 1988 (where I heard it) and at the American Philosophical Association meeting in December 1988. A much shorter version of the lecture was printed in *The Journal of Philosphy* and, with the exception of reporting Derrida's provocative comments on a "democracy still to come," I have restricted myself to the published text. Thomas McCarthy (1988 and 1989) has published two responses to "The Politics of Friendship," both of which object to Derrida's politics on grounds very similar to my own. Tobin Siebers (1988 chap. 4) offers a reading of violence in Derrida that parallels mine in several ways. Unfortunately, I did not know his work until after completing this book.

counter is "asymmetrical and heteronomical," precisely where Habermas's political hopes rest on making that encounter reciprocal and egalitarian.

We would expect "asymmetry" in Derrida to serve as a protection of difference, but in this essay on politics, asymmtery is also a trace of a domination that appears inescapable. I pick up where the passage quoted in the preceeding paragraph left off.

> What is taking place at this moment, the disquieting experience we are having, is perhaps just the silent unfolding of that *strange violence that has since forever* [my emphasis] insinuated itself into the origin of the most innocent experiences of friendship or justice. We have begun to respond. We are already caught, surprised [*pris, surpris*] in a certain responsibility, and the most ineluctable of responsibilities—as if it were possible to conceive of a responsibility without freedom. We are invested with an undeniable responsibility at the moment we begin to signify something (but where does that begin?). This responsibility assigns us our freedom without leaving it with us, if one could put it that way. And we see it coming from the Other. It is assigned to us by the Other from the Other, before any hope of reappropriation permits us to assume this responsibility in the space of what could be called *autonomy*. (1988c 634)

This meeting of subject and Other is asymmetrical because the other is not only (or even) another subject, but the Lacanian Other (with a capital O), the order of signification that "assigns" responsibility, freedom, and personhood to the subject. The version of freedom found in this passage is completely positive, and we find the denial of individual autonomy that almost invariably accompanies descriptions of positive freedom. But the reference to the "strange violence" that marks the subjection of the subject to the conditions imposed by the Other already suggests that Derrida intends to protest against the very terms of political and social life that he presents as "ineluctable." The tragic stance manifests itself in the revelation of laws and necessitites that are insufferable.

Derrida develops this tragic conviction through a discussion of friendship as the singular relation of a particular subject to a particular other; what distinguishes this relationship is that I love this other who is my friend for what is unique in him. (In the tradition, as Derrida notes, the friend is never "her," and this exclusion must be taken into account in reevaluating the tradition.) Lacan, of course, distinguishes between the other and the Other, where the first is another person and the second is the order of the Symbolic. Derrida refuses this distinction (although not explicitly) by writing "Other" with a capital O throughout his essay. His point is that this distinction cannot be maintained, that the very possibility of a relationship to an other is dependent on the relationship to the Other. Yet this impossibility of extricating the singular other from the generalizing order of the Other manifests the "aporia" of friendship.

> Of these two dimensions [personal friendship and the more abstract social bond] of the relation to the Other, the one maintains the absolute singularity of the Other and of 'my' relation to the Other, as well as the relation of the Other to the Other which I am for him. But the relation to the Other also passes through the universality of the law. . . . Does not my relation to the singularity of the Other as Other pass through the law? Does not the law command me to recognize the transcendent alterity of the Other who can only ever be hetero-genous and singular [an odd conjunction], hence resistant to the very generality of the law? But this co-implication, far from dissolving the antagonism and breaking through the aporia, aggravates them instead—at the very heart of friendship. (1988c 640–41)

This particular deconstruction of a tradition of political thought that attempts to take friendship as the model for desirable social relations reveals that the ideal of friendship as a respect for a singular other—"there is no friendship without 'respect of the Other' " (1988c 640)—conflicts with the very social order that is deemed necessary to make any social relation at all possible. In the public lecture titled "The Politics of Friendship," Derrida suggests that this *aporia* in the political calls for an entirely new model of politics, a "democracy still to come" whose shape we cannot specify right now. This explicit use of *democracy* to name what might prove an acceptable politics interests me, but Derrida had little to say beyond a gesture toward an uncertain future, and there is no reference to democracy at all in the printed (shorter) version of the lecture. Instead, that version ends with a footnote that returns us to mystical grounds, to the dream of protecting the other's (and our own?) singularity by keeping the other aloof from any order of representation. "The 'Who?' of friendship moves off into the distance beyond all these determinations. In its 'infinite imminence,' it even exceeds the interest of knowledge, science, truth, proximity, even life and the memory of life. It is not yet an identifiable 'I,' either public or private" (1988c 644n.). The only avoidance of the violence of metaphysics, of representation, and of the politi-cal/social bond of responsibility is this complete escape. But it is hard to reconcile this image of escape with the necessity of being "always already" caught in the relation to the Other that is "perhaps the very essence of the law" as presented in the body of the essay.

One tragic strain in Derrida, then, calls on us to resist the continually enacted defeat of pure difference, even while reminding us of the inevitablity of that defeat. Another, and less often noted, tragic strain in Derrida admits that pure difference has its own characteristic violence, and that freedom can be gained only in the Pyrrhic victory of death. If violence is ineradicable, that is because both the philosophy of the same and the play of *différance* are violent, although in different ways. The early Derrida suggests that we merely have a choice of violences, not a hope to avoid violence altogether.

There are good reasons for the historic suppression of play, *différance*, and writing; they are difficult to affirm because they carry terrible burdens. What Artaud and Bataille both recognized in their extreme art and their fascination with violence and death is that to embrace play, the unsettling of metaphysic's conservative representations, is to encounter "mute and nonproductive death" (1978 255), "a kind of potlatch of signs that burns, consumes, and wastes words in the gay affirmation of death: a sacrifice and a challenge" (1978 274). Only if Artaud and Bataille "rush headlong into death pure and simple" (1978 255) can they disrupt the mastery of death characteristic of Hegelian dialectics. "I am speaking of a relationship between a *différance* that can make a profit on its investment and a *différance* that misses its profit, the *investiture* of a presence that is pure and without loss here being confused with absolute loss, with death. Through such a relating of a restricted and a general economy the very project of philosophy, under the privileged heading of Hegelianism, is displaced and reinscribed" (1982 19). The philosophy of the same has protected us from "absolute loss," from death, through its recuperation of the essential from mere transitory appearances. To affirm play must be to affirm death. *Différance* introduces "the *economy of death*" (1982 4).

We have seen that metaphysics is violent because it appropriates the other, reducing it to the same, in a representational logic that repeats what can be subsumed and condemns to death, declares useless waste, that part of the other which cannot be put to work in the "labor of the negative." Derrida recognizes that this work of thought takes place *within* writing, "a writing within which philosophy is inscribed as a place within a text which it does not command" (1976 286). But philosophy plays out only part of what writing makes possible (which is why philosophy is a "restricted economy"); philosophy's characteristic violence is directed toward the other in order to preserve the same. The model of mastery and of violence in philosophy is that of Hegel's master/slave dialectic, a relationship that ultimately proves as binding to the master as it is to the slave. Crucially, the master/slave dialectic would dissolve once the fear of death was overcome, once the slave did not exchange his subservience for his continued life, and once the master did not associate his immortality with his power over others. The wider realm of play, which is also inscribed in writing (always already there), opens up a "general economy" that is characterized by a different sort of violence, the dissolution of presence, of identity, of the same. This violence might be called openness toward one's own death (to echo a Heideggerian theme), as opposed to the infliction of death upon the other. Certainly, sacrifice is a crucial theme in Artaud and Bataille, from whom Derrida draws the concept of a general economy, while the pull toward mysticism in this acceptance of dissolution should also be clear.

The choice, then, is not between a violent metaphysics and a nonviolent writing or play. The Derrida of the "Afterword" tries to get around this stark ubiquity of violence in his early texts by protesting that "the repression at the origin of meaning is an irreducible violence. It is difficult to call it 'bad' or to condemn it from a moral or political point of view" (1988a 150). (This formulation—with its appeal to norms that would differentiate 'bad' from not-bad violence—raises more questions than it answers.) In *Of Grammatology*, Derrida outlines three "moments" of violence: the originary violence of writing, as "arche-violence, loss of the proper, of absolute proximity, of self-presence, in truth the loss of what has never taken place, of a self-presence which has never been given but only dreamed of and always already split"; then the second violence of metaphysics "that is reparatory, protective, instituting the 'moral,' prescribing the concealment of writing"; and finally, a third violence that is potentially the violence of deconstruction itself, a "violence of reflection" which "reveals the first nomination [the arche-violence] which was already an expropriation, but it denudes also that which since then functioned as the proper the so-called proper . . . the reassuring seal of self-identity" (1976 112).

Thus deconstruction offers us not an escape from violence but a return to (or a replaying or a representation of) an originary violence within writing that metaphysics has, in turn, attempted to violently repress. It is difficult to affirm this violence (as writing or as play) because it is difficult to affirm one's own death. Metaphysics embodies the logic of self-preservation; *différance* points toward self-dissolution. But this affirmation of play is not without its rewards, most notable of which is a radical negative freedom. What attracts Derrida so strongly in Bataille's work is the image of escape from the hateful, calculating, petty dialectics of the restricted economy. Once shorn of self-concern, the (non)self (which now attains what Bataille, significantly enough, calls "sovereignty") steps completely outside the master/slave dialectic, completely outside the realm of work, and completely outside discourse. This last escape is a necessary consequence because Derrida insists that all discourse is representative; there is no alternative within language to representational discourse, even though writing carries within it traces of *différance* that disrupt representation. In the absolute terms employed in the early essays, the internal strategy is doomed to failure because the discourse of representation

cannot be unsettled; it always returns, and the best one can get is an oscillation between moments of disruption and moments of stability, without any
progress toward some more desirable condition. The external strategy provides the only possibility of a real freedom, but this escape (this sovereignty)
can be had only at the price of, at the moment of, death. What we must
recognize here is that the rule of philosophy, of the dialectic, of representation, has been made so complete in Derrida's thought that only death provides
an escape—and the result is that death is erotized insofar as freedom, at
whatever price, remains desirable. Derrida, like Bataille, is fully aware of the
paradoxes of this view, since it aims for a freedom that is achieved in the very
moment that there is no self to enjoy that freedom. The essay on Bataille
pursues these paradoxes ruthlessly, positing a desire that is recognizable by its
being "indifferent to any possible results" (1978 264). Only in such indifference is sovereignty attained, since the tragic circumstances in which we
find ourselves cannot be altered. All desire is focused on mastery itself—a
mastery that must include relinquishing that investment in the self and its
survival which makes Hegel's slave the dominated one. Freedom, as in
Nietzsche, lies entirely in our response to a world we cannot change; not
caring becomes the sign of the strongest self, the self that can accept anything
existence dishes out with equanimity, the self that can affirm death.

Gerald Graff and others have criticized Derridean play as the very embodiment of postmodern consumer capitalism. The argument is that Derrida and
his followers are picking on a straw man when they attack the restricted
economy and work ethic characteristic of traditional thought and representation. Rather, the very play that the poststructuralists present as disruptive
should be recognized as the dominant form discourse takes in a society in
which the manipulation of images (an economy of reproduction or of signification) takes precedence over processes of actual production. The peculiar
violence of advertising—with its radical decontextualization of images from
their history, their production, or their normal use (which, in a Wittgensteinian way, we could associate with their ordinary meaning)—owes a lot to
the techniques of surrealism. Bataille and Artaud both had strong ties with
surrealism, and their fascination with the eroticism of violence and death
suggests how the violence of dismemberment, mutilation, unorthodox juxta-
positions, and decontextualization (all characteristic of disruptive play within
significative systems) can also arouse certain desires. Some part of the self
wants its own death (a statement Freud would recognize), and postmodern
society has learned how to capitalize on that desire just as it has on all others.
The very strategy of a disruptive play only becomes possible within a postmodern economy that has already assured that such play is safe and profit-

able. Of course, such a diagnosis only increases our paranoia, our sense that the postmodern monolith is always there ahead of us, always having already colonized those terrains we are attempting to mark out as the spaces for some kind of freedom. But when one considers the triumph of poststructuralism in the academy and the immense institutional rewards and backing now provided for poststructuralist work (play?), such paranoia often seems justified.

In any case, whether supportive of the postmodern consumer economy or not, Derridean play opens up a space that is recognizably tragic, since, at the very best, it registers a protest against a certain order without being able to effect the transformation of that order. Play can be experienced as liberation from the hateful, calculated restricted economy of the dialectic, but that liberation will always be tainted by the tragic realization that a full escape from the realm of representation, of the *Aufhebung*, is impossible. "To think the closure of representation is to think the tragic: not as the representation of fate, but as the fate of representation. Its gratuitous and baseless necessity. And it is to think why it is *fatal* that, in its closure, representation continues" (1978 250). One manifestation of tragic necessity is the inability to achieve the dreamed-of liberation; no full negative freedom, no completely free play, no pure consumption is possible. The other manifestation of tragic necessity is that such desideratum as play and pure consumption are, strictly speaking, "unthinkable" and "untenable" (1978 268), only imaginable in the extreme formula of "the gay affirmation of death" (1978 274). Only in annihilation could we experience the liberation that play appears to promise. To desire play is to desire the impossible, as summed up in Bataille's notion of our fundamental desire to consciously witness (experience) our own death. We are prisoners of an order (of thought, of representation) that we can escape only through death, and Derrida calls upon us to affirm that death as a means toward unsettling the order. But nothing suggests that such a move will be very successful (the order eternally returns), and certainly it would be highly problematic to describe such an affirmation as liberating.

Derrida's work has been so crucially important to postmodernism because it presents so forcefully the processes by which the monolith has appropriated everything, while also searching resolutely for strategies that would activate the plural. These themes become especially provocative when "hierarchy within envelopment" is seen as the characteristic strategy not only of Western metaphysics but also of the Western construction of its political, economic, and sexual orders. Contemporary radicals' attempts both to understand the way these orders have constituted the subjects within them and to develop possible ways to disrupt the order have been greatly influenced by Derrida's work, even though he continually undermines the hope for any fundamental

transformation of the current order. To work within the system in a deconstructive mode is merely to highlight a play that was always there, although'
(perhaps) more hidden in the past. To reach outside the system is to move
toward mysticism, since language itself is synonymous with the order of
thought. There is no ontological fulcrum point outside language or the
human order that might facilitate a change (as, say, "anomalies" motivate
changes in Kuhnian paradigms). And when Derrida does make what appear
to be ontological claims about the nature of language, of human signifying
orders, he suggests that language at all times and in all places has been subject
to these exact same constraints, so there is no reason to expect some transformation either in the game's rules or in the moves characteristic of various
players. Instead, freedom is envisioned as a disengagement from the system's
law, and Derrida masterfully demonstrates how such moves are continually
brought back into the fold.

Finally, his antihumanism, his reduction of subjectivity to a "function" or a
"position" within the system, is not linked to an examination of capabilities
the subject acquires by virtue of its location within the system.[17] The subject
experiences freedom not in the playing out of the possibilities the system
affords it but in affirming the tragic (negative) freedom of the "pure death"
that play offers at its extreme limit. A lingering trace of humanism, however,
makes itself felt within Derrida's determinedly antihumanist thought in the
strongly implied complaint about philosophy's appropriation of the other; his
work often points toward something "irreducible" that is to be valued precisely for its difference, its irreducibility. And Derrida exhibits the standard
postmodern privileging of democracy as a goal that we neither can question
nor need argue for, linking his stress on the plural to an attempt to make
democracy appear.[18] Surely this ethical and political ideal of a democratic
pluralism relies on the Kantian definition of the human being as that individual entity which should not be treated as a means, whose difference should be
respected and preserved. Derrida would never accept this violation of his own
difference from Kant, of course, and the politics that would stem from a
Derridean emphasis on human differences would differ drastically from the
Kantian recuperation of those differences within the categorical imperative.

[17]Derrida does not claim that the subject does not exist, only that "there is no subject who is
agent, author, and master of *différance*, who eventually and empirically would be overtaken by
différance. Subjectivity—like objectivity—is an effect of *différance*, an effect inscribed in a system
of *différance*" (1981 28).
[18]On the connection of democracy to a true pluralism—and Derrida's belief that neither yet
exists—see "The Ends of Man" (1982 114–15). Derrida has recently taken up this topic more
explicitly and at greater length, as he tries to envision a "democracy still to come" in "The Politics
of Friendship" (1988c).

But the outrage that precipitates Derrida's attack on metaphysics does imply that the West violently overrides some sanctity, some right, that resides in the other's difference. The valuing of such difference is a recognizably humanist theme, even if we accept the antihumanist insistence that humanism did not value (and protect) difference enough. (After all, Kant's humanism was directed against what he perceived as a threatening tyranny of the same— religious intolerance.) What humanism provided was some grounding principle for the privileging of the other's irreducibility. The complaint (with which I am sympathetic) of the antihumanists is that humanism all too often erects a prescriptive definition of what counts as human that serves to justify exclusion and maltreatment of those who are not up to snuff. But that complaint often leaves antihumanism reduced to appealing to its audience's implicit understanding of what is right and wrong. (The point is not to return to assertions of grounding principles, but to begin to theorize about the fact and nature of the implicit understandings embedded in social groups.) In Derrida's thought, the very possibility of the other is constantly put in doubt because the processes of thought, language, and representation constantly assimilate the other into the same. At the same time, the desire to preserve otherness that drives his whole enterprise can only be presented as a psychological fact, poised against the perhaps stronger psychological fact that humans also desire a metaphysics of the same.

FOUCAULT AND THE ETHOS OF PERMANENT CRITIQUE

The similarities of Foucault's work, from the writing of *Madness and Civilization* to the beginning of *The History of Sexuality*, to that of Derrida suggest how, despite the significant differences between them, the two writers served to set out a problematic that reverberates throughout postmodernism. Like Derrida, Foucault suggests that humanism and reason have functioned in the West as definitive, exclusionary terms, and that a society's or an epoch's identity is formed vis à vis what it forcefully excludes. Foucault's histories provide a wider view of the conflicts and fields within which practices of definition and exclusion occur, thus making evident the relation of reason to madness or the relation of the self-examining, self-regulated bourgeois to the vagrant in the workhouse. The included and the excluded, the same and its other, are revealed as dependent on one another within the larger dynamics of the constitution of identities within a social whole that privileges some identities over others. Peter Stallybrass and Allon White convey the thrust of this perspective when they quote Barbara Babcock's assertion that "what is so-cially peripheral is often symbolically central" and go on to comment that a society's representation of the other "is not simply a powerful image but fundamentally constitutive of the categorical sets through which we live and make sense of the world" (1986 23). Foucault thus points us beyond the binary opposition of the same and its other toward the larger economy of the discursive and social practices that create and enforce the distinctions of (and the hierarchies that stem from) the binary opposition.

The heroic view of Foucault's early work, a view found most fully in Alan Sheridan's book,[19] sees him as giving voice to or opening a space for the hitherto silent other to make its presence felt. Stallybrass and White's book on the carnivalesque captures the sense that these transgressive alternative artic-ulations "may become a primary, highly charged intersection and mediation of social and political forces, a sort of intensifier and displacer in the making of identity. . . . A fundamental rule seems to be that what is excluded at the overt level of identity-formation is productive of new objects of desire" (1986 25). The site where the other speaks is a transgressive site at which "symbolic dissonances" within the society, outlawed desires, and refashioned categori-cal schemes may be brought into the economy of the same by a counterlogic of transgression that is reminiscent of Bataille's attempt to disrupt the restricted logic of the Hegelian dialectic. The other possesses energies and potential that identity both needs to survive and views as dangerous, always in need of being kept under strict control. Stallybrass and White are careful to state that no simple translation of the carnivalesque's symbolic transformations into political transformation is possible, a point that Derrida tries to make about his own counterlogic of *différance*: "Deconstruction is inherently neither 'conservative' nor the contrary. . . . Deconstruction does not exist somewhere, pure, proper, self-identical, outside of its inscriptions in conflictual and differentiated contexts; it 'is' only what it does and what is done with it, there where it takes place" (1988a 141).

To portray Foucault simply as the champion of the downtrodden, however, is to vastly underestimate the extent to which his understanding of the general economy that relates the other to the same dictates whatever the other might say. Like Derrida, Foucault severely questions the very possibility of a pure

[19]Sheridan offers this description of Foucault's early work on madness: "The whole concep-tual basis of psychiatry . . . is turned on its head, sabotaged from within, in the name of its victims. The real heroes are not the sober, white-coated scientists . . . but rather those literary 'madmen' who, repudiating the language of reason, crossed over into the territory of 'unreason' and, in a language beyond and prior to both, testified to an experience that lay, not beyond the boundary of true humanity, but at its heart" (1980 7).

other.[20] Since so many commentators stress how fully Foucault neutralizes the concept of "otherness," however, it is worth taking a few moments to indicate what justifies a view such as Sheridan's. In other words, Foucault evidences, like Derrida, an oscillation between identifying an other to the characteristic strategies of identity formation (particularly by societies) and denying that such an other can exist. In some instances, the other remains a crucial ingredient in the hope for freedom in Foucault, because "attention" to the "illegitimate" (as defined by the dominant discourse) "knowledges" of the excluded can provide the material for those genealogies that Foucault insists will render apparent the "contingency" of existing social forms, the possibility that things could be otherwise.

> Let us give the term *genealogy* to the union of erudite knowledge and local memories which allows us to establish a historical knowledge of struggles and to make use of this knowledge tactically today. . . . What it really does is to entertain the claims to attention of local, discontinuous, disqualified, illegitimate knowledges against the claims of a unitary body of theory which would filter, hierarchise, and order them in the name of some true knowledge and some arbitrary idea of what constitutes a science and its objects. (1980b 83)

How we are to weigh these alternative claims remains unclear, while presumably the facts of conflict and resistance that a genealogical investigation uncovers justifies the assertion that the "unitary body of theory" is based on "some arbitrary idea." In any case, genealogy here appears dependent on the voices of the "disqualified" in order to disrupt the serenity of what is. In his later years, Foucault mostly drops this appeal to the testimony of the other, but he remains adamant that genealogy reveals "contingency," as opposed to necessity, and that such contingency opens up the possibility of freedom. In the late essay "What Is Enlightenment?" Foucault contrasts his critical practice to that of a transcendental, Kantian critique that indicates necessary conditions.

> This criticism [i.e., Foucault's own] is not transcendental, and its goal is not that of making a metaphysics possible: it is genealogical in its design and archaeological in its method. . . . This critique will be genealogical in the sense that it

---

[20]In *Discipline and Punish* Foucault makes it clear that the excluded are never outside: "The carceral network does not cast the unassimilable into a confused hell; there is no outside. It takes back with one hand what it seems to exclude with the other. It saves everything, including what it punishes. It is unwilling to waste even what it has decided to disqualify. In this panoptic society of which incarceration is the omnipresent armature, the delinquent is not outside the law; he is, from the very outset, in the law, at the very heart of the law" (1979 301). This is a general, unrestricted economy with a vengeance.

will not deduce from the form of what we are what it is impossible for us to do and to know, but it will separate out, from the contingency that has made us what we are, the possibility of no longer being, doing, or thinking what we are, do, or think. It is not seeking to make possible a metaphysics that has finally become a science; it is seeking to give new impetus, as far and wide as possible, to the undefined work of freedom. (1984 46)

Genealogy reveals that history could have been *other* than what it has been; history, in keeping with Nietzsche's use of genealogy, is shown to be the product of successive power struggles that are understood as discontinuous. And Foucault here explicitly links this revelation of contingency to the possibility of freedom, a freedom that remains "undefined" but involves "the possibility of no longer being . . . what we are." It is not clear if this late formulation of the notion of genealogy remains dependent on some kind of access to or articulation of an other to the official histories in order to demonstrate contingency against the official claims of inevitability. Foucault usually avoids appeals to an other that might be seen as somehow pure. Instead, like Derrida in his meditations on the "margins" of philosophy and Said in his notion of "marginalization,"[21] Foucault hopes "to move beyond the outside-inside alternative; we have to be at the frontiers. Criticism indeed consists of analyzing and reflecting upon limits. But if the Kantian question was that of knowing what limits knowledge has to renounce transgressing, it seems to me that the critical question today has to be turned back into a positive one: in what is given to us as universal, necessary, obligatory, what place is occupied by whatever is singular, contingent, and the product of arbitrary constraints? The point, in brief, is to transform the critique conducted in the form of necessary limitation into a practical critique that takes the form of a possible transgression" (1984 45). The problem appears to be more how those on the inside can struggle away from the center out to the margins (if not outside) than gaining access to others who are already outside and can somehow help our movement to the frontiers. We cannot deny, however, that Foucault has used meditations on the excluded (the mad and criminals) to precipitate criticism's outward movement. He presents this critique to be performed at the margins as the "attitude of modernity" he wishes to endorse: "a philosophical ethos that could be described as a permanent critique of our historical era" (1984 42).[22]

---

[21]See Derrida (1982 ix–xxix) and Said (1976 37–38) for these two writers' discussions of margins.

[22]Foucault's description of the "attitude of modernity" in "What Is Enlightenment?" is remarkably close to the description of modernity found in Habermas with which I have been working in this book. This similarity clearly stems from Foucault's reconciliation with Kant in this late essay, a reconciliation that contrasts strongly with the submerged debate with Kant that informs the much more hostile description of modernity found in *The Order of Things* (1973).

Genealogy, as an alternative to transcendental theory of the Kantian sort, also entails a new description of the intellectual.[23] Foucault labels the traditional theorist a "universal intellectual" who, whether a Marxist or a Freudian psychiatrist or a liberal economist, possesses an overarching theory that allows him to delineate the total arrangement of social (or psychic) forces with which we have to contend and thus the correct moves for their transformation. Because he possesses this knowledge, the intellectual must take the Leninist position of leader; only his accurate, theoretical insight can prevent mistakes from being made. The epistemological privilege attached to theoretical knowledge serves to legitimate antidemocratic hierarchy; the reign of experts that characterizes high-tech, postindustrial society is reproduced in radical politics as well. (Bernard Shaw called every profession a conspiracy against the laity.) An opposition to traditional theory and the critique of intellectuals' power combine in Foucault's insistence that every production of knowledge serves the interest of some power. The general, theoretical knowledge produced in medicine, economics, psychiatry, anthropology, and the other human sciences since their establishment at the dawn of modernity is part of the power of the social institutions that have grown up around these disciplines: the market, colonial administrations, the university.

Associating theory with the claim to universal applicability, Foucault proposes instead the nontheoretical work of the specific intellectual, whose work is directly related to a particular social struggle. Such work (usually described by Foucault as a genealogical account of the alignment of and choices made by various groups who now find themselves in contention) makes no pretense of being disinterested; it is produced for use in a particular situation and toward a particular end. The specific intellectual makes no claim to produce generally valid conclusions. (Just how this modesty pertains to Foucault's own work is, of course, not apparent.) The specific intellectual's work pertains only to the situation at hand and is placed at the service of those in the struggle. Crucially, Foucault is wary of the intellectual's offering any recommendations for action. Although Foucault's account sometimes makes it appear as if the intellectual is divorced from the struggle itself, acting as an aloof outsider who provides information, what he wants is a model of intellectual work that is motivated primarily by the intellectual's own involvement in particular struggles. The ideal, it seems, is to combat the habitual abstraction of intellectuals from the local by focusing instead on the kind of intellectual work that is produced as one necessary tool in a social conflict; we might say that Foucault is deeply troubled by the whole concept of an intellectual and

---

[23]See Foucault (1980b 126–33) for his discussion of the distinction between the universal and specific intellectual.

would prefer that we think of intellectual work as being done by anyone who happens to be in the particular circumstances that call for such work. One's primary identity would be something quite different and quite concrete, and one's intellectual work would be undertaken only at times when that primary identity required the support of intellectual work in pursuing some particular end.

The model of the specific intellectual assumes the fact of political and social struggles, but the primary complaint against Foucault's work has been that his view of power offers no way to explain how successful opposition of power could ever occur. In Edward Said's account, Foucault portrays a monolithic power that "is everywhere. It [power] is overcoming, co-opting, infinitely detailed, and ineluctable in the growth of its domination" (1986a 150); oppositional voices in Foucault's work "are absorbed and institutionalized almost routinely by the very structure one might have thought they had permanently disabled" (1986a 152). Despite Foucault's protests that such was not his intent, many readers have experienced *Discipline and Punish* as, in Frank Lentricchia's words, "the most persuasive, if depressing, statement yet published, from radical quarters, on the apparently endless stamina, the perfect flexibility, and the bottomless cunning of capitalism to sustain itself" (1988 86). No less than Derrida, Foucault is a master of the logic of recuperation. If the monolith haunts postmodernism, it is because writers such as Derrida can reveal the eternal repetition of Western metaphysics' themes and writers such as Foucault can reveal the complicity of even the actions we most habitually validate as oppositional with the aims of power. It is now becoming apparent, less than ten years after his death, that Foucault is going to be one of those writers—like Yeats or Wittgenstein—whose work will be divided into periods. The "middle" Foucault of *Discipline and Punish* and the essays and interviews collected in *Power/Knowledge* has been a highly influential figure (as I discuss below), but we are only just beginning to sort out what the "late" Foucault of roughly 1978 to 1984 was trying to do in the three volumes of *The History of Sexuality* that deal with the ancient world and in the numerous interviews and essays of these years. (The first volume of *The History of Sexuality* begins to look more and more like a transitional work, with its relentless recuperation of "liberated" sexual practices back into the dynamics of disciplinary power, but with its discussion of power in the chapter titled "Method" already more fully directed to theorizing the possibility of resistance.) In certain respects, the late Foucault appears to be groping for an escape from the monolith, just as such writers as Said and Lentricchia are, despite his continual denials that any of his earlier works offer any monolithic view. Foucault explicitly shifts his interest from power to the subject, even though he does not admit that this shift is a response to such criticisms as Said's. The path Foucault carves out for himself in the late works is far from clear. What follows is my attempt to reconstruct certain strands in the late work and to indicate in what relation to one another these strands lie.

Without examining them in detail, we must recall three characteristics of power in the middle Foucault: it is productive; it is only exercised by individuals but never possessed by them; and it is involved in every social relation.[24] Taking the last two points first, the middle Foucault's view of power appears to deny the possibility of agency (hence Foucault provides an example of the poststructuralist "death of the subject") and to accept the Nietzschean insistence that power is omnipresent. On the individual, Foucault writes: "The individual . . . is not the *vis-à-vis* of power; it is, I believe, one of its prime effects. The individual is an effect of power, and at the same time, or precisely to the extent to which it is that effect, it is the element of its articulation. The individual which power has constituted is at the same time its vehicle" (1980b 98). The individual does not stand apart from power or prior to it as a traditional, dualistic model would suggest, that is, a model that views the individual as submitting to or opposing the dictates of a power that stands over or above her. The dualistic model accords the individual an autonomy, an existence, and an identity independent of power that Foucault's model denies. Rather, the individual is constituted by power—hence, individual existence and identity are among power's effects. And the individual never possesses power to act out her own autonomous desires or goals. The individual exercises power at certain times and in certain places as a functionary of power's intentions, not her own.

> There is no power that is exercised without a series of aims and objectives. But this does not mean that it results from the choice or decision of an individual subject; . . . the rationality of power is characterized by tactics that are often quite explicit at the restricted level where they are inscribed (the local cynicism of power), tactics which, becoming connected to one another, attracting and propagating one another, but finding their base of support and their condition elsewhere, end by forming comprehensive systems; the logic is perfectly clear, the aims decipherable, and yet it is often the case that no one is there to have invented them, and few who can be said to have formulated them. (1980a 95)

Hence the claim that the individual is "the element of power's articulation," not the intentional agent who puts power into play. A fully three-dimensional

---

[24]I am assuming that the middle Foucault's discussions of power are by now too familiar to require rehearsing here. Apart from reading *Discipline and Punish* and *Power/Knowledge*, the reader who wants a guide to this material would be well advised to read the excellent commentaries found in Hoy (1986a), Dews (1987), Taylor (1986), and Dreyfus and Rabinow (1983).

model of power (to recall Steven Lukes's work) appears at work here. The "comprehensive systems" that power forms overwhelm individual aims or objectives. The very possibility of critique and of resistance is hard to justify theoretically, and even if their existence is asserted, the capability to counter effectively the dictates of power appears limited, to say the least.

When Foucault insists that "a society without power relations can only be an abstraction" (1983 222–23) or that "there are relations of power throughout every social field" (1987 123), he, like Nietzsche before him, is making a transcendental claim of a precisely Kantian sort despite his claim that he, "in studying these power relations . . . in no way construct[s] a theory of Power" (1988 38), and his hope that genealogy will reveal contingencies, not necessities. Is the inevitable fact of power relations meant to be seen as one of those limits a "permanent critique" invites us to transgress? Little in Foucault indicates such a utopian hope. Instead, Foucault inclines toward the tragic view that power—although its particular shapes and practices vary—is, in itself, ineluctable. This view is tragic because the middle Foucault strongly implies rhetorically, even if never stating explicitly, that power is inimical to freedom and that freedom is what we desire, even if we cannot get it.[25] The late Foucault sometimes tries to escape a tragic view by claiming that some types of power are "not evil."

The notion of power as productive requires more of our attention because it indicates a path that the late Foucault follows to some extent, but not fully and not to the exclusion of other paths that I believe are contradictory to it. Productive power stems from Foucault's insistence that the dualistic vision that pits an inhibiting power against an autonomous, oppressed subject misunderstands the relation of power to its subjects. "It seems to me now that the notion of repression is quite inadequate for capturing what is precisely the productive aspect of power. . . . What power holds good, what makes it accepted, is simply the fact that it doesn't only weigh on us as a force that says no, but that it traverses and produces things, it induces pleasure, forms

---

[25]Fraser (1981 and 1983), Taylor (1986), and Habermas (1987a 238–93) have all called attention to Foucault's implicit normative judgments against power in the name of a freedom that is never named. I think their argument about the middle Foucault's "cryptonormativism" is convincing; it is interesting to see what a more sympathetic commentator on Foucault's work does with this objection. John Rajchman writes: "The question of freedom is one Foucault constantly, if tacitly, poses. It does not figure prominently either in his own presentations of his work or in the secondary literature about it. Yet I wish to argue that it is found in what he *does*, motivated by his search for a new role for philosophy in the 'ethic of the intellectual.' . . . Our real freedom is found in dissolving or changing the polities that embody our nature, and as such it is asocial and anarchial. No society or polity *could* be based on it, since it lies precisely in the possibility of constant change. Our real freedom is thus political, though it is never finalizable, legislatable, or rooted in our nature. Foucault's philosophy is the critical appeal to this real freedom" (1985 121, 123).

knowledge, produces discourse" (1980b 119). In this holistic model, "there is no outside" (1979 301). There is no disinterested or objective knowledge, just as there is no autonomous self. "Perhaps we should abandon a whole tradition that allows us to imagine that knowledge can exist only where power relations are suspended and that knowledge can develop only outside its injunctions, its demands and its interests. . . . We should admit rather that power produces knowledge . . . , that power and knowledge directly imply one another; that there is no power relation without the correlative constitution of a field of knowledge, nor any knowledge that does not presuppose and constitute at the same time power relations" (1979 27). The denial of independent knowledge is linked, in the middle Foucault, to the denial of independent individuality. Power/knowledge has constituted the form of subjectivity—with our belief in interiority, an unconscious, and a psychological identity that needs to be discovered by a probing interpretation—that characterizes modern man from around 1780. The human sciences (psychology, anthropology, history, sociology, linguistics, and the rest) develop both this concept of subjectivity and the methods to explain and explore it, thus creating a terrain in which power intervenes from the outset. The terrible logic of this collusion between disciplinary power and the academic discourses that most intellectuals utilize is one of the most compelling things about *Discipline and Punish*. Far from being autonomous entities, knowledge, power, and the subject are shown to be intimately related to one another within a single productive process; that Foucault usually calls this the productive process of power indicates that power is the primary force among the three.

As portrayed in *Discipline and Punish*, this symbiotic relationship between power and knowledge makes the disciplinary power of the modern era appear invincible. The deep self of modernity is created only along with the techniques for its surveillance and control. In the first volume of *The History of Sexuality* and in various subsequent interviews, however, Foucault develops a description (a theory?) of freedom that mitigates the apparently monolithic sway of power in the prisons book. Given the holistic premises of productive power, the description of freedom Foucault offers is recognizably a variant of positive freedom, although he never uses that term. "Where there is power, there is resistance and yet, or rather consequently, the resistance is never in a position of exteriority in relation to power" (1980a 95). "By definition, they [resistances] can only exist in the strategic field of power relations" (1980a 96). In the chapter "Method" in the first volume on sexuality, Foucault tries to insist that resistance is not doomed to futility just because it is inside power. Much like Derrida, he wants to open up a disruptive internal strategy as opposed to reliance on some external, autonomous other. "Power is co-extensive with the social body; there are no spaces of primal liberty between the meshes of its network. . . . There are no relations of power without resistances; the latter are all the more real and effective because they are formed right at the point where relations of power are exercised; resistance to power does not have to come from elsewhere to be real, nor it is inexorably frustrated through being the compatriot of power. It exists all the more by being in the same place as power; hence, like power, resistance is multiple and can be integrated in global strategies" (1980b 142). "Aside from torture and execution, which preclude any resistance, no matter how terrifying a certain system may be, there always remain possibilities of resistance, disobedience, and oppositional groupings" (1989 264). But it is crucial to see that these possibilities are generated by the constitution of the whole field; resistance and the "practice" of liberty are found within a social terrain that is always traversed by power relations. The places resistance is likely to occur and the strategies it will adopt are fully "situated" in this version of liberty in Foucault's work.

Before moving to a consideration of those texts in which Foucault advocates a more negative freedom, one that contrasts with the holistic notion of a power that produces resistances along with control, I want to articulate three reservations about Foucault's version of situated freedom. First, Foucault's emphasis on liberty as a practice makes it peculiarly contentless. Foucault often appears to believe that once he has assured us that resistance is possible—that subjects can act oppositionally, can adopt various strategies and practices that counter the positions into which power tries to maneuver them—he has successfully introduced freedom into the disciplinary society (or into any social field produced by power). But this notion of freedom is rather empty, since it does not suggest a capacity for purposive action, that is, for the achievement of particular purposes. There is usually something more at stake in social conflicts than simply the possibility to act, and we measure power (in part) by the capacity to gain one's objectives. Surely, freedom is not only the ability to strive but also the ability to achieve. If one is constantly thwarted, one can hardly be said to be free. The trouble with a model of continual conflict (which Foucault inherits from Nietzsche) is that it refuses any value to resting points or to activities and goals that are not directed toward gaining ascendancy in the conflict. Foucault understands the criticism that his view of power is monolithic to mean that it renders certain subjects docile, unable to play in the games of power, and he thinks he has restored freedom when he claims that all can play, that some possibilities are always open. But that answer does not address the complaint that some players are positionally disadvantaged in certain social orders—and that disadvantage is measured by losing what one wants to hold on to and by failing to gain what one wants to attain. For all his talk of power and resistance, Foucault continually shies away from the issue of evaluating the relative opportunities for successful purposive action that different social orders afford their subjects.

The focus on freedom as an activity apart from any goals is merely the flip side of the notion that power primarily takes the attainment of power as its end. Foucault's blind spot here stems, I think, partly from the same Nietzschean impulse to valorize nonteleological activity that leads Derrida to a similar celebration of a contentless play, and partly from the sticky problem of accounting for, within a notion of productive power, the intentions and desires exhibited by individuals within power relations. If the subject is constituted by power, what could explain the diversity of goals? Sometimes, in Nietzschean fashion, Foucault appears to suggest that the only goal individuals have is to have power, "to determine the conduct of others" (1987 131), and that diversity is merely explained by the different strategies employed toward that end by subjects in different positions. (Of course, to talk of subjects' motives even in this fashion requires backing away from the earlier position that power has aims and intentions, but the subjects who exercise power cannot be identified with those intentions. The late Foucault is much more willing to locate individual action and motives within power relations. "That brings us back to the problem of what I mean by power. I hardly ever use the word 'power' and if I do sometimes, it is always a short cut to the expression I always use: the relationships of power. . . . I mean that in human relations, whatever they are . . . power is always present: I mean the relationship in which one wishes to direct the behavior of another" [1987 122].) But Foucault is never fully comfortable with this reduction of human striving to the will to power. His work is clearly motivated by a desire to mitigate power, and he speaks of the goal of "avoid[ing]" the reproduction of "the effects of domination" (1987 129) in one's activities as a teacher in one interview, while, in a discussion of homosexuality in 1981, he speaks of gay men trying "to invent . . . friendship; that is to say, the sum of everything through which they can give each other pleasure" (1989 205). He claims that "these relations [of friendship] short-circuit it [the institutional form of male relations] and introduce love where there's supposed to be only law, rule, or habit." But these indications of a goal other than the active participation in the play of power need to be teased out of Foucault's texts, because he has difficulty accounting for these goals' existence, because he has no very good way of talking about power as the capacity to achieve goals, and because he is continually nervous that any positively stated goal will become, like the well-intentioned, universalizing tenets of

Kantian humanism, established as a standard that legitimates exclusion, hierarchy, and domination. He apparently hopes that associating freedom with a contentless and goalless activity will protect him from reinstating the forms of domination that his work is designed to combat.

One result of this reticence is a complete inability on Foucault's part (putting the unique instance of his discussion of gay friendships to one side) to talk about any social bonds other than power. The refusal to countenance any positively described tie between individuals (such as love, responsibility, a common purpose) lends some credence to the charge made by Frank Lentricchia that Foucault's failure to imagine collective actions or a positive collectivity "points directly to what may be his most cherished (if generally unannounced) principle—that of the sanctity of the individual in his or her isolate freedom" (1988 75). Foucault's anarchistic fear of all collective forms and his concomitant fear that any moral norm must prove oppressive lead him to adopt a position not very distinct from deontological liberalism in its refusal to bind individual actions and choices to anything outside the self. In other words, even in Foucault's version of a situated freedom, he refuses to grant legitimacy to, even as he acknowledges the fact of, the power that constitutes selves. All power in Foucault is equal, just as all resistance is approved. The self is justified in any and all efforts to reverse, resist, and otherwise disrupt the power relations in which it is embedded, and those very activities of disruption are portrayed as its experience of freedom.

My second reservation about Foucault's version of situated freedom is that he still bifurcates power and resistance, with freedom exercised in resistance, not in power. In other words, he maintains an (ethical? or theoretical?) dualism within his holistic model insofar as he associates freedom with what resists institutions. Thus, in the discussion of gay friendship, Foucault can valorize this social tie only by insisting that "it can yield intense relations not resembling those that are institutionalized" (1989 207), while stressing that this friendship takes place "outside of institutional relations" (1989 204). This distinction between the institutional and the extrainstitutional appears ethical because it suggests that intentional actions *within* institutions do not deserve the name of freedom because they perpetuate a given order. But there seems no reason, theoretically speaking, to believe that freedom could not be practiced in preserving an institution or tradition as well as in resisting it.[26] As

---

[26]In an interview found in *The Foucault Reader* (conducted by Paul Rabinow, Charles Taylor, Martin Jay, Richard Rorty, and Leo Lowenthal), Foucault is asked whether he "recognizes" two "possible sides of power," namely the "relations among people that allow them to accomplish things they would not have been able to do otherwise" as well as the "relations of domination of certain people over others" (1984 378). Foucault's answer is confusing; it is not very clear that he

his linking of "permanent critique" with "transgression" indicates, Foucault habitually associates that of which he approves—critique, freedom, resistance—with transgression, while retaining, despite all his protests to the contrary, a distinctly negative charge in his term *power*. The result is a bifurcation between power and resistance, deplored conservative action and approbated transgressive action, that leads toward a notion of negative freedom.

My third reservation is that, once he declares "there are relations of power throughout every social field" (1987 123), Foucault is almost inevitably led (as Derrida is in his meditations about "irreducible violence" [1988a 150]) to distinguish between bad and not-so-bad power. One form this distinction takes is a differentiation between "domination" and "power" in some of Foucault's texts, where "domination" refers to the situation in which "an individual or a social group manages to block a field of relations of power, to render them impassive and invariable and to prevent all reversibility of movement" (1987 114), while "power" merely indicates the fluid, reversible set of relationships in which all humans always find themselves. "In human relations, whatever they are . . . power is always present: I mean the relationship in which one wishes to direct the behavior of another. . . . These relationships of power are changeable relations, i.e., they can modify themselves, they are not given once and for all" (1987 122–23). Foucault states that, in contradistinction to "domination," "power is not an evil. Power is strategic games. . . . To exercise power over another, in a sort of open strategic game, where things could be reversed, that is not evil" (1987 129). The possibility of reversal, not the object sought or achieved, differentiates not-evil power from domination. In certain places, Foucault appears about to extend this formula of differentiation into a fairly traditional notion that legitimates certain "systems of constraint" in terms of their accountability to the individuals within it. "Well, the important question here, it seems to me, is not whether a culture without restraints is possible or even desirable but whether the system of constraints in which a society functions leaves individuals the liberty to transform the system. . . . A system of constraint becomes truly intolerable when the individuals who are affected by it don't have the means of modifying it" (1988 294). But this idea is never developed in Foucault's work, while we should note the characteristic stress on modifica-

---

is answering the question asked. Significantly enough, however, he again resorts to the example of the "pedagogical relation" when asked to consider a more positive notion of power as capacity, and he seems to agree that power does have two sides. I think it fair to say that he rarely, if ever, considers this positive type of power in his work; he remains too obsessed with the notion of "resistance." (See 1984 378–79.)

tion of the system rather than on the grounds for accepting any particular set of restraints, even though Foucault insists that some such system will always be in place.

In the interview in which Foucault states that "power is not an evil" he offers two examples of not-evil power relations. The first is the "open strategic game" that is "part of love, passion, of sexual pleasure" (1987 129). The second is the relation of teacher to student. "I don't see where the evil is in the practice of someone who, in a given game of truth, knowing more than another, tells him what he must do, teaches him, transmits knowledge to him. . . . The problem is rather to know how you are to avoid in these practices—where power cannot not play and where it is not evil in itself—the effects of domination which will make a child subject to the arbitrary and useless authority of a teacher, or put a student under the power of an abusively authoritarian professor, and so forth." Quite a problem, indeed, since Foucault, like most postmodern writers, lacks any criteria for distinguishing "arbitrary and useless authority" from the "not-evil" variety and since his basic legitimating principle of "reversibility" (which distinguishes domination from power) does not address what gets achieved in the teacher-student relationship, even though that achievement is clearly what makes the authority in this case "not evil." Even though he has far less good to say about law than does Derrida, we find Foucault at this point, where he feels (for once) the need to legitimate a form of authority, falling back on institutional guidelines. I pick up the passage where the last sentence quoted left it. "I think these problems should be posed in terms of rules of law, or relational techniques of government and of *ethos*, of practice of self and of freedom" (1987 129–30). Foucault here indicates his need for a norm to differentiate evil from not-evil power and his need for social institutions to embody, protect, and enforce that norm, but his work never sufficiently addresses this need.

Given these anarchistic tendencies even within his version of positive freedom, it is not surprising to find Foucault drawn to the more dualistic model provided by negative freedom. In his late works, Foucault continually insists that power was never his primary interest. "It is not power, but the subject, which is the general theme of my research" (1983 209). In addition, he tells us that power relations only constitute one "axis" along which the nature of the social field within which individuals act should be examined. The "practical systems" within any society "stem from three broad areas: relations of control over things, relations of action upon others, relations with oneself. This does not mean that each of the three areas is completely foreign to the others. . . . But we have three axes whose specificity and whose interconnections have to be analyzed: the axis of knowledge, the axis of power, the axis of ethics" (1984 48). We are to understand the "middle" works, Foucault tells us, as explorations of the axis of power that never meant to deny the existence or validity of the other axes or to suggest their subordination to power as the final determinant. The argument that power in the middle Foucault was an equal partner in a triumvirate composed of power, knowledge, and ethics belies what Foucault actually said in those works. Of more interest to me than this attempt to alter retrospectively the import of *Discipline and Punish* is Foucault's need to propose what I take to be a (vague) version of "semiautonomy" (although he never uses that Althusserian term) in order to begin the task of combatting the monolithic vision of power he presented earlier. How he imagined the "interconnections" between the "axes" that are not "completely foreign" to one another is something he unfortunately never got around to specifying. But we can recognize that just as Althusser uses "semiautonomy" to mitigate the reductionism of economic determinism, Foucault introduces the three axes to deny the reduction of everything to power relations. Less concerned than Althusser with maintaining a holistic perspective, the late Foucault uses his new subdivision of the whole to emphasize distance and autonomy, thus reaping the benefit of heterogeneity. But Foucault is unable simply to abandon his earlier, more holistic views, and thus he continually makes gestures toward the interconnection of the three axes, even though he ignores the problem of defining those interconnections in favor of using the separation to gain the desired pluralism.

In discussing the two new axes and their separation from power I shall begin with the axis of knowledge. "We can show, for example, that the medicalization of madness, i.e. the organization of medical knowledge around individuals labeled as 'mad' has been linked, at some time or other, to a whole series of social or economic processes, but also to institutions and practices of power. This fact in no way impairs the scientific validity of the therapeutic effect of psychiatry. It does not guarantee it but it does not cancel it out either" (1987 127). Foucault does not specify how we might determine "scientific validity" or sort out what elements in a scientific discourse are primarily effects of power and what elements concern what he calls elsewhere "the search for truth" (1984 381). He does point to the notion that truth is a "game," by which he means "an ensemble of rules for the production of the truth. . . . It is an ensemble of procedures which lead to a certain result, which can be considered in function of its principles and its rules of procedure, as valid or not" (1987 127). To describe truth as a "game" obviously shifts the tone from the earlier talk of a "regime of truth" (1980b 132). In an interview conducted shortly before his death, Foucault suggests, in distinguishing between the polemicist and the serious searcher for truth, that a line can be drawn between the writer who tries "to come as close as possible to a difficult truth" (1984 382) and the polemicist who seeks only "to bring about the triumph of a just cause he has been manifestly upholding from the beginning" (1984 383). The ability to maintain this distinction comes to rest on what can be considered an ethics of discussion, one that suggests certain procedural guidelines that keep the dialogue moving toward the difficult truth, avoiding a swerve toward prejudice, interest, or the causes one might hold dear.

> In the serious play of questions and answers, in the work of reciprocal elucida-
> tion, the rights of each person are in some sense *immanent* in the the discussion.
> They depend only on the dialogue situation. The person asking the questions is
> merely exercising the right that has been given to him: to remain unconvinced,
> to perceive different postulates, to point out faulty reasoning, etc. As for the
> person answering the questions, he too exercises a right that does not go beyond
> the discussion itself; by the logic of his own discourse he is tied to what he has
> said earlier, and by the acceptance of dialogue he is tied to the questioning of the
> other. Questions and answers depend on a game—a game that is at once
> pleasant and difficult—in which each of the two partners take pains to use *only*
> the rights *given to him by the other* and by the *accepted form* of dialogue. (1984
> 381–82; my emphasis)

This passage is remarkable for several reasons. For one thing, it offers a much more positive image of intersubjective processes than we find anywhere else in Foucault.[27] Here the relation between two people enables a process of discovery in ways that make talk of power almost irrelevant. Which, of course, is much of the point. The game of truth (the axis of knowledge) is here circumscribed, separated from power relations on the basis of its own "imma-nent" procedures and agreements, and on the basis of the acceptance by both participants of the rules of the game. Similarly, the passage suggests how rules and procedures can be creative rather than stifling, offering a more positive image of what it might mean for a social context to be "productive." With the stress on procedures and the intersubjective agreement that guarantees ad-herence to them, Foucault's description of dialogue here is strikingly similar to Habermas's description of the ideal speech situation.

Furthermore, like Habermas, once Foucault has somewhat isolated the

---

[27]Dews (1987 192–99) offers a particularly cogent account of Foucault's persistent neglect of "the reciprocity specific to the social domain" (198), insisting that Foucault's account of the constitution of subjects by power "fails to register the fact that socialization, the formation of subjects, depends upon a mutual recognition of subjects, however distorted." Instead of seeing two subjects confronting one another, the middle Foucault poses an impersonal power vis-à-vis the subject. The late Foucault is somewhat more open to considering relations between subjects, but the emphasis on the relation of self to its own self in "the care of the self" once again diminishes the place for intersubjectivity in Foucault's thought.

game of truth from power, he is drawn to finding in that game the possibility of freedom. The compulsion to adhere to the rules of the dialogue, of the search for difficult truths, can subvert the status quo. Foucault suggests that the autonomy (or semiautonomy) that the game of truth has enjoyed in the West marks a difference between the West and other societies that is measured by an openness to change. "There is always a possibility, in a given game of truth, to discover something else and to more or less change such and such a rule and sometimes even the totality of the game of truth. No doubt that is what has given the West, in relationship to other societies, possibilities of development that we find nowhere else. Who says the truth? Individuals who are free, who arrive at a certain agreement and who find themselves thrust into a certain network of practices of power and constraining institutions" (1987 128). The "agreement" individuals reach here is unclear. Is it an agreement that shapes the rules of the game of truth or an agreement that comes from following those rules? In either case, that agreement is reached in freedom, and the relative autonomy of the game of truth in the West to follow to the end the questions one takes up in searching for knowledge makes possible changes that might be unattainable in societies where the game of truth enjoys less autonomy.

Foucault more globally associates "thought" with "freedom" in the interview where he distinguishes between the polemicist and the searcher for truth.

> It seemed to me there was one element that was capable of describing the history of thought: this was what one can call the element of problems or, more exactly, problematizations. What distinguishes thought is that it is something quite different from the set of representations that underlie a certain behavior; it is also something quite different from the domain of attitudes that can determine this behavior. Thought is not what inhabits a certain conduct and gives it its meaning; rather, it is what allows one to *step back from* this way of acting or reacting, to present it to oneself as an object of thought and question it as to its meaning, its conditions, and its goals. *Thought is freedom in relation to what one does*, the motion by which one detaches oneself from it, establishes it as an object, and reflects on it as a problem." (1984 388; my emphasis)

The model of thought here is recognizably Kantian, with the disengagement characteristic of reflection making a transcendent investigation of experience—"its meaning, its conditions, and its goals"—possible. The differences from Kant lie in Foucault's emphasis on "problematization," as opposed to Kant's preference for definitive solutions, and in Foucault's identification of thought as freedom in contrast to Kant's use of thought to identify that area outside of knowledge where freedom lies. By stressing "problematization,"

Foucault once again demonstrates his fear that any determinate results of intellectual work would form a possible basis for new varieties of domination; it follows that the activity of thought, not anything that it might accomplish, is freedom. "The ethos of permanent critique" is not out to achieve anything but its own permanence. Permanent critique in this way bears some resemblance to permanent revolution; the project is geared against all those forces in the social body (the forces of "normalization") that harden representations and meanings, that resist and try to control a thought that problematizes. Hence the "philosophical ethos" of permanent critique does not pursue "the Kantian question . . . of knowing what limits knowledge has to renounce transgressing," but "takes the form of a possible transgression" (1984 45). Thought is posed dualistically against everything that would deny its freedom, its questioning, its transgressions.

Foucault comes close to presenting this agon, this antagonism, between thought and that which would limit it as an eternal struggle. Foucault links the ethos of permanent critique to modernity, but "wonder[s] whether we may not envisage modernity rather as an attitude than as a period of history" (1984 39). And consequently, Foucault writes, "rather than seeking to distinguish the 'modern era' from the 'premodern' or 'postmodern,' I think it would be more useful to find out how this attitude of modernity, ever since its formation, has found itself struggling with attitudes of 'countermodernity'" (1984 39). Presumably, "countermodernity" embraces all the forces of normalization and conservation in a society as posed against the transgressive forces embodied in critique. By associating freedom solely with critique and transgression, Foucault adopts an anarchism whose experience of transgression as liberty is based on the certainty that there will always be social forms to transgress. Such an anarchism problematizes, but it never transforms, since it has located freedom in the negative and thus cannot risk any positive achievement. And this anarchism seems to me to abandon the most interesting and potentially fruitful aspect of Foucault's meditation on power: his holistic account of productive power. Foucault replaces the notion that the capacities of thought are products of power *and* that thought's own categorizations and conclusions will become productive as they connect with power relations within the social body with an account that detaches thought from these social processes. As distinct from his earlier work, he now believes thought can operate apart "from the set of representations that underlie a certain behavior" (1984 388), not producing such representations itself, but merely reflecting upon them and problematizing them. All the positive, productive elements of Foucault's model of society are now ascribed to "countermodernity," while the intellectual who adopts the "attitude of modernity" achieves the purity of an indeterminate negativity that is associated with freedom. And thus Foucault is led, in describing "the attitude of modernity," to recognize the logic of modernist aestheticism. The characteristic elements of modernity, as epitomized by Baudelaire, cannot "have any place in society itself, or in the body politic. They can only be produced in another, a different place, which Baudelaire calls art" (1984 42). Frightened by the potential for domination that inhabits any social order (a potential that, in his productive view of power, is only the flip side of the potential for freedom), Foucault turns away from his earlier willingness to accept that political action involves changing one "institutional regime of truth" (1980 133) for another. Instead of risking that a new institutional regime will lessen the chances for domination and will allow the positive accomplishment of democratically formed purposes, Foucault now leaves this positive work and proposes "to take oneself as object of a complex and difficult elaboration: what Baudelaire, in the vocabulary of his day, calls *dandysme*" (1984 41), where this work of "invent[ing] himself" (1984 42) takes place apart from the "body politic" and in "the practice of a liberty that simultaneously respects . . . reality and violates it" (1984 41). (By "respect" here, Foucault means "grasping" reality "in what it is" [1984 41].)

This goal of self-invention brings us directly to the axis of ethics, which places the self at center stage and involves Foucault's rethinking of his earlier position on the constitution of the subject as one of productive power's "effects." The late texts are obscure here; not the least of our worries should be how fully we are to take the activities of the classical Greeks and Romans as some kind of proposed model. Asked in one interview if he finds the Greeks "admirable," Foucault replies "No," and adds that "all of antiquity appears to me to have been a 'profound error'" (1989 319). The context shows that Foucault is to some extent joking, but there still remains the issue of what in ancient history is of use in the very different circumstances of late twentieth-century postmodernity. The late Foucault is clearly striving to develop an ethics out of the notion of "the care of the self"—a notion he finds in antiquity and describes as "an exercise of self upon self by which one tries to work out, to transform one's self and to attain a certain mode of being" (1987 113). The axis of ethics, Foucault tells us, raises the question of "how we are constituted as moral subjects of our own actions" (1984 49), where morality is understood as "the practice of liberty, the deliberate practice of liberty" (1987 115). (From his earlier reticence about freedom, it is obvious that the late Foucault may have begun to err too far in the other direction. He tends to stress the importance of whatever activity he is describing—be it reflection, the search for truth, care of the self, the attitude of modernity, or ethics—by associating it with freedom.) For the Greeks (in Foucault's account), ethics involved the "labor of self on self" and is connected to liberty in a "measure where being free means not being a slave to one's self and to one's appetites, which supposes that one establishes over one's self a certain relation of domination, of mastery, which was called *arche*—power, authority" (1987 117). Thus Foucault substitutes a power one develops over one's self for the power that social forms have over the self. In other words, the ancient Greeks disciplined themselves, whereas nineteenth-century selves were disciplined by the institutional forms of micropower. (We should note that only certain elites in Greek society practice this ethos of self-mastery, according to Foucault, and the achievement of self-mastery "renders one competent to occupy a place in the city, in the community or in interindividual relationships" (1987 118), including the place of mastery over others—such as wives and slaves— who do not practice the ethos of self-mastery. But once the situation is described this way, the difference from a nineteenth-century society in which the bourgeoisie practiced the disciplines of delayed gratification, hard work, and strong control over various appetites while employing a disciplinary power over the unruly lower orders becomes harder to locate.)

The focus on ethics, then, considers "how the subject constituted himself" (1987 121), where the shift to the active voice from the passive description of a subject constituted by power indicates a dramatic change in Foucault's emphasis. When questioned about this shift, Foucault implausibly replies: "If it is true, for example, that the constitution of a mad subject can in fact be considered the result of a system of coercion—that is the passive subject— you know full well that the mad subject is not a non-free subject and that the mentally ill constitutes himself a mad subject in relationship and in the presence of the one who declares him crazy" (1987 122). Such a statement might very well reflect the inevitable intersubjective matrix within which any identity is shaped, but the word *freedom* loses all meaning (as the active employment of purposive strategies toward gaining a particular end) if we claim that every subject in that intersubjective situation is "not non-free." The problem is how to think through the issue of freedom in relation to "a system of coercion."

More plausibly, Foucault suggests that we must consider the options, possibilities, and capacities afforded the individual by a given social order. The constitution of subjects need not mean that they are all monolithically stamped out according to the same pattern; rather, it can mean that their identities are constructed within a social field that limits the range of possible practices. "I would say that if now I am interested, in fact, in the way in which the subject constitutes himself in an active fashion, by the practices of the self, these practices are nevertheless not something that the individual invents by himself. They are patterns that he finds in his culture and which are proposed, suggested and imposed on him by his culture, his society and his social group" (1987 122). This middle ground, which avoids both absolute passivity and absolute activity in understanding how selves are formed, strikes me as being on the right track, and I try to develop my own version of this model in my final chapter. I believe that such a model is dependent upon the notion of semiautonomy that also appears to be indicated by Foucault's description of the three axes. Furthermore, in my view, the problem of freedom can most fruitfully be pursued in terms of a positive freedom that takes as axiomatic that identities are shaped within and through intersubjective processes.

As with the axis of knowledge, Foucault often pushes the axis of ethics toward full autonomy, instead of keeping in view its "interconnection" (1984 48) with power relations and games of truth. Thus the "attitude of modernity"—Foucault tells us that an "attitude" is "a bit, no doubt, like what the Greeks call an *ethos*" (1984 39)—is linked to "the constitution of ourselves as autonomous subjects" (1984 43). To the determinate forms of selfhood that humanism in various places and at various times has imposed Foucault contrasts "the principle of a critique and a permanent creation of ourselves in our autonomy" (1984 44). There is no need to belabor the point. I think that Foucault's association of transgression with freedom must lead him to pose some independent entity against the social and institutional forms that are to be transgressed, and thus it is hardly surprising that he is led to images of disengagement and of an autonomous self as he moves from the holistic model of productive power to the dualistic model of transgressive action against the powers that be. This revised view of power relations posits a recalcitrant will that stands in relation to power but does not appear as a product of it. "The relationship between power and freedom's refusal to submit cannot therefore be separated. . . . At the very heart of the power relationship, and constantly provoking it, are the recalcitrance of the will and the intransigence of freedom. Rather than speaking of an essential freedom, it would be better to speak of an 'agonism'—of a relationship which is at the same time reciprocal incitation and struggle; less of a face-to-face confrontation which paralyzes both sides than a permanent provocation" (1983 221–22).

In contrast to this agonistic, dualistic view stands what Foucault in "What Is Enlightenment?" calls the "paradox of capacity and power" (1984 47). This paradox calls attention to "the simultaneous and proportional growth of individuals with respect to one another" in the West since the Enlightenment, a growth that both increases the (or introduces new) capabilities of the self *and* opens up the spaces that "disciplines" and "procedures of normalization"

(1984 48) colonize. Just as the proletariat in Marx's work is both exploited by and placed in a position to transform capitalism, so the modern individual in Foucault is both subject to disciplinary power and the possessor of new capacities for the resistance against that power. Both individual subjection and freedom are products of the self's situation in a new set of circumstances; situated or positive freedom calls on us to think this "paradox." But the late Foucault no longer appears prepared to follow out the difficult theoretics of power suggested by the first volume of *The History of Sexuality*, where "discourses are not once and for all subservient to power or raised up against it, any more than silences are. We must make allowance for the complex and unstable process whereby discourse can be both an instrument and an effect of power, but also a hindrance, a stumbling-block, a point of resistance and a starting point for an opposing strategy" (1980a 100–101). Against this emphasis on strategic moves internal to the play of power, the Foucault of "What Is Enlightenment?" responds to the paradox of the relations of capacity and power by stating: "What is at stake, then, is this: How can the growth of capabilities be *disconnected* from the intensification of power relations?" (1984 48; my emphasis).

This tension between negative and positive versions of freedom, between a model of disengagement and a model of exploring the strategies and capabilities productive power makes available, also surfaces in Foucault's ambivalent attitude toward theoretical thought. An intellectual practice that opts for genealogy as opposed to a transcendental critique of the Kantian sort emphasizes contingency, "the undefined work of freedom," experimentation, and local, "specific transformations" (1984 46). Foucault believes we "must turn away from all projects that claim to be global and radical" (1984 46)—an interesting conjunction of terms. But Foucault is not ready to embrace some version of methodological anarchism or to abandon all claims that his work provides knowledge of a general sort. He insists that his difference from traditional theory "does not mean that no work can be done except in disorder and contingency. The work in question has its generality, its systematicity, its homogeneity, and its stakes" (1984 47).

Antitheory, in Foucault's case at least, is not to be given over entirely to contingency. And as we might expect from Foucault's earlier, more monolithic work, the generality, systematicity, and homogeneity to which he refers here point toward a retained belief that certain systems of practices cohere in particular social orders and/or in particular epochs, so that certain kinds of generalizations are permissible, even if we must now emphasize not the necessity of these generalities but their problematization by the inquiries to which Foucault urges us. As for genealogy's "stakes," the term appears to introduce a purpose, a telos, into the process, which is meant to combat the "risk" that a random, local critique might let itself "be determined by more general structures of which we may well not be conscious, and over which we have no control" (1984 47). A general knowledge and an awareness of the purposes that motivate one's strategies are necessary because the forces to be confronted are still—despite all Foucault's talk of micropower—seen as possessing a daunting generality.[28] Just as Derrida, in "The Ends of Man," must caution against naive attempts to disrupt Western metaphysics that merely reinstate its hold upon us, so Foucault must acknowledge that the resources of a local criticism might prove inadequate to the task he proposes for it.

Foucault's attempt to balance the claims of the local and the general in his work mirrors the balance he seeks to strike between the individual and society in his description of the "antiauthority struggles" (1983 211) and the "anarchistic struggles" that he sees as characteristic of contemporary politics; the so-called new social movements (i.e., feminism, various civil rights groups, and other mass movements that gather around particular issues that are usually neither economic nor best understood as matters of class interest) are described by Foucault as

> struggles which question the status of the individual: on the one hand, they assert the right to be different and they underline everything which makes individuals truly individual. On the other hand, they attack everything which separates the individual, breaks his links with others, splits up community life, forces the individual back in himself and ties him to his own identity in a constraining way. These struggles are not exactly for or against the "individual," but rather they are struggles against the "government of individuation." . . . All these present struggles revolve around the question: Who are we? They are a refusal of these abstractions, of economic and ideological state violence which ignore who we are individually, and also a refusal of a scientific and administrative inquisition which determines who one is. (1983 211–12)

The crux here is whether legitimate individualism is formed by oneself in a care for the self, a process of self-mastery such as Foucault finds in the Greeks, or is shaped in communities that somehow escape being "abstract" or being "administrative inquisitions." Foucault is right, I think, in noting that the new social movements are torn between models of individual autonomy and images of more satisfying communities. His own work appears torn in similar ways, but finally (especially in the late work) is weighted toward the

[28]See Foucault (1984 47–49) for a full discussion of the generality and systematicity he believes a genealogical investigation will uncover.

side of autonomy, of self-mastery and self-constitution as a disengagement from power that offers the best chance for freedom. The fear of the oppressive potential of communal life overwhelms any urge in Foucault to imagine positive images of community.

In keeping with this emphasis on the individual, Foucault's image of what the intellectual accomplishes also turns inward. "For me intellectual work is related to what you would call aestheticism, meaning transforming yourself. . . . But if I refer to my own personal experience I have the feeling knowledge can't do anything for us and that political power may destroy us. All the knowledge in the world can't do anything against that. . . . My problem is my own transformation" (1988 14). Expressed this way, care of the self looks like the political quietism of the post-sixties' turn to jogging, transcendental meditation, and other forms of self-cultivation. From this perspective, Cornelius Castoriadis reads Foucault's message as "the death of politics" (1987 23) and claims that the success of Foucault's work (and of poststructuralism generally) is "fundamentally due to the *failure* of May '68," since postmodern theory justifies the "limits of the May movement" (1987 25), particularly its failure to seize power and to think through an alternative political order. A more sympathetic reading of Foucault's individualism will pay heed to his notion that "the undefined work of freedom" is carried forward by those, intellectuals or not, who are willing to "experiment," to perform a "work done at the limits of ourselves" designed "to grasp the points where change is possible and desirable, and to determine the precise form this change should take" (1984 46). There is more than a little of the myth of the avant-garde here, especially when we remember that this work is linked to transgression. After providing us, in his early and middle works, with some of the most compelling postmodern portraits of the intellectual's inevitable participation in the power relations that structure and traverse a social order, the late Foucault can appear to be opting for the strategy of personal transformation in isolation that was chosen by so many modernist radicals. But I sympathize with Foucault's notion that our future as a society needs to be *realized* in actual lives rather than merely thought, and we should recognize how fully the notion of individual experimentation in Foucault stems from the sense that all our received notions about *the* revolution and a desirable social order need to questioned severely in light of the disastrous results of so many modern utopias. Given our present uncertainty and the murders that certainty has sponsored in this century, Foucault's portrait of the ideal intellectual may suggest an appropriate model for our specific time. "I dream of the intellectual who destroys evidence and generalities, the one who, in the inertias and constraints of the present time, locates and marks the weak points, the openings, the lines of force, who is incessantly on the move, doesn't know exactly where he is heading nor what he will think tomorrow for he is too attentive to the present; who, wherever he moves, contributes to posing the question of knowing whether the revolution is worth the trouble, and what kind (I mean, what revolution and what trouble), it being understood that the question can be answered only by those who are willing to risk their lives to bring it about" (1988 124). I only worry that Foucault at times elevates being "incessantly on the move" as the defining characteristic of freedom, instead of seeing it as an activity suited to this particular stalled moment in Western history. When he emphasizes the questioning and the destroying over the answers that we are seeking and the goods that we wish to see prevail, Foucault too often portrays freedom as the restless practice of an eternal negation by a self who keeps and cherishes his distance.

THE LITERARY LEFT: JAMESON, EAGLETON, SAID

The postmodern literary left can loosely be defined as those writers who reexamine the relation of art to radical politics within the problematics generated by contemporary theory. These writers have come to politics through their original engagement with literature and are heirs to the tradition (from Blake and Shelley to Breton and Brecht) that art can foster and guide the revolution. Marx is also crucially important to these writers, of course, but except for Jameson, the literary left tends to use Marx for its own purposes without much allegiance to the orthodox tenets of Marxist theory. Similarly, the left has tried to shape structuralism and poststructuralism to its own aims, using these French innovations where they aid the cause and refuting them when they appear inimical to a radical politics. The literary left has often been accused of being too academic, partly because of its interest in theory, partly because of its focus on academic audiences. Certainly, this left has fought a constant battle to control the reception of the new French theories by the literature departments in English and American universities.

Fredric Jameson's *Prison-House of Language* (1972) was the first guidebook to the new theories. Jameson's text simultaneously linked criticism to politics in ways no work had done since the 1930s, and evaluated (often negatively) writers few Americans had ever heard of (among them Derrida, Barthes, Foucault, and Lacan) in terms of their works' political consequences. Jameson's troubled relationship to French antitheory carries through the rest of his work, from his extensive use of Althusser and Lacan to rewrite Marxist theory in *The Political Unconscious* to his inclusion of poststructuralism as one of the cultural phenomena he deplores as part of postmodernism. Edward Said's *Beginnings* (1975) demonstrated how structuralist work on narrative could, when read in conjunction with Foucault's histories, offer new ways to consider the individual's relation to tradition, where tradition designates not only the artistic past but also the culture in which the author/agent finds herself. Said's work after *Beginnings* continues to probe both the synchronic and diachronic determinants of representation, how the place from which something is uttered alters its meaning and how a body of truisms (especially concerning excluded, silent others) acquires authority by virtue of its repetition over time. Meanwhile, Said has been prominently associated with the Palestinian cause, thus providing one of the most crucial models of the engaged intellectual in our time.

Frank Lentricchia's *After the New Criticism* (1980) follows the path indicated by Said's *Beginnings* in many ways, especially in its focus on history and on the cultural situation in which artists and critics find themselves. Lentricchia's strong attack on American criticism from New Criticism (Cleanth Brooks, W. K. Wimsatt, John Crowe Ransom) to myth criticism (Northrop Frye) to the Yale deconstructionists (J. Hillis Miller, Paul de Man) is based on his insistence that each of these critical paradigms stresses the artwork's immunity from historical/political processes. Like Said, Lentricchia finds a hero in Foucault, but unlike Said, Lentricchia also valorizes Derrida, insisting that it is not Derrida's work that is ahistorical, anarchistic, and in search of a hedonistic freeplay but that of his irresponsible American followers. The publication of the English translation of *Discipline and Punish* in 1979, along with the work of Jameson, Said, and Lentricchia, ushered in the "new historicism" that dominated Anglo-American literary criticism, especially any criticism with the slightest political pretensions, throughout the 1980s. In the early 1980s, Said dramatized the choice for criticism as being between Derrida and Foucault, a choice that in America was between the new historicism and the Yale school. Very often this choice (as in Lentricchia's book or in Barbara Johnson's work) was played out in reading Derrida's work itself, with one side trying to show that Derrida was concerned with indicating social/historical determinants and the other side insisting that Derrida's work ironized any easy, noncontradictory understanding of a text's relation to a constitutive context. The fact that most young critics and almost all feminists had, by the year of de Man's death (1983), opted for historicism over the Yale school explains in part the great outpouring of tributes to him on that occasion. De Man had so often been publicly whipped by the left in his last years that his friends/followers felt a particular need to honor him. And, of course, it was the memory of these disputes that made the revelations in late

1987 about de Man's Nazi past elicit such emotional responses, with his detractors feeling vindicated in their earlier denunciations of the political consequences of his work and his defenders insisting (as others have done for Pound and Heidegger) that the leap from the work to the political allegiance cannot be made so easily (especially in de Man's case where, unlike Pound's or Heidegger's, the association with fascism came years before any of the work). In any case, an explicit attempt to link criticism to a leftist politics dominated American literary theory throughout the 1980s, an open staging of political allegiances and hopes that contrasts strongly with the reticent submergence in the text's subtleties characteristic of the first deconstructive readings in America during the 1970s. And certainly the problematic of postmodernism itself is a product of these renewed political concerns. The new historicism requires a description and a label for historical context, so that postmodernism comes to designate not only an artistic period but also a phase in Western history. At the same time, postmodernism indicates the left's disparaging/despairing portrait of a contemporary reality that, in the 1980s, was dominated by Thatcherism and Reaganism and the disappointing regime of Mitterand. The heightened political awareness of the 1980s' literary intellectuals must be tied to the right's political triumphs throughout the decade.

Terry Eagleton's *Literary Theory: An Introduction* (1983) rounds out my quartet of leftist introductory texts to the new French theories. Appearing in the same year as Said's *The World, the Text, and the Critic* and Lentricchia's *Criticism and Social Change*, Eagleton's work aims to consolidate the emerging portrait of the critic as agent of social transformation and inadvertently bears testimony to how fully the left's image of the world has been influenced by Foucault's theory of power. (Of course, the new historicism, especially as practiced in the journal *Representations*, has usually adopted wholesale the middle Foucault's historical schemas and theory of power.) In a follow-up volume published the next year, *The Function of Criticism*, Eagleton attempts to delineate the social space within which the critic can operate. Both of Eagleton's books, like those of Said and Lentricchia, struggle against the more pessimistic and monolithic conclusions of much postmodern theory, since they need to preserve some freedom for the critic. Significantly enough, Said and Lentricchia have felt compelled to announce publicly a disenchantment with Foucault's work because it so drastically delimits the possibilities of any escape from disciplinary power,[29] and the literary left in general, even while adopting Foucault's views about the constitution of selves and knowledge by

[29]See Said (1983 178–247 and 1986a 149–55) and Lentricchia (1988 29–102).

power, has argued against his apparent pessimism. The logic of the monolith haunts the work of the left even as they try to deny it and to theorize a kind of critical freedom. I have neither the space nor the inclination to discuss Lentricchia fully here,[30] so will limit myself to considering how Jameson, Eagleton, and Said address the possibility of freedom as they attempt to negotiate a theory of social transformation within the multiple determinants uncovered by contemporary theory.

Jameson has been the leftist theorist most willing to hold on to the totalizing claims of a traditional Marxism that identifies an economic base or a mode of production as the unitary determinant of all social forms. Against the fashionable denigration of totalizing theories, Jameson declares: "I do want to argue that without a conception of the social totality (and the possibility of transforming a whole social system) no properly socialist politics is possible" (1988a 355). This insistence on the need for a vision of the whole is tied to an essential faith in the powers of critical reason. Postmodern reality (contemporary, global capitalism) has proved so resistant to change precisely because it "involves our insertion as individual subjects into a multidimensional set of radically discontinuous realities" (1988a 351) that prove increasingly difficult to grasp in their totality. We experience the world and ourselves as fragmentary and disconnected, "which in lived experience makes itself felt by the so-called death of the subject, or, more exactly, the fragmented and schizophrenic decentering and dispersion of this last" (1988a 351). Only a recovered ability to "cognitively map" the "local positioning of the individual subject and the totality of class structures in which he or she is situated" (1988a 353) will bring back onto the stage of history a subject capable of acting politically. "The incapacity to map socially is . . . crippling to political experience. . . . It follows that an aesthetic of cognitive mapping in this sense is an integral part of any socialist political project." For Jameson, criticism still pursues the time-honored role of providing knowledge about the ways of the world, and action predicated on that knowledge still stands the best chances for success. His work evidences little of the ironic suspicion of purposive action achieving what it aims that paralyzes theory from Nietzsche on. And Jameson also advocates a fairly straightforward Shelleyan view of art as providing images of a possible future. A full Marxist hermeneutic must not only "negatively" recognize the ideological content of a text, its function in a "war of position" to maintain hierarchy and exploitation, but also exercise a "positive . . . decipherment of the Utopian impulses of these same still

[30]*Criticism and Social Change* is a beguiling, intriguing, and (I find) ultimately frustrating book, raising many of the right questions, but somehow never quite engaging them in ways that seem helpful. For good discussions of the book and its problems, see Kucich (1985) and Kadvany (1985).

ideological" texts (1981 296). We value works of art for their utopian, "antic-
ipatory" representation of collective social forms, for their tackling "the task
of trying to imagine how a society without hierarchy, a society of free people, a
society that has at once repudiated the economic mechanisms of the market,
can possibly cohere" (1988a 355).

Jameson recognizes how far we are currently from anything like Utopia,
and his recent work on postmodernism is, to a certain extent, a work of
despair, a work that describes just how fully we are in the thrall of distopia.
Socialism in late-twentieth-century America is reduced to the most fundamental groundwork before it can even begin to bring the negative and positive
poles of its hermeneutic to bear on contemporary political reality. Right now,
"while people know that a socialist discourse exists, it is not a legitimate
discourse in this society. Thus no one takes seriously the idea that socialism,
and the social reorganization it proposes, is the answer to our problems. . . .
Our task . . . has to do with the legitimation of the discourses of socialism in
such a way that they do become realistic and serious alternatives for people"
(1988a 358–59). Pluralist critics of Jameson, however, most notably Cornel
West, have argued that his hostility to postmodern theory is a function of his
insistence that theory must provide totalizing explanations, an insistence that
ignores concrete political action in favor of chasing long-familiar philosophical conundrums.[31] Jameson himself alludes to the danger of totalized explanations at the beginning of his major essay, "Postmodernism, or The Cultural
Logic of Late Capitalism": "There is a strange quasi-Sartrean irony—a
'winner loses' logic—which tends to surround any effort to describe a 'system,' a totalizing dynamic, as these are detected in the movement of contemporary society. What happens is that the more powerful the vision of some
increasingly total system or logic—the Foucault of the prisons book is the
obvious example—the more powerless the reader comes to feel" (1984b 57).
Having indicated his awareness of the problem, Jameson goes on to defend
his notion of "a cultural dominant":

> I have felt, however, that it was only in the light of some conception of a
> dominant cultural logic or hegemonic norm that genuine difference could be

---

[31]See West (1986), whose major complaint is that "Jameson's works are too theoretical; his
welcome call for a political hermeneutics is too far removed from the heat of political battles"
(1986 140). West attributes this failure to Jameson's urge to take on the philosophical issues of
totality, idealism, the nature of the referent, and the like, whereas West claims that "what is
distinctive about the Marxist project is that it neither resurrects, attacks, nor attempts to 'go
beyond' metaphysical, epistemological, and ethical discourses. It aims rather at transforming
present practices—the remaining life—against the backdrop of previous discursive and political
practices, against the 'dead' past. Marxism admonishes us to 'let the dead bury the dead' " (1986
138).

measured or assessed. I am very far from feeling that all cultural production today is 'postmodern' in the broad sense I will be conferring on this term. The postmodern is however the force field in which very different kinds of cultural impulses . . . must make their way. If we do not achieve some general sense of a cultural dominant, then we fall back into a view of present history as sheer heterogeniety, random difference, a coexistence of a host of distinct forces whose effectivity is undecidable. (1984b 57)

Much depends here on whether we accept Jameson's either/or, the choice between a systematic notion of the "force field" and undecidable random forces. His logic is Hegelian: the insistence that "genuine difference" can be perceived only within a set of relationships. But he is also arguing that the very ascription of identifying names to historical periods depends on some sense that the context within which particular acts take place has changed. Only if we have some general description of that context can we even identify the fact of historical change. Random differences finally turn all historical times into one—or at least make their distinctive differences from one another unnamable, in what Martin Jay has described as the poststructuralist "night of endless *différance* in which all cows [are] piebald" (1988 148).

Determined to resist this poststructuralist anarchism, Jameson is confronted with two crucial theoretical problems. First, he must justify his privileging of "history," conceived as a determinant and totalized social context, as "the ultimate ground as well as the *untranscendable limit* of our understanding in general and our textual interpretations in particular" (1981 100; my emphasis). Second, if he is to preserve the possibility of change he must, like Derrida and Foucault, either fragment his monolith from within or appeal to an outside. And for Jameson, even more than for Derrida or Foucault, not just any change will do; he wants the intended, planned change to a socialist future.

Jameson's justification of history as "ground" and "untranscendable limit" of thought finally rests on a rather bald assertion of a reality principle, an assertion that can be traced back to the realism of a Marxist interpretation that distinguishes ideology from the facts. In one way, Jameson appears to accept the Althusserian reinterpretation of "ideology" as "a representational structure which allows the individual subject to conceive or imagine his or her lived relationship to transpersonal realities such as the social structure or the collective logic of history" (1981 30). Formulated this way, we all live an imaginary (in the Lacanian sense) relationship to History; there is no "other" to ideology. But this necessity of ideology does not, in the end, prevent the Marxist critic from recognizing the real facts. "The aesthetic act is itself ideological, and the production of aesthetic or narrative form is to be seen as an ideological act in its own right, with the function of inventing imaginary or formal 'solutions' to unresolvable social contradictions" (1981 79). The Marxist hermeneutic uncovers contradictions within the text that reflect the *fact* of social contradiction; ideology, on the other hand, credits the facile solutions to those contradictions that the text offers. (Jameson explicitly derives this model from Lévi-Strauss's theory of myth.)

The articulation of "a text's fundamental contradiction may then be seen as a test of the completeness of the analysis" (1981 80), proof that this version of historicist interpretation has gotten outside the text to "external reality" (1981 81). But Jameson recognizes that contemporary theory has deprived him of any easy access to that reality; he accepts that "history is inaccessible to us except in textual form" (1981 82), which means "that the social contradiction addressed and 'resolved' by the formal prestidigitation of narrative must, however reconstructed [by the critic], remain an absent cause." But Jameson insists that this recognition "that our approach to [history] and to the Real itself necessarily passes through its prior textualization, its narrativization in the political unconscious" (1981 35) does not mean that we lose history altogether to the play of tropes, to the prison-house of language and textuality. He refuses to "draw the fashionable conclusion that because history is a text, the 'referent' does not exist." But his proof of history's existence comes down to assertion. "One does not have to argue the reality of history: necessity, like Dr. Johnson's stone, does that for us" (1981 82). "History is therefore the experience of Necessity, and it is this alone which can forestall its thematization or reification as a mere object of representation or as one master code among many others. Necessity is not in that sense a type of content, but rather the inexorable *form* of events. . . . History is what hurts, it is what refuses desire and sets inexorable limits to individual as well as collective praxis, which its 'ruses' turn into grisly and ironic reversals of their overt intention" (1981 102). To link history with *Ananke*, while it gives Jameson a reality principle to hold (Dr. Johnson style) against the textual idealists, also moves him toward the tragic ground occupied by Nietzsche and Freud.

Jameson believes that his unapologetic embrace of utopianism will preserve him from the hopeless, albeit defiant, acceptance of unalterable necessity found in tragedy. Against inexorable necessity, the history that hurts, Jameson posits "a single great collective story" that illustrates "a single fundamental theme—for Marxism, the collective struggle to wrest a realm of Freedom from a realm of Necessity" (1981 19). "It is in detecting the traces of that uninterrupted narrative, in restoring to the surface of the text the repressed and buried reality of this fundamental history, that the doctrine of a political unconscious finds its function and its necessity" (1981 20). To take the most ungenerous view, we can say that Jameson reacts to the apparent lack of any revolutionary socialist fervor among the peoples of the contemporary West by insisting that the desire for collective social forms is always present, although unconscious, and is always striving to push history in a certain direction: toward a socialist society. Thus he manages to sidestep the issues of contemporary political aspirations and of intentionality in one move. He also disentangles himself from Marxist humanism, by removing the question of political desires to the order of the unconscious. The evidence for these desires' existence now becomes, as in Freudian analysis, not the subject's self-reported desires but the interpreter's recognition of the subject's "true" desires. The Marxist hermeneutic will reveal to us the future that we really want, but did not know that we wanted. Such an odd notion is appealing to Jameson because it combines the repudiation of humanism found in Althusser (and in structuralism/poststructuralism as a whole) and a way to address the lack of any strong socialist political presence in the Western democracies.

Even if we grant the rather dubious notion of a political unconscious, there remains the recalcitrant history that has been associated with unresolvable contradictions and with necessity. Utopian desires and the brutal facts of hierarchical, exploitative society are shown by Jameson's Marxist hermeneutic to confront one another, but a model for resolution is never provided. And this failure to sketch the next move appears linked to Jameson's theoretical twisting. He has refused to reduce history to mere textuality, but he has also claimed we only have access to history through texts. As a result, he appears to believe that mere textual resolutions of "real" historical contradictions cannot actually solve these experienced necessities; the suggestion seems to be that more than textual resolution, more than textual action, would be needed. That is, only some kind of political action by a collective group (not a solitary author) can effect social change. But Jameson is going to have serious problems giving us a theoretical account of such action upon history because he has said our only access to history is textual. His refusal to allow history to be completely swallowed into textuality has given him an epistemological grounding for his theorizing a Marxist hermeneutic, but his concession that we always approach history through texts has left him without a model of nontextual action. And in fact Jameson at times appears to believe that the next revolution will come through the work of artists and intellectuals. He talks of "cultural revolution" (1981 95–98) as occurring at times when "the dynamics of sign systems of several distinct modes of production can be registered and apprehended" (1981 98). Jameson's speculations here have led to contemporary criticism's interest in "transcoding" or "recoding" as the textual work on social forms that re-presents them with a difference, slanted toward alternative possibilities.[32] More usually, Jameson appears skeptical that such textual work on history can on its own usher in a new historical order.

In *The Political Unconscious*, Jameson strives to use history to undermine any sense of the social order's inexorable necessity, which is one reason it seems odd that he then connects history so intimately to necessity. History is liberating for Jameson for much the same reason it is for Foucault; the fact of diachronic diversity indicates both the possibility of change and the fact that alternatives have existed. Furthermore, Jameson insists that, synchronically, there is always more than one mode of production (1981 95) at work in any society, thus providing simultaneously existing alternative models. Finally, within any given mode of production there are different social positions (employer versus employee, for example) occupied by different subjects, so that a diversity of interests is generated within what might at first appear a monolithic order. (Generally speaking, their allegiance to confrontational models of politics and to the notions of "class positions" within social systems has provided the literary left with one argument against Foucault's more amorphous notion of power, with its refusal of the categories "ruling class" and the "dominated.") There is plenty of theoretical room, then, in Jameson's totalized social order for resistant voices and alternative imaginings. He simply insists that the significance of such differences can be recognized only within a larger understanding of their relationship to the prevailing social order. In his most orthodox moments as a Marxist, Jameson can even insist that truly revolutionary discourse/action can come only from the subject position occupied by the working class, an insistence that denies the radical potential of the new social movements.[33]

Recently, Jameson has also defended himself against the critics of his

[32]Foster (1985) provides a particularly impressive example of a writer who tries to enact the possibilities inherent in "transcoding" or "recoding." He defines "'cultural revolution'" as the "critical activity that reactivates the conflictual history of sign-systems so as to break through the (ahistorical) logic of the code as well as the formalist discourse of academic disciplines" (1985 177). He adds: "Theoretically at least, such an irruption would not play into the hands of the code, would escape recuperation, precisely because these new and old signs would contest the code as absolute sign-system" (1985 178).

[33]The conclusion to Jameson's essay "Periodizing the 60s" reveals him at his most unimaginative and orthodox. He argues that the "prodigious release of untheorized new forces" in the sixties, including "the ethnic forces of black and 'minority,' or Third World movements . . . [and] the student and women's movements . . . can perhaps best be explained in terms of the superstructural movement and play enabled by the transition from one infrastructural or systemic stage of capitalism to another" (1988b 208). Now that this transitional moment is over, "the 80s will be characterized by an effort, on a world scale, to proletarianize all those unbound social forces that gave the 60s their energy." The moral of the story, then, is that the New Left and the new social movements were only the transitory products of an odd moment of historical anarchy, but now things are back to normal and only the Marxist concentration on issues of class struggle and the historical role of the proletariat offers the royal road to the true revolution.

"totalizing" approach to postmodernism by insisting that the "war on totality" in contemporary theory "rests on a confusion between levels of abstraction" (1989 34). The "idea" of "a system that constitutively produces differences" does not mean that "such a system [is] supposed to be in kind 'like' the object it tries to theorize, any more than the concept of dog is supposed to bark." (1989 34). Only thought that moves to this more abstract level of generalization, to the region of the concept, can ever hope to comprehend contemporary existence. Thus Jameson insists that the current hostility to totality cannot simply be accepted without examination. "Does the current taboo on totality simply result from philosophical progress and increased self-consciousness? Is it because we have today attained a state of theoretical enlightenment and conceptual sophistication, which permit us to avoid the grosser errors and blunders of old-fashioned thinkers of the past (most notably Hegel)? That may be so, but it would also require some kind of historical explanation . . . namely, why is it that 'concepts of totality' have seemed necessary and unavoidable at certain historical moments, and on the contrary noxious and unthinkable at others" (1989 36)? Not only do I find Jameson's position here convincing, but his differentiation of levels of analysis also has the unexpected, but much appreciated, bonus of dissolving the hard distinction between reformist and revolutionary action that has so debilitated leftist politics. "The old antithesis between reform and revolution does indeed strike me as disastrous; but there is no need to make it, and Mao Zedong used to talk about 'walking on two legs.' Local struggles and issues are not merely indispensable, they are unavoidable; but as I have tried to say elsewhere, they are effective only so long as they also remain figures or allegories for some larger systemic transformation. Politics has to operate on the micro- and macro-levels simultaneously" (1989 44). I am not so sure that politics *must* operate on both levels at once in every instance, but am convinced that local, reformist concerns are almost always where a radical politics starts, and that these concerns always have the potential to open out toward more elaborate and total questioning of current arrangements and imagining of alternatives. Radical politics ignores reformist concerns at its own peril, cutting itself off from the very groups that are its most likely constituency.

   Jameson also ascribes to the Althusserian notion of "semiautonomy," of which he provides a brilliant account in *The Political Unconscious*. Semiautonomy allows for significant differentiation within the totality, while also insisting on the interconnectedness of the whole. I return to this concept in the next chapter, where I use it to further my own model of critical intervention in the present. What we need to pursue here is whether all of the expedients just listed save Jameson from utter despair when he turns to a discussion of postmodernism as the cultural logic of late capitalism.

Two key features identify postmodernism for Jameson. The first relies on connecting contemporary "cultural" (meaning artistic, intellectual, and popular culture) forms with the description of "late capitalism" put forward by Ernest Mandel. Jameson presents Mandel's identification of "three fundamental moments in capitalism: . . . market capitalism, the monopoly stage or the stage of imperialism, and our own—wrongly called postindustrial, but what might be better termed multinational capital" (1984b 78). Far from being some kind of transcendence of capitalism's logic, the global economy "constitutes on the contrary the purest form of capital yet to have emerged, a prodigious expansion of capital into hitherto uncommodified areas." Because "aesthetic production today has become integrated into commodity production generally" (1984b 56), any modernist hope for an autonomous, or even semiautonomous, realm of culture (i.e., artistic production) is no longer feasible. (Jameson believes that modernist strategies did, in their own time, provide a "provocative challenge to the reigning reality- and performance-principles of early 20th century middle-class society" [1983 124].[34]) More generally, the "global deployment of capital around the world" which characterizes multinational capitalism has "effectively destroy[ed] the older coherence of the various national situations. . . . The total system [of late capitalism] is marked by the dynamism with which it penetrates and colonizes the two last surviving enclaves of Nature within the older capitalism: the Unconscious and the precapitalist agriculture of the Third World—the latter is now systematically undermined and reorganized by the Green Revolution, whereas the former is effectively mastered by what the Frankfurt School used to call the Culture Industry, that is, the media, mass culture, and the various other techniques of the commodification of the mind" (1988b 47).[35] Capital-

[34]In an earlier version of the essay on postmodernism published in *New Left Review*, Jameson much more explicitly contrasts the "oppositional art" (1983 123) of modernism to a postmodernism that has lost any critical edge. (The earlier version, a talk presented at the Whitney Museum in New York, is reprinted in Foster [1983].) "Whatever the explicit political content of the great high modernisms," Jameson writes, they "were always in some mostly implicit ways dangerous and explosive, subversive within the established order" (1983 124). "Postmodernist art is going to be about itself in a new kind of way; even more, it means that one of its essential messages will involve the necessary failure of art and the aesthetic, the failure of the new, the imprisonment in the past" (1983 116). Jameson concludes: "There is some agreement that the older modernism functioned against its society in ways which are variously described as critical, negative, contestatory, subversive, oppositional, and the like. Can anything of the sort be affirmed about postmodernism and its social moment? We have seen that there is a way in which postmodernism replicates or reproduces—reinforces—the logic of consumer capitalism; the more significant question is whether there is also a way in which it resists that logic. But that is a question we must leave open" (1983 125).

[35]Significantly, Jameson adds as an afterthought that late capitalism has invaded a third domain which now joins "the last surviving enclaves": "I should also add that this enormous new quantum level of capital now menaces that other precapitalist enclave within older capitalism, namely the nonpaid labor of the older interior or home or family, thereby in contradictory fashion

ism's global expansion joins with universal commodification to bring previously unsubjugated areas of social life under its domain. Much of this
appropriation, especially of our unconscious desires, fears, and hopes (including, presumably, our political unconscious), takes place in the realm of
the sign, so that the characteristic machines of late capitalism are "indeed
machines of reproduction rather than of production" (1984b 79).

The second key feature of postmodern late capitalism is the loss of any
place from which a critical discourse can be launched. Jameson thematizes
this loss as the "death of the subject," the "effacement of history," and the
"abolition of critical distance." (Each of these phrases appears in "Postmodernism, or the Cultural Logic of Late Capitalism.") Postmodern art's ran-
sacking of the past for the motifs, styles, and themes it recycles effectively
strips the past of any significance as a lived alternative; the past now simply
serves as a fund of images for the "society of the spectacle." And the subject
confronted with this parade of images can only be described as "schizophrenic," where that term is understood (following Lacan) "as a breakdown
in the signifying chain" (1984b 71–72); the meaning of utterances is produced by their interrelationship in a chain of mutually differentiated signs,
and "when the links of the signifying chain snap, then we have schizophrenia
in the form of a rubble of distinct and unrelated signifiers" (1984b 72).
Postmodern culture, with its endless projection of disconnected, decontex-
tualized images, breaks down the systematic underpinnings of meaning, and
Jameson can only conclude that poststructuralist celebrations of the random
and heterogeneous merely reinforce this larger cultural dynamic. "If, indeed,
the subject has lost its capacity actively to extend its pro-tensions and re-
tensions across the temporal manifold, and to organize its past and future into
coherent experience, it becomes difficult enough to see how the cultural
productions of such a subject could result in anything but 'heaps of fragments'
and in a practice of the randomly heterogeneous and fragmentary" (1984b
71). For Jameson, the fact that such a subject now exists is comprehensible,
but he sees no reason to identify the disease as the cure. The problem of late
capitalism's "total system" is that it is so large and so complex that the subject

---

unbinding and liberating that enormous new social force of women" (1988b 47). What is
significant here is not only that Jameson thinks of the situation of women after the main argument
has been made, but also that his need to acknowledge the political potential of the women's
movement leads him to see a more contradictory, more conflictual, and less monolithic social
result stemming from late capitalism's invasion of the family than his description of the colonization of Third World agriculture and of the unconscious had implied. Furthermore, if Jameson
were to pursue the whole issue of the family and its relation to consumer capitalism, he would
necessarily be brought face to face with a whole spectrum of populist issues that his own version
of Marxism resolutely evades.

can no longer "think the impossible totality of the contemporary world system" (1984a 80). To think fragments instead only indicates the desperate straits we are in.

We have seen how Jameson's theoretical concessions to postmodern theory in *The Political Unconscious* deprive him of a model for action that is not textual; now we find his theory of postmodernism depriving him of any politically active subject. Neither the working class nor any other agent steps forward as harbinger of a future beyond late capitalism or as the group that can lead us from necessity to the realm of freedom. Instead, Jameson rests what little hope he can muster on the dialectic itself. "The dialectic requires us to hold equally to a positive or 'progressive' evaluation of its [late capitalism's] emergence" [1984b 88], in keeping with the "well-known passage" in which "Marx powerfully urges us to do the impossible, namely to think this development positively *and* negatively all at once" (1984b 86). The historical dialectic is moving forward and we can only accept (Jameson even uses the Nietzschean term "affirm" (1984b 88)) what it brings, recognizing that such old notions as "the possibility of the positioning of the cultural act *outside* the massive Being of capital" (1984b 87; my emphasis) are no longer operative, but that new, unforeseen possibilities will be made available by this new historical constellation. We find here Jameson's attempt to think—and to think positively—what Foucault calls "the paradox of the relations of capacity and power" (1984 47).

In the meantime, critics and artists appear the most important agents in the socialist game plan, because the immediate task at hand is "pedagogical and didactic" (1984b 89). Critics must make us aware of the nature of late capitalism, "of which it has never been said here that it was unknowable, but merely that it was unrepresentable, which is a very different matter" (1984b 91). Artists must strive to find ways to represent what currently exceeds representation. Meanwhile, the revolution is on hold, until "a breakthrough to some as yet unimaginable new mode of representing [multinational capitalism]" allows us to "again begin to grasp our positioning as individual and collective subjects and regain a capacity to act and struggle which is at present neutralized by our spatial as well as our social confusion" (1984b 92). Freedom and agency have only been temporarily suspended, and we look to criticism and art to get the grand narrative of the political unconscious moving perceptibly forward once again. In the meantime, we must rest our faith on the dialectic and the possibilities it opens up.

In his earlier work, Jameson resolutely held onto the belief that the defeat of capitalism would come from *inside* the system, propelled by those social groups (notably, the proletariat) whose position gave them a privileged insight into the existing order's insufficiencies. But the despair found in his view of postmodernism, with his claim that culture no longer enjoys any autonomy from the dominant order and that the schizophrenic self no longer has any critical distance from the whole, leads Jameson, in "Third-World Literature in the Era of Multinational Capitalism," to look outside the West for salvation. He tells us that this essay "forms a pendant to the essay on postmodernism which describes the logic of the cultural imperialism of the first world and above all of the United States" (1986 88 n. 26). The linchpin of the connection between the two essays is Jameson's allegiance to the epistemological "argument" in Lukács's "*History and Class Consciousness*, according to which 'mapping' or the grasping of the social totality is structurally available to the dominated rather than the dominating classes" (1986 87–88 n. 26). The loss of a revolutionary working class to the mass confusion that characterizes postmodernism makes Jameson look elsewhere for a possible agent of transformation. In his response to Jameson's essay on Third World literature, Aijaz Ahmad cogently objects to Jameson's "suppression of the multiplicity of significant difference among and within both the advanced capitalist countries and the imperialised formations" (1987 3). Jameson has allowed Marx's essentialist and overly schematic connection of the potential for action and knowledge to one's class position lead him into both a facile despair (about the Western masses) and a facile optimism (about the possibilities embodied in the peoples of the Third World).

But this lapse is not, to my mind, an inevitable consequence of Jameson's theoretical convictions, and I think he is more to be emulated than chastised for his resolute retention of the image of collective action and the necessity of interpreting both the possibility of action and its appropriate strategies on the basis of a theoretical attempt to comprehend the social whole. Jameson's failure to appreciate the potential of the new social movements and his sometimes less than subtle characterizations of the working class, of women, and of Third World peoples are disappointing but remain preferable to the more individualistic models of action found in Eagleton and Said. Freedom in Jameson is more positive than negative, since the capacity to act grows out of one's social position, not out of disengaging oneself from social constraints. Jameson's problem is how to explain that this positive freedom is not currently being exercised to upset the order of late capitalism. He posits the particularly (spectacularly) oppressive hegemony of late capitalism (a hegemony he calls "postmodernism") as the answer. But for the most part, even in his despair, he resists imagining liberation as an escape from that hegemony. Rather he accepts that, just as Marx affirms capitalism even while deploring it because capitalism provides new opportunities that are the seeds of the future, contemporary Marxism must affirm the postmodern condition while remaining attuned to the unexpected possibilities it will open up. That Jameson himself cannot right now indicate those possibilities or even provide a very satisfactory model of political action still does not justify a model based on negative freedom's escape from society and history.

In the absence of the collective revolutionary subject for which Marxist theory calls, it is no surprise that contemporary radicals fall back on a model of individual action. But this reliance on the individual runs counter to the literary left's own theoretical demonstrations of the individual's submission to the social whole. Terry Eagleton's works provides us with a particularly clear example of this contradiction, but I believe that Said, Lentricchia, and countless other contemporary critics are bedeviled by a similar problem, what I will call "the paradox of power and interest." The prevalence of this usually unnoticed paradox can, I think, be traced to Foucault's immense influence on the literary left, but I do not think Foucault himself can be entirely blamed, since he avoids the paradox himself.[36] (The comments about Foucault in the rest of this section refer to the "middle" Foucault, whose work informs the "new historicism." The texts by Eagleton and Said that I discuss here were written before Foucault's later reflections on power and the individual.)

Eagleton insists that "all theory and knowledge . . . is 'interested'" (1983 207), and his justification for this assertion recalls Foucault's notion of knowledge/power and follows a logic that is prevalent in much contemporary criticism:

> All of our descriptive statements move within an often invisible network of value-categories, and indeed without such categories we would have nothing to say to each other at all. It is not just as though we have something called factual knowledge which may then be distorted by particular interests and judgements, although this is certainly possible; it is also that without particular interests we would have no knowledge at all, because we would not see the point of bothering to get to know anything. Interests are *constitutive* of our knowledge, not merely prejudices which imperil it. The claim that knowledge should be 'value-free' is itself a value-judgement. (1983 14)

The phrase "although this is certainly possible" in this passage is odd, and indicates that Eagleton, unlike the middle Foucault, is not quite prepared to accept that the assertion that interests are constitutive of knowledge means that all appeals to an nonrelativized order of truth are thereby ruled out. For

---

[36]The middle Foucault avoids the paradox of interest and power because he has a unitary vision of power. He never appeals, as many on the left do, to an individual or class interest that somehow opposes itself to power, or to the interests of another, dominant individual or class.

Eagleton, "rhetoric" names "the received form of critical analysis" that "examined the way discourses are constructed in order to achieve certain effects," but this does not mean that rhetoric "ignored the truth value of the discourses in question, since this could often be crucially relevant to the kinds of effects they produced" (1983 205). Just what "truth-value" could possibly be, or how it could be separated from a discourse's "effects," is not clear.

In any case, having embraced the ubiquity of interest, Eagleton's aim is to make a virtue of necessity. In the first place, the acknowledgment of interest places the critic on Marx's side (the determination of consciousness by interest) against Kant's attempt to prove art's disinterestedness in *The Critique of Judgment* and Matthew Arnold's attempt to maintain criticism's disinterestedness in "The Function of Criticism." One of literary criticism's abiding sins, for Eagleton, has been its resolute unconsciousness of its own implicit politics. "Literary theories are not to be upbraided for being political, but for being on the whole covertly or unconsciously so—for the blindness with which they offer as a supposedly 'technical,' 'self-evident,' 'scientific' or 'universal' truth doctrines which with a little reflection can be seen to relate to and reinforce the particular interests of particular groups of people at particular times" (1983 195). Eagleton's political hermeneutic supplies the "little reflection" necessary; his advice is that we openly embrace criticism's inevitable political nature, where we "mean by the political no more than the way we organize our social life together, and the power-relations which this involves" (1983 194). Literary criticism and theory are participants in the conflictual struggles in which social life is shaped, although Eagleton feels compelled to remind us that there are other, more crucial and more immediately effective struggles. "Those who work in the field of cultural practices are unlikely to mistake their activity as utterly central. Men and women do not live by culture alone; the vast majority of them throughout history have been deprived of the chance of living by it at all, and those few who are fortunate enough to live by it now are able to do so because of the labour of those who do not. Any cultural or critical theory which does not begin from this single most important fact, and hold it steadily in mind in its activities, is in my view unlikely to be worth very much" (1983 214). Having acknowledged the literary intellectual's eccentric and privileged position, Eagleton feels that the intellectual's particular task is straightforward: to pursue directly those theoretical/critical discourses and practices that further her interests. "It is a matter of starting from what we want to *do*, and then seeing which methods and theories will best help us to achieve these ends" (1983 210). (The "we" here somewhat belies how individualistic this advice is, but Eagleton never tries to present some account of what the interest of critics as a class might be. Rather, he seems to be granting each critic the freedom to determine her own interest and then to act upon it.)

The paradox of power and interest makes itself felt, however, the moment we begin to question how, given Eagleton's comments on power, we could ever be expected to have any simple conception of our own interest. Eagleton appears to believe that we have some kind of Cartesian "clear and distinct" intuition of our interests. Yet the very notion of power makes no sense at all unless it refers to the ability of an outside force to alter the behavior of the self, while the alignment of power with discourse systems that is characteristic of poststructuralist thought must deny the individual any direct or unclouded apprehension of personal mental states, be they desires, interests, or intellectual constructs. Eagleton's adherence to such constitutive theories of power is often evident. He believes that "departments of literature in higher education . . . are part of the ideological apparatus of the modern capitalist state" (1983 200), and that "becoming certificated by the state as proficient in literary studies is a matter of being able to talk and write in certain ways. It is this which is being taught, examined and certificated, not what you personally think or believe, though what is thinkable will of course be constrained by the language itself" (1983 201). It is hard to see how the category of what you "personally think" can be maintained when what is "thinkable" is "constrained" by a language that is given to us by institutions that are part of the state's ideological apparatus. As a result, Eagleton must find ways to soften this monolithic suggestion of mind control. He insists that literature departments are "not wholly reliable apparatuses, since for one thing the humanities contain many values, meanings and traditions which are antithetical to the state's social priorities" (1983 200). He also argues that literary critics are not merely literary critics; hence, what they use literary criticism to do is related to wider sets of social circumstances. But conceding these points still does not recover any possibility of some simple access to a personal interest; presumably, power has constituted the languages of any number of different social fields, and even if we grant that these languages are not "wholly reliable" instruments of power, that does not mean that resistance stems from anything remotely like clearly perceived interest. If the language of literary studies is shaped by power so "that certain meanings and positions will not be articulable within it" (1983 201), as Eagleton claims, then where are we to find a language distanced enough from power that some pure, personal, and antithetical interest could be articulated? Instead, as Foucault recognizes, resistance in such cases involves occupying the strategic positions that power has made available; only this description of resistance remains faithful to such phrases as "we think only what the available language makes thinkable." In

using interest as the motivational basis of a committed criticism, Eagleton
uses a humanist tenet that poststructuralism does not allow him precisely to
combat the more distressing consequences of that form of thought.

Eagleton faces this theoretical difficulty much more directly in "Capitalism, Modernism and Postmodernism." He has little to offer, however, beyond
the assertion that contemporary individuals function simultaneously as autonomous agents and as creations of discursive power. "The subject of late
capitalism, in other words, is neither simply the self-regulating synthetic
agent posited by classical humanist ideology, nor merely a decentered network of desire, but a contradictory amalgam of the two. The constitution of
such a subject at the ethical, juridicial and political levels is not wholly
continuous with its constitution as a consuming or 'mass cultural' unit" (1986
145). The argument is that contemporary society still requires its subjects, in
some social fields, to operate as classical humanist individuals, even while
constituting that same subject as the postmodernist, decentered consumer in
other fields. (Note that even the humanist subject is constituted by society in
Eagleton's formulation.) Eagleton clearly believes that this contradiction can
be productive. He is less willing to say, however, what seems to be the case:
that his political hopes rest on exploiting the abilities to decide and to act that
characterize the humanist subject.[37] Instead, he only holds out "the emergence of a transformed rationality" (1986 147) as the ground for hope, albeit a
hope that we cannot as yet fully articulate since this "quite different rationality . . . still newly emergent, is not even able to name itself" (1986 144).

More generally, Eagleton is willing to ascribe the inability to resolve such
theoretical difficulties to "the site of contradiction we still inhabit" (1986
146), a site characterized by him in ways very close to my notion of an
oscillation between monolithic and pluralistic explanations:

> There is, of course, no question of some triumphant theoretical synthesis,
> which could only be premature and intellectualist. Such a synthesis would be
> untrue to what is in my view the essentially transitional nature, theoretically
> speaking, of the situation in which we now find ourselves, strung out as we are,
> for example, between certain essentialistic notions of social totality which are
> plainly discreditable, and an equally ineffective politics of the fragment or
> conjuncture. The fact that such matters . . . are not at the moment susceptible of
> satisfying theoretical resolution is a sign that they are indeed much more than

[37]Eagleton appears to recognize the problem in the following comment, although he has not
offered much in the way of a solution. "What one is asking for is less a rethinking of the subject
than, to use an old term, a rethinking of the agent, a rethinking of the subject as agent in a context
where unworkable ideas of agency, the agent as transcendental source, have been properly
discredited" (1986 134).

theoretical—that these dilemmas are the mark at the level of theory of certain real deadlocks and difficulties at the level of political history, and in part await for their successful resolutions upon developments in that latter realm. (1986 5)

The theoretician/intellectual caught in postmodernity must wait upon history.

Eagleton's attraction to the hybrid solution of a subject that is both autonomous agent and passive consumer stems from his desire to identify the "ideological" or political interests of cultural work while at the same time being unwilling to sacrifice a firmer oppositional portrait, a clearer demarcation between oppressor and oppressed, than poststructuralism (with its more dialectical logic of recuperation) will allow. To maintain such a clear oppositional portrait requires that certain agents occupy certain identifiable positions fairly consistently, and that such positions can be evaluated by some firm standard of judgment, which is why (I suspect) Eagleton reveals a hankering for some "truth-value" separate from power/knowledge and why he is also willing to appeal to various moral norms. "Socialists are those who wish to draw the full, concrete, practical applications of the abstract notions of freedom and democracy to which liberal humanism subscribes" (1983 208). I am fully sympathetic with Eagleton's aspirations here, but this linking of socialism's goals with the ideals of liberal humanism suggests a continuity not indicated by his usual contrast between the bourgeois world and the needs and desires it represses.

That Eagleton's oppositional view, finally, requires the traditional (realist) Marxian distinction between "true consciousness" and "false consciousness" becomes apparent in *The Function of Criticism*. When it comes to describing the populace in Thatcher's England, Eagleton cannot assert that the people's interests are obvious to themselves. What "socialist intellectual work today" needs is a "counterpublic sphere, one based upon . . . institutions of popular culture and education" (1984 112). Eagleton recognizes that such a sphere does not currently exist; instead, we have "mass culture"—an "ideologically powerful *homogenization*, an *ersatz* sociality which is little more than the levelling effect of the commodity" (1984 121–22). The "function of criticism" becomes a battle for the hearts and minds of the people. Eagleton quotes (with approval) John Brenkman: " 'The constructing of a proletarian public sphere . . . requires a persistent struggle against the symbolic forms by which the mass-mediated public sphere constitutes subjectivity and puts it under the dominance of the commodity' " (1984 123). In *Walter Benjamin*, Eagleton declares that "the primary task of the 'Marxist critic' is to actively participate in and help direct the cultural emancipation of the masses" (1981

97), a statement made in a paragraph that begins by quoting Lenin. Eagleton concludes *The Function of Criticism* with the claim that "the role of the contemporary critic is to resist that dominance [of the commodity] by reconnecting the symbolic to the political, engaging through both discourse and practice with the process by which repressed needs, interests and desires may assume the cultural forms which could weld them into a collective political force" (1984 123). The appeal to "repressed needs, interests, and desires" here indicates Eagleton's distance from Foucault's model of power; contemporary subjectivity may be constituted by the symbolic realm of mass culture, but there is a "repressed" reality that is available to a counterdiscourse. The masses can be brought out of subjection to mass culture and back to this reality. Critical thought is the activity that can return the people's true, albeit repressed, interests to the surface.

The heroic critic who, like Moses, will lead the masses out of their captivity to the commodity is, Eagleton's work suggests, himself strangely immune to the workings of symbolic power. Eagleton's good critic is peculiarly innocent; once liberated into "the counter-public sphere" that ideal criticism would create, any worries about criticism's institutional ties to "ideological state apparatuses" is dispelled, while the alignment of criticism with some sort of "universal interests" (in the sense in which Marx speaks of the proletariat as the "universal" class) also seems assumed. Eagleton never explicitly makes these claims, of course, but I think that they are strongly implied. For one thing, the critic is less governed by interest than anyone else; the oddity of the critical task that Eagleton assigns us is that we are to work not in our own interest, but in the interest of the masses or the proletariat. Eagleton has eloquently explained how the current social arrangements make writers and intellectuals a privileged caste; thus, if we really consulted our interests as he advises us to do, we would hardly work for a socialist future. Eagleton's implicit (and sometimes explicit) appeal, then, is to the intellectuals' consciences, not to their interests.

More important, Eagleton clearly still believes in the power of criticism to uncover repressed truths, to bring back onto the stage of history those contents that ideological power (i.e., capitalism, or what he calls "the bourgeois state" [1984 124]) has tried to obliterate. And he appears to associate this ability to be a critic with a certain detachment from the immediate struggle. *Literary Theory*'s last paragraph rather amazingly undermines three-quarters of the book's argument. "I shall end with an allegory. *We* know that the lion is stronger than the lion-tamer, and so does the lion-tamer. The problem is that the lion does not know it. It is not out of the question that the death of literature may help the lion to awaken" (1983 217).

The remarkable point here is the elevation of the "we" to spectatorship above the conflict of lion and lion-tamer. The critic has the distanced, totalizing view unavailable to the participants, and "the function of criticism" turns out to be to find some way to hand that knowledge over to the lion as a replacement for the "disinformation" being given to him by the "lion-tamer." And the allegory suggests that the critic's knowledge is to be trusted more than the lion-tamer's, because the critic is a nonparticipant; that is, the critic is distanced and disinterested. This last statement may be pushing Eagleton's "allegory" too far, but I do think it fair to say that Eagleton has painted himself into a rather tight corner once he argues that social discourses, such as mass culture and education, constitute selves and knowledge. It is not surprising in that case that freedom becomes identified with an interest that is portrayed as unproblematically personal or that the critic's knowledge, in the allegory, seems to stem from his transcendence of social circumstance. Only some such negative escape from the discourses of power will provide access to essential realms of truth and justice or, more mundanely, assure a true consciousness of one's interests.

Edward Said's work has explicitly championed models of escape. For Said, criticism should "stand between culture and system" (1983 26). By "system," Said means the totalizing and reified forms often taken by thought. "Criticism deals with local and worldly situations, and it is constitutively opposed to the production of massive, hermetic systems." Criticism, we might say, must oppose itself to theory. By "culture," Said means "to suggest an environment, process, and hegemony in which individuals (in their private circumstances) and their works are embedded, as well as overseen at the top by a superstructure and at the base by a whole series of methodological attitudes" (1983 8). Said is fully capable of making the generalizations about culture's enormous power that we find throughout postmodern thought; he writes of "the power of culture by virtue of its elevated or superior position to authorize, to dominate, to legitimate, demote, interdict, and validate: in short, the power of culture to be an agent of, and perhaps the main agency for, powerful differentiation within its domain and beyond it too" (1983 9). "There is no reason to doubt that all cultures operate in this way or to doubt that on the whole they tend to be successful in enforcing their hegemony" (1983 14). Where Said differs greatly from poststructuralism and Jameson is his overt reliance on "individual consciousness" as the necessary location of criticism. What Said attempts to theorize, or at least to make possible, is this individual consciousness, distanced from both culture and system, a distance achieved, in part, by its location *between* the two.

Said's descriptions of the individual, critical consciousness sound much like modernist images of the "alienated" intellectual, while also relying heavily on spatial metaphors of "distance," "exile," and "margins." The crux of criticism appears to be a reflective evaluation of cultural norms instead of a mere thoughtless adoption of them. "On the one hand, the individual mind registers and is very much aware of the collective whole, context, or situation in which it finds itself. On the other hand, precisely because of this awareness—a worldly self-situating, a sensitive response to the dominant culture— the individual consciousness is not naturally and easily a mere child of the culture, but a historical and social actor in it. And because of that perspective, which introduces circumstance and distinction where there had only been conformity and belonging, there is distance, or what we might also call criticism" (1983 15). This identification of criticism with distance would not be peculiar if Said were presenting some (modernist) vision of art's transcendence of local circumstances. And in fact Said often indicates that some such vision of the intellectual is important to him. "There is some very compelling truth to Julian Benda's contention that in one way or the other it has often been the intellectual . . . who has stood for values, ideas, and activities that transcend and deliberately interfere with the collective weight imposed by the nation-state and the national culture" (1983 14).

But in many other places, of course, Said is deeply involved in the new historicist critique of all forms of criticism (or intellectual activity in general) that lose sight of their specific location in certain social circumstances. "To repeat: the critical consciousness is a part of its actual social world and of the literal body that the consciousness inhabits, not by any means an escape from one or the other" (1983 16). Said must justify the existence of this "distance" that makes criticism possible, while also showing that he is not talking about some fantasized escape. Bruce Robbins has characterized this dilemma as the tension in Said's work between "homelessness and worldliness."[38] The critic must be resolutely in the world, but he must never feel at home there. Part of this worldliness is criticism's inevitable involvement in questions of values and politics. Criticism "is by no means . . . value-free. Quite the contrary, for the inevitable trajectory of critical consciousness is to arrive at some acute sense of what political, social, and human values are entailed in the reading, production, and transmission of every text" (1983 26).

Said has described himself as "temperamentally antisystemic and antischool" (1976 46), and a certain impatience with the theoretical presuppositions of his own position often makes itself felt in his work. His tendency to appeal to transcendent values like freedom and justice conflicts with his

[38]See Robbins (1983).

adherence to the doctrine that "there is no point of view, no vantage, no perspective available like an Archimedean principle outside history" (1987b 19) that allows for disinterested knowledge. Clearly, the relativism that this theoretical position about knowledge appears to validate disturbs Said. He insists that "there can be no neutrality or objectivity," but adds in the next sentence that "this is not to say that all positions are equal"; he goes on to discriminate among different positions on the basis of whether one is "engaged openly on the side of justice and truth" (1987b 22). Said's parting advice in this particular lecture is to "enjoin" his audience "to call justice justice and truth truth."

Similarly, Said often appeals to an objective reality to ground the knowledge claims made by criticism and scholarship. "If it is not to be merely a form of self-validation, criticism must intend knowledge and, what is more, it must attempt to deal with, identify, and produce knowledge as having something to do with will and with reason" (1983 202). In part, Said's concern with knowledge is a clear-sighted attempt to face a dilemma that Foucault usually sidesteps: the status of the discourse that uncovers the workings of power/ knowledge. As with all ideology critique, Foucault's work is open to the charge that it is itself merely an instance of power and thus has no greater truth value than the discourses it critically examines. Foucault appears to accept the inevitability of this equality in status between criticism and the discourses it studies.[39] Said rejects this equality, insisting instead that "the conjunction between power and knowledge" is "a reality to be confronted and examined" (1988c 17). Admittedly, the knowledge that criticism produces is "openly contentious" (1983 224), "inhabiting a much contested cultural space" (1983 225), but the political uses to which that knowledge will be put can still be separated from the question of its truth value. Thus Said wants to discredit the "spurious scholarship" of certain Zionist texts, these "rewritten histories" that are "completely at odds with the realities" (1988c 8).

These more recent passages signal a retreat from the more stringent theoretical purity of *Orientalism* (1978). In that work Said is very clear that, although the "lives, histories, and customs [of the people who live in the Orient] have a brute reality obviously greater than anything that could be said about them in the West" (1978 5), the crucial point is "that the Orient is not an inert fact of nature" (1978 4). Instead, the Orient is "produced" by a discourse that "*is*, rather than expresses, a certain *will* or *intention* to under-

---

[39]This generalization about Foucault needs to be qualified by acknowledging certain indications that, near the end of his life, he was moving toward a position on knowledge and truth that was much closer to the one that I am ascribing to Said. See especially Foucault (1984 381–83).

stand, in some cases to control, manipulate, even to incorporate, what is a manifestly different (or alternative and novel) world" (1978 12). Like history in Jameson, the Orient exists for Said but is unavailable except through humanly produced representations of it. And the ethical denunciation of the Orientalist discourse of the West is based not on some violation of the facts or truth of the Orient in itself, but on the identification of the less-than-admirable intentions that are operating in the production of the discourse. The only cognitive claims made in this theoretical model of discourse are that knowledge is a product of interests, not of some unmediated apprehension of an object, and that the discourses of knowledge have an awesome power to reproduce themselves over time since they shape the expectations and utterances of each subsequent investigator who goes to look at the object in question "for himself." What comes to appear monolithic in *Orientalism* is the cultural system of representation itself, a set of clichés that is repeated solemnly as original insight by each new speaker on the subject.

Within such a scenario, the appropriate response is not to appeal to the Orient's neglected reality but to produce a counterdiscourse to the discourse one abhors. "One doesn't just write: one writes against, or in opposition to, or in some dialectical relationship with other writers and writing, or other activity, or other objects" (1976 35). Even when he consistently denied himself assertions about truth and reality, however, Said did want to retain the ethical universals that motivated his work and allowed him to judge other discourses. "I guess what moves me mostly is anger at injustice, an intolerance of oppression, and some fairly unoriginal ideas about freedom and knowledge" (1976 36). And in the eighties, as his work became less concerned with literary theory and more directly connected to the Palestinian cause, Said has found the nonrelativistic standards supplied by the notions of truth and reality necessary.

Certainly, Said has found the discourse of "rights" most helpful in presenting the Palestinian case. "The first dispossession bred a whole series of sustained exclusions, by which Palestinians were denied their primordial rights not only in fact; they were also denied those rights in history, in rhetoric, in information, and in institutions" (1987b 20). And the foundation for possessing such rights is being a human being. "The avoidance of the Palestinian as a human being" (1987a 32) justifies, in American and Israeli eyes, the denial of basic rights. "They try to deny our humanity. This is a true part of being a Palestinian. Not only are you denied your political sovereignty and rights, but also your history is denied and your reality as a suffering human being is pooh-poohed or ignored completely" (1987a 33). Where the assertion of differences is used for the old-fashioned purpose of suppressing or excluding certain groups, the postmodern fear of an all-inclusive monolith and the postmodern celebration of difference as freedom appear rather irrelevant. What is arguable is whether Said's appeal to universals is merely the appropriate strategy for the particular political struggle in which he is engaged or says something about the need for universally applicable notions of justice and equality and freedom in all political battles.

The same ambiguity resides in the term that I find most fruitful in Said's recent political writing: *recognition*. "The essence, obviously, is mutual recognition. They have to recognize us. And we, who think what they have done to us is outrageous and illegitimate and illegal, have to recognize them. It's very difficult, but it has to be done. Otherwise, there will be killing and endless instability for years to come" (1987a 33). "Recognition," with its Hegelian overtones, could work without any appeal to transcendent categories. The recognition of an other's right to exist is made from within a culture and on grounds supplied by that culture's traditions and discourse. In this case, it would not be a question of which culture represents the Orient truly, but of an acknowledgment that other experiences, other representations, of the Orient are not only possible but are *lived* by others. And such recognition has the very practical consequence of providing us with a way of living in a world where others, with different ways of living, manifestly exist. "The main task for American intellectuals is not to attack Libya or denounce Soviet communism, but to figure out how this country's staggering power can be harnessed for communal coexistence with other societies rather than for violence against them. Certainly such a task cannot be helped by trading in metaphysical abstractions while we charge around the world as if we were the only people who counted" (Said and Hitchens 1988 158). In this formulation, the "abstractions" work against the very possibility of "recognition," with its respect for the concrete, lived differences between peoples. But it is hard not to make "recognition" itself just such an abstraction, one that is based on the ethical imperative to grant full humanity to all other members of the species. We know from anthropology how common it is for human groups to deny the humanity of outsiders. The ethical complaint against this reflex appears based on a universal humanism, a will to extend the rights and privileges of being human to all.

I return to the difficulties and the hopes that reside in the concept of recognition in my final chapter. Here, I want to finish tracing Said's contradictory impulses toward postmodern localism and a reliance on transcendent categories of truth and ethical universals. We can recognize the tensions in his work in favorite terms such as *beginning, affiliation*, and *marginality*. The stress on beginnings takes place within a theoretical description of genealogy, of our embeddedness in a history that makes all attempts at a fresh start a willful forgetting (à la Nietzsche) of all that has gone before and has shaped the circumstances in which we now find ourselves. Beginnings in Said are undertaken within a theoretical context that stresses how difficult, even impossible or illusionary, the act of beginning is. Similarly, "affiliation" names our inevitable connection to the network of interests and institutions that go along with our cultural position, yet Said continually hopes to sidestep these affiliations by gaining the critical distance of exile. Finally, Said exploits the pun of "marginality" to express spatially the critic's ideal distance from a culture's hegemonic arrangements, but with a full ironic awareness that such distance makes the critic marginal, tangential, to the processes that influence the paths hegemony takes.

Catherine Gallagher has succinctly described the epistemological impasse Said encounters once he asserts that all representations are interested: "He writes of distortions of reality while denying the existence of a reality beneath the distortions. He notes that knowledge is always bounded by place but insists that there is an epistemologically privileged locus of displacement called exile" (1985 37). I have suggested that Said might be able to sidestep these epistemological dilemmas by accepting a full-scale relativism accompanied by universal tolerance, although his desire to hold on to a notion of "knowledge" undermines this strategy. More crucially, such a strategy requires the ethical universal of tolerance, and Gallagher argues that such "abstract universalism" only acts to empty "the category of the political" (1985 40). "Complete unspecifiability is the most striking feature of [Said's] politics, the feature that emerges most starkly from the rootlessness, the *disengagement*, inherent in critical affiliation" (1985 39).

Gallagher's critique appears confirmed by certain rather chilling comments made by Said on the nature of belonging and of exile. In an essay on Michael Walzer's *Exodus and Revolution*, Said tries at first to have it both ways. He contests Walzer's praise of Camus as a "connected" intellectual, rooted in a particular community and forming his fundamental commitments on the basis of that membership. Said validates "critical distance" instead, but then raises the question of "whether the position of critical distance [Walzer] rejects could not also, at the same time, entail intimacy *and* something very much like the insider's connectedness with his or her community? In other words, are critical distance and intimacy with one's people mutually exclusive?" (1988d 175). Said clearly wants to claim that they are not mutually exclusive, thus holding out the hope that universalism and localism can coexist in critical consciousness, just as he constantly hopes that our inevitable affiliations do not completely bias our critical judgments. The critic, as an individual, is charged to achieve what neither culture nor system can accomplish, a loyalty to universal principles of justice and tolerance linked with an affective commitment to the needs, history, and survival of her own community. Systems have ignored the local, while cultures have been intolerant of the different; but critical consciousness, between the two, can call both to a better destiny. By the end of the essay, however, Said has found this intermediary position too difficult to sustain and appears to now answer his question about mutual exclusion differently. Said now "thanks" Walzer for reminding us of the "tragic" fact "that you cannot 'belong' *and* concern yourself with the Canaanites who do not belong" (1988d 178). We must make a choice between belonging and exile, and Said defends his own choice by claiming that "the strength of the Canaanite, that is the exile position, is that being defeated and 'outside,' you can perhaps more easily feel compassion, more easily call injustice injustice, more easily speak directly and plainly of all oppression, and with less difficulty try to understand (rather than mystify or occlude) history and equality."[40]

This necessity of choice (for or against a culture's self-understanding and self-legitimation) stems from Said's acceptance (which he derives from poststructuralism and shares with most literary leftists and many feminists) that cultures posit "the particular authority of certain values over others" (1983 53), in the process inevitably subordinating certain groups within an inequitable hierarchy.[41] Such a universal claim about the inevitable tyranny with which every social group defines itself means that no legitimation of cultural identity is possible. This position has the advantage of undermining

[40]In an interview Bruce Robbins asks about this passage from the essay on Walzer, and Said concedes that "there's belonging, and then there's belonging. One can certainly belong to communities in ways that don't always involve rapacity, exploitation, and the denial of equal rights to other communities. That's the second point. The third point I want to make is that I never said anything about rootlessness and exilic marginality as excluding the possibility of, shall we say, sympathetic—I'm using a very simple word—sympathetic identification with a people suffering oppression. Especially when the oppression is caused by one's own community or one's own polity" (1988a 49–50). The striking point here is that Said misses what is at stake. Walzer's worry may be that exile makes one less sympathetic, but it is clear that Said does not believe such is the case; the claim is not that Said has slandered exile, but that he has slandered belonging. At issue is whether "belonging" necessarily makes one less sympathetic, more blind to the harm one's community does to those it excludes, to those it does not recognize as members. Said, despite his attempt here to distinguish between "belonging and belonging," strongly implies throughout his work that any movement from a position of exile into a community constitutes a kind of tragic fall into blindness and away from ethical purity.

[41]See Said (1988b 55–57) for what is perhaps his most vehement description of "the logic of identity" as "the modern social or state order . . . in which authority is based principally upon the organization of coercive power, and neither upon national consent nor upon a benignly ordained and preexistent harmony" (1988b 55). Rather, "social order and identity" is enforced by "the confinement of disorderly energies by the fearful terror of Jove's power" (1988b 54).

(delegitimating) all existent social forms but points only to an anarchic "politics of difference" as an alternative. Even if we accept that a "politics of difference" names a possible and desirable political hope, the delegitimation of collective identities provides us with no way to get from here to there. How are the social groups who will work for a politics of difference to be formed? How will they formulate their goals, legitimize them, and shape the strategies appropriate to achieving them without employing any of the tyrannical means of group formation that the advocates of difference see as universally prevalent? A reliance on individual action hardly offers an effective alternative.

Perhaps because he is involved in a very concrete political struggle, Said sees these difficulties with a politics of difference very clearly—and he also has tried to articulate the real goal for which such a politics aims. He accepts that under current conditions the Palestinians must first gain an identity that has been denied them; they must be "recognized" both as partakers of a general "humanity" and as specific members of a country and/or nationality. Only this prior accession to identity could grant the Palestinians any political effectiveness. But Said goes on to make it clear that he endorses this achievement of a national identity only as a means, not an end. "I'm not sure, in any event, that I believe in what would have to be at the outset a partitioned Palestine. . . . I do not believe in partition, not only at a political and demographic level, but on all sorts of other intellectual levels, and spiritual ones. . . . I certainly believe in self-determination, so if people want to do that [i.e., create a separate Palestinian state] they should be able to do it: but I myself don't see any need to participate in it" (1987c 129). Said would prefer to take a stand "*against* the notion of partition and . . . [try] instead to realize a democratic Jewish/Palestinian state. . . . We really can't talk about separate peoples, because our lives are interlinked in so many ways, at this moment principally by the dominance of one group over the other. But the whole idea of a separate, differentiated polity is a travesty of justice and of what was believed to be liberalism and a great social experiment. That's where the future is: in the evolution, over time, of notions of community that are based on real interdependent experiences, and not on dreams that shut out the other person and half of reality" (1987c 130).

For Said, then, the politics of difference has its culmination in a community of tolerance and interdependence; as his reference to liberalism makes clear, Said sees the politics of difference as achieving that universal tolerance that liberalism preaches, but fails to achieve. If this is what the politics of difference means, then I find it an appealing and coherent ideal, even if one we are very far from realizing. (Said calls himself "a great optimist, let's say for my son's generation" [1987c 130].) But I don't see that this statement of the final goal really entails repudiating all the mechanisms by which a community constitutes itself. Rather, Said appears to me to be presenting his own version of the standard romantic strategy of repudiating existing wholes by reference to a larger, more inclusive whole (a fully tolerant community of interdependent citizens). The standards for the condemnation of the existing community are internal to it; liberalism does not live up to its own claims to universality. I believe that this tactic of internal critique is much more likely to succeed than some venture into the unknown territory of *différance*, and it seems that Said, as a practical matter, agrees.[42]

In the interim, however, Said will keep his distance. He is determined to have this fully acceptable universalism or nothing. He will not "participate" in a Palestinian state but will retain his characteristic position of critical outsider until the day when a truly all-inclusive polity is formed. In a world of communities where identity is founded on violence, the ethically minded critic decides that it behooves him to always be on the outside, on the losing side. Said takes as axiomatic that the critic's allegiance must be not to existing social arrangements but to "the voices dominated, displaced, or silenced" (1983 53) by those arrangements.

We have seen how both Derrida's and Foucault's work makes it much more difficult to identify the distinction between insiders and outsiders within our social totalities. Said, like much of the left, wants to maintain a firmer distinction between oppressors and oppressed than poststructuralist theory, with its extremely sensitive notions of appropriation and complicity, would allow. Said posits a version of the postmodern monolith insofar as he finds that worldliness and interest delegitimate all existing social forms and that all cultures have enormous powers of "identity-enforcement," but he also claims a heroic disentanglement from such determinants for the critic. His persistent individualism prevents him from ever considering the possibility that different points of view, different interests, exist within the monolith by virtue of the fact that subjects are relegated to varying positions within the whole. Such an

---

[42]Thomas McCarthy insists that the politics of difference can only be a "politics of the ineffable," because it turns its back upon any of the existent political codes or strategies available to groups that wish to work for political transformation. "A general reminder of the myriad forms of violence that have accompanied the march of the universal through history is not a sufficient basis for restructuring politics and society. It is sheer romanticism to suppose that uprooting and destabilizing universalist structures will of itself lead to letting the other be in respect and freedom rather than to intolerant and aggressive particularism. . . . Enlarging the social space in which otherness can be, establishing and maintaining a multifarious and spacious pluralism seems, on the contrary, to require that we inculcate universalistic principles of tolerance and respect, and stabilize institutions that secure rights and impose limits. Otherwise, how is the tolerance of difference to be combined with the requirements of living *together* under *common* norms [i.e., the norm of tolerance]?" (1989 158).

explanation ensures that the (after all) obvious fact of resistance and conflict within societies is not theoretically opaque or only the product of those who, by force of circumstance or by will, are outside the society.

Three factors appear to govern Said's unwillingness or inability to entertain this alternative theoretical model of resistance. The first, on which there is no need to dwell any longer, is his desire for foundational, universal legitimations for the values offered by criticism against current practices. To stress that social conflicts arise from differential subject positions within society removes any independent foundations, while also implying a fairly strict determinism about people's ideas and beliefs. The second is Said's apparent belief that any resistance that is structurally dependent on the given social arrangements must necessarily be ineffective. This belief is at the bottom of much of the left's need to distance itself from Foucault and of its concomitant continuing search for a pure Other. The left needs to discover ways to outflank complicity; as I have stressed earlier, postmodernism as a cultural phenomenon has a lot to do with a despairing conviction that complicity is a more complex and more intractable problem than previously thought. Since Foucault's work so often appears to guarantee the triumph of existing power, its ability to recuperate all apparent resistances, the left has, not surprisingly, looked for other theoretical models of resistance. But the disturbing thing about Eagleton's, Lentricchia's, and Said's work is that it has not examined thoroughly enough the possibility of its own complicity, namely in recognizing the consequences of the third factor that governs their privileging of critical thought as the best model of resistance: a residual and foundational individualism.

Said's work is important in part because he has spearheaded the valorization of "the Other" so prominent in much contemporary social criticism, but the compatibility of this search for an other with an unexamined individualism too often goes unnoticed. One prominent response to poststructuralist strategies of demonstrating inclusion is to search further and further afield for an other. The current vogue for the Third World among literary intellectuals follows the logic that the West's only savior must come from the outside and that the true outside can still be found if only we get far enough away from what Said calls "metropolitan culture." Feminist discourse and strategies in particular are often contested around the question of whether women are a "true" other to the patriarchal systems they inhabit or are firmly within such systems. If Said's insistence that oppressed groups are not included (albeit in subordinate positions) but are simply excluded by dominant cultures more accurately describes the dynamics of social power than the constitutive, appropriative models found in Derrida and Foucault, then the tensions and dilemmas of postmodern theory may in fact be irrelevant to everyone but

would-be dissenting Western men.[43] Assured of their otherness, the sub-
alterns in today's world need not confront the sticky issues of possible coopta-
tion or complicity, or the possibility that their strategies of resistance actually
reinforce the system.

I think, however, that Said and other searchers for and champions of the
Other to Western culture have paid far too little attention to how parasitic the
whole concept of an other is on liberal traditions of individualism. To put it
another way, to imagine the other as distant and separate is profoundly
undialectical. The poststructuralist skepticism about claims made for and
about the existence of otherness stems from an acute awareness that the other
participates in a relationship that defines him as other. The very notion that
otherness affords some kind of purity or freedom rests on an assumption of
self-sufficiency, of an identity forged in the absence of social ties. That
identity is possible in such isolation, and that the true and free self is only
achieved apart from outside influences, provides the founding principle of
liberal individualism and its justification for the stress on autonomy and the
priority accorded negative liberty. In an interview, Said affirms a similar
principle of perpetual nonalignment as the way to preserve freedom. "I've
never really had to face the problem of solidarity in this way myself, because
the causes with which I've been associated—like the Palestinian movement,
for example—well, they're losing or at least underdog causes. . . . Some third-
world groups and states have tried to co-opt me. They aren't very difficult to
resist. And even in the case of the Palestinian movement itself I've made it a
point never to accept an official role of any sort; I've always retained my
independence. Sometimes I worry whether that's a kind of irresponsibility
that I can afford, thanks to the freedom guaranteed by a professorship at
Columbia. But I think it's right" (1986b 6–7). W. J. T. Mitchell quotes Said as
saying, "My goal is to bring the Palestinian nation into existence so that I can
attack it."[44]

It is crucial to see that such individualism follows quite easily from the
"tragic" conclusion that all societies establish a hierarchy of values that they
enforce in such a way as to exclude or disadvantage (to use the mildest,
euphemistic term) certain people. Individuals can be just, ethical, innocent;
societies can never be. Where no social arrangements are legitimate, the only
possible legitimate position for intellectuals or for others must be assumed

[43]See Said (1989) for his rather convincing argument that Lyotard's notion of postmodernism
"stands free of its own history" by essentializing the condition of the West: "He *separates* Western
postmodernism from the non-European world, and from the consequences of European
modernism—and modernization—in the colonized world" (1989 222).
[44]See Mitchell (1987 17).

apart from the society. (The logic of Thoreau's famous comment that the only place for a just man in an unjust society is jail applies here.) Permanent opposition, permanent individualism, becomes the only palatable option. (Oddly enough, Said's position thus becomes remarkably similar to Camus's notion of the rebel, although Camus protests endlessly against the conditions of existence whereas Said protests against man's inhumanity to man.) "Were I to use one word consistently along with *criticism* (not as a modification but as an emphatic) it would be *oppositional*. If criticism is reducible neither to a doctrine nor to a political position on a particular question, and if it is to be in the world and self-aware simultaneously, then its identity is its difference from other cultural activities and from systems of thought or of method" (1983 29). Embracing this "identity" of "difference" safeguards the critic's position as eternal outsider; it follows that " 'ironic' is not a bad word to use along with 'oppositional' " (1983 29). Said senses that such a resolutely negative definition of criticism might prove unsatisfactory and tries to provide some more positive guidelines. "For in the main—and here I shall be explicit—criticism must think of itself as life-enhancing and constitutively opposed to every form of tyranny, domination, and abuse; its social goods are noncoercive knowledge produced in the interests of human freedom." What's odd here is the insistence on a dichotomy between the "oppositional" critic and the oppressors, as if to take a stand for life enhancement and human freedom is controversial. Everyone claims to be working for such goals. At issue is how to activate these rather vague norms in specific circumstances so that they can serve to limit actual tyrannies.

Said's work presents, I believe, the most extreme form of the literary left's postmodern vicissitudes, but he is hardly an unrepresentative figure. Armed with postmodern theory's wholesale denunciations of the disastrous results of a Western rationalism and humanism that has hidden behind facile assertions of disinterestedness, the literary left has proved adroit at revealing how any culture privileges and protects certain groups at the expense of others. But the very universality of the charge—repeating in new jargon the old sociological commonplaces about how communities achieve solidarity by finding some group to deem inferior—prompts the left, in Norberto Bobbio's words, to adopt "a wishy-washy, half-baked anarchism" in order to avoid "the fact that political power can be exercised in various ways, and it is necessary actually to decide on which one is to be preferred to the others" (1987a 114).

I am not, I hope, simply repeating the shopworn and illegitimate objection that critics of current arrangements must have something positive to propose before offering any negative evaluations. My point is rather different: that the half-baked anarchism of the literary left is necessarily accompanied by a version of individualism that is, I believe, theoretically unsound and politically counterproductive. This point can be best made by teasing out the implications of Said's acceptance of the word *irony* as a description of the critical attitude. Irony, in relation to tragedy, can mean that an individual's actions have unintended consequences. Oedipus tries to avoid killing his father, but the actions he takes to evade his fate actually ensure its occurrence. In the tragic circumstance of all societies being oppressive, even the intellectual with the best intentions will find that her work, her production of knowledge, will serve some power.

At this point, with the severance of intention from actual consequence, irony breaks into two forms, which we can conveniently call Hegelian and Kierkegaardian irony. Hegelian irony is a hermeneutic that focuses on the illusion of intention, the illusion that the individual by himself can be said to choose what to do and to exercise some control over what is achieved by that doing. It is the totality, the "cunning of reason" or Oedipus' fate, that rules; Hegelian irony reveals that rule to individuals who continually make the mistake of believing in their own independence. Jameson, almost alone among contemporary leftists in the literary world, practices a Hegelian hermeneutic of this sort, and even he does not do so consistently.

A Kierkegaardian irony is determined to preserve the integrity of the self in the face of the unintended consequences of its actions. (Existentially, we might say, unintended consequences prove that the individual is part of something bigger than she is—to use the old movie cliché.) In Kierkegaard, irony becomes a strategy for disassociating the self from its actions, a refusal to allow what the self says or does to serve as definitive of some "true" self that remains behind or beneath the worldly appearances. (Kierkegaard's favorite metaphor for irony is, in fact, a disengaged self "hovering above" the nitty-gritty of daily entanglements, a metaphor relevant to Eagleton's allegory of the critic.) Kierkegaardian irony has remained a continual temptation for leftists because it is the habitual strategy within the individualist tradition by which the production of contents not determined by culture is understood. Irony works hand in hand with negative liberty to create that space in which the nonidentity of the self with language, social role, institution, or interest can be asserted.

The literary left uses irony to create a distinction, to create two camps, but the conflict they thereby construct is the old liberal standby of the individual versus society. Of course, such a position abandons Marx's own vehement anti-individualism, while also ignoring the antihumanism of poststructuralism. What I am suggesting is that the retreat to individualism becomes inevitable once all societies are condemned as constellations of power that are repugnant. Criticism cannot hope to change this grim fact; therefore, it must construct a nonsocial repository of value, a negative place, that it can occupy in order to at least attempt to preserve its own innocence. The same dynamic, albeit without the appeal to irony, appears at work in the late Foucault.

   In the next chapter I have more to say about the theoretical grounds for denying that the self has any identity apart from the intersubjective and social context in which it is formed. Here, I want to discuss why oppositional individualism is politically counterproductive. To begin with, individualistic disengagement is a strategy of despair. What is wonderful about Kierkegaard's work or Dostoyevsky's *Notes from Underground* is that they demonstrate how pathological and painful the alienation celebrated by liberal theory becomes when it is actually put into practice. A criticism that promotes oppositional disengagement courts such unhappy results. More frequently, such criticism is actually disingenuous about its own desires, on what we might call both the macro and the micro levels. On the macro level, oppositional criticism is a luxury available to a certain class in historical circumstances that make a revolution highly unlikely. The Kierkegaardian strategy of going through the motions of daily life while insisting that it is inauthentic is possible only when one is perfectly confident that existing structures are in no serious danger of collapsing; those structures will be influenced neither by the individual's sincerity nor his irony in carrying out his daily routines. I am not accusing leftists of hypocrisy. A fully experienced despair/anguish (something else Kierkegaard knew plenty about) over our society's injustice and the sordid pettiness of our daily concerns afflicts many contemporary intellectuals (among whom I would include myself), but an ironic and individualistic response to that despair is only appropriate when one is convinced of the inefficacy of any collective strategies for change. On the micro level, it is disingenuous not to recognize that staged opposition is an entrance requirement in various intellectual and artistic communities. By ignoring the intersubjective origins of oppositional stances, the critic reinforces the assumptions of an individualism that his own practice and institutional affiliations refute. Again, the issue is not hypocrisy; rather, it is our deep-seated habit of associating criticism with oppositional, negative, and individualistic stances, a habit that blinds us to the intersubjective grounds of those very stances.

   Finally, if we accept that individual identities and our everyday practices are generated by the social relations in which we participate (willingly or not), then oppositional individualism looks like a merely neurotic or childish attempt to withhold consent. (I revert to Freudian terms here because they provide the clearest model for describing the dynamic at play, not because I want to associate certain political positions with neurosis and others with health or maturity. My criterion for judgment is potential effectiveness, not putative psychological well-being.) Norman O. Brown describes the resolution of the Oedipal complex as the acceptance that one is not self-generated or self-sufficient; in recognizing the facts of sexual differentiation and of the father's role in conceiving a child, the child recognizes its dependence on others, its entanglement in a network of relationships that Lacan calls the Symbolic.[45] One way to describe mental illness would be to call psychosis the refusal ever to recognize or accept this fact of dependence, while neurosis is the refusal to accept responsibility for the self fashioned in the family and social network that the neurotic never asked to join. The neurotic is an ironist, continually insisting that he has been a passive victim of the powerful others in his life and that his true, but unexpressed, identity lies elsewhere. This neurotic/ironist is a perpetual child, convinced that the symbolic (fetishized as the phallus) is the perpetual possession of the Other (think of Kierkegaard's problems with marriage and with his father), and inventing alternative identities for himself while firmly enmeshed in the (often tyrannical) family matrix that defines him. The Freudian cure is premised on the notions that freedom can begin only with the acceptance of responsibility for what the past has made one and that this freedom can then be used to construct different patterns of relationship (hence a different self) in the future. Transference is crucial precisely because it is the workshop in which the patient must recognize that, even outside the family, he repeats certain patterns that he claims are imposed upon him and in which, subsequently, his ability to alter those patterns is demonstrated. I offer this Freudian detour not to endorse all its details or strategies but in order to indicate the essential passivity of political irony and negative freedom. To be oppositional is always to cede power to the Other and attempt to absolve oneself of responsibility. The literary left often appears most concerned with maintaining its purity as victim, a purity that only noninvolvement in all positive social ties can ensure, a refusal of any responsibility for the social self that one is. Irony becomes the strategy of disinvestment by which responsibility is evaded and, pushed to its extreme, results in an assertion of an essential, self-sufficient individualism, but an individualism that can never be put into play because any social interaction falsifies it.

I do not want to suggest, in the style of Christopher Lasch and Daniel Bell, that authority stands in need of defense today because our times validate negative, "liberated," models of identity. On the contrary, I believe that authority's seemingly immovable entrenchment in our time generates the

---

[45]See Brown (1959 110–34) for his discussion of "the Oedipal *causa sui* project" (1959 128).

proliferation of negative behaviors. Authority is in no danger; and as Lasch recognizes in his more lucid moments, the strategy of disengagement followed by various liberation movements reinforces authority rather than threatens it. Thus the left's model of an oppositional space apart from the dominant culture, while repeating a recognizably modernist strategy, assumes a different meaning in the postmodernist context. Modernist isolation was not primarily ironic, not adopted out of weakness but out of a felt strength. (Kierkegaard's weak irony is a reaction to the Hegelian totality, just as postmodern irony reacts to the totality of global capitalism.) The modernist's separation from the dominant culture allowed her to enter into a clearer dialogue with the formal exigencies of her art; isolation proved a productive, not a primarily defensive, strategy, as is evident in countless artworks of the period and in the modernists' optimism that the revolutions in art could be transported back into society. That optimism only turns sour in the postmodernist context, where the construction of a separate space looks much more like a retreat, a way of avoiding implication in the barbarities of the dominant culture. The modernist could still affirm her art; the oppositional postmodernist can only affirm his distance as a token of an innocence that cannot be preserved once any positive action is taken. In this respect, Jameson's inability to supply any model of action becomes as symptomatic as Eagleton's lifting of the "we" of criticism above the fray and Said's endorsement of an endless exile, even though Jameson still theoretically retains a notion of positive freedom that Eagleton and Said repudiate.

Postmodern Pragmatism

The most fervent postmodern antifoundationalists have been the neopragmatists, best represented by Jean-François Lyotard in France and by Richard Rorty, Stanley Fish, Steven Knapp, and Walter Benn Michaels in America. While recognizing their affinities with antifoundationalist theorists such as Derrida and Foucault, the pragmatists believe that even poststructuralism has not gone far enough because it is still tied to universalizing general assertions. The postmodern pragmatists' strategy has been to deny the possible cogency of any universal laws or constraints that "govern" particular utterances or acts of interpretation.[46] I highlight the word *govern* because much of the pragma-

---

[46]Thus Knapp and Michaels begin their essay "Against Theory": "By 'theory' we mean a special project in literary criticism: the attempt to govern interpretations of particular texts by appealing to an account of interpretation in general" (1985a 11). Rorty expresses his acceptance of this definition, including the word "govern," and "their [Knapp's and Michaels'] view that

tist animus against theory derives from the conviction that it illegitimately attempts to tyrannize over individual choices and acts. Such an understanding of theory is misleading, I argue, while also considering what appear to me to be serious flaws in the pragmatist position.

Rorty has recently sought to appropriate the term *postmodernism* to describe our culture's ascension to the true way of pragmatism,[47] while Lyotard's widely read *The Postmodern Condition* served, along with Jameson's essays on the subject, to place postmodernism at the center of critical discussion in the arts and in literary criticism by the early eighties. Some of the confusion about what postmodernism could possibly mean stems from Lyotard's and Jameson's use of the term to describe fundamentally incompatible things, a fact made abundantly clear in Jameson's foreword to the English translation of *The Postmodern Condition*. For disciples of Lyotard, my discussion of postmodernism in this book will seem to have missed all the important points, since I have devoted my attention (until now) to writers who still manage, in Rorty's paraphrase of Foucault, "to find Hegel waiting patiently at the end of whatever road [they] travel (even if [they] walk backward)" (1984 11). This emphasis in my work reflects my adherence to the Jamesonian insistence that postmodernism as a temporal term designates a historical period that is to be identified by a set of characteristics that operate across the whole historical terrain. Like Jameson, I am not only suspicious of claims that postmodernism means the acceptance that no such general operators exist any longer in our culture, but also committed to interpreting the very desire to make such claims as a primary symptom of the general conditions whose prevalence signals postmodernism's uniqueness. Jameson (rightly, I think) argues that Lyotard's postmodernism is merely a recycled version of "modernism as its first ideologues projected it—a constant and ever more dynamic revolution in the languages, forms, and tastes of art" (1984a xvi) and that in taking this position, Lyotard is "paradoxically enough" fairly close to the position of Habermas, who is supposedly Lyotard's main target.

Lyotard is determined to defend the local against the universal, and he takes theory as a primary instance of totalitarian terror. "Reason and power are one and the same thing. You may disguise the one with dialectics or prospectiveness, but you will still have the other in all its crudeness: jails,

---

'theory' . . . has got to go" (1985c 132). Similarly, Fish endorses Knapp's and Michael's definition and sets out explicitly to refute "theory [which] can be seen as an effort to govern practice" (1985 110).

[47]The essay "Postmodern Bourgeois Liberalism" makes it clear that Rorty primarily associates postmodernism with antifoundationalism, with the belief that there "are no ahistorical criteria" for moral or intellectual judgments. That Rorty sees such a position as Hegelian (as opposed to Kantian) highlights the oddity of calling it "postmodern" instead of the condition of "modernity."

taboos, public weal, selection, genocide" (1984a 11). Reason here is understood as aiming "for the unification of diversities." Theory, as the essential rationalistic activity, wants to establish a common vocabulary by which all things can be explained, located, and evaluated; successful theory constructs a hierarchical grid for arranging particulars that looks suspiciously like the surveillance techniques of disciplinary power as described by Foucault. "The notorious *universality* of knowledge, generally understood as an *a priori* condition of theoretical discourse's communicability is . . . a mark of the destruction of personal identities" (1974 295). As we might expect, Lyotard is particularly hostile to all forms of the dialectic; against dialectic syntheses, Lyotard champions the "*différend*," which he defines as "a case of conflict between (at least) two parties that cannot be equitably resolved for lack of a rule of judgment applicable to both arguments" (1988a xi).[48] Throughout his career, Lyotard has searched for "*différends*," for unassimilable particularities that stand over and against discursive totalities. Most notably, he has poised the visible figure against discourse itself (in *Discours, Figure*) and, later, the opacity and force of desire against the order of speech (in *Economie Libidinale*).[49] The continuity of this search with other poststructuralist attempts to identify an "other" to Western reason is obvious, but Lyotard's work more easily and consistently declares this other has been found than the more systematic and Hegelian ironies of Derrida's or Foucault's thought allow. In this respect, Lyotard is much closer to Deleuze than to the other two writers, in his fervent hostility to any form of dialectical thought, in his penchant for declaring an ontology of particularity, and in his belief that desire can provide the anarchic, system-resisting singularity he wants to find.

   In the work explicitly on postmodernism, to which I confine myself here, the principle of particularity is embodied in the concept of "incommensurability." The fundamental theoretical assertion of *Just Gaming* and *The Postmodern Condition* is that "no common measure" (1985c 50) exists among different language games. Language use is not subject to a set of universal rules but is organized instead into a number of smaller, more local purviews, each of which operates according to its own set of conventions, procedures, and goals. Pragmatics names the processes by which the local rules of the

   [48]On his enduring and formative hostility to Hegel, see Lyotard (1983 120–26). The speculations on the sublime in *The Postmodern Condition* and the *Artforum* essays are particularly indebted to Kant's *Critique of Judgment*, while, in general, the enterprise to construct incommensurate realms can be seen as an extension of Kant's differentiation of knowledge from morals and from art.
   [49]Dews (1987 109–43, 200–219) provides an excellent account of Lyotard's earlier work and his persistent "anti-dialectical dualism" (1987 130), his continual "search" for "the ineffably singular" (1987 136).

game are established. Nothing significant (either as universal rule or necessary constraint or predictive law) can be said about the general functioning of all language games; purely local conditions determine the direction that any particular game takes. (Lyotard appears to believe that this theoretical claim about the purely local nature of determinants justifies the very different assertion that nothing sets limits to the directions in which the game can go; localism becomes associated with endless "experimentation," a highly desirable situation in Lyotard's view.) Theory is understood as the illegitimate attempt to violate the independent uniqueness of each language game.

In *The Postmodern Condition*, the constraints that theory would impose are linked to the unifying pretensions of "grand narratives," which grant legitimacy only to local activities that bolster the unified communal identity that the narrative projects as the nation's or humanity's true (or best) self. Postmodernism is the pluralistic condition that arises when the practitioners of local games no longer pay heed to the constraints suggested by the grand narratives but instead pursue the logics of their own activities unmindful of nonimmediate purposes and consequences.

Lyotard makes it clear that the category of grand narratives includes not only nationalist stories of manifest destiny and humanism's celebration of autonomous selves but also Marxist schemas of emancipation—in other words, any generalizing explanation or purpose (*telos*) to which local action must be answerable. Needless to say, such a conclusion appears scandalous to most humanistic intellectuals, especially since, in *The Postmodern Condition*, this position is adopted specifically in relation to scientific research. Lyotard believes (apparently) that the way to disconnect scientific discoveries from their use for lamentable purposes is not to tighten the restrictions on what scientists can study according to some generalized moral formula but to sever completely the connection between research and the other language games of nationalist politics, morality, and the economic exploitation of technological innovations. It is the current answerability of research to such external concerns, Lyotard suggests, that produces results calculated from the start to be used by the defense department or the technocrat. Of course, Jameson would argue that the presumption that science could somehow remain clear of such constraints merely reinstates the by-now-discredited modernist faith that some kind of separate sphere of intellectual endeavor can be maintained. Lyotard himself eventually appears to concede that each language game's independence will be difficult to achieve and to maintain.

In addition to liberating language games from external, theoretically imposed (or identified) limitations, Lyotard also (in most cases) wants to downplay the existence of internal constraints. For him, postmodernism is an honorific epithet earned by those players of a language game who, through relentless "experimentation," invent "new rules of the game" (1984c 80). Modernity, according to Lyotard, can be described as the discovery that no unifying theory, no grand narrative, provides a foundation for our various activities. The modernist nostalgically mourns this loss or tries to reconstruct a language that would provide a foundational motivation. The postmodernist, on the other hand, practices a kind of Nietzschean affirmation, "the emphasis placed on the increase of being and the jubilation, which result from the invention of new rules of the game." Thus postmodern and modern cannot be distinguished from each other temporally, as Lyotard freely admits; they exist simultaneously, referring to two different responses to modernity.[50] In art, Lyotard consistently associates the postmodern attitude with the avant-garde, which he describes as obsessed (as he believes it should be) with the problematic of the "sublime," understood as the continual effort to capture in art "ideas of which no presentation is possible" (1984c 78). The avant-garde persistently stretches the language of art in its efforts "to make visible that there is something which can be conceived and which can neither be seen nor made visible."[51]

Even this brief summary of Lyotard's position suggests some of its problems, many of which he addresses in the remarkable set of dialogues with Jean-Loup Thébaud found in *Just Gaming*. First, we should note that the mysticism implicit in Lyotard's version of the sublime (as in his earlier notions of "figure" and "desire") is both obscurantist and crucial to his progressivism. Edward Said complains that Lyotard "*separates* Western postmodernism from the non-European world," thus "misread[ing] . . . the major challenge to the great narratives and the reason why their power may now appear to have

---

[50]See not only "Answering the Question: What Is Postmodernism?" (1984c 71–82) for this denial of any temporal specificity for the terms *modern* and *postmodern*, but also the essay "Historie Universelle et Différences Culturelles" (1985b), where "modernity" is presented as "not an epoch, but more a style . . . of thought, of utterance, of sensibility" (1985b 559).

[51]As we might expect, Rorty has no patience at all for Lyotard's speculations about and attachment to the sublime. "The desire for the sublime makes one want to bring the philosophical tradition to an end because it makes one want to cut free from the words of the tribe. Giving these words a purer sense is not enough; they must be abjured altogether, for they are contaminated with the needs of a repudiated community" (1985b 175). This insight brings Rorty to the edge of condemning negative freedom altogether. "Lyotard unfortunately retains one of the Left's silliest ideas—that escaping from such institutions is automatically a good thing, because it insures that one will not be 'used' by the evil forces which have 'coopted' these institutions. Leftism of this sort necessarily devalues consensus and communication, for in so far as the intellectual remains able to talk to people outside the avant-garde he 'compromises' himself" (1985b 174). Unfortunately, Rorty cannot see that his condemnation of "silliness" here applies as much to his own portrait of the ironist's private self-creation as to Lyotard's notion of an avant-garde in relentless and endless pursuit of the sublime. Rorty's *Contingency, Irony, and Solidarity* celebrates the sublimity of genius.

abated" (1989 222). To generalize Said's point: Lyotard's appeal to a sublime unrepresentable willfully neglects the very concrete "others" who have constantly prodded Western discourses to innovation. Lyotard wants to domesticate change, to portray it as the result of a purely internal process, or at least to understand the external as some mysterious other from the realm of Ideas. The very presence of the other in Lyotard's thought reflects his theoretical need to explain how or why a particular language game should ever change at all. Once freed from the oppression represented by a totalizing reason, there is nothing to motivate a local change in the rules of the game unless some kind of "anomaly" (to use Kuhn's term), some kind of inadequacy, appears. The "other" in Lyotard, that which is irreducible to the terms of any discourse, thus serves double duty as that which defeats the pretensions of theory and that which guarantees that the local will not be experienced as boring and deadly stasis. By making the anomalous other so vague, Lyotard can easily affirm, as a matter of principle, *all* the experiments of the avant-garde, while also ensuring the eternity of experimentation, since it will always remain "impossible to represent the absolute" (1982 68), a fact that underlies the "infinity . . . inherent in the very dialectic of search" (1982 69). Of course, the mystic can always defend his vagueness by claiming that imprecision is precisely the point; the experience of something that cannot be adequately represented by discourse suggests discourse's limits, even while it cannot be fully expressed.

But we should recognize that avoiding a concrete identification of an other that is understood as "absolute" entails avoiding a more concrete assessment of what specific strategies experimentation has devised to deal with those others. This problem surfaces in Lyotard's attempts to differentiate the "bad" postmodernism from the "good" postmodernism, where the first is represented by the art market and "techno-science" and the second is practiced by the avant-garde and research scientists.[52] Lyotard recognizes that the good postmodernists' constant attempt to extend the limits of language inevitably looks like bad postmodernism's (i.e., capitalism's) continual drive to appropriate everything and, using the universal language of commodity exchange, convert it into something marketable. Apart from philippics on "the habits of magazine readers [and] . . . the sensibility of the supermarket shopper" (1982 69) joined with noble pronouncements about art's "honor," the only substantial distinction between the two is that capitalism continually succeeds, whereas the avant-garde (in both art and science) continually fails. The

[52]For his various attempts to distinguish good from bad postmodernism, see Lyotard (1982, 1984c 73–81, and 1984d).

Lyotardian avant-garde protects its honor by continually pointing toward, but never actually grasping, those others that now lie beyond discourse, while greedy, insensitive capitalism simply yanks those others onto its terrain.

Which raises a second, and much more crucial, problem in Lyotard's account of language games. His whole polemic is directed against the tyrannies of theory and power, tyrannies that presumably demonstrate that the universalism that he declares is fundamentally impossible to achieve not only can be accomplished but can also be made institutionally, politically, and socially real. The trouble with "incommensurability" as a theoretical assertion of a necessary state of affairs is that the concept is so obviously constructed to combat the actual functioning of its opposite in today's world. "The plural, the collection of singularities, are precisely what power, kapital, the law of values, personal identity, the ID card, responsibility, the family and the hospital are bent on repressing" (1984a 10). That's an impressive array of forces ranged against pluralism, and it is rather hard to believe that assertions of "incommensurability" are going to do the job of liberation. This is Jameson's point. Lyotard wants to reenact the modernist solution of retreating to a separate space, apart from the terrors associated with the universalistic vocabularies of reason, of commodity, or of the nation. But such a retreat is a tribute to the powers that be (leaving the social totality in their hands). Furthermore, this retreat renders *postmodernism* an almost completely meaningless term, since only a prevalent sense that modernist strategies are ineffective and self-defeating justifies the insistence that something after modernism now informs the attitudes toward their work and its relation to society among most contemporary intellectuals. The oddness of *The Postmodern Condition* is that it popularized an essential postmodernist goal—pluralism—while advocating a modernist strategy to achieve that goal. The book's success is perhaps due to the assurance with which it offers that strategy, combined with its upbeat insistence that the goal has been reached. More cynically, we can argue that the book reassures intellectuals (and I think all humanistic intellectuals are in this position) who work hard at their particular fields without any firm sense of how that work contributes to society's movement in any specific direction that their devotion to their specialities is the very stuff of pluralism and is the way that the latest thing, postmodernism, is ushered into being. Such a view contrasts quite strongly with the agonies of postmodernism for more skeptical souls like Jameson, who view the goal of a democratic pluralism as farther away than ever and who proclaim that effective strategies for the achievement of that goal still elude us.

Why won't Lyotard's old wine in new bottles do? Several fundamental ambiguities haunt his version of pragmatism and, I argue, the version being

promulgated in America. First, there is the instability of the concept "language games" or its close cousin "speech communities." To protect the
notion of "incommensurability" (which is also a key concept in Rorty's work),
the walls between games or communities have to be rather high. The "incommensurable," in Rorty's version, is the "unfamiliar" in the sense that its
conventions are unknown to us and we do not share its goals or its grounds for
the adjudication of disputes.[53] The illustrating cases for such incommensurability are almost always drawn from one of two disciplines: history and
anthropology. That a different culture acts, or a different historical period
acted, out of fundamentally different assumptions is by now an almost universally accepted truism in the humanities and the social sciences. (It is worth
noting, however, that contemporaneous with the triumph of historical and
cultural relativism over the older humanist assertion of the "eternal verities"
to be found in the "great books," a new universalism has also arisen in the
disciplines attuned to what is called "cognitive science." Among the academic
human sciences, psychology, linguistics, and philosophy have proved especially open to claims that certain ways of processing information are universal
because dependent on the way the human brain functions.) For practitioners
in the humanities and human sciences who accept some version of the
incommensurability of foreign cultures and different historical periods, the
pressing question has been what could possibly overcome these barriers and
provide some adequate understanding of this other world view. Rorty provides the following advice on the appropriate way to approach the fundamentally unfamiliar, a world view with which we share no common ground: "If
there is no such common ground, all we can do is to show how the other side
looks from our own point of view. That is, all we can do is be hermeneutic
about the opposition—trying to show how the odd or paradoxical or offensive
things they say hang together with the rest of what they want to say, and how
what they say looks when put in our own alternative idiom" (1979 364–65).

I have no desire to pursue the epistemological agonies involved in trying to
figure out if such translation from their idiom to ours can ever be (theoretically or practically) possible when we begin from the premise of no common
ground.[54] I want to consider a different point: namely, how many different
language games or speech communities can be said to exist if the criterion of
identification is incommensurability.

Lyotard addresses this issue in *Just Gaming*: "When I say: there is no

[53]Rorty's fullest account of incommensurability can be found in *Philosophy and the Mirror of Nature* (1979 316–21).
[54]For important attempts to grapple with the epistemological dilemmas raised by notions of incommensurability, see Geertz (1979) and Bernstein (1983 79–108).

common measure, it means that we know of nothing in common with these different language games. We merely know that there are several of them, probably not an infinite number, but we really do not know. In any case, the number is not countable for the time being, or if it is, it is provisionally so" (1985c 51). The difficulty lies in making the generalizing terms *incommensurable* and *unfamiliar* concrete. What differences can be said to constitute full incommensurability? Pushed to one extreme, we get a particularism akin to Hume's skeptical universe (or Nietzsche's description of sense impressions in "Of Truth and Lies in an Ultramoral Sense"), in which no connection between any speech act and another can be established, an endless proliferation of "private languages." Pushed to the other extreme, all the members of a single nation, or the speakers of a single language, or even the inheritors of a single tradition can appear to share a fundamental world view. (In this last strategy the buck almost always stops at some fundamental East/West distinction. Jews and Catholics do not really appear to occupy incommensurate speech communities because they share something plausibly labeled the Judeo-Christian tradition; but no one talks of a Judeo-Muslim tradition or a Hindi-Christian tradition. The theoretical point is that justifying commensurability in the one case and its opposite in the other two would prove awfully difficult in the concrete; the practical point is that, the pieties of translators aside, we really do not pragmatically [i.e., as a matter of daily practice and belief] believe that the cultures of the West—Italian, German, French, English—are incommensurable. Given this practical assumption, a habitual enthnocentricity that crosses national boundaries, it is hard to see how incommensurability is going to generate any great plurality of games in the West.)

Neopragmatism, it seems to me, gets pulled in both directions, both toward an infinite particularism and toward a holistic incorporation of all utterances and all speakers within some definitive "form of life" (to use Wittgenstein's famous phrase). Knapp and Michaels take the particularist position: "Our insistence . . . that language is always intentional is no more than the positive side of the denial that preexisting forms, rules, or conventions are essential conditions of language" (1985b 145). Citing Donald Davidson's denial that "conventions . . . are essential to language," Knapp and Michaels can deny the aggregate notions of language games and speech communities (what they quote Rorty as calling "a system of community intentions") altogether in favor of an infinite variety and unpredictability of individual speech acts.[55] Yet Knapp and Michaels think of themselves as allies of Stanley Fish, who offers an equally (albeit diametrically opposed) strong insistence on the priority of

---

[55]The relevant essay by Davidson is "Communication and Convention" (1984).

the conventional: "You will always be guided by the rules or rules of thumb that are the content of any settled practice, by the assumed definitions, distinctions, criteria of evidence, measures of adequacy and such, which not only define the practice but structure the understanding of the agent who thinks of himself as a 'competent member.' That agent cannot distance himself from these rules, because it is only within them that he can think about alternative courses of action or, indeed, think at all" (1985 113).

Pragmatism swings between these two poles, depending on whether the writer is trying to emphasize the freedom/pluralism generated by the denial of metadiscursive conditions that constrain the production of particular speech acts or trying to explain how we happen to communicate with one another so successfully most of the time. Poised against Humean skepticism is Wittgensteinian holism. Rorty admits that his version of pragmatism has "no criterion of individuation for distinct languages or vocabularies to offer," but then calmly adds, "but I am not sure that we need one" (1989b 7).

Lyotard swings rather wildly between the particularist and holistic poles, thus enacting his own version of poststructuralism's inability to decide if a demonic monolith or a joyous heterogeneity best characterizes our current condition. In his most recent work, Lyotard has abandoned the term *language game* in favor of "phrase" and "genre." Incommensurability now exists among the various genres of discourse or even among its various phrases.[56] Obviously, the insistence that "a sentence presents a universe" (1983 129) greatly increases the number of incommensurate particularities; just as obviously, this proliferation of particulars breeds a new urgency for the question of how they are related to one another. Thus the new vocabulary of phrases and genres is accompanied by a new interest in "interlinking" (1983 129) and in what facilitates the "passage" (1984b 18) from one phrase to another. Even more astounding, since it seems to go against the major thrust of Lyotard's work, has been his description of *"petites histoires"* (1985b 564)—"small stories" in which particulars (represented by the proper name) are lodged. These *petites histoires* are, of course, contrasted to the *grand récits* of Western humanistic rationalism, the "universal histories" (1985b 559) that overlook local differences in favor of a global version of common humanity. However, Lyotard's example of *petites histoires*—the storytelling rituals of the Cashinahua Indians—explains how these narratives create a "communal identity sheltered from the events of 'right now'" (1985b 565) and how at the same

---

[56]Lyotard writes: "When I speak of *incommensurability*, I do not have in view the plurality of languages, but the plurality of genres of discourse. . . . I say that one can always pass from one genre to another, can change genres, but one cannot translate from one to the other" (1985a 581).

time the narratives create their own legitimacy. "The narrative authorizes itself. It authorizes a collective 'we,' outside of which there is only a 'they'" (1985b 566).

Lyotard completely endorses this result, insisting that "such an organization [of a culture and its identity] is in every way opposed to those of the grand narratives of legitimation which characterize Western modernity" (1985b 566). The unanimity achieved by small communities is neither tyrannical nor undesirable, apparently. Only larger, "cosmopolitan" abstractions are to be shunned. As with the distinction between "good" and "bad" postmodernism, Lyotard places himself here in the position of having to distinguish between good and bad narratives, good and bad achievements of a unifying cultural identity. And he never even considers the argument that the possibilities for pluralism are much greater in the modern West than in traditional cultures. We do not live in the golden age of pluralism—as Foucault's and Jameson's work makes abundantly clear—but to look to small, highly integrated, traditional communities for a better model of pluralism hardly seems the right way to go. Lyotard's affirmation of Cashinahua cultural identity indicates that a holistic goal of communal integration conflicts in his thought with his more usual championing of pluralistic particularism.

Furthermore, Lyotard, as another result of his ties to poststructuralism, realizes much more fully than his American counterparts that pluralistic particularism can in no way be linked to individualism. Once neopragmatism asserts (as it must, once it repudiates the notion of a "private language") that the lines between incommensurate language games do not coincide with the lines between individual selves, then pragmatist pluralism does not offer individual freedom of any sort. "We also know that there are games that we can enter into but not to play them; they are games that make us into their players, and we know therefore that we are ourselves several beings (by 'beings' is meant here proper names that are positioned on the slots of pragmatics of each of these games). . . . The fact that I myself speak of this plurality does not imply that I am presenting myself as the occupant of a unitary vantage point upon the whole set of these games, but simply that these games have the capacity of talking about themselves" (1985c 51).[57]

---

[57]Lyotard explains his switch from talk of "language games" to talk of "phrases" as explicitly motivated by the need to emphasize that individuals are not masters of the plurality his work desribes: "It seemed to me that 'language games' implied players that made use of language like a toolbox, thus repeating the constant arrogance of Western anthropocentrism. 'Phrases' came to say that the so-called players were on the contrary situated by phrases in the universes those phrases present, 'before' any intention. Intention is itself a phrase, which doubles the phrase it inhabits, and which doubles or redoubles the addresser of that phrase" (1984b 17).

Lyotard's comment here shows that taking incommensurability seriously, combined with the insistence that individuals themselves do not define the boundaries of incommensurability, leads to a notion of the self very close to the schizophrenic model put forward by Deleuze and Guattari, since the neopragmatist is positing parts of the self that cannot talk to one another, that have no common ground. Such fragmentation results in a very passive self, one that is simply "positioned" in each of the games it plays and is never able to gain a "vantage point" on the whole of its activities. Only an anarchist belief that random, disconnected action (or play) will disrupt the status quo can turn this passivity into a political asset.[58] Radical incommensurability offers no other way to imagine a self capable of altering the circumstances in which it finds itself positioned. The freedom of pluralism in Lyotard comes down to the freeing of each language game to play out its own internal dynamic. In certain ways, this view comes close to positive freedom; the positioned self works within the possibilities afforded by the concrete circumstances of a given situation and task. The language game, like Hegel's Spirit, moves down the grooves of its own logic. But where Hegel identifies the self with Spirit to allow for freedom, Lyotard dissolves the very notion of a self who is able to experience freedom.

Rorty sidesteps this problem by never acknowledging its existence. He simply combines certain fundamentally individualistic assumptions with an equally fervent adherence to Wittgensteinian holism. The radicals' charge against Wittgenstein has always been that he grants the speech community complete ascendancy over thought and self, thus assuring complete stasis. Rorty aligns himself with "the holistic point" that he claims Dewey, Wittgenstein, and Heidegger "hammer away at": "that words take their meanings from other words rather than by virtue of their representative character, and the corollary that vocabularies acquire their privileges from the men who use them rather than from their transparency to the real" (1979 368). Once this viewpoint is adopted, only two criteria for truth remain: coherence and the endorsement of one's statements by the community of one's peers. "Nothing counts as justification unless by reference to what we already accept, and . . . there is no way to get outside our beliefs and our language so as to find some test other than coherence" (1979 178). "Our only usable notion of 'objectivity' is 'agreement' rather than mirroring" (1979 337). Rorty lucidly recog-

---

[58]In the *Diacritics* interview of Lyotard conducted by Georges Van Den Abbeele, the first question asks for Lyotard's response "to the charge of seeking the new for its own sake. In the political sphere, the charge would be that of pursuing a liberalist pluralism, if not anarchism" (1984b 16). Unfortunately, Lyotard evades the question completely, never even addressing the issue of anarchism.

nizes that his pragmatism raises specifically the question of what "authorizes," what makes legitimate the assertions found in our utterances, and he insists that we should now realize that all such authority is social. There is no metaphysical, foundational, or independent truth apart from the social. To search for such transcendent sureties is to try to become God, to escape the very defining limits of humanity, of our rootedness in a social and temporal context. To embrace nonfoundationalist pragmatism "would be to abandon the hope of being anything more than merely human" (1979 377). (We find here the transcendental moment in Rorty's thought, his identification of the defining limits of the human.)

Obviously, Rorty's antifoundationalism, combined with his insistence on our being determinately embedded in the social and historical, is quintessentially postmodern, completely in sync with the ways I have been suggesting that we use that term. My argument, then, is not with Rorty's holism but with his apparent disregard for its consequences. The potential tyranny of social authority does not trouble Rorty because he ignores the anti-individualistic implications of Wittgenstein's work. Rorty simply adopts the dualistic position that "the public and private . . . [are] forever incommensurable" (1989b xv). Efforts at self-creation—like those found in "edifying philosophy," avant-garde art, and other attempts to shape new "final vocabularies"—are "wildly irrelevant to the attempt at communicative consensus" (1985a 174) that characterizes the effort to construct a *polis*. Such creative activities are confined "to us relatively leisured intellectuals, inhabiting a stable and prosperous part of the world" (1979 359). Just what allows "us intellectuals" to slip the nets of social authority and enjoy an individualistic quest unimpeded by the determinants identified by holism remains unclear. "Socialization, to repeat, goes all the way down" (1989b 185), but "the ironist—the person who has doubts about his own final vocabulary, his own moral identity, and perhaps his own sanity . . . has these doubts and needs because, for one reason or another, socialization did not entirely take" (1989b 186). If you assume a self standing over against a society that socializes as the originary situation, then incommensurability can cover a lot of theoretical sins.

A portrait of the liberal intellectual as perpetual ironist dominates Rorty's *Contingency, Irony, and Solidarity*. To protect the privileged individualism of the intellectual, Rorty divides human activities into a public and a private sphere and then posits novelty as the creative achievement of the private self. "This book tries to show how things look if we drop the demand for a theory which unifies the public and private, and are content to treat the demands of self-creation and of human solidarity as equally valid, yet forever incommensurable" (1989b xv). As we might expect, the pursuits of the private sphere are associated with "irony" and "autonomy." And what the ironist does has little consequence for anyone else. The ironist "is not in the business of supplying himself and his fellow ironists with a method, a platform, or a rationale. He is just doing the same thing that all ironists do—attempting autonomy. He is trying to get out from under inherited contingencies and make his own contingencies, get out from under an old final vocabulary and fashion one which will be all his own. The generic trait of ironists is that they do not hope to have their doubts about their final vocabularies settled by something larger than themselves. This means that their criterion for resolving doubts, their criterion of private perfection, is autonomy rather than affiliation to a power other than themselves" (1989b 97). A poor thing, perhaps, but at least mine own. Of course, Rorty also "reminds" us in the same book "of Wittgenstein's point that there are no private languages" (1989b 41). However, in presenting Nietzsche, Heidegger, and Derrida to us as "exemplars, as illustrations, of what private perfection—a self-created, autonomous, human life—can be like" (1989b xiv), Rorty never suggests (as Nietzsche's and Derrida's own works strongly imply) that the search for autonomy is riddled with contradictions and probably doomed to tragic failure.

Rorty carries the contradiction between the denial of a private language and autonomous self-creation more lightly. The statement that "for one reason or another, socialization did not entirely take" (1989b 186) in the ironist is no more helpful than Adorno's conclusion in *Negative Dialectics* that only "a stroke of undeserved luck" can explain what "has kept the mental composition of some individuals not quite adjusted to the prevailing norms" (1973 41). Rorty's final appeal is to the timeworn notion of the genius who transcends his age. In the case of Nabokov, Rorty refers to the novelist's "specially wired brain" (1989b 153 n. 15), a phrase hard to take seriously except that it gets repeated: "He [Nabokov] was a hero both to his parents and to himself—a very lucky man. He would have been a merely self-satisfied bore if it were not that his brain happened to be wired up so as to make him able continually to surprise and delight himself by arranging words into irridescent patterns" (1989b 155).

The sublimity of genius or, more mundanely, the tendency of contemporary intellectuals to be ironists results in a "widened gap between the intellectuals and the public" (1989b 82). Rorty reads Habermas's polemic against postmodernist thought (in *The Philosophical Discourse of Modernity*) as a protest against this gap, to which Rorty's proposed response is to make "a firm distinction between the private and the public. Whereas Habermas sees the line of ironist thinking that runs from Hegel through Foucault and Derrida as destructive of public hope, I see this line of thought as largely irrelevant to public life and political questions. Ironist theorists like Hegel, Nietzsche, Derrida, and Foucault seem to me invaluable in our attempt to form a private self-image, but pretty much useless when it comes to politics" (1989b 83). Nietzsche, and perhaps the late Foucault (with his talk of self-transformation), might accept this insulation of their work from all public consequence, but Hegel and Derrida surely would not endorse it. Philosophy in our time, Rorty believes, is "pursued as private meditation" founded on the "tacit admission that social prophecy, and the task of putting forward new imaginary significations, has now passed into other hands" (1989a 30), namely those of the novelists. Just why this reversal of the nineteenth-century association of philosophy with the public and the novel with the private and domestic should have occurred Rorty does not speculate; he displays a similar lack of interest in how, why, and in what specific times and places autonomy comes to function as the primary goal of private life.

Rorty's individualism, which is tied to his self-proclaimed bourgeois liberalism, would hardly be of much interest if it were not presented along with perhaps the most useful contemporary version of Wittgensteinian holism. I find what Rorty has to say about morality absolutely right—both in its reintroduction of the question of ethics into postmodern discourse and in its emphasis on the communal foundations of moral norms and their connection to issues of identity (communal identity and self-identity). Rorty insists that we "think of [morality] as the voice of ourselves as members of a community, speakers of a common language" (1989b 59). This view entails "that morality is a matter of what he [Wilfrid Sellars] calls 'we-intentions,' that the core meaning of 'immoral action' is 'the sort of thing *we* don't do.' . . . In Sellars's account, as in Hegel's, moral philosophy takes the form of an answer to the question 'Who are *we*, how did we come to be what we are, and what might we become?' rather than an answer to the question 'What rules should dictate my actions?'" (1989b 59–60). Morality is the contingent creation by a community of its own identity. At issue is how the private forging of an autonomous identity can be related to this communal act of creation. Rorty tries to finesse this gap by claiming that "the heroes of liberal society are the strong poet and the utopian revolutionary," not because they are "alienated" from society but because "the poet and the revolutionary are protesting in the name of the society itself against those aspects of the society which are unfaithful to its own self-image" (1989b 60). This formulation, as Rorty notes, places these heroes squarely *within* the social, thus effacing the distinction between reformer and revolutionary, a consequence I fully applaud. What Rorty does not acknowledge is that this formulation makes nonsense of the public/private distinction he tries to maintain elsewhere in the book. The strong poet's actions are not private, because they are based on and uphold a public ideal. The private is public and political in liberal society insofar as that society is constructed to ensure individualistic freedom and is legitimated by its success in that endeavor. It is one thing to insist that everything is not political—a position I believe it is important to endorse. Various decisions by selves and various social activities are not matters submitted to the procedures of political decision making, nor need they be. But the recognition of intersubjective relations that are not political is very different from the attempt to define a private sphere that isolates the individual from formative relations with others. It is the belief in the possibility of such a privacy that I would contest and that I understand as being denied by Wittgenstein's argument that a private language is impossible.

Rorty's assurance of the individual's possession of an identity apart from any particular community allows him to be completely vague about what constitutes a speech community. The criteria for truth, he writes in one place, "are just the facts about what a given society, or profession, or other group, takes to be good ground for assertions of a certain sort" (1979 385). If the individual were subordinated to the group, there would be serious consequences indeed if a "profession" were truly incommensurate with a "society," and Rorty would be forced to consider more carefully just how incommensurability might be experienced by selves. Instead, despite his reliance on the term, Rorty chooses not to take incommensurability very seriously. Faced with Lyotard's much more stringent (and hence much more consequential) version of the term, Rorty protests that "incommensurability is nothing more than a temporary inconvenience" (1985a 574), one that is overcome as soon as the individual finishes learning the initially incommensurate language game.[59]

This portrait of the individual who somehow escapes the consequences of social embeddedness is complemented by Rorty's dualism between systematic and edifying philosophy. Rorty appropriates Kuhn's distinction between

---

[59]The movement from an extreme understanding of "incommensurability" to an assurance that it is "only a temporary inconvenience" takes the bite out of the concept. Hilary Putnam (1981 113–19) offers a succinct critique of the thesis of incommensurability, specifically directed against Feyerabend's formulation of that thesis, but equally relevant to Rorty's and Lyotard's as well. Feyerabend's response (1987 265–72) appears to me, like Rorty's paling before the extreme version of incommensurability to which Lyotard adheres, to water down the whole notion to the point where it says little more startling than that it takes us some time to figure out the logic of a new or different mode of thought. I am dubious about the merits of the strong version of incommensurability but am merely perplexed by Feyerabend's and Rorty's desire to save the term, with all its far-reaching implications, for a condition that is so innocuous and is only temporary.

"normal" (systematic) and "abnormal" (edifying) discourses to elucidate the distinction he wishes to present. "Normal discourse is that which is conducted within an agreed-upon set of conventions about what counts as a relevant contribution, what counts as answering a question, what counts as having a good argument for that answer or a good criticism of it. Abnormal discourse is what happens when someone joins in the discourse who is ignorant of these conventions or who sets them aside" (1979 320). The key to Rorty's use of this Kuhnian distinction is that he thinks of the two as existing simultaneously, while Kuhn (to put it a little strongly) thinks of the two as mutually exclusive. In Kuhn, the triumph of an abnormal discourse necessitates that complete change in the prevailing normal practices which he calls a revolution. On the other hand, Kuhn recognizes that daily immersion in normal discourse acts as a strong impediment to the development of abnormal discourses. For this reason, revolutions are often associated with the young, with outsiders, or with newcomers to a field. Kuhn's holism leads him to see the normal and the abnormal as dialectically related opposites and to insist that the development of abnormal discourses is an exceptional occurrence and one with dramatic consequences.

For Rorty, however, abnormal discourse is something that happens alongside normal discourse, more a supplement than an antithesis. (Rorty's supplement, unlike Derrida's, is not presented as necessarily unsettling the assumptions of normal discourse.) "Abnormal and 'existential' discourse is always parasitic upon normal discourse . . . [and] the possibility of hermeneutics [which Rorty associates with 'edifying philosophy'] is always parasitic upon the possibility (and perhaps upon the actuality) of epistemology [which Rorty associates with 'systematic philosophy']" (1979 365–66). Similarly, the recent discussion of private genius accepts that "no project of self-creation through imposition of one's own idiosyncratic metaphoric can avoid being marginal and parasitic" (1989b 41). In Rorty's view, our need to be socially embedded, to know that the ground of the normal is there beneath our feet, is primary. "To attempt abnormal discourse *de novo*, without being able to recognize our own abnormality, is madness in the most literal and terrible sense" (1979 366). Instead of a Kuhnian revolutionary, Rorty's edifying philosopher is social man on a brief vacation, playing with new combinations and possibilities but not confusing them with the conditions that constitute daily life. Not surprisingly, then, edifying philosophy in Rorty becomes associated with all the attributes modernists such as Oscar Wilde or the New Critics ascribed to art. Philosophy (to paraphrase Auden) makes nothing happen, a position that Fish, Knapp, and Michaels have championed even more vociferously than

Rorty,[60] while edifying philosophy has "no goals outside itself" (1979 362). Rorty draws the parallel with modernism explicitly: "Pragmatism is the philosophical counterpart of literary modernism, the kind of literature which prides itself on its autonomy and novelty rather than its truthfulness to experience or its discovery of pre-existing significance" (1982 153). Rorty's confusion over whether pragmatism is modernist or postmodern accurately reflects the dualism of his thought; pragmatism is postmodern insofar as it is holistic, modernist insofar as it tries to protect edifying discourse's or private self-creative irony's "autonomy" from the social whole.

If edifying philosophy has any social role to play, that role, like the one Said assigns to criticism, is entirely negative. "Edifying philosophy is not only abnormal but reactive, having sense only as a protest against attempts to close off conversation by proposals for universal commensuration through the hypostatization of some privileged set of descriptions. The danger which edifying discourse tries to avert is that some given vocabulary, some way in which people might come to think of themselves, will deceive them into thinking that from now on all discourse could be, or should be, normal discourse. The resulting freezing-over of culture would be, in the eyes of edifying philosophers, the dehumanization of human beings" (1979 377). We live our lives on the terrain of normal discourse or, in Said's terms, within a culture. But the negative discourse of criticism or edifying philosophy (a gadfly) makes sure that we never feel so at home in normality that we refuse the possibility of change. We can see here why Rorty rejects Kuhn's dialectic of normal and abnormal discourse. Rorty does not want abnormal discourse to become the basis for the next normal discourse; rather, he wants abnormal discourse to function perpetually to unsettle the normal without ever constituting a new ground. The emptiness of this negative formulation rests in the fact that Rorty appears to endorse all change, anything that keeps the conversation rolling in new directions. Along with the fear of tyrannically imposed stasis, there also appears a fear of boredom (as Rorty's continual use of the word *interesting* to praise the new suggests). The moral imperative in Rorty's work (the avoidance of inhumanity) attaches not to any particular arrangement of our social world but to the continual willingness to abandon current arrangements in favor of new ones. Change, no matter to what or from what, earns his approval. As we have seen, there is much to be said for the argument that this point of view toward change presents the basic world view of dynamic, advanced capitalism, not some oppositional challenge to it.

[60]Fish's essay "Consequences" (1985) provides the fullest and most convenient summary of the neopragmatist contention that theory has no consequences.

Of course, Lyotard and Rorty are not merely apologists for capitalism, and I will now argue that they implicitly endorse a particular, positive model of society. But their inability to make this endorsement specific is typical of the problem I insist inflicts postmodern theory as a whole: the association of any established or definitive order with tyranny. The persistent belief that freedom can only be achieved through disengagement works against the holism that pragmatism puts forward. Neither Lyotard nor Rorty resolves the tension between that holism and the negative vision of freedom found in their work.

The first point to be made is that both writers rather misplace the locus of responsibility when they blame theory or systematic philosophy for the suppression of pluralistic freedom. True, theory can be exclusive and dismissive; true, theory can be seen as working in ways analogous to or reflective of power. But it is foolish to believe that theory simply legitimates itself within a particular social order. (Just as it is equally foolish to think that somehow the successful abolition of theory by the pragmatists or anyone else will end social tyranny.) We would be better off gauging the legitimated theory in any society as a symptom of that society's self-understanding and its self-constitution. Rorty seems on the verge of taking this tack, both when he presents postmodern pragmatism as the appropriate philosophical ideology of "bourgeois liberals" at this historical moment (1983 585) and when he identifies the real threats to edifying philosophy as coming "not . . . from science or naturalistic philosophy" but "from the scarcity of food and from the secret police" (1979 389). Yet Rorty never follows through on the import of these observations. He comes closest in "Postmodernist Bourgeois Liberalism" and (especially) his *Critique* essay on Lyotard's work, "Le Cosmopolitisme sans emancipation." But in the first case he allows his usual fight against foundational philosophy to derail him, and his defense of Wittgenstein against what he sees as Lyotard's distortions blurs his focus in the second. The crucial point he almost articulates is that it requires a particular, entirely specific social order to promote and guarantee pluralism. Rorty calls this order "bourgeois liberalism," partly to be provocative, but also to indicate an allegiance to traditions of individual rights and to democracy. The name is not at issue here; the important thing to note is that the negative endorsement of change, of the ever continuing conversation, is dependent upon and presupposes a much more positive vision of the social world that the conversationalists inhabit.

Disappointingly, Rorty's recent book once again reveals his blind spot on this issue. The ironist, he insists, inevitably has "an inability to empower. . . . She [the ironist] cannot claim that adopting her redescriptions of yourself and your situation makes you better able to conquer the forces which are marshalled against you. On her account, that ability is a matter of weapons and

luck" (1989b 91). What Rorty misses here (even though his comment about
the strong poet's speaking on behalf of of part of society suggests this possibility)
is that power within a social context is susceptible—not always, but also not
never—to persuasion, to protests about its illegitimate violation of prevailing
norms. In Rorty's work, once power enters the picture conversation ends and
we resort to "weapons and luck," which is why conversation is a luxury mostly
available "to us relatively leisured intellectuals, inhabiting a stable and prosperous part of the world" (1979 359). Rorty does not see how conversation, a
collective sense of grievance, or appeals to violated social norms, laws, and
procedures might be of use in struggling against instances of brute force.
Again, I stress that such means are no surefire solution to abusive power; but
neither are they negligible.

John Keane makes much the same complaint about Lyotard's position in
The Postmodern Condition, but even more strongly. "Postmodernism" of
Lyotard's sort, Keane argues, "*implies* the need for democracy, for institutional arrangements which guarantee that protagonists of similar or different
forms of language games can openly and continuously articulate their respective forms of life" (1987 13). The alternative to such institutions is anarchy
and/or the resolution of conflicts through the use of force. Incommensurate,
even incompatible, "forms of life" can exist side by side only where a positive
social order is built upon a general (holistic) consensus that these different
forms of life are inviolable *and* authority is vested in institutions that protect
that inviolability. Keane continues: "Postmodernism further *implies*, no doubt,
the need for *political* mechanisms (of conflict resolution and compromise)
which *limit* and *reduce* the serious antagonisms that frequently issue from
struggles among incompatible forms of life. Postmodernism does not imply
anarchism, for active and strong political institutions, as Tocqueville pointed
out against his contemporaries who dreamt of a withering away of the state,
are a necessary condition of preserving the democratic revolution" (1987 13–
14).

Infatuated as they are with enjoying the freedom of pluralism in spaces as
far from the normal as possible, neither Lyotard nor Rorty takes on the
question of the political arrangements required to create or maintain pluralism. But Rorty's endorsement of liberalism does include a positive reference
to "the institutions of Western liberalism" (1985a 571), a comment that
perhaps can be tied to his cryptic remark elsewhere about "the attempt at
communicative consensus which is the vital force which drives [a] culture"
(1985b 174). He recognizes that some kind of shared ethos must lie at the
foundation of a society's ability to tolerate differences ("an idea (in the
Kantian sense) . . . of tolerance" [1985a 571]), and even suggests that a

consensus about tolerance's priority/desirability must ground pluralistic liberalism. "The social glue holding together the ideal liberal society . . . consists
in little more than a consensus that the point of social organization is to let
everybody have a chance at self-creation to the best of his or her abilities, and
that that goal requires, besides peace and wealth, the standard 'bourgeois
freedoms'" (1989b 84). The casualness of this statement is matched by his
earlier description of "civility" or "civic virtue." "Hermeneutics views them
[people] as united in what he [Michael Oakeshott] calls a *societas*—persons
whose paths through life have fallen together, united by civility rather than by
a common goal, much less a common ground" (1979 318). But Rorty has
almost nothing to say about this principle that unites people who have passively just happened "to fall together." He appears to accept civility as unproblematically given in liberal societies at the very same time that he is
energetically deconstructing any other kind of unity (of knowledge or of
purpose) proposed by philosophers. That civility is not just given but may
actually have to be constructed is just barely suggested in the following
formulation, which begins with the admission that it might be missing at some
times and in some places: "What is needed is a sort of intellectual analogue of
civic virtue—tolerance, irony, and a willingness to let spheres of culture
flourish without worrying too much about their 'common ground,' their
unification, the 'intrinsic ideals' they suggest, or what picture of man they
'presuppose'" (1985b 168).

No wonder that the specter of brutal power (the "secret police" mentioned
at the very end of *Philosophy and the Mirror of Nature*) haunts Rorty's work as
the barely spoken. The gentle virtue of tolerance needed to keep the conversation going hardly seems up to the challenge of preserving civility against the
various versions of fanaticism or *Realpolitik* that view tolerance only as weakness. Lyotard's hypersensitivity to power's encroachment on free conversation, contrasted with Rorty's continual attempt to affirm that real conversa-
tions (the priority of "persuasion over force" [1985a 578]) do take place in our
Western world, provides the fundamental difference highlighted by their
Critique debate. Lyotard depends on the self-directed activities of independent language games to defeat power's unifying aims, whereas Rorty relies on a
general ethos of tolerance to protect individual differences. Neither writer
considers the concrete political and institutional work required to make
norms of civility and tolerance effective against threats to them.

The notions of civility and of solidarity reintroduce holism into Rorty's
pluralistic pragmatism. And this foundational civility, to which all must subscribe if pluralism is to survive, is hardly contentless. Appearances to the
contrary, tolerance is not a purely negative category. Even if we disregard

Keane's insistence that strong and active institutions are needed to ensure civility, we must recognize (as Rorty does) that his definition of the civic virtues would appear ridiculous to a Roman in the year 100, not to mention a neoconservative in the year 1990. But we concede far too much to the conservative if we attempt to deny that a culture's health, its ability to live in peace and pursue the normal activities of daily life undisturbed by internecine conflicts, depends on its maintaining a strong group identity. The distinction between conservative and pluralist here is not the promotion of group identity by the former and its denial by the latter; rather, the pluralist works to construct and preserve a different identity, one built not on ethnic, religious, or racial grounds, but on the commitment to the civic virtues required to make democracy and tolerance work. The 1980s suggested that the pluralist may be at a terrible disadvantage in this attempt; she is asking the group to rally around an identity that often does not appear to have the immediate gut-level appeal of the conservative banners. But we should also not underestimate how deeply the culture of democracy is rooted in American culture (to bring the issue directly home for a moment) and how successful appeals to that democratic culture can be at times when it is threatened. This assurance, of course, does not solve any problems in itself, and the struggle over how Americans define themselves and how they understand the ground rules of the civility that underlies their interactions will continue. The theoretical point to be made is that the pluralist promotion of tolerance should not and cannot be seen as simply dissolving any common identity shared by the members of a society. In other words, edifying discourse (or criticism) cannot simply be content to keep normal discourses from ossifying. Like it or not, abnormal discourse also has to make a positive case for why it should be tolerated and become involved in forging that "communicative consensus" which produces a social order in which it will be tolerated. We can view this necessity of making a positive case at those moments when Said and Rorty are pushed to the wall and associate criticism with what is "life-enhancing" (or edifying discourse with accepting what it means to be human), or imply that tolerance is the road to reducing cruelty.

Lyotard, like Rorty, demonstrates that he half recognizes this necessary positive component to his project, both in his celebration of the Cashinahua Indians' cultural identity and in the more strictly philosophical musings of *Just Gaming*, a text that shifts the neopragmatist discussion from the endless epistemological debates about theory's legitimacy to the ethical consideration of pragmatism's political and moral ramifications. Lyotard states the issue quite clearly in the following consideration of what the principle of incommensurability and the resultant pluralism might mean politically.

The picture that one can draw from this observation [of incommensurability] is precisely that of an absence of unity, an absence of totality. All of this does not make up a body. On the contrary. And the idea that I think we need today in order to make decisions in political matters cannot be the idea of the totality, or of the unity, of the body. It can only be the idea of a multiplicity or of a diversity. Then the question arises: How can a regulatory use of this idea of the political take place? How can it be pragmatically efficacious (to the point where, for example, it would make one decision just and another unjust)? Is a politics regulated by such an idea of multiplicity possible? Is it possible to decide in a just way in, and according to, this multiplicity? And here I must say that I don't know. (1985c 94)

Not surprisingly, as soon as he pursues these questions, Lyotard moves toward formulating a general principle of tolerance. He identifies "terror" as the primary threat of our age, defining its occurrence as "when . . . a language game begins to regulate language games that are not the same as itself" (1985c 99). Such interventions must necessarily be "assisted by the sword," since the fact of incommensurability ensures that no language game could ever enter into a dialogue with another. "That is why it is just to maintain this plurality. And any attempt to state the law, for example, to place oneself in the position of enunciator of the universal prescription is obviously infatuation itself and absolute injustice, in point of fact" (1985c 99). Lyotard's intention here is clear enough: a kind of pluralism of universal tolerance and noninterference. Lyotard's response to the threat of abusive power is to declare *all* uses of force illegitimate and unjust. And his ontological grounding for this principle of illegitimacy is the "fact" of incommensurability. Given the extreme vagueness of incommensurability and the very dubiousness of its existence, the practical enactment of Lyotard's position appears hopeless. How do we know which language games count as truly incommensurate? Does invasion of incommensurate language games really describe the terror practiced by Nazi anti-Semites or by leftist guerrillas in Peru and right-wing death squads in El Salvador? If, as Lyotard's work half implies, force can be legitimately used against groups that try to violate incommensurability, then clearly discernible boundaries between language games must be identified (so we know when violations occur) and a universally binding prescription against violation must be in place as the foundation of legitimate force.

Lyotard appears to accept reluctantly that he cannot evade this last point. "Yes, there is first a multiplicity of justices, each one of them defined in relation to the rules specific to each game. . . . And then the justice of multiplicity: it is assured, paradoxically enough, by a prescriptive of universal value. It prescribes the observance of the singular justice of each game" (1985c 100). Only a universal prescription of tolerance as the essence of

justice can protect the multiplicity of language games against the encroachments of terroristic power. Thus, in order to preserve multiplicity and incommensurability, Lyotard is forced to contradict these very principles and to
produce a rule that applies to all language games.

Lyotard recognizes the fact of this contradiction, as his use of the word
paradoxically indicates, as does his tortuous, if finally unsuccessful, attempt to
avoid this conclusion during the dialogue that constitutes *Just Gaming*. And,
in *Peregrinations*, he signals his recognition that the contradiction extends to
any vision of a society able to uphold this principle of justice. "It seems to me
that the only consensus we ought to be worrying about is one that would
encourage this heterogeneity or 'dissensus'" (1988b 44). The phrasing here
emphasizes the paradox but cannot obviate the fact that some basic consensus
must lie at the foundation of a political community: we have to agree to
disagree. A liberal or anarchist theory built upon an assertion of "incommensurability" or the absolute distinction between the public and the private finds
itself pushed into recognizing the public, social constitution of these separa-
tions (of one language game from another, of one self from another) once that
theory eschews any metaphysical claim about incommensurability or autonomy. Only some political order, organized around some consensus, can
preserve incommensurability or privacy in a world where power or a different
kind of social order is always capable of violating these separate spaces.
Where there are no metaphysical guarantees, there can be only communal,
political ones, and that means that the conditions of action and of freedom
must be the products of a social order, not the result of an achieved distance
from that order.

To raise the issue of a prior social consensus that establishes the conditions
for freedom of language games or conversation or individual action is to
emphasize how close the neopragmatists are to Habermas. This convergence
is, in one way, not surprising, since Habermas is deeply indebted to the same
pragmatic tradition from which Rorty and Lyotard derive much of their
inspiration. Even more crucially, Lyotard's explicit concern with the issue of
legitimacy and Rorty's desire to preach the superiority of persuasion to force
means that each must provide a way of distinguishing what counts as acceptable social practice and what does not. Lyotard often appears to want to avoid
this necessity; he veers from declaring everything illegitimate (power infects
everything) to declaring everything acceptable (a moral anarchism grounded
by the relativism introduced by incommensurability). But his use of the
vocabulary of legitimacy continually pulls him back from this kind of monism.
Thus what I would consider the honorable contradiction expressed at the end
of *Just Gaming* stems from Lyotard's willingness to accept that his whole

enterprise needs—indeed, is predicated upon and motivated by—a norm, even though his ontological pluralism does not entitle him to that norm. Foucault, as we have seen, steadfastly took the opposite approach for most of his career, refusing to admit the normative foundations of his work. Rorty, unafflicted by poststructuralist worries about how our ideas are constituted by social power, can unabashedly endorse the norms appropriate to Western liberalism.

Insofar as Rorty and Lyotard explicitly understand themselves as writing against Habermas's position, however, the affinity between their thought and his is odd.[61] I think that the cause of the confusion is the misleading understanding of theory to which the postmodern neopragmatists subscribe. Habermas comes up in *Philosophy and the Mirror of Nature* when Rorty argues that contemporary thinkers should "give up any hope of the 'transcendental'" (1979 381). Habermas is a prime example for Rorty of a philosopher who will not give up this hope, and Rorty quotes his description of transcendental theory (in *Knowledge and Human Interests*) in order to attack it: "Habermas says that for a theory to 'ground itself transcendentally' is for it to 'become familiar with the range of inevitable subjective conditions which both make the theory possible *and* place limits on it, for this kind of transcendental corroboration tends always to criticize an overly self-confident self-understanding of itself'" (1979 381). Rorty's objection to Habermas's transcendentalism is that it partakes of "the primal error of systematic philosophy": the "attempt to answer questions of justification by discovering new objective truths" (1979 383). The theoretical philosopher "substitut[es] pseudo-cognition for moral choice."

Rorty has constructed a straw man here, especially if we focus on Continental philosophy from Kant to the present. Plato and Descartes, along with

---

[61]Rorty has slowly moved from seeing Habermas as an opponent to a recognition of their affinity. The discussion of Habermas in *Contingency, Irony, and Solidarity* (1989b 61–69, 83–88) recognizes that Habermas and Rorty do not have "any political disagreement . . . [only] what are often called 'merely philosophical' differences" (1989b 67). The complaint remains, as we would expect, that Habermas still wants to rely on "universalism or rationalism" to ground "democratic society," whereas Rorty "is content to call 'true' (or 'right' or 'just') whatever the outcome of undistorted communication happens to be, whatever view wins in a free and open encounter." From my point of view, Rorty's obsession with Habermas's talk of reason blinds Rorty to the more important point that procedures and norms for determining what counts as "free and open encounter" must be operative in the culture *before* we can accept the outcomes of such encounters. That Habermas labels such norms and procedures "rational" obscures the issue, as do his appeals to their universal character, but these objections do not mean that we give up the transcendental task of delineating the specific norms and procedures that prevail in a particular social context or that we have no ways of assessing the relative benefits and desirability of different sets of norms and procedures. See Habermas (1986 158) for his sympathetic account of Rorty's work.

that branch of academic Anglo-American philosophy which has somehow managed to ignore the fact that Wittgenstein's *Philosophical Investigations* was ever published, may make systematic philosophy's primal error, but it would be hard to see how critical philosophy does. Inevitably, since "transcendental" is the focal point for Rorty's attack, Kant is the proper name he uses again and again (in both *Philosophy and the Mirror of Nature* and in his essays) to designate the attempt to locate foundational, eternal principles that make choice unnecessary. Yet Rorty is constrained to admit parenthetically in *Philosophy and the Mirror of Nature* that moral choice in Kant is "not based on *knowledge*, since our grasp of the categories is not a *cognition*" (1979 383), just a few sentences before he blasts the "ever more complicated post-Kantian attempts to reduce freedom to nature, choice to knowledge" (1979 384).

Two major—and completely contradictory—positions stem from this caricature of transcendental theory. Both positions are found in Rorty, whereas (more consistently) Stanley Fish has become the major exponent of the one and Lyotard the standard-bearer of the other. The first position declares the whole theoretical project impossible, and hence inconsequential (in the strictest sense). Theory, the argument goes, aims to provide ahistorical and permanent grounds for practices that are always only local, ad hoc, and variable. As a result, theory is just a peculiar intellectual mistake that afflicts Western intellectuals and has absolutely no impact on the actual behavior of human beings, not even on the theorists themselves. Just why Fish, Knapp/Michaels, and Rorty should expend so much energy refuting pointless theorizing is unclear. The second position, of course, is that theory is tyrannical, that it governs practice (or at least tries to). Knapp and Michaels are clearly motivated by their anger at theory's pretensions, even though their own position assures them that those pretensions are preposterous and completely unrelated to anything theory could accomplish in fact. Lyotard (like Derrida and Foucault) takes theoretical tyranny's potential success much more seriously, mostly through adopting the French propensity to establish a continuity between theoretical thought and the mechanisms of dominance and exclusion found in social arrangements. Rorty waffles here, often chiding the French for being paranoid but not always sure that the philosophers have done no harm. It is tempting to ascribe this difference between the French and American positions to the relative attention and prestige accorded to intellectuals in the two countries.

If we return to Habermas's description of transcendental thought, however, we can recognize that the neopragmatists set themselves against a type of theory that Habermas himself does not advocate; among post–World War I European thinkers, only the structuralists and possibly Karl-Otto Apel present a theory that makes any claim to governing the variety of possible actions. Pierre Bourdieu's attack on structuralism in *Outline of a Theory of Practice* upbraids structuralist theory for the same faults that neopragmatism assigns to theory *tout court*. Bourdieu, however, both portrays the position of his specific target much more accurately than the neopragmatists do and avoids their mistake of thinking that the implausibility of one kind of theory invalidates all theoretical thought. In particular, Bourdieu's essential argument— that practice is the contingent use of strategies rather than a determined following of rules—in no way rules out either the validity or the utility of transcendental thought.[62] In delineating the conditions within which the multiplicity of acts takes place, transcendental thought does not *govern* those actions. Rather, transcendental thought indicates the limits that define whether a particular action counts as an action of this category or does not count.

This point can be illustrated by considering a game—say, basketball. The transcendental part is the rule book, but the rule book does not govern what players actually do on the court, what strategies they adopt at particular moments in the game. The rule book, however, does define what actions can count as playing basketball; these actions do not necessarily even constitute a finite set. Endless innovation in basketball might be possible (as the "moves" of a great player suggest), but the transcendental conditions allow us to identify whether an entirely novel move counts as playing basketball or not. In any case, I hope it is obvious how foolish it would be to claim that the rule book "governs" the actions of the players on the court; the rule book only delimits the terrain in which their contingent strategies are shaped and enacted.

When we move from games where a rule book has been explicitly drawn up and can be referred to when the boundaries of what counts are in dispute to a social world in which the transcendental conditions are less clear, matters become much more complicated. (Of course, the whole notion of using a constitution to ground a social order derives from the hope of avoiding the more debilitating of these complications.) When transcendental thought sets itself forward as describing the defining conditions of some social sphere or some social action-type, of course, the specifics of its formulation of those conditions can always be questioned. And inevitably, that questioning will always raise the charge or the worry that the processes of transcendental thought have been infected by the interests (political, social, or economic) of the thinker. Thus we can argue that Kant's division of the epistemological from the ethical, his claim that different ground rules define what counts as

[62]See Bourdieu (1977), especially chaps. 2 and 3.

knowledge and what counts as morals serves to sever the technological from the moral, to the great advantage of capitalist industrialists. But it is crucial to see that such arguments in no way question the validity of transcendental thought as a theoretical activity. The only way to attack transcendental theory as an activity is to deny the cogency or validity of drawing distinctions between different spheres or categories of activities. In other words, only a truly global monolithic holism obviates the need for the distinctions to which transcendental thought attends. As soon as any notion of differentiated spheres of social activity enters, a theory that identifies the principles of differentiation becomes possible, perhaps even necessary.

It certainly could be argued that my description of transcendental thought in the preceding paragraph makes much more modest claims for its goals and its accomplishments than Kant wanted to put forward. I am taking for granted, for starters, that transcendental thought can be historicized without losing any of its essential characteristics. In fact, by stressing transcendental thought's function in delineating the various conditions that obtain in different social spheres, I am making a case for its being a particularly suitable tool for the identification of historical differences. Kant, with his commitment to universal conditions, would not have welcomed this transformation.

Similarly, Kant undoubtedly had a stronger sense of how the categories of pure reason (for example) governed perception than I am allowing to transcendental thought here. But in that case my argument is that Kant, like the structuralists, misunderstood the relation of rules or conditions to the contingencies of practice. That Kant made this mistake does not invalidate transcendental theory as an activity, only some aspects of Kant's own theorizing. Habermas, like Bourdieu, attempts to salvage theory from its past excesses, and I think both succeed in demonstrating that there is no necessary connection between the theoretical delineation of transcendental conditions and a tyrannical or foolish (because doomed to failure) attempt to govern individual practices. Habermas explains his transcendental position as identifying "conditions of symmetry and reciprocal recognition which are unavoidable presuppositions of communicative action" (1986 206–7), but insists that, even after the transcendental identification is made, "the common business of political discourses among citizens nevertheless stays what it is. It [i.e., political discourse] is not a philosophical enterprise. It is the attempt of participants to answer the question 'what now?'—in these circumstances, for us particular people, what are or would be the best institutions" (1986 204–5). Identifying the conditions within which discourse takes place has no influence on the specific content of the discourse or the conclusions (or impasses) it might reach.

With this last comment, I seem to have swung to the other pole of the neopragmatist attack on theory. In refuting the notion that theory tyrannically governs practice, I now seem to accept that theory has no consequences. I think the actual situation might be better characterized by saying that theory aspires to reform practice, and that it believes that changing the way we think about the fundamental conditions in which practice takes place will precipitate reform. (I am tempted to add that this belief is in itself a transcendental condition, a sine qua non, of intellectual life. This condition would be captured by accepting Castoriadis's description of intellectuals as "those who, by their use of speech and through their explicit formulation of general ideas, have been able or are now able to attempt to have an influence on how their society evolves and the course of history" [1988 163]. We intellectuals only do what we do in the hope that it can make some difference.)

Kant wants to reveal the limits of what can count as knowledge in order to prevent the impossible quest for certainty of a particular kind and in particular spheres, a quest whose inevitable (according to Kant) frustration justified Humean skepticism. Kant cannot prevent the practice of seeking such knowledge, but he can try to reform us, to make us see that such practices are futile and pointless. Similarly, Rorty's delineation of the limits of the human is meant to discourage the attempt to gain the universal, ahistorical viewpoint traditionally attributed to God. But such reformism is not equivalent to making such misguided practices impossible, or outlawing them. Rather, theory is the name for a particular procedure (that of transcendental thought) for identifying the limits placed upon and conditions under which human action takes place; under the conditions of modernity, this identification of limits only claims to apply to human action here and now.

Practice has countless other procedures for making the same investigation. Theory's uniqueness, we might say, comes from its belief that it can make this identification by not doing anything, just by thinking. And theory is committed to justifying its conclusions by not only marshaling empirical and historical evidence (these aims have been achieved, these have proved unattainable), but also by providing arguments formed according to the canons of rationality. Viewed this way, it is much more fruitful to see Habermas's project as the description of the conditions of communication that *already exist within* a society, that serve as that society's fundamental ties of inclusion, rather than to view him as trying to achieve, through prescriptive rules, a desired but thus far unattained consensus. Habermas wants to see what the agreements we already possess as members of a particular society enable us to do, not to force some new agreement on us. Of course, Habermas's attempt to detail meticulously the terms of that existing agreement and his attempt (less evident in the more recent works) to tie those terms to "universal reason" has distracted many of his critics, who object (as I do) to some of the specifics of his formulation. But this argument over specifics is an argument against theory per se only if we insist that every statement of limits introduces a "false necessity," that our actual birthright is an "absolute freedom" that theory's identification of limits seeks to rein in illegitimately. Finally, I should stress that, while I believe in the existence of existential limits (the amount of oxygen we need in the air in order to survive), the crucial limits identified by transcendental theory are historical and social, the delineation of what is possible in a specific intersubjective setting.

Neopragmatism's true significance, then, lies not in its abandonment of theory, but in its forceful identification of the individual speech act's location within the constraints of social authority and social possibility.[63] Obviously, the notion of incommensurability in Lyotard, the description of theory's impossibility in Fish, and the designation of human limits in Rorty all function as transcendental statements of the confines of the possible and are aimed at reforming practice. These writers are all transcendental in exactly the way described by Habermas. But this inconsistency is not the most interesting thing about their work. Rather, it is their need to think through and to theorize the social limitations on thought, speech, and action once the notion of universal, natural limitations is discredited. Lyotard's attempt to construct a principle of justice, Fish's recent interest in the institutional settings of discourse, and Rorty's notion of the judgments of one's peers and of civility indicate a recognition that anarchy is both a highly unusual historical/social circumstance and a highly undesirable one.

In trying to articulate the social grounds for conversation, the neopragmatists share the fundamental research goal of Habermas. Their inability to recognize this affinity resolves, I believe, into three related blindnesses. First, they practice a version of transcendental thinking, even while they eschew it. Second, the neopragmatists devote their energies to refuting objectivism, universalism, and other theoretical tyrannies, instead of focusing on ways to act politically to counteract the threats of power and force. This strategy creates a need to deny their own theoretical moments, or at least to pass over the more positive components of their thought (Lyotard's principles of incommensurability and justice, Rorty's notions of civility and tolerance) too quickly. Habermas, on the other hand, openly acknowledges his need of positive theoretical conclusions about the conditions of social interactions to combat power. Caught up in their negative, antitheory polemics, the neoprag-

---

[63]Knapp and Michaels are the exception here, since they refuse to grant any authority to context and convention.

matists thus see Habermas as on the other side. Finally, the neopragmatists' fear of theory's tyrannies means that they devote almost all their attention to the negative disentanglement from the conditions and limits theory identifies. Their own theoretical assertions remain undeveloped and vague in the course of their attacks on more specific theories, like those of Habermas. Temperamentally, the neopragmatists are ashamed of or frightened by their own need to resort to theory at times. (The tortured process by which Lyotard finally forces himself to enunciate a principle of justice in *Just Gaming* is a perfect illustration.) Thus Habermas's cheerful acceptance of theory's necessity and his very specific description of the social conditions needed for communication untainted by power clash with neopragmatism's gut-level suspicions of theory, despite the fact that Habermas' specifics are closely related to such notions as civility and tolerance.

Neopragmatism, like the other postmodern theories, remains caught between a theoretical vision of the inevitable placement of subjects within historical and social conditions and the notion that freedom resides in breaking through the limits of those conditions. This allegiance to negative freedom has resulted, in the intellectual world, in a repudiation of theory itself, because theory is identified with the limits it designates. (Theory, as the bearer of the message of limits, is killed for bringing bad news.) Yet, as the more astute (and more tortured) postmodern theorists recognize, their own work can hardly claim not to be doing theory. The postmodernists proceed (despite Derrida's experimental texts and Rorty's claim about abandoning arguments in favor of telling stories) according to forms of rational argument practiced since Descartes's time and now institutionally established in the West's universities; similarly, they transcendentally identify limits, if only to demonstrate the impossibility of "traditional" theory's claims. The result is an inevitable legitimation crisis among intellectuals, who appear doomed to keep practicing an art (called theory) about whose utility they are dubious (often claiming that it is positively harmful) and whose procedural canons appear indefensible. No wonder that dreams continually resurface of somehow escaping the whole mess. I am convinced, however, that not only is the pursuit of negative freedom logically inconsistent with everything postmodernism tells us about the relation of subjects to the social worlds that they inhabit, but it also has the undesirable consequence of continuing (all the contemporary claims to the contrary notwithstanding) the modernist separation of the intellectuals from the political lives of the nations to which they belong. In the next chapter I present an alternative model, one that tries to find for the intellectual a recognizable and constructive role in a society's politics.

4

Positive Freedom and the Recovery of the Political

In the preceding chapter, I tried to indicate that postmodern theory aims to discover some alternative principle of action to that offered by contemporary Western society, but that this aim is vitiated by the habitual association of opposition with distance and exteriority. Internal strategies of disruption and of generating pluralism are only fitfully employed by the writers I discuss. On the whole, these writers remain wedded to modernist notions of distance and disengagement as enabling radical critique, notions that their own attack on autonomous models of selfhood render inoperable.

What we need instead is an account of the self's inevitable immersion in the social that also explains how selves can experience themselves as integral agents capable of dissenting from or choosing alternative paths among the options social situations present. The fundamental point is that a holistic view of society does not eliminate the possibility of differences (as Hegel struggles to indicate). The prevailing conviction among contemporary intellectuals, however, has been that holism is equivalent to tyranny and to an undifferentiated monolith. Poststructuralism, with its "grand theory" portraits of Western metaphysics and disciplinary power, has been largely responsible for the prevalence of such unsophisticated images of social totality among literary intellectuals. But we should not discount the continuing strength of the liberal tradition in the West, with its abhorrence of holistic thought and its fundamental fear of the social abrogation of what it deems the individual's prerogatives. The oddity of postmodern thought is that it has clung to a liberal image of negative freedom even while deconstructing the self who could embody that freedom.

TOWARD A POSTLIBERAL DEMOCRACY

An adequate holistic social theory will have to be more complex, more differentiated, than the social model found in most postmodern texts, while also adopting the postmodern attack on liberal individualism. Following Samuel Bowles and Herbert Gintis, I will call the model this chapter presents "postliberal democracy." To a certain extent, this model functions as a Weberian "ideal type," since it exists at a level of abstraction above the particular circumstances in each different Western democracy. My model does not claim to be universal, however, because it assumes conditions of possibility that prevail only in those countries where Western liberalism and Western democracy have had some sway (even if not always, or not very often, dominant) over the past one hundred years or more. In other words, the model is meant to be both descriptive (at a very general level) and prescriptive, the first insofar as it indicates fundamental principles within which the democratic societies of the West proceed, the second insofar as it indicates that certain features of liberalism should be jettisoned because they hinder the movement toward an even more fully realized democracy. My mixture of the prescriptive and the descriptive in this chapter is, I grant, questionable. What I have in mind is an attempt to bring the ethical to bear within the political, a process that cuts both ways, as I try to consider the form of a *polis* that is responsible to an ethical imperative of democracy and to consider the political exigencies of actual community decision making to which ethical imperatives must submit. My understanding of the "political" and the "ethical" is taken from Tobin Siebers:

> If Aristotle was correct . . . the ethical and the political should not differ considerably, and when they differ, it should be largely in the nature of the community that they address. The ethical aspires to a wholly inclusive community, and it is therefore oriented toward the future and possesses a more theoretical and abstract dimension. It is interested in the realm of practice, although its notion of practice might be better described as an essentially hypothetical operation geared toward obtaining an ideal state of human cohesiveness. The political also aspires to a wholly inclusive community, but it exercises itself on a community already in existence and therefore tends to restrict itself to the temporal and geographical limitations of that community. (1989 219–20)

Even an ethics of difference, which might insist that the ideal of a wholly inclusive community is not its aim, would have to practice a politics of appeal to existent communities in order to get its ethic adopted.

In taking democracy as the primary good, I am accepting the postmodern ethical a priori. In the ensuing discussion, the word *democracy* is used to designate social arrangements that guarantee that public decisions are made through processes that allow for the full and equal participation of each citizen. Anthony Arblaster ties democracy to the

> idea of popular power. . . . What is distinctive about the politics of the past century [is that] . . . the consent, acceptance, or support of 'the people' has increasingly become the principle source of legitimacy for governments and regimes. . . . Invocations of popular support or consent may be baselss and even blatantly dishonest. But 'hypocrisy is the tribute vice pays to virtue,' and in the twentieth century democracy represents political virtue. Those who pay lip-service to a principle they do not intend to put into practice always run the risk of being outflanked by those whose homage is more sincere. Hence the idea of democracy, or of popular power, however much and however easily it is abused and exploited, still retains a radical potential. There will always be some who are apt to ask whether existing electoral arrangements do conform to the basic principle of popular power; or whether this principle should not be applied in areas of privilege and power hitherto untouched by it. (1987 8–9)

I take it for granted that the basic civil liberties of the Western democracies as well as an equality of status among all citizens/participants are essential preconditions for any possible establishment of a democratic society.[1] Post-liberal democracy, however, does not base the civil liberties on any notion of natural rights or the inviolability of autonomous individuals but justifies them as necessary means to the desired end of democracy. The social adoption of the specific goal of democracy contrasts with deontological liberalism and points toward the insistence that positive action, not just the negative removal of constraints, is required to create and sustain a democratic society. I argue that the best ways to promote a more democratic society lie along holistic paths that postmodernism and liberalism have spurned. Finally, postliberal democracy entails adopting a version of the radical critique of liberalism's way of defining the distinction between public and private concerns. The possibility of democracy is undermined by the inequities generated in spheres that liberalism deems private and therefore beyond the jurisdiction of public decisions.[2]

[1]See Arblaster (1987 90–98) for a succinct discussion of how (historically) and why (logically) democracy comes to include a notion of civil liberties as a necessary part of its program.

[2]I have already argued against the category of the purely private, but the question of what activities are open to the political jurisdiction of society as a whole is clearly a fundamental determination of legitimate action that must continually be established, reexamined, and reconstituted. A major complaint against liberalism is that it denies in theory a whole series of interventions (in the economy, in the family, in education, and elsewhere) that it nonetheless practices—and always has practiced. The ideal, laissez-faire state has never existed. Within capitalism, as within all other societies, the economic still remains a subset of the political and not

Postliberalism begins with the rejection of two primary (and interrelated) liberal tenets: incommensurability and individualism. *Incommensurability* is not a term the founding fathers of liberalism used, of course, but (as Lyotard's most recent work suggests) there is ample reason to think of Kant—in his identification of the spheres of pure reason, of practical reason, and of aesthetic judgment—as preaching a version of incommensurability. Similarly, the classical liberal insistence that the processes of decision making that prevail in the public political sphere are inappropriate to the private economic realm represents another assertion of incommensurability. Finally, we can recognize that "deontological liberalism" is based not only on a notion of autonomous selves but also on a stronger notion of incommensurate selves. The negative conclusion that the political order must be built upon the refusal to stipulate ends follows from the assumption that individuals' goals are peculiar to themselves and could not be rationally justified in some public forum. For the deontological liberal, there is no accounting for goals, in the way that our proverb says there is no accounting for taste. (In Kant's case, in fact, taste is much more accountable than goals.) In this last instance, incommensurability becomes just another name for individualism. In the wider sense, incommensurability expresses the prevalence of division as the characteristic mode of liberal thought. As Michael Walzer puts its, liberalism is "the art of separation. . . . Liberalism is a world of walls, and each one creates a new liberty" (1984 315).

Marxism, of course, has waged the most relentless battle against liberal separatism, but Marxist reductionism yields the clumsy theoretical monolith (where everything is economics or everything is power or everything is politics) that so handicaps would-be radical discourse among contemporary humanist intellectuals. Oddly enough, those in the West who actually call themselves Marxists are in some ways least susceptible to this reductionism. Certainly Jameson, Raymond Williams, and Stuart Hall, to name three prominent Marxists, have much more subtle versions of domination and of the multiple causes of cultural phenomena than those found in Foucault, Said, or Derrida. In particular, following Althusser's lead, the Marxists have tried to escape economic determinism by articulating an acceptable notion of "semi-autonomy"—a tricky, hybrid concept that falls between the walls erected by

---

a realm isolated from it. The debilitating effect of liberal theory's denial of this relationship of the economic and the political resides in the liberal society's inability to face squarely the fact of intervention and then think through which interventions are desirable and make its decisions on those interventions in a public, democratic forum. Instead, the liberal state must intervene indirectly and surreptitiously. Tax incentives are a perfect example of the disastrous results of this policy; not only are these incentives based on highly fallible guesses about what effect these indirect measures will have on economic behavior, but they also result in a tax code too complicated for most citizens to understand—hardly a way to promote democracy.

liberal incommensurability and the all-out reductionism of "vulgar Marxism." Jameson's interpretation of "semiautonomy" stresses that "Althusser's real polemic target is at one with that of Hegel":

> The notion of "semi-autonomy" necessarily has to *relate* as much as it *separates*. . . . It is clear that he [Althusser] means to underscore some ultimate structural interdependency of the levels, but that he grasps this interdependency in terms of a mediation that passes through the structure, rather than a more *immediate* mediation in which one level folds into another directly. . . . Althusserian structure, like all Marxisms, necessarily insists on the interrelatedness of all elements in a social formation; only it relates them by way of their structural *difference* and distance from one another, rather than by their ultimate identity, as he understands expressive causality to do. Difference is then here understood as a relational concept, rather than as the mere inert inventory of unrelated diversity. (1981 41)

Let me use a concrete example to illustrate what I take to be the import of semiautonomy and the plausible complexity it can add to our notion of the various demands among which any institutional sphere of activity or any self maneuvers. An American Catholic's religious belief, if taken as "semiautonomous," is understood as participation in a traditional network of tenets and institutions that has its own historical development, its own distinctive manner of preserving and reproducing itself, and its own distinctive practices. These distinctions (or differences) are definitive; to be a Catholic is to belong to a certain community that confers a certain identity on its members, and that identity cannot be reduced to economic class or any simple calculus of interests pursued by all Americans, whether Catholic or not. This identity, however, is necessarily lived (made public) in the context of the social whole. The Catholic cannot avoid participating in economic, political, and other identity-constituting activities that he must interrelate (as best he can) with his religious beliefs. Thus, politically, a Catholic might join the sanctuary movement for Central American refugees or become an antiabortion activist. Economically, the Catholic president of a drug company may decide that his firm will not produce birth-control pills. The point is not that Catholicism and the economic or the political stand in contradiction or collusion; rather, the relation between religious beliefs and activities in other spheres must be negotiated at every turn. The unpredictability of these negotiations (only in very large aggregates is the position of Catholics on a particular issue predictable, and even then, large percentages—almost always more than 25 percent—will take the minority position) stems precisely from the hybrid character of semiautonomy. The separate development and history of Catholicism make its concerns "other" than those of different spheres, so that the terms of its negotiated settlements with them cover a wide spectrum of possibilities.

But there is no question of incommensurability here, since such negotiations cannot be avoided; a decision must always be made and some ground for it always found, since one's Catholicism is always part of one's social being.

In fact, the notion of incommensurability only hides the decision about negotiation among the spheres that the liberal has reached. Liberalism attempts to avoid the possible conflicts among spheres and the different codes of conduct they embody by emphasizing the spheres' separation; this strategy is justified by the assertion that such separation results in greater freedom of activity within each sphere and for the selves that live at various times in different spheres. This appeal to freedom provides the common ground, the commensurate principle, that underlies liberal separatism. A nonreductionist postliberalism needs to emphasize the different logics and histories of the separate spheres while also considering the specifics of how these spheres are interrelated in particular cases within particular societies. The transcendental, theoretical claim of postliberalism is that the spheres must be interrelated, because they occupy positions within a social whole and because selves within that whole must negotiate the relations among the spheres in which they participate.

Liberal individualism is ultimately founded on a particular model of choice. The classic liberalism of Smith and Kant understands both rationality and freedom as the product of choices made by unconstrained, uninfluenced, autonomous selves. A very similar notion of freedom underlies the liberal origin myth of the social contract; society, which places various constraints upon individuals, can be legitimated only if completely unconstrained individuals made the original choice to construct a social order. The postliberal objection is that individualism simply gets the facts wrong. The unconstrained individual never existed anywhere and if something approximating such a creature can be found, she will always be at the end of (as a product of) a long social process, not at the beginning of the social.

This point can be made in two ways. First, we know that human individuals undergo a far longer developmental period than any other animal. The child is intimately connected to others (usually a family) from whom she acquires any number of prejudices, preferences, and interests. The ability to make choices for oneself comes much later, if at all. The more theoretical point is that choice itself is not possible until one's identity has been shaped by this early intersubjective setting. *Pace* Kant, the very act of choice makes no sense if there are no prior commitments, experiences, knowledge, goals, or prejudices to guide choice. Take a trivial example: how is the utterly contentless Kantian self expected to make a consumer's choice between tomato and potato soup? The postliberal insists that such a choice can only be made in relation to the self's commitment to its past and to its sense of itself. Choices are self-affirming and serve to reinforce identity by enacting it. I choose tomato soup because I liked it before; I choose potato soup because I fancy myself an intrepid searcher for new sensations. Only our prior identity means that something is at stake in making a choice, and that prior identity must be recognized as a social product, not a product of earlier, autonomous choices. Even the "self-preservation instinct" that motivates Hobbesian man to make the social contract is not an autonomous, presocial possession of every self. We have ample evidence, in the behavior of parents and of soldiers, that social settings can call forth self-sacrificing as well as self-preserving behavior; there is no reason to accord one of these some kind of ontological or instinctual priority.

But doesn't this rejection of individualism simply lead me back to a holistic portrait of a self constituted by the social monolith? Yes and no. The poststructuralist version of socialization is too drastic, too monolithic, for reasons I must now provide. On the other hand, the poststructuralist version has the strong virtues of dramatically denying liberal individualism (which it calls humanism) and of raising the essential question of power. Two basic considerations temper the poststructuralist monolith: the dynamics of recognition and identity formation within social communities and the consequences of semiautonomy within the social whole. I devote the bulk of this chapter to these two issues, before concluding with a final reexamination of the intellectual's role within a society understood in these terms. It might help the reader to keep in mind what is at stake in the whole discussion: the delineation of the possibility of action that can properly be called political within the social whole. The argument is that such political action must, at a bare minimum, intend the creation and maintenance of democracy if any more substantial action is to be possible, and that even this minimal action requires a model of positive freedom to become possible. The final question will be whether the activities of intellectuals can be understood as differentiated from other types of political action and as having anything of particular value to add to the social goal of democracy.

RECOGNITION

Recognition, of course, is a key Hegelian concept, but one that has only fitfully found favor with twentieth-century theorists.[3] I believe that recogni-

---

[3]Dews (1987 45–86) offers an interesting reading of Lacan that suggests that recognition plays a role in his early work but is less important in the later work. The argument is that French phenomenology, influenced by Alexandre Kojève's lectures on Hegel (particularly on the master/slave dialectic), showed an interest in the dynamics of intersubjective recognition, but that

tion provides a crucial corrective to both poststructuralist and Wittgen-
steinian/neopragmatist thought. Recognition names the primal, usually (but
not always) unspoken "acknowledgement" (to use Stanley Cavell's version of
the concept) that one is a member of the group. If we accept the postliberal
insistence that individual identity is constituted in an intersubjective context,
then recognition stands at the very beginning of the process. It is, we might
say, the act of intersubjective mutuality that enables all subsequent social
interactions. In this sense, recognition looks somewhat like the mythical social
contract, except, of course, its enactment is rarely as explicit as a formally
concluded contract would be. (Various social subgroups do have explicit
ceremonies of recognition; degree conferral or the acceptance of an application for membership offer two examples. But even in such cases, these

---

structuralism, with its notion of a self as an effect of impersonal social rules (the Symbolic in
Lacan), loses interest in the intersubjective. Dews (1987 239–42) also digs out the few places
where Habermas has explicitly addressed the issue of recognition, noting correctly that Habermas's notions of communicative action and of the lifeworld often appear to imply strongly a need
for recognition. However, Habermas's focus on the *conditions* of the ideal speech act have tended
to lead him away from the more dynamic portrait of social interaction that the notion of
recognition would suggest. Two of the best commentators on Habermas's work, Seyla Benhabib
and Thomas McCarthy, often use the term *recognition* in ways similar to my own, but neither of
them (to my knowledge) has discussed the reasons for this usage explicitly. Interestingly enough,
one of the best modern discussions of recognition can be found in Berlin's essay "Two Concepts
of Liberty" (1969 154–62). Berlin realizes that the concept of recognition is fatal to his own wish
to champion negative freedom, and thus he argues that recognition involves the achievement of
"equality and fraternity" but not of "liberty" (1969 154). "This desire for status and recognition . . . is something no less profoundly needed and passionately fought for by human beings—it
is something akin to, but not itself, freedom; although it entails negative freedom for the entire
group, it is more closely related to solidarity, fraternity, mutual understanding, need for association on equal terms, all of which are sometimes—but misleadingly—called social freedom"
(1969 158). Of course, what Berlin never considers, given his individualistic premises, is that
recognition might be constitutive of the self, not just a desire that the self possesses as it possesses
various other capacities and aims. Finally, my list of modern commentators on the concept of
recognition can be rounded out with the addition of Stanley Cavell, who develops his notion of
"acknowledgement" out of a reading of Wittgenstein. I can hardly hope to summarize Cavell's
complex argument here, one that takes Wittgenstein's meditations on pain and private language
for a starting point. The key essays are "Knowing and Acknowledging" (1978 338–66) and "The
Avoidance of Love: A Reading of *King Lear*" (1978 267–353). In *The Claim of Reason*, Cavell
describes the point of these two essays as follows: "I said that acknowledgement 'goes beyond'
knowledge, not in the order, or as a feat, of cognition, but in the call upon me to express the
knowledge at its core, to recognize what I know, to do something in light of it, apart from which
this knowledge remains without expression, hence perhaps without possession. To avoid acknowledgement by refusing this call upon me would create 'the sense of the sense it makes to say
that I cannot step outside' ('go beyond') my feat of cognition. In 'The Avoidance of Love' I said
that acknowledgement of another calls for recognition of the other's specific relation to oneself,
and that this entails the revelation of oneself as having denied or distorted that relation" (1979
428). On the basis of the other's "pain behavior" I cannot know for certain whether he is *really* in
pain. But this skeptical question about my ground for knowledge misses the point that pain
behavior is about the other's call for my help, my response, my sympathy, not about the other's
trying to give me certain information.

ceremonies usually only set in motion or summarize more implicit processes by which respect and acknowledgment are won from the group.) The rather nebulous notion of a speech community begins to make sense if we think of such communities as constituted by those who have a recognized right to speak and to be heard. The boundaries of the community are defined by those who are completely ignored, and the principles of inclusion define its canons of procedure. Recognition, not incommensurability, establishes the boundaries of different language games. We are born into some of these games; others we enter through a process that, again, is analogous to the social contract, in that the self abides by certain canons (if only to ensure being heard) while the group extends its recognition of that self as a member.

The crucial difference between recognition and the social contract is that the former introduces the whole question of social power in a way that the latter—with its presupposition of freely contracting parties—does not. Recognition is a psychological as well as sociopolitical category and thus intersects with the issues of the cultural production of meaning that dominate much literary theory. At stake in recognition is the ability to be a person at all, the terms on which personhood is constituted in a given society. The self can exist only if recognized by some social group, which provides the group with a tremendous power over individuals. Recognition, even within a family, is always experienced as to some extent provisional; the self must behave in expected and established ways to retain its existence in the eyes of others. As Hegel's reliance on recognition to explain the master/slave relationship makes clear, the need to be recognized can place the self in a highly vulnerable position vis à vis the social order and its established hierarchies. In this way, social power contains an emotional hold over selves that underscores the relevance of Freudian musings on family dynamics to political theory and supplements Foucault's hyperrational account of power's dominion. The great threat that power holds in reserve is not suppression but nonacknowledgment. The appeal of nationalism and of fascism, especially when contrasted to liberal individualism, can be located in their extension of membership in a social group that provides duties, praise, and an acknowledged position, an extension most likely to attract those who benefit least (economically and socially) from the negative liberties offered by liberal anomie. The fundamental unit of social recognition is, of course, the family. Conservatives are almost invariably willing to use the family explicitly as their model of what other social arrangements should look like, while liberals just as invariably are hostile to the perceived tyrannies and stultification of family life.

Hegel so often appears a conservative because his holistic model of society can make the State look like a sublated version of the family, discovered at a further dialectical stage and now established in power over the social whole. Marxism's ambivalence about social totality reflects its dual inheritance of Hegelian holism combined with the intellectuals' hatred of conservative pieties. What we need to recapture is the radical potential within the concept of recognition; otherwise, radicals abandon the vast emotional power latent in issues of social membership to reactionaries and demagogues. As usual, Hegel's dialectical understanding undercuts any one-sided view of a concept. Recognition, even in the most extreme instance of the master/slave relationship, is never simply conferred by one entity upon the other; recognition must work both ways. Where the slave recognizes the master's power, the master confers life on the slave. Each is dependent upon the other, even though the relationship is hardly equal. Within the master's dependency, however, resides a certain potential power for the slave, an opening that he can exploit, a potential that provides certain (albeit circumscribed) options for action. The vulnerability of the powerful (which complements the vulnerability of the dominated in this dialectical relationship) increases when we move from the master/slave reliance on brute force to the much more usual social situation of legitimate authority. The group's procedural canons and its enforcement of them are legitimated by the members' acceptance of those canons.

The members' acceptance is not, however, always gained in a simple exchange of acceptance for inclusion. There are various social groupings in which inclusion precedes such acceptance, where a person is established as a member or a subject or a citizen prior to having explicitly granted the legitimacy of the social authority embodied in the group. In these instances, the subject has gained the right to make a judgment about legitimacy that cannot be simply denied when a negative judgment is made. Of course, a declaration of exclusion is one strategy by which a group can deal with a member who now questions its procedures. But in the case of families and of nations, disinheritance, exile, or execution are not very satisfactory solutions, because they can rarely be carried through without damaging the legitimacy of authority. To revoke the primal act of recognition that formerly included these individuals is to lose certain witnesses to the group's procedures and to admit that the group is not organized in such a way as to benefit or satisfy all of its members. Legitimacy is severely weakened when authority cannot plausibly claim to be working for the general welfare. The American civil rights movement showed that the resources of action open to included groups are not negligible. The only legitimate way to deny certain black claims, especially about voting rights, was to revoke recognition of their claims to citizenship, an extreme course that the nation as a whole could not stomach. (Of course, liberal separatism meant that the blacks' political claims and gains could not be easily translated into claims and gains in the economic sphere.) Thus, while recognition enhances the hold of social power over selves in some ways, it confers at the same time a greater potential for *effective* action on the part of the recognized within the communities of which they are members. We know, as a grim historical fact, that every conceivable violence can be justified against the unrecognized, which is why Said's plea for mutual recognition between Israelis and Palestinians is completely appropriate, as is Foucault's concern for those marginal groups in our societies (the insane or criminals) who are often deemed unworthy of recognition. Such concerns about the practical effects of exclusion only underline the protections and potentials for freedom and action that come with inclusion, with recognition—which are consequences worth pondering when Western intellectuals start romanticizing or fantasizing about the pure other they wish they could find.

Within a politics grounded by recognition we can, in Kuhnsian fashion, distinguish between revolutionary and normal politics. Normal politics are the activities of the already recognized to alter prevailing arrangements, to reorganize the social order so that it more fully serves the general welfare. Obviously, different subgroups among the recognized will have different notions of what the best organization of the social would be, but their negotiations toward that end will, for the most part, be nonviolent because of the general agreement on the right of all those involved in the discussion to take part according to the procedural canons of the group. Revolutionary political action involves the very issue of who is to be recognized or not as a member of the group or of the society. Here the potential for violence is much greater because there is a much greater possibility that what is at stake are the very principles that define the boundaries of inclusion and exclusion. The radical, or conflict, model of society calls attention to how often such fundamental incompatibilities surface in social life. Clearly, the model I offer here emphasizes instead how much of our lives is led within the boundaries of the normal; however, I am also striving to do full justice to the tendency of power to disrupt normal interchanges and of societies to resort to strategies of exclusion at times of stress.

What my holistic model highlights is that civil war or other forms of violence, while always the possible result of social conflict, are very often avoided; violence is less the norm than the exception. The extreme conflict theorist can only explain this tempering of conflict by insisting that compromises, negotiated settlements, or resolutions between parties to a social dispute are imposed by one side on the other by a threat of violence, or that they are accepted by one side as the result of a cognitive mistake like "false consciousness," a mistake often fostered by the manipulative rhetoric (ideology) of the other side. My position—which allows for legitimate canons of resolution and for procedural norms accepted by all members of the society—can only appear naive to the conflict theorist.

The conflict theorist's decision to write a book must, however, be seen as an example of what Habermas calls a "performative contradiction." What possible motive could explain their expending so much energy to persuade the nonconflict theorist that she is wrong? If she is duped by notions of legitimacy, then that merely gives them a greater advantage on the social battlefield. Furthermore, their very use of arguments and words to persuade the non-conflict theorist depends on a different, nonviolent and (presumably) non-fraudulent means of resolving disagreement about how society functions.[4]

As Roberto Mangabeira Unger reminds us, "most of what passes for normative skepticism represents an attack upon one form of normative argument by the proponents of another. Behind such attacks we are likely to find disagreements over what personality and society are really like and how we may live in society as who we really are. . . . The only true normative skeptic is the maximalist one, who denies that the result of this or any other dispute should guide our actions" (1986 97). The conflict theorist presents a normative account that justifies berating the illegitimate (because premature and falsely perceived) resolution of conflicts in favor of a determined engagement in struggle that is open and to the end, usually with the accompanying implication that all nonviolent forms of struggle mask the true animosity between the parties, as do any agreements. All intermediate stages of civility between the extremes of civil war and complete unanimity are deemed equally illegitimate. What the "naive" position I am advocating looks for instead are the institutional and procedural means by which societies manage in many cases to weather conflicts without either entering a civil war or fully resolving the disputes. The consensus I am describing only accrues to those institutional and procedural means, not to the particular content of disputes, and of course there is never any guarantee that even this minimal consensus will last. Violence is always possible, but societies do have ways to avoid it that (I believe) stem from a general will to maintain the peace that relies on legiti-

---

[4] I take the notion of a "conflict theorist" from Randall Collins's *Three Sociological Traditions* (1985). The other two traditions Collins identifies are the social order tradition (associated with Durkheim and Parsons) and the interactionist tradition that begins with Charles Sanders Peirce and, especially, George Herbert Mead. Clearly, it is within this latter tradition that my own work here belongs, and I regret not having the space to take up explicitly the work of Mead, Garfinkel, and other interactionists. The reader interested in an overview of this tradition should read the excellent essays by Heritage (1987) and Joas (1987) as well as Collins. For one example of Habermas's use of the notion of "a performative contradiction," see the section on Derrida in *The Philosophical Discourse of Modernity* (1987a 185–210).

mate means of communal decision making. As Unger puts it, a community is "a zone of heightened mutual vulnerability" (1986 66), and the fact of that vulnerability gives all members of the community a stake in preventing violence.

SEMIAUTONOMY AGAIN

The theorist of the social monolith can still argue that, even if we grant "the recognized" some room for action, they are recognized only by virtue of their accepting a social identity and place that guarantees the social order's stability. In other words, the threat of exclusion (even if used sparingly in certain extreme but exemplary cases), plus the positive force of one's conferred identity, immobilizes any internal resistance to the social order. Identity, in other words, is the linchpin of social discipline—a position derived from the middle Foucault and found throughout contemporary radical thought.[5]

Obviously, the concept of semiautonomous spheres of activity is crucial to the refutation of this monolithic portrait; the principles of recognition differ at different social sites, and any self is recognized at a number of different social sites. Because of this proliferation of sites, socialization is never precisely calculable. (Foucault calls our attention to the multiplicity of sites but then insists that one type of power—disciplinary power—and its distinctive techniques can be found at each site.) In striking contrast to Lyotard's praise of traditional culture over universal modern culture, Habermas (following Max Weber) recognizes an increasing differentiation of spheres of activity as culture becomes modernized. We need to be careful here, since Habermas develops this idea in certain ways that are objectionable. I would not contest that modern Western culture is certainly less pluralistic than traditional culture *externally*; that is to say, the West has far less tolerance (or at least has been in a position to act more forcefully on its intolerance) of alternative cultural orders than traditional cultures have been. Hence the West has aggressively exported its cultural arrangements around the world. On the other hand, modern Western culture is far more pluralistic *internally*; the West's characteristic mode of appropriation, combined with the differentiation over time of separate spheres of activity, has multiplied the groups to which an individual might belong. Once we take semiautonomy seriously, it makes a real difference whether one is a Catholic or not, and it is obvious that

---

[5]Judith Butler (1990 ix–34) offers a very complete version of the argument that all forms of identity are oppressive and that the true path of radical politics lies in the disruption of identity.

there are many more differences of this sort within modern Western cultures than within a traditional culture. None of which denies that some basic principle of recognition remains that still enacts inclusion/exclusion within the culture as a whole. The very notion of culture makes no sense if such boundaries cannot be drawn *as a matter of daily practice* by the members of the culture. But, especially in such multiethnic nations as the United States and Canada or in vague (but very real) cultural entities like "the West," the *theoretical* delineation of that principle of inclusion becomes increasingly difficult. Rather, the membership and allegiance of different individuals to different subgroups within the nation or culture becomes the more obvious fact.

"Semiautonomy" attempts to capture theoretically this precarious balance between the fact of a social totality (since all these individuals are recognized and recognize themselves as "Americans") and the fact of a wide diversity of membership in subgroups, be they ethnic, religious, occupational, or geographic. Habermas has been particularly interested in distinguishing three spheres: the juridicial/administrative sphere of the state, the technocratic/economic sphere of commodity production/distribution, and the aesthetic sphere. Habermas' rationalistic bias is evident here, since he identifies spheres by their development of rationalized (in Max Weber's sense of the term, not Freud's) procedures and their serving the need of "functionally intermeshing action *consequences*" in order to promote *"system integration"* (1987c 150). Within such a scheme, it is not surprising that Habermas has devoted far less attention to the aesthetic than to the state and economic spheres, while his comments on religious, educational, ethnic, and other possible spheres have been even more sparse.[6] Perhaps these other, less systematic concerns belong more properly to the lifeworld and its emphasis on "social," as opposed to system, "integration." But it is unclear just how much differentiation Habermas would be willing to introduce into the holistic notion of the lifeworld.

In any case, whether we differentiate three spheres or fifteen, my version of semiautonomy (which is faithful to neither Jameson nor Habermas, although influenced by the thought of both) has several crucial ramifications. The first is a denial of any simple, monolithic view of contemporary society. Habermas

---

[6]See Jay (1985 125–39) for an attempt to puzzle out what place the aesthetic may hold in Habermas's work. Jay finds Habermas vague and ambivalent on the key question of whether the autonomy of the aesthetic within modernity is potentially emancipatory or only another example of a systemic sphere cut loose from the lifeworld. He purports (1988 137–48) to see in some of Habermas's more recent work a clearer statement that "he contends that the utopian dedifferentiation of art *by itself* is insufficient to undo the pathologies of modernization" (145).

has a tendency to argue that a different kind of "reason" is operative in each sphere, which then allows him to contend that the Frankfurt School's and poststructuralism's attack on reason makes the mistake of identifying the "instrumental" reason of the economic/technological sphere as the totality of reason. The threatened hegemony of instrumental reason in the West should be contested in the name of a wider vision of reason's own different manifestations, not by a condemnation of reason or an uncovering of its inevitable aporias. Furthermore, the refusal of semiautonomy to collapse one sphere into another (or Habermas's refusal to reduce his various types of reason into one form of reason) rejects a holistic thought that does not also recognize complex differentiations. In addition, the notion of separate spheres suggests how critique is possible and why it is not surprising that intellectuals attached to the aesthetic sphere have been among the primary critics of both the state and capitalism. The separation of this sphere offers the possibility (although hardly the necessity) of viewing the state's and the economy's activities from the viewpoint of a different logic and a different set of goals. Finally, an insistence on semiautonomy denies the Marxist tradition of economic determinism and its pessimistic rebirth in postmodernist visions of a globally ascendant capitalist "world-system."

This resistance of economic determinism necessitates a rethinking of the state's role in modern society. The democratic state has traditions, procedures, institutions, and self-produced responsibilities that do not make it a simple tool of the ruling classes or a mere superstructural reflection of economic realities.[7] Bowles and Gintis describe the conflict between the democratic state and capitalism as occurring between personal rights and property rights. The expansion of these two sets of rights brings them increasingly into conflict with one another. Marxist theory explains capitalism's continual drive to expand property rights; the dynamics of democratic politics (which Marxists continually underestimate) explains the expansion of personal rights as more and more segments of the population demand full enjoyment of the personal liberties promised to all. The democratic state must respond to these political claims even when they pose a threat to, or at least are contrary to the interest of, capitalism.[8] This argument does not deny

[7]My comments on the state in late capitalism are indebted to C. B. Macpherson's superb essay "Do We Need a Theory of the State?" (1987 55–75). See also Nicos Poulantzas (1980 251–65) for another leftist discussion of the state that avoids the orthodox Marxist refusal to countenance it in any form.

[8]Bowles and Gintis (1987 27–63) offer a succinct history of the contest between property rights and personal rights in American history and of how the political necessity to accommodate the demands of various groups has limited the sway of property rights. They see both personal rights and property rights as naturally tending to expansion and thus coming into greater and

that the liberal democratic state is committed to the preservation of capitalism; the argument only contends that the separately developing logic of the state's own commitments, institutions, and strategies for self-perpetuation open up political demands that are not in capitalism's interest, and that the state, caught among various pressures, does not invariably serve capitalism. A view of the state as yet another instance of a semiautonomous entity allows us to recognize the various possibilities among which it (like the Catholic in my earlier example) must negotiate at every turn. Thus the democratic state is hardly likely to be monolithically serving one set of interests or another. In fact, as C. B. Macpherson notes, the political events of the past decade in England and America show that the state now has a harder time justifying its existence and activities to the capitalists than it does to the populace. "The state, whether or not it is seen as jointly parasitic with capital, is still sufficiently different from corporate capital to have to justify its activities to the latter. . . . This seems to me to be the central problem of the advanced capitalist state" (1987 70). One of the oddities of our times is that radicals, who theoretically abhor the state, almost invariably vote for the political parties that endorse *more* state action, while capitalists, who supposedly have the state in their back pocket, almost invariably vote for the parties that preach a minimalist state. This fact registers the role the contemporary state plays, albeit imperfectly and inconsistently as a counterforce to capitalism.

The specifics of whether the contemporary state's activities check capitalism or in fact merely ensure its continuance by correcting the potentially disastrous (to capitalism) consequences of its short-sighted greediness can be debated endlessly, and have been. The principle of semiautonomy only insists that democratic politics (even in the watered-down and circumscribed varieties available today) and the state it fosters produce demands and pressures within modern society that would not have arisen from the existence of capitalism alone. Furthermore, having accepted the desirability of democracy and the civil liberties traditionally associated with it, I extend the argument to claim that we can recognize the legitimacy (according to the principle of democracy) of certain aspects of the modern Western state. This extension of the argument has important practical and theoretical consequences. On the practical level, it means accepting that Western states, especially in the past

---

greater conflict over time. I am suspicious of such a continuous history of escalation. A discontinuous account that considers the different strengths available to each side at different times (because of the world situation or economic cycles or other external factors), the different temporary compromises politically negotiated, and the social, technological, and political changes over the past two hundred years would, I think, more accurately portray the different forms this conflict has taken.

thirty years, have been remarkably successful in maintaining personal liberties. This is not to say that there has not been any abuse of these liberties in the West; the endless revelations of FBI surveillance and harassment of even the mildest political dissidents destroys any easy belief in liberty's triumph. And it is not to say that Western freedom does not largely depend on the prosperity gained from economic exploitation of the "underdeveloped" world that (literally) cannot afford the freedoms enjoyed in the West. But even with these disclaimers, it seems to me foolish to deny that the liberties of the West are, and must remain, a crucial ingredient of any more just and more democratic society of the future. It seems equally foolish to deny that the rule of law has proved the best (even if still imperfect) guarantee of these liberties, beginning with the recognition of all citizens as having equal status before the law. As a practical matter, then, not only will political dissidents in the West find their own best safeguard in the law, but they should recognize the law's desirability in any future they envision. Where the West is culpable of hampering, or even preventing, the legal principles and the practical enjoyment of civil liberties and democratic decision making in the rest of the world, the goal must be to act in ways that make such conditions possible everywhere, not to undermine their partial achievement in the West.

Theoretically, this recognition of civil liberties and the juridicial/state sphere's role in maintaining them brings the issues of legitimacy and positive freedom to the fore. The Marxist denies all legitimacy to the state in capitalist society because that state merely reflects the interest of the ruling class, not the social whole. Foucault denies any legitimacy to the state and its legal apparatus because they are merely further manifestations of disciplinary power. What these visions deny is that the state and its legal apparatus could ever possibly serve as a legitimate form of authority that serves to protect liberty against encroachments by other types of power. (This formulation is still only a negative image of legitimate power, although it implies a model of positive freedom for selves; I present a more positive image of legitimate power in my discussion of power.) Following Quentin Skinner (who is following Machiavelli, who is following Cicero), we can say that the embrace of positive freedom begins with the acceptance that civil liberties are best promoted and protected in a *particular* type of society and, among other things, that type of society is one organized to defend those liberties against various threats. In other words, society must be empowered to deal with other forms of power that threaten liberty; and that empowerment inevitably constrains individuals and even imposes certain duties upon them.[9] The denial of

9See Skinner (1986 193–221).

legitimacy and an attachment to negative liberty go hand in hand, which is one prime reason that liberalism as a political philosophy is so rife with contradictions; it is always trying to justify a state that its own deepest commitments reject. The truly consistent liberal (like Thoreau) is an anarchist, except that anarchism cannot explain how negative liberty (or equality) will be protected or preserved. The Marxist denial of legitimacy also pushes it in the anarchist direction, while at the same time leading to the implicit embrace of negative liberty in most leftist writing, even though Marx himself was an advocate of positive liberty.

Only the acceptance of legitimacy allows the endorsement of some form of social authority and the resultant acceptance of a positive responsibility for its maintenance. I hope it is clear that such a statement implies no endorsement of the current state or even, for that matter, of the state as absolutely necessary. Tribal societies exist without anything we can properly label a state; but of course that hardly means that they do not have any constituted social order or authority.[10] My position here only reiterates the point made in my discussion of neopragmatism: the reign of tolerance and of other civil liberties that ensure civility and conversation depends on specific social arrangements. These arrangements must be organized in such a way as to protect them against threats, and that this situation necessarily implies the legitimacy of the authority that responds to threats and the illegitimacy of the forces that pose the threat. Under modern circumstances, legitimate authority is almost always vested in a legal order and in a state, and democracy is a primary good precisely because it assures full access to the processes by which these legitimate orders are negotiated, constituted, and reformed. Finally, if we accept that civil liberties and equality are likely to be threatened by powers that seek forms of advantage that will violate those liberties and equality, then we must accept that the political and social world we wish to inhabit cannot be achieved through negative freedom alone.[11]

The objection that semiautonomy merely reinstates liberal separatism must

---

[10]I remain agnostic about the future possibility of societies without a state; the return to such a condition in the West would necessitate, at the very least, a massive decentralization. For an illuminating discussion of "tribal societies" without states, preindustrial societies with states, and the class and state society of capitalism as the three basic types of societies history has known, see Giddens (1981 90–229).

[11]Admittedly, I offer no theoretical account here of why abuses should occur. Strictly speaking, I need to consider the social causes of such behavior if I am not to adopt simply the Machiavellian position described by Skinner (1986), namely that human nature is such that every society must protect itself against greed and self-seeking violence. In the absence of a theoretical account, however, the safer course certainly appears the adoption of safeguards against dangers that experience indicates are all too common, instead of an insistence that such safeguards should be unnecessary.

be considered. As a hybrid concept, semiautonomy insists on the state's independence of the economic but does not deny the economic sphere's influence on the state, as my portrait of the state's responding to various pressures suggests. What is trickier is the suggestion that the state is better the more it is separated from capitalism, which may appear to make the wall between state and economy higher. At this point Hegel is both a help and a hindrance. He is a hindrance insofar as he accords the state (as the fullest embodiment of reason) an autonomy from and a superiority to civil society and the family, both of which must finally synchronize their logics (or wills) with those of the state. I want to maintain the full semiautonomy of various spheres without granting the state any special status among them. It is the social as a whole, not the state (which is just one sphere in that whole), that establishes and guarantees the conditions within which the activities of the various spheres take place. In other words, the organization of the state/legal sphere to protect civil liberties and equality gains its impetus and legitimacy from the will of the social totality for democracy. The state does not coincide with the social whole, and thus its own logic of development can move it in undemocratic directions and its susceptibility to the influence of other spheres can undercut its protection of democracy.

Hegel is a help insofar as he reminds us that the spheres remain answerable to the social whole, which is one way of stressing that their autonomy is far from complete. My argument is that within a democratic culture the social totality is identified with democratic procedures and principles. Just as the state's legitimacy is predicated on its activities adhering to and preserving this democratic ground, so the legitimacy of activities in other spheres is answerable to democratic principles. This does not mean that the activities in other spheres are similarly motivated or are answerable to identical canons of rational procedure. It is easy to confuse the state with society as Hegel did because the state much more directly follows the dictates of the prevailing social norm. The other spheres do not pursue democracy directly and their activities are shaped by the procedures that appear to further their immediate goals. But these other spheres remain answerable to democratic norms; certain possible procedures, perhaps even the most efficient ones, are deemed unacceptable because too obviously in conflict with the democratic ethos. Thus I believe that the history of Western capitalism, far from exhibiting the unadulterated triumph of the capitalist mode of production, is more the story of the continuing struggle over what economic practices are still compatible with democratic ideals. That all the various participants in this struggle (capitalists and workers, if you like, although the actual groups involved are more various and more complex) share the commitment to democracy identifies them as members of the same social whole and has meant that negotiated settlements are at least as frequent as violent confrontations in this two-hundred-and-some-year history.[12] Of course, the exact meaning of democracy and the exact potential of any practice to enhance or hinder democracy are, and will remain, matters of political dispute and negotiation. The argument is merely that the walls erected by semiautonomy, unlike the walls erected by liberal separatism, are always permeable by the prevailing social norm of democracy. The liberal state, in practice, has never been able to practice the laissez-faire program toward the economic (or toward other private realms like the family) that liberal theory preaches. This failure, I contend, is theoretically explained by the continual pressure of the values constitutive of the social whole on any of the semiautonomous spheres within that whole.

SOCIAL NORMS AND THE SOCIAL WHOLE

The insistence that a social whole exists, to which all activities are answerable, raises two fundamental theoretical problems. The first is how the existence of this social whole can be made plausible to those who deny it. In fact, the very fact of their denial appears to refute the claim, unless it is argued that the totality exists and functions apart from any conscious recognition by the selves within the society. Hegel, of course, uses the concept of alienation to explain that selves are unconscious, with *Geist* manifesting itself openly as the social whole only at the end of history. Such a solution hardly helps the contemporary philosopher or political theorist who wants to use the social whole to provide the norms to which all social activities are answerable. The contemporary tactic has been, instead, to try to demonstrate that certain principles are tacitly or implicitly accepted by all members of the relevant group, a position that is sometimes accompanied by the even stronger claim that these tacit principles could be teased out of any competent member of the group if a

[12]The universality of the norm of democracy in the West is indicated not only by the increased appeal to democracy as primary good in postmodern socialist writings but also by the felt need of neoliberals such as Frederick Hayek and Milton Friedman to legitimate capitalism and the principle of noninterference in the economy on the ground that a fully functioning capitalist order is a necessary precondition of democracy. Recent events in Russia, Eastern Europe, South Korea, China, and the Philippines also suggest how strong a rallying cry democracy can be outside the West. The development of strong democratic traditions or cultures in the countries still suffering from the aftershocks of colonialism offers fewer examples to which one can point with hope. The potentially disastrous ethnic conflicts in Eastern Europe suggest that these countries, as they emerge from Russia's thrall, may experience the violent struggles over boundaries of inclusion that have devastated so many of Britain's former colonies.

version of Socratic questioning (the *Meno* offers a perfect example) were employed. This position of implicit recognition of the social whole and its constitutive principles raises the second, and in my opinion more troubling, problem. If the principles exist, why are they more honored in the breach than in the observance? We slip from the descriptive to the prescriptive when the fact of the social whole becomes the source of social norms that we are then meant to uphold. In the discussion below I do not consistently separate out these two problems, a failure that I hope will not prove too burdensome on the reader.

For Habermas, the implicit norm to which all subscribe exists as a counter-factual, as a principle to which social actors can appeal when confronted with an action that they wish to deem socially unacceptable. The difficulties of this position become apparent if we return to the analogy of a basketball game. The norms in basketball are unambiguously (for the most part) contained in a rule book and it is only rarely in anybody's interest to break the rules. True, it might help a player to win if she "gets away with" an infraction of the rules, but wholesale infraction (advancing the ball without dribbling, for example) does not help one to win but ends the game altogether—if one team doesn't dribble but the other team does, it is no longer basketball. Clearly, a social norm does not work in the same way. First, what counts as properly demo-cratic action is continually a matter of controversy. Players of the social game will argue over what democracy means, and even when they agree on this meaning, they will argue about whether or not a given action is democratic. Second, the best strategy for individuals or groups who wish to enhance their power or their economic well-being might very well be to ignore democratic procedures. Social life, unlike basketball, does not come to an end if different agents are guided by different imperatives and motives. The very existence of semiautonomous spheres makes it highly likely, if not inevitable, that social spheres of action will develop that have goals, and strategies for achieving those goals, that are reconciled with democracy only with difficulty.

The Habermasian norm, then, is invoked as a court of appeal, not as a transcendental limit that no action can violate. The norm does not state what actions are possible and what actions are impossible; rather, it serves as the fundamental appraisal of actions within a specific social whole. (We would expect norms to vary from society to society and from one historical period to another.) The norm exerts an influence over action only to the extent that the members of a particular community desire to have their various actions *recognized* by the group as congruent with its prevailing values. We should not underestimate the force of this concern; in the United States, for example, the charge that an action is fundamentally undemocratic is taken seriously by virtually everyone. All agents will strive to represent their actions as compatible with democracy. Within such a consensus about norms, ethics becomes a matter of meaning more than of values. The norm of democracy is not at stake, but the meaning of democracy and the interpretation of particular actions as compatible with it or not is at issue.[13] Various sanctions—from disapproval to forceful cessation of action—follow upon the community's unfavorable response to particular actions. But, of course, none of these sanctions, nor the existence of the norm, can prevent actions that violate it from occurring. Thus the norm cannot be said to govern action; instead, it establishes the parameters within which actions are interpreted and judged.

Readers of Habermas will realize that I am adopting the general form of his understanding of the pragmatic functioning of a cultural norm but am neglecting both the specific description he offers of that norm and his defense of an expanded, and necessary, rationality in human communication. This neglect stems quite simply from my belief that Habermas's notion of communicative reason, with its concomitant appeal to an "ideal speech situation," is derived from a particular philosophical/theoretical tradition whose claim to universal validity or acceptance is hard to credit. I believe that Habermas is right to argue that this philosophical brand of rationality is distinct from instrumental reason, but this very differentiation of reason (embodied in different semiautonomous spheres) renders suspect his attempt to retain the Hegelian identification of the social whole (in Habermas's case, the grounding social norm) with reason. There is a tension between the differentiation of reason into various types in Habermas and his urge to retain a totalized view of society.[14] Of course, Habermas recognizes this tension in his discussion of the severance of "system" (the semiautonomous spheres) from "lifeworld" (the lived immersion in the social). It seems more obvious that different

---

[13]Let me remind the reader of Rorty's description of "morality as a set of practices, *our* practices," rather than a matter of following rules. Our actions are chosen and are judged by their "congruence with our deeper understanding of ourselves and our aspirations" (see Rorty [1989b 57–60]). What I am arguing is that *democracy* names that deepest aspiration in our political culture, and that we justify our actions by offering interpretations of them that reveal their congruence with democracy, interpretations that may also involve new versions of what democracy may or should mean. But this introduction of interpretation doesn't turn the social ground on which these judgments are made into a free-for-all; our justifications and interpretations, after all, have to be made plausible to the audience who we hope will *recognize* our self-description of our actions as accurate. Charles Altieri's essay "From Expressivist Aesthetics to Expressivist Ethics" (1987) offers a stimulating and convincing portrait of what an ethics of meanings established through intersubjective determinations of value would look like.

[14]Martin Jay has been the most persistent commentator on Habermas's fluctuations between the hope (or temptation) of "a single meta-narrative of normative totalization" (1988 12) and the more modest realization that such totalities are both impossible to attain and self-defeating (to our dearest political hopes) if achieved. See Jay (1988 10–13, 137–48).

communities within the lifeworld accept different forms of reason, that is, have different criteria for what counts as a successful utterance. In this instance, I think the neopragmatist critique of Habermas is correct and that Rorty, for example, offers a better model for considering the varieties of acceptable communication in different social subgroups, including intellectuals.

As is obvious by now, however, I want to retain the Hegelian/Habermasian vision of the social whole, shifting from reason to democracy the burden of providing the social norm to which all subgroups and spheres render allegiance. At issue is whether it makes sense at all to insist that some kind of tacit acceptance by all of certain fundamental ground rules stands as a sine qua non of communal life. Wittgenstein, of course, argues for this necessary agreement among those who share a language, a condition Stanley Cavell has called "attunement."[15] Rousseau raises this question most forcefully within the traditions of political theory. How, he asks in *The Social Contract*, could we ever establish legitimate authority if there was not a prior agreement by all as to what constituted legitimacy? "The law of majority-voting itself rests on a covenant, and implies that there has been on at least one occasion unanimity," Rousseau writes in the chapter titled "That we must always go back to an original covenant" (1968 58–59). But even this requirement of a one-time unanimity does not express the full extremity of the case, since there is the even earlier issue of who is to be included within the group that has to achieve unanimity. "We ought to scrutinize the act by which people become *a* people, for that act, being necessarily antecedent to the other, is the real foundation of society" (1968 59). Rousseau cannot imagine any procedure (since the legitimacy or illegitimacy of the procedure itself would have to be decided) that can explain how this prior agreement about what (and who) constitutes the

[15]Cavell's discussion of "attunement" highlights how mysterious, and yet how necessary, this concept is. What we hope to explain is "the astonishing fact of the astonishing extent to which we *do* agree in judgment; eliciting criteria goes to show therefore that our judgments *are* public, that is, shared. What makes this astonishing . . . is that the extent of agreement is so intimate and pervasive; that we communicate in language as rapidly and completely as we do; and that since we cannot assume that the words we are given have their meaning by nature, we are led to assume they take it from convention; and yet no current idea of 'convention' could seem to do the work that words do—there would have to be, we could say, too many conventions in play, one for each shade of each word in each context. We *cannot* have agreed beforehand to all that would be necessary. . . . So I should emphasize that, while I regard it as empty to call this idea of mutual attunement 'merely metaphorical,' I also do not take it to prove or explain anything. On the contrary, it is meant to question whether a philosophical explanation is needed, or wanted, for the fact of agreement in the language human beings use together, an explanation, say, in terms of meanings or conventions or basic terms or propositions which are to provide the foundation of our agreements. For nothing is deeper than the fact, or the extent, of agreement itself" (1979 31–32).

polis or its method of making political decisions is reached.[16] Rather, that agreement is always already there—a fact that completely undermines the notion that humans ever existed in some kind of presocial state of nature. The very fact of communities, just like the very fact of language, points to agreements and attunements outside of which human life is simply not conceivable. Thus the attempt to describe the origins of language or of society leads to an infinite regress or to paradox, a point Derrida's work has emphasized. Extreme examples like the wild boy of Aveyron reinforce the belief that human life is impossible outside of language and community.

A minimalist version of Rousseau's notion of the "general will" insists that some kind of fundamental social consensus is a transcendental condition of language and of communal life. (A maximal reading of "general will" goes on to argue, as Rousseau does in the later sections of *The Social Contract*, that the consensus it embodies should be enacted in each decision a democratic society makes. I am adopting the minimal, not the maximal, reading.) Norberto Bobbio states clearly the necessity of a general agreement about procedures in any functioning democracy.

> The decision to submit [a] question . . . to an agreed set of procedural rules . . . presupposes a consensus on the desirability of those rules, and the conviction that the result obtained from a good procedure is automatically a good one. It should be noted that, in this case, contrary to what is generally believed, it is not the desirable outcome which justifies the means, even when these are dubious ones, but the good means (or at least what are held to be good ones) which justify the outcome, or at least make the outcome acceptable even to those who voted against it (i.e., to those who would have considered the outcome in itself bad, but for the means by which it had been arrived at). (1987b 67–68)

Only some such consensus about the procedures of decision making can explain how some disputes are settled without violence, even in the cases

---

[16]Rousseau's solution to this problem (found in chap. 7 of book 2 in *The Social Contract*) is the "extraordinary" figure of the lawgiver, who founds the society—"a task which is beyond human powers" and which depends upon "a non-existent authority for its execution" (1968 86). Since the general will is a product of the social contract, the lawgiver cannot appeal to its authority to legitimate his establishment of the laws or rules within which a general will could be recognized and enacted. "It is this which has obligated the founders of nations throughout history to appeal to divine intervention and to attribute their own wisdom to the Gods; for then the people, feeling subject to the laws of the state as they are to those of nature . . . obey freely and bear with docility the yoke of the public welfare" (1968 87). Rousseau's explanation of this ruse places him within modernity's recognition that the social order has only human origins, while his sympathy with the ruse reveals Rousseau's perplexity over how self-legitimation might be carried out. I am suggesting that abstract legitimation of this sort never proves necessary, is never a real question. Instead, we always find ourselves in an already constituted social order and at issue is legitimating this specific order, a task we undertake by appealing to norms, procedures, and principles of legitimation that are also available to us from various traditions and social interactions.

where those who do not get their way remain unpersuaded. The general will means that the alternatives are not, as Rorty presents them, between persuasion and violence; the grounding consensus makes a third option possible: the acceptance of particular decisions that are reached in such a way as to affirm the agreed-upon, legitimate procedures. To sum up in a phrase: in democracy, the means justifies the ends.

How such a consensus originates must remain mysterious. It cannot be created by fiat; the inscription and ratification of a democratic constitution does not guarantee a culture capable of sustaining democracy, while the ratification procedures themselves appeal to some prior sense of legitimate decision making. The procedures of a democracy (and the norms of equality and justice that make those procedures desirable) must have some extra-constitutional, cultural basis if a democracy is to survive. And we can recognize that the fact of social consensus is inseparable from the concept of legitimacy, from what its norms allow the culture to accept as appropriate and ethical action, and what to reject. The very distinction between violent, coercive forms and acceptable forms of reaching decisions is dependent on a definition of legitimacy. That such a definition often rests on intuitive, emotional, and unexamined grounds reflects the primal and often unarticulated (hence tacit) consensus on which the judgments of legitimacy are based. On the other hand, once *within* a social group whose members are bound to one another by mutual recognition and by certain agreed-upon procedures of social intercourse, the terms of consensus are certainly open to explicit examination, articulation, questioning, and change. The construction of a social identity may be dependent on the preexisting identity (the very fact of some defined social group), but, although that construction does not take place in "absolute freedom," it is not doomed to exact reproduction either. The articulation of what was previously implicit may in itself provoke change.

This theoretical insistence on an existing consensus both grants a historical dimension to notions of community and allows us to move beyond what Roberto Unger calls "an impoverished conception of community . . . [which] defines communal life largely negatively, as the absence of conflict" (1986 66). Rather, communities are dynamic, historical entities whose norms and procedures are shaped over time through a variety of conflicts, experiments, and experiences. Michael Walzer attempts to sum up the multiple means by which, over time, "consensus and shared understanding" are produced: "That process includes political struggle . . . negotiation and compromise, law making and law enforcement, socialization in families and schools, economic transformations, cultural creativity of all sorts" (1989 192). Thus our contemporary notion of the good society includes a commitment to civil liberties.

These liberties are not ahistorical, "natural" rights but the product of a complex political and historical process. No claim can or should be made for the current agreements' necessity, perfection, or permanence. The claim is only that, synchronically, some set of mutually understood agreements does hold the community together, does provide the terms within which it conducts its political life and the conflicts of that life, and does provide the terms on which the community makes judgments about ethical and legitimate action.

Unger uses the term *formative context* to designate this consensus (which Habermas calls the "lifeworld," and Bourdieu the "habitus") and attempts to show how such a notion allows us to move beyond the "impoverished" notion of community as transcending or repressing conflict or differences. The "formative context" provides the minimal set of interconnections that make disagreements possible; thus, in my terms, it provides the "situation" that makes action, argument, and meaning possible in the way theorized by the notion of "situated freedom." Unger writes:

> In every society we can distinguish between the repetitious activities and conflicts that absorb much of the people's effort from the formative institutional and imaginative order that usually remains undisturbed by these routines and gives them their shape. The routines include the habitual limits to the use of governmental power, the available ways of combining labor and capital, and the accepted styles and criteria of normative argument. . . . Formative contexts do not exist as facts open to straightforward observation like the atomic structure of a natural object. Nor does their existence depend entirely upon illusions that a correct understanding might dispel. Rather, they subsist and become entrenched in a practical sense, by gaining immunity to challenge and revision in the course of ordinary social activity. (1986 92–93)

Unger's emphasis lies with considering ways to "disentrench" current formative contexts, where "disentrenchment means not permanent instability, but the making of structures that turn the occasions for their reproduction into opportunities for their correction" (1986 93). In his account, the fact of an underlying consensus is enabling, even necessary; what is required, however, is a fuller, conscious intervention in the complex social and historical processes by which that consensus is shaped.[17] That intervention must take place at the site of social reproduction, to which I now turn my attention.

---

[17]Unger is the chief spokesman of the highly influential "critical legal studies movement." As my use of his work here indicates, I find his reliance on a normative politics (not surprising for someone coming out of the legal tradition) helpful, as well as his distinction between routines and formative contexts. I am skeptical, however, of the reductionism involved in declaring that "formative contexts . . . represent frozen politics" (1986 92), since such a formula privileges conflict over other possible social interactions. Needless to say, I am in full sympathy with Unger's general goal of making formative contexts more susceptible to intervention and revision.

SOCIAL REPRODUCTION IN THE CONTEXT OF LEGITIMACY

The obsession, on the part of the postmodern writers I have discussed, with the other, the excluded, either blinds them to social consensus or makes them believe that such consensus is achieved only by the forceful imposition of one group's will upon the other groups within the social whole. Where no vision of a possible legitimate social order is offered, the writer inevitably adopts the tragic vision of perpetual strife, of endless appropriation and the hopeless effort to escape it, that we find in Nietzsche and the middle Foucault. For these writers, as for Marxists who focus on the imminence of the revolution, the issue is often the persistence of the imposed social arrangements, a topic thematized as "social reproduction." The question these writers raise is how a ruling group (usually numerically inferior to those over whom it rules) manages to maintain an order so obviously disadvantageous to the vast majority. Even more mysterious is the garnering of that majority's consent to these social arrangements, so that only a minimum of overt force is needed to preserve it. Social reproduction names the processes by which that consent is manufactured and retained. A greater concern with modes of reproduction than with modes of production may be *the* hallmark of Western Marxism and is certainly a prominent feature of all postmodern meditations on the social.

For those who deny the legitimacy of contemporary societies, social reproduction must rest on some kind of trick, as the naked use of power would generate immediate and widespread resistance. For Marxists, ideology masks the workings of power so that they are not apparent to most (if not all) members of the society; there have been countless descriptions of the specifics of ideology's functioning, of which Jameson's insistence that the complex totality of global capitalism is unrepresentable is just one version. In Derrida, the very grammar of our language keeps returning us to modes of thought that perpetuate the characteristic structures of Western life. Foucault explains society's stability by locating power in an institutional order that is invisible, unapproachable, and unassailable. In all three cases, no site for lucid, conscious consent emerges. The social reproduces itself according to mechanisms that function apart from the participation of society's members. Instead, those members are simply slotted into the preestablished subject positions of the social structure. This structure, and the process of its reproduction, is not answerable to any norms or any social consensus about either procedures or ends. It blindly enacts the imperatives of power or of habit.

The account of social institutions that the postmodern version of social reproduction requires points toward these theorists' devaluation of citizens' participation in the mundane daily activities that give a social order its lived reality and reinforce its unquestioned, self-evident character. Neither Derrida nor Foucault offers a very satisfactory account of time or of change. For Derrida, Western metaphysics simply repeats itself in various guises over a two-thousand-year period. Foucault tries much harder to encompass the fact of change in his work, but his social vision never successfully incorporates a temporal dimension. He understands that institutional structures do "enable" subjects, enhancing and giving scope to certain of their capacities, just as he recognizes that these engendered capacities might prove complicitous with the institution or resistant to it. But he has no way of explaining how specific complicitous or resistant action might impede change or cause it. Power in *Discipline and Punish*, apart from the mysterious moment of total transition from one type of power to another, has the unchanging, immovable placidity of Kafka's Law. Surprisingly enough, despite his brilliant critique of structuralist thought's unreal abstraction from the everyday practice of agents, Pierre Bourdieu's Marxism leads him to portray an institutionally embodied power that remains stagnant in much the same way that Foucaultian power does. In contradistinction to traditional societies, in which the possessor of power must continually reestablish his power by extraordinary actions of generosity and strength, the modern institutional order creates, according to Bourdieu, "a social world which, containing within itself the principle of its own continuation, frees agents from the endless work of creating or restoring social relations" (1977 189). Nothing could be more wrong. The social order, whether characterized by a relative paucity or a relative abundance of institutionalized procedures and rules, is never freed from the endless task of re-creation. The temptation to think otherwise, to portray an ossified institutional (bureaucratic) order, stems from a commitment to Marxist concepts of reification and alienation, concepts that seek to extract large segments of the population from any part in the social consensus, any part in the daily reproduction of the social order.

Agents simply do not have the kind of negative freedom that the theory of alienation proposes, a fact that Foucault's formulation of resistance half recognizes and that Bourdieu's concept of the habitus fully recognizes. Agents' identities, their very existence, are tied to their participation in the social order. Resistance, where it occurs, must therefore take place in the daily practice of the social routines embodied in work, in family relations, and in various economic and social exchanges. Agents are not alienated from these activities. (The concept of alienation rests on an appeal to some "true self" apart from prevailing social routines, a self that is violated by these routines. I am, of course, denying that the notion of a "true self" makes any sense.) Instead, in exactly the way that Bourdieu relates theory to practice, agents pursue various distinctive strategies within the social situations in which they find themselves. At most, within a highly differentiated modern society, a student (for example) might be "alienated" from his family by adopting the procedural canons and norms of his college world as the guiding principles of his behavior. A more generalized alienation from society as a whole could be explained (as Habermas insists in his work on Foucault) only by an (at least implicit) appeal to a norm that one derives from the social consensus.

Anthony Giddens neatly sums up the crucial significance of daily *practical* action within the social, institutional order when he writes that "social life is inherently recursive" (1979 217). Significantly enough, Giddens reaches this conclusion as a gloss upon Bourdieu's notion of the habitus and the question of how it might be reproduced, a circumstance that suggests how fully Bourdieu's vision of modern institutional order conflicts with the rest of his "theory of practice." The habitus, like Habermas's concept of the lifeworld or Cavell's notion of what a society's members share through "attunement" or Unger's "formative contexts," designates, in Giddens's words, the "mutual knowledge employed [by social actors] such that interaction is 'unproblematic,' or can be largely 'taken for granted'" (1979 219). Habermas describes the "lifeworld" as "a reservoir of taken-for-granteds, of unshaken convictions that participants in communication draw upon in cooperative processes of interpretation. . . . We can think of the lifeworld as represented by a culturally transmitted and linguistically organized stock of interpretive patterns" (1987c 124). According to Giddens, the recursive reproduction of the lifeworld is "*not a motivated phenomenon*" (1979 219). Rather, the simple repetition of various routinized activities reinforce the lifeworld without agents consciously intending that reinforcement or, for that matter, consciously reflecting on the whys and wherefores of their actions. "Where routine prevails, the rationalisation of conduct readily conjoins the basic security system of the actor to the conventions that exist and are drawn upon in interaction as mutual knowledge. This is why, in routinised social circumstances, actors are rarely able, nor do they feel the need, in response to the inquiries they make of one another in the course of social activity, to supply reasons for behavior that conforms to convention."

To locate social reproduction in the daily repetition of actions that take conventions, mutual knowledge, and social hierarchies for granted introduces temporality into our model of society. Some changes in the lifeworld— Giddens offers linguistic change as the prime example—will occur simply as the unintended result of use. Daily routines will never be repeated exactly, so changes will be introduced, albeit accidentally. More important, this insistence that reproduction depends on repeated actions by agents opens up the possibility of "conscious social innovation" (1979 221). Motivated (as contrasted to unmotivated) change will generally be accompanied by a sense of crisis, with an appeal to external exigencies or to a new interpretation of social purposes serving as the justification for new practices. Inevitably, only part of the lifeworld can be called into question at any particular moment; the appeal for change will itself take for granted other parts of the shared knowledge and values that reside in the lifeworld. Particular situations, conflicts, or contradictions (between two different spheres, for example) can bring some usually unnoticed component of the lifeworld to the attention of those engaged in a specific intersubjective exchange, forcing the renegotiation of the consensual grounds that allow that exchange to take place.

I want to be careful not to make this process appear too reflective. Giddens rightfully stresses unmotivated reproduction as primary, because agents, acting for completely different reasons, also serve to reproduce the lifeworld; however, the location of the responsibility for reproduction in agents' hands does explain how the social order is created over time by its members and does indicate the possibility of their active, conscious intervention in that creation at certain moments. The great advantage of Giddens's account is that change takes place in practice, not thought, and on the site of the routines made possible by social conventions and institutions. Nothing in Giddens's model prevents the influence of thought (or theory) on practice, but thought without practice would leave the recursive social milieu untouched, while practice external to the lifeworld (if such a negative freedom were even possible) would fail to confront the status quo on its most fundamental and persistent level. In other words, Giddens's model of social reproduction indicates both that the other, some untainted external agent, is not in a very good position to intervene in the temporal process of social change and that a conflict of ideologies (the refutation of existing justifications in favor of justifications that call for different conventions, institutions, and practices) would similarly miss that most crucial part of social reproduction which takes place beneath or apart from thought in the daily exchanges between agents on institutional sites.

One conclusion we might draw from the notions of the lifeworld and recursive reproduction is that a radical vision of change will attract a large popular response only when it takes concrete existence as a lived alternative at a social site where certain types of alternative exchanges are enacted. The power of examples, in which some people can be shown to be living out alternatives, greatly exceeds the power of the abstract representations provided by thought. For writers like Michel de Certeau and Charles Altieri, the aesthetic takes up its peculiar, and essential, social place exactly here. As Certeau phrases it, stories "are *repertories of schemas of action* between partners [that] . . . teach the tactics possible within a given (social) system" (1988 23). Naismith is the lawgiver, the system builder of basketball, but Michael Jordan is its artist/storyteller. For Altieri, the aesthetic thus expresses particular possibilities that are staged as examples of attitudes that an agent might wish to adopt.[18] Theories cannot adequately convey the "thick" texture of lived social existence or the sense of security actors gain from their reliance on everything within the lifeworld that they can take for granted. The legitimacy of a social order in the eyes of its members derives as much from its provision of this thick context that makes daily interchanges unproblematic as it does from abstract questions of justice or equality. In other words, legitimacy is conferred not only by the congruence between social procedures and social norms but also by the successful achievement and maintenance of a social identity, a shared lifeworld that social members ratify each day in their routine activities. By ignoring this daily immersion in the lifeworld and by holding society solely accountable to abstract, disembodied norms (which they despair of ever seeing embodied), the postmodern theorists both misunderstand the nature of legitimacy and discount the accrued legitimacy of contemporary Western society. Paradoxically, this attitude leads them to both underestimate and overestimate the possibility of change. In their manic, euphoric moments, they believe in absolute revolutionary transformation, writing as if pure thought can foster such change and its historical moment is upon us. In their more despairing moments, these same writers announce the tragic inev-

---

[18]Altieri (1981 270–307, and 1987) accounts for literature's rhetorical power and its ability to make significant contributions to our meditations on ethical matters by the prevalence of "exemplars" or "types" in literature over arguments. The appeal of this position lies both in its explanation of the literary critic's usually unformulated sense that literary works embody ideals and viewpoints not found elsewhere (or at least not in as satisfactory a form) and its providing a connection between a particular type of discourse (literature) and the activity of morals understood as "properties displayed in performance" (1981 279) before others. Altieri (1990) faults "oppositional postmodern" painting (exemplified by Hans Haacke's work) for its attachment to "a language of resistance [which] allows neither self-representation nor the respect for the other necessary" to "shape a significant particularity" (22–23). (I quote from a typescript of this forthcoming essay kindly sent my way by Professor Altieri.) The similarity of this complaint to my own and McCarthy's (1989) account of Derrida's "politics of the ineffable" is noteworthy. A reliance on examples over abstract arguments recalls the central revelation of the revolutionary, Pietro Spina, in Silone's *Bread and Wine*, the lesson he learns from his old teacher, Don Benedetto: "I am convinced that it would be a waste of time to show a people of intimidated slaves a different manner of speaking, a different manner of gesticulating; but perhaps it would be worth while to show them a different way of living. No word and no gesture can be more persuasive than the life, and, if necessary, the death, of a man who strives to be free, loyal, just, sincere, disinterested; a man who shows what a man can be" (1946 256).

itability of oppression, of perpetual illegitimacy, and of the untroubled reproduction of the current unjust arrangements.

SOCIAL AND INDIVIDUAL IDENTITY

We can extend Giddens's model of recursive reproduction by adopting Bowles and Gintis's observation that "the *constitutive* character of social action—the fact that social actors are transformed by their very acts—entails that social choice transforms not only the rules of the game, but the subjects of social life themselves" (1987 118). Applied to communities, this notion of action, while recognizing that "groups of people . . . come together for instrumental reasons (the Hobbesian community)" or "for reasons of common concern (. . . the sentimental community)," emphasizes that communities exist "for reasons of identity" (1987 230 n. 29).[19] The shared lifeworld that is reinforced in daily actions constitutes a shared identity; liberal individualism and the leftism that stresses ideological mystification both have continually underestimated the strength of commitments to communities that provide an identity along with a way of life. If resistance to change can be tied to interest, it certainly cannot be tied to anything narrowly understood as economic interest. As the traditional conservatism of the peasantry or the contemporary conservatism of American blue-collar and clerical workers reveals, threats to settled social identities often outweigh purely economic considerations in shaping political attitudes. Postliberalism represents, among other things, an attempt to capture this crucial aspect of social life, most fully articulated by Edmund Burke, from its almost exclusive association (to date) with conservatism.

To recognize commitment to social identity as an important (although not exclusive) motive for agents is necessarily to question the explanatory power of interest. In fact, interest, no matter how defined, has proved an almost completely worthless tool in predicting political or social behavior, and the term, so beloved of many contemporary literary theorists, would best be abandoned altogether.[20] When the term is not used tautologically to name

---

[19]Bowles and Gintis are following the lead of Michael Sandel here. Sandel describes "the constitutive conception" of community as entailing for a group's member "not just what they *have* as fellow citizens but also what they *are*, not just a relationship they choose (as in a voluntary association) but an attachment they discover, not merely an attribute but a constituent of their identity" (1982 150).

[20]See Reddy (1987) for a good summary of the empirical and theoretical arguments against the explanatory or predictive power of notions of interest.

what motivates an action (as in Stanley Fish's work), it usually functions as a red herring, highlighting one particular type of motive without considering the range of other motives. Attempts such as Bourdieu's to supplement economic interest with a concept of "symbolic interest" merely offer some concession to the existence of noneconomic motives without justifying the maintenance of the overarching term of *interest*. (Bourdieu retains the word *interest* because, in the final instance, he maintains that the symbolic can always be converted back into the economic.) Finally, the very notion of interest carries a theoretical bias toward liberal individualism, since in the work of Adam Smith and Jeremy Bentham it assumes an agent who acts from motives constituted apart from social circumstances. Marx, of course, introduces the notion of class interest to overcome liberalism's asocial individualism, but the abject failure of class interest to manifest itself in history has revealed the clumsiness of the term. Furthermore, Marx's version of interest, like liberalism's, theoretically ignores the formation of identities (be they class or individual identities) through constitutive communal action and thus underestimates the stake that a class or an individual can have in maintaining that identity.

This last point brings me to the reconsideration of individualism that I believe is essential to understanding the possibility of freedom and of political action. As with the notion of semiautonomy, postliberalism attempts to steer a plausible path between liberal, humanist individualism and the poststructuralist deconstruction of the self. To summarize briefly, the poststructuralist critique rests either on holistic statements of how the self is constituted by language, power, or some such monolithic entity or on the ontological priority of diversity, arguing that any unified notion of the self is a later imposition (of tyrannical Western/capitalist reason) on this primordial flux. My position is that individual identity, like communal identity, is a construct and, more particularly, a construct created through constitutive action. The transcendental, theoretical aspect of my argument is that action must necessarily be constitutive; in other words, a self-identity must be constructed by any individual who is "thrown" (to use Heidegger's term) into a network of intersubjective relations. The resulting self is the product of a process, is radically nonautonomous, but is differentiated from other selves and possesses an identity that unifies its disparate experiences, guides the presentation of the self to others, and forms the context for the various choices that the self makes.

We can take the family as the primal scene (which is why feminist work on the family is so crucial) in which the construction of identity takes place, but a similar process occurs within other social groupings in which the individual finds herself or with which, in later life, she chooses to align herself. The child has no choice but to occupy the position of "daughter," "sister," "niece," and so forth, and these relational names highlight her dependence on the others in the household for the first indications of identity in the world. The details of how the child then grows into this identity, and the ability (always less than total) she has to alter it, vary from one psychological theory to another; I take as axiomatic that this self-identity is formulated in relation to others, that the process still leaves various moves or strategies open to the self, that the self must go through some process (in adolescence or at another time) of recognizing its identity as its own, and that the alternative to identity formation (what we call psychosis or schizophrenia) is not a matter of choice and is never experienced as anything but painful. Within contemporary psychological theory, I think it safe to say that the first of these axioms is completely noncontroversial. Even ego psychology grants some kind of individualist autonomy to selves only at a date long after their formative childhood experiences; liberal individualism accommodates this perspective by not recognizing the self as a fully autonomous "chooser" until it has reached some designated "age of reason."[21] My other three axioms are more controversial. Let us consider each of them in turn.

Freud and subsequent psychologists have often written as if determinate paths of identity formation are laid out for the whole species, with particular crucial hurdles that are either cleared or not. (The Oedipal complex is only the most famous instance.) Yet the wonder of Freud's case histories lies in their particularity, in the distinctive experiences of his patients and the theories, symptoms, defenses, and character traits they devise to deal with those experiences. Even within a culture in which familial patterns are fairly uniform, there still remains a wide variety of possible responses, with a resultant wide variety of individual personalities. The monolithic theorist must either take the rather implausible tack of denying the existence of this diversity or, more usually, argue that the differences are insignificant since they do not locate individual selves outside the general character type that the culture produces for its own purposes. In this latter case, differences are utterly trivialized. It is one of the oddities of postmodern thought that it is obsessed

[21]See Bowles and Gintis (1987 chap. 5) for an account of liberalism's need to distinguish between "learners" (those still incapable of fully rational choice) and "choosers" (fully constituted, "mature" and rational beings). Such an account becomes particularly pernicious when not only children but also "primitive" peoples, women, and other socially marginal groups are denied full political participation on the basis of their not being ready or able to act as choosers. Bowles and Gintis argue that the constitutive character of action means that we are all learners and choosers all the time; no threshold of passage from one condition to the other could ever be identified.

with difference at the same time that it so often argues that the differences we experience in everyday life are insignificant. We could, of course, explain this obsession and the search for a "real" difference, a true other, as the obvious consequence of the belief that differences have disappeared in a monolithic world; but this explanation avoids that other part of postmodern thought that continually proclaims that differences are everywhere.

My third and fourth axioms go right to the heart of a reconstructed postliberal individualism. Obviously, I am following up on my earlier comments on Kierkegaardian irony. Because an identity is constructed in an intersubjective process that takes place in the self's earliest years, the self, at a later time, can easily experience that identity as given or imposed and as inadequate to some other sense of self. Lacan has been the most brilliant theorist of this experience of alienation, locating its genesis in the very earliest moments of childhood, in the mirror stage. But I must admit that Lacan's formulation of the matter does not satisfy me, because his version still rests on a contrast between the imposed identity (the unified image in the mirror) and some vague, but still foundational, reality (the child's amorphous experience of her uncoordinated body). I want to portray the process as much more fundamentally social. The experience of alienation from the earliest identity (or earlier identities) stems from the creation of new identities in new intersubjective contexts, not from some existential split between the social and the true self. It is the need to reconcile old and new or to scuttle one in favor of the other that produces identity crisis or alienation. The ironic position of Kierkegaard, it seems to me, indicates a negative (in the Freudian sense of the term) awareness of identity's fundamental social character by indulging in the fantasy of escaping all social bonds. That such a fantasy is probably more the result of feeling caught between two or more seemingly incompatible sets of social demands, rather than the result of some intuition of a true self, helps explain Kierkegaard's willingness to give up the whole struggle in the faithful acceptance of an all-embracing religious obligation. In other words, even negative identity must be staged for someone and Kierkegaard must imagine an ideal audience—his readers or God—when the demands of the audiences he faces directly each day become too conflicting. Self-identity exists for me only insofar as its exists for others. When the context of my social interactions shifts, so does my identity; the famous identity crises of adolescence come from moving out of the family into other social worlds, and those conflicts subside when one settles down once again into a set of fairly stable social positions.

But why, as my fourth axiom insists, is identity a necessity? Why do we feel the need to reconcile the various selves we are in various settings? Why do I argue that the serial self or the schizophrenic self are conditions that we cannot will? My position here returns to the fundamental role of social recognition. Just as the self is recognized by a community as a member of that group who occupies a certain position and possesses certain abilities, so the self must recognize the individual recognized by the group as himself. The self's very existence rests on this dual recognition. Despite the romantic nonsense to the contrary, the schizophrenic who fails to negotiate the various (often conflicting) roles and demands associated with different social contexts can only experience that failure as terrifying, as a condition to be rectified. The schizophrenic is merely the repository of other voices, unable to recognize a voice to call his own in the cacophony. Jameson seems to me completely right on this score. The multiplication in the late twentieth century of social groupings, of images, and of voices, coupled with the destruction of the limiting, binding force of tradition, makes schizophrenia *the* malady of the age—and to embrace the malady as the cure is absurd. Schizophrenia serves the purposes of consumer capitalism precisely because it is such a highly anxious state; the self without an identity will be constantly in search of one, seeking through compulsive consumerism to obtain the identities that society portrays as accompanying possession of this or that item.

Romantically considered, schizophrenia can look like the most absolute rejection of the social. The schizophrenic refuses to adopt as his own any of the identities that various social contexts have conferred on him. I believe, however, that this refusal cannot be willed; no one can choose or desire to be a schizophrenic. But even if I am wrong in this belief, the condition of schizophrenia is completely dysfunctional, a stance in the world that completely abolishes the individual's capacity to act, since action is predicated on the individual's assuming an identity that can be recognized by the group. Schizophrenia, then, could be theorized as the achievement of exclusion, which might seem desirable to those in search of the other but which carries all the anxieties and disabilities of exclusion without, as far as I can see, any of its advantages, since the effective other still operates from some social context that is itself other than the context he wishes to transform.

The successful recognition of identity on the part of the self involves, then, a reconciliation to the necessary social bases of the self, a construction of identity that manages (albeit in many cases fragilely and with difficulty) to tie together the self's various social roles, and that establishes the self's ability to act purposively and meaningfully. This process is fully dialectic. To paraphrase Marx, we can say that the self constructs itself but not in circumstances of its own making. Only where the self recognizes as its own the identity that it has for others can it act constitutively. The self constructs its identity by enacting it before others; that others witness its actions and recognize them as signs of its identity establishes the purposive ground of action. The self does not move from one random reflection of temporary impulse to the next but makes decisions based upon the identity it wishes to stage for others.[22]

Firmly situated within the social whole, the self gains access to the social codes by which identities are constituted and, through its actions, can shape the social identity it projects. Two cautions are needed here. The first must stress that my use of the phrase *gain access* might seem to suggest that the self has some kind of autonomous existence before it gains access. Such is not the case. I only want to suggest that sometime in adolescence the self begins to acquire a greater input into the process of identity formation, an ability to reflect upon a range of possible courses of action made available by the social contexts into which the self is born or that it now seeks out. However, and here is the second caution, the self obviously never gains anything like total control of this intersubjective process. The codes for the interpretation of action are still social, the ability to restrict the interpretations others place on one's actions is limited, and the identity one tries to project is influenced by the available models and mores of the social group as well as by the identity one carries from the past. Nevertheless, these constraints can be theorized as impediments to freedom only where the possibility of constitutive, purposive action outside of this intersubjective arena is asserted. The argument for positive freedom rests on the insistence that meaningful action by selves can take place only where a social group registers the import of that action and where the identity of the self vis-à-vis both itself and others is always part of what is at stake in any action. It is because our primary motivations are social that the range of those motivations is restricted by the social world we inhabit, but that situation looks like unfreedom only when we believe that there can exist nonsocial motivations forged in the smithy of our true, authentic, autonomous selves.

[22]I understand my whole description of personal identity formation as a restatement, in twentieth-century terms, of Hegel's discussion of the will, freedom, and right in the Introduction to his *Philosophy of Right* (1967a 14–36). Charles Taylor is the contemporary philosopher who has most fully indicated the significance of Hegel in discussions of identity and I am particularly indebted to Taylor's insistence that humans are "self-interpreting animals" who have second-order intentions directed toward the establishment of a certain kind of self, not just first-order intentions geared toward the satisfaction of immediate needs. Taylor has specifically linked this strong version of identity to the insufficiency of a concept of negative liberty in his justly famous essay, "What's Wrong with Negative Liberty?" (1985b 211–29). See also Taylor (1976, and 1985a 1–44, 97–114, and 248–292) for discussions of "agency," of "person," and of the communal bases of meaning that are, I believe, the most lucid and convincing accounts of these notoriously tricky issues to be found in contemporary work.

NEGATIVE FREEDOM, THEORY, AND MODERNITY

If negative freedom is impossible, why is it such a persistent fantasy? I think the answer lies in the historical conjunction of modernity and liberal individualism. Modernity's attack on tradition stems, in large part, from its simultaneous encounter (after 1492) with diverse cultures around the globe and its multiplication of semiautonomous spheres within a single culture. As a result of this proliferation of available social sites, the definition of both social and individual identities came to rely increasingly on contrast. The Greeks differentiated themselves from the barbarians, of course, and we know that almost no cultures anywhere have ever existed in isolation. The boundaries of recognition, of inclusion/exclusion, have always rested to some extent on the contrast between them and us instead of on some intrinsic quality possessed by members. What appears distinctive about modernity is that the difference between selves moves (not completely, of course) from being marked by different positions occupied in the social whole to being marked by contrastive assertions about defining qualities such as intelligence, talent, moral rectitude, industriousness, and the like.[23] With the proliferation of semiautonomous spheres and the resultant social mobility, the internal qualities of selves can be seen as explaining where on the social map they finally take up residence. Bourdieu has brilliantly outlined how taste can function as one of these mysterious inner qualities that explains social diversity and stratification; taste in modern societies is fundamentally contrastive, achieving its significance only in relation to the awful tastes of others that it spurns.[24] Any meritocratic justification of social differences must be based on an appeal to inner qualities (as opposed to inherited advantages, given social places, or sociohistorical determinants). Thus liberalism both explains and justifies the new kinds of social/economic differences characteristic of modernity by contrasting individuals one to another rather than by contrasting social orders or contexts. The individual, we might say, is now encouraged to define herself in the negative, contrastive way that was once reserved for the way one culture viewed itself in relation to another. Thus, from a rather different perspective, I am urging a historical account of individualism rather similar to Foucault's. Modernity isolates the individual by encouraging the notion of autonomous, innate (or at least self-developed) qualities that then explain the individual's social accomplishments; the necessary corollary of this isolation is an institu-

---

[23]I have tried to describe this historical shift from external to internal determinants of personal worth in my essay on Jane Austen (1985). McKeon (1985) focuses on the same shift in his discussion of Richardson and the rise of the novel.
[24]See Bourdieu (1984).

tional order that examines, differentiates among, and rewards these various selves. The dream of negative freedom makes sense only within a social context in which the greatest prestige and material rewards go to those who most successfully transcend the more local bonds of commitment to others in a community. Autonomy is socially created and socially rewarded in modernity.

The issue of the isolated modern individual permeates classical sociology, most memorably in Tönnies's famous distinction between *Gemeinschaft* and *Gesellschaft* and in Tocqueville's concern about the erosion of intermediate social groupings that could dissipate the intensity of the pure confrontation between the solitary self and the state/social whole. Habermas now offers his own version of this issue in differentiating between lifeworld and system. For Habermas, the autonomous, systemic spheres that characterize modernity are abstract, norm free, and oriented toward successful, efficient action in a way that contrasts markedly with the lifeworld's orientation to intersubjective mutuality and the reproduction of the social integration founded on social consensus.

> These systemic interconnections, detached from normative contexts and rendered independent as subsystems, challenge the assimilative powers of an all-encompassing lifeworld. They congeal into the 'second nature' of a norm-free sociality that can appear as something in the objective world, as an *objectified* context of life. The uncoupling of system and lifeworld is experienced in modern society as a particular kind of objectification: the social system definitively bursts out of the horizon of the lifeworld, escapes from the intuitive knowledge of everyday communicative practice, and is henceforth accessible only to the counterintuitive knowledge of the social sciences developing since the eighteenth century. (1987c 173)

Thus Habermas's description of our contemporary situation focuses on the invasion of the lifeworld by the different forms of reason characteristic of the economic system of production and the administrative system of the great bureaucracies. "The tasks of passing on a cultural tradition, of social integration and of socialization require adherence to what I call communicative rationality. But the occasions for protest and discontent originate precisely when spheres of communicative action, centered on the reproduction and transmission of values and norms, are penetrated by a form of modernization guided by standards of economic and administrative rationality—in other words, by standards of rationalization quite different from those of communicative rationality on which those spheres depend" (1983 8). For Habermas, the project of modernity, of the Enlightenment, was "to develop objective science, universal morality and law, and autonomous art according to their inner logic" (1983 9), but "the Enlightenment philosophers also wanted to utilize the accumulation of specialized culture for the enrichment of everyday life."

"The project of modernity has not been fulfilled" (1983 13) because the autonomous spheres have separated themselves too drastically from the life-world, at times overwhelming it, at other times deforming it. The solution Habermas urges is not to abandon ourselves to a proliferation of incommen-surate activities but to continue the second half of modernity's project: the connection of systems and lifeworld. "The life-world has to become able to develop institutions out of itself which set limits to the internal dynamics and imperatives of an almost autonomous economic system and its administrative complements." Within this perspective, the role of theory, of philosophy, is rethought. "Philosophy . . . might do well to refurbish its link with totality by taking the role of interpreter on behalf of the lifeworld. It might then be able to set in motion the interplay between the cognitive-instrumental, moral-practical, and aesthetic-expressive dimensions that has come to a standstill today" (1987b 313).[25]

The modern individual experiences himself as confronting the various systems in an abstract form that places his isolated self in relation to a set of procedures, rules, and outcomes that, if embodied, find form only at distant institutional sites. (The frequent inadequacy of these sites as representations of system is evident as soon as we ponder the question of where "the market" is embodied; similarly, the act of voting as one's single input to political processes is awfully abstract.) Modernity, then, not only proliferates the contexts in which the self can act but also introduces a new kind of context that is not shaped around a visible community that shares a set of taken-for-granted norms. Postmodernity, from this Habermasian perspective, only names the heightened complexity of our own moment of modernity joined with a new set of intellectual and artistic responses to that complexity. Habermas deplores these responses, since he believes that they accede to the multiple differentiations of our time (hence his notorious labeling of Lyotard and Foucault as "young conservatives" [1983 14]). Instead, Habermas wants

---

[25]Habermas's essay "Philosophy as Stand-In and Interpreter" (1987b) lays out clearly the claims he believes philosophy (theory) can and still must make even within the context of contemporary antifoundationalism. In this essay, Habermas sets out what aspects of the Kantian, transcendental project he wishes to save, as well as his understanding of the Hegelian and pragmatist objections to the Kantian project. Crucially, Habermas rejects any notion that philosophy might "ground" cultural practices or cultural knowledge; "epistemic authority" belongs "to the community of all who cooperate and speak with one another," not to philosophy (1987b 314). Instead, he proposes for philosophy the task of attempting to mediate among the various spheres, with their different forms of rationality.

to retain the Enlightenment hope of combining the expanded sites of action afforded by differentiation with a nondeformed, fully holistic lifeworld.

Marx and numerous subsequent writers have made us aware of how the shattering of the old, traditional communities can be experienced both as exhilaratingly liberating and as disorienting and frightening. Certainly, this transformation fosters that type of negative freedom enjoyed by selves who escape from ties to a visible community to constitute themselves in relation to an invisible community, whose very invisibility makes it (at times) appear nonexistent. One good example of the consequences of this shift is the liberation from the constraints upon how much wealth one can amass; in a traditional community, where others are direct witnesses of one's wealth, limits (achieved through redistribution techniques such as potlatches and charities) are almost invariably set. But the escape from such communities into the abstract world of the market effectively demolishes such limits. Of course, the self could probably never abandon the lifeworld altogether, but liberal individualism embraces modernity's offer of constituting the self within much more abstract social frameworks.

Habermas and Alvin Gouldner also offer reasons for associating the birth of theory itself with the same conditions of modernity that foster the liberal model of negative freedom. The splitting off of various spheres from the lifeworld, along with the questioning of traditional mores that resulted from the encounter with so many other cultures, meant that the lifeworld lost much of its taken-for-granted character. Everyday practices are subjected to more scrutiny and must be more explicitly justified, hence the development of the social sciences. In particular (at least according to Habermas) the abstract spheres do not possess the "intuitive" rightness of the lifeworld, and therefore must be legitimated. The whole discourse of legitimation requires reflection upon grounds and, in Gouldner's view, produces the class of intellectuals whose job it is to produce the ideologies that justify the social order.[26] Finally, the self's participation in various spheres gives it not only the task of reconciling its practices and activities within each of those spheres with its sense of its identity but also a multiplicity of perspectives from which it can reflect on the characteristics of the various spheres and on the various components of its own identity. Theory is the self-consciousness generated when selves inhabit multiple social contexts.

[26]The connection of industrialization's destruction of traditional communities to the emergence of ideological discourses produced by intellectuals to legitimate the new order is the basic theme of Gouldner's *The Dialectic of Ideology and Technology* (1982a). Thus Gouldner sees intellectuals as from the start distanced from the communities in which the lifeworld functions so smoothly that no explicit account of its workings or its legitimacy is ever required.

Such a formulation, then, suggests that theoretical thought and an attachment to negative freedom go hand in hand, both born out of the abstract relation to disembodied social systems that, with modernity, increasingly play a larger role (even though they do not entirely replace traditional communities) in the self's constitutive confrontations with the social. And Gouldner's work suggests that this combination is particularly characteristic of the intellectuals who embrace, articulate, and legitimate modernity's dramatic break with the past and with the local. Postliberalism does not advocate a conservative (or neoconservative) return to traditional communities or authorities; rather, it stresses that the abstract spheres are still social contexts, thus denying that liberal individualism achieves the kind of autonomy negative freedom claims to have gained, while also striving to bring the abstract spheres back into accountability to the social consensus and norms. It recognizes this agenda as quintessentially political; but before attempting to describe the features of this politics, I must address the understanding of power that my postliberal model of society proposes.

POWER

Power manifests itself at the point of connection between the constitutive action of individuals and the sites within the semiautonomous spheres (or systems) where that action takes place. Recall that the various spheres have their specific procedures, institutions, and canons of rationality. These arrangements are putatively instrumental, allowing for the smooth (i.e., not stymied by irresolvable conflict or counterproductive complication) social achievement of particular ends. In a perfect world this smooth achievement fosters power in its positive sense: the capacity to reach a specific destination through purposive action. The almost complete absence of this positive notion of power (whose opposite is impotence) in most postmodern theory is noteworthy. Apparently, the twentieth century's repeated experiences of social tyranny have led to a loss of faith in the power to do certain things that can be achieved only collectively, not individually. Needless to say, despite the refusal to articulate theoretically positive power, contemporary intellectuals endorse it practically all the time, especially in their reliance on educational institutions and communications media. Giddens's model of recursive reproduction explains how individuals can participate every day in these social institutions without ever accepting that they are participating in the positive social maintenance of these sites. The drama of staging one's identity for family, peers, or other groups takes place on these social sites, but the individual's stake in becoming a writer or a basketball player can be distinguished from society's stake in preserving, maintaining, reforming, or changing the institutions and procedures that mark these sites. What Giddens's model makes us realize is that by pursuing her individual course of action, the individual contributes to social reproduction.

Of course, we hardly inhabit a perfect world, and the spheres do not always function to maximize the communal power to achieve particular goals or the individual's attempt to forge a recognizable identity. We can recognize four negative forms of power. (Power in this sense is linked not to capacity but to domination, and its opposite is freedom, not impotence.) The first instance of negative power occurs when the procedural imperatives of the spheres overwhelms the lifeworld contexts of identity formation. Habermas dwells on this particular problem, of course, and I do not spend much time on it here. Agents experience this power when they feel pressured by incompatible demands, one set of which emanates from the formal, impersonal, even legal, requirements of participation in corporations, bureaucracies, or educational institutions, while the other set stems from personal relations to family, friends, coworkers, or peers. Habermas thinks of the formal systems as "language-independent" (1987c 318), since they are structured formally and legally apart from the ongoing communicative interactions of the lifeworld. Inevitably, such a vision of the systems leads Habermas to talk of reification,[27] and in my opinion to underestimate the opportunities that recursive reproduction gives agents to modify and resist institutionalized systems just as they maneuver in the lifeworld. To the extent that institutional arrangements predetermine an agent's range of options and, more important, cause him to abandon an identity previously assumed, we can identify an instance of power as domination. (The key theoretical point here, which sometimes appears to get lost in Foucault and some of his followers in literary theory, is that it makes no sense to talk of power and domination unless power works upon something that the subject of power wants to hold on to but is forced to give up.)

The second instance of power manifests itself where institutional arrangements establish an inequality among agents participating in the activities enabled and organized by the institution. Power as domination exists where the procedures of any sphere place certain agents in positions of advantage or disadvantage in their interactions. In such a case, the outcomes of intersubjective encounters on the institutional site "get prejudged for participants in a typical fashion," to use Habermas's phrase (1987c 187). We should dis-

---

[27]See Habermas (1987c 332–73) for his use of the concept of "reification" to denote "a pathological de-formation of the communicative infrastructure of the lifeworld" (1987c 375).

tinguish here between a teleological and a structural explanation of power. A teleological explanation stresses how certain groups manipulate, forge, or maintain particular social arrangements to their advantage. The Marxist notion of a ruling class is the most obvious example. The structural view, to be found in Foucault and Bourdieu, tries to evade teleological inference, focusing instead on the specific power over another that accompanies a given position in a social sphere. The individual possesses that power only as long as she occupies that position, and the advantages gained from that temporary occupation are far from obvious. The individual is a functionary of power, is used by it. The only teleology in this view appears to be power's own desire to maintain itself. The problem here, of course, is the oddness of talking about power's desires apart from any particular human agents. The middle Foucault makes very little effort to justify this personification of power or to indicate how he gains interpretive access to power's needs and wants.

These problems aside, the structural view highlights the crucial fact that the hierarchical and stratified arrangements within the semiautonomous spheres characterize a social site in which the intersubjective exchanges through which recognition and identity formation are achieved are not carried out between equals. This fact, however, can be a matter of indignation that justifies a call for radical remedial action only if we accept an egalitarian norm. The existence of hierarchies and of structural inequities can be easily legitimated if efficiency, productivity, or social order are the prevalent social norms. Structural power becomes delegitimated only where the egalitarian norm is recognized as applicable to each social sphere. In other words, the economic goals of production/distribution and the educational goals of transmitting and producing knowledge can be legitimately pursued only within the bounds prescribed by the fundamental social norm of equality. We can decry structural power only in the name of a principle that defines its illegitimacy, and that principle can be socially efficacious only where it represents a fundamental social consensus. A utilitarian justification of equality may appear to escape this appeal to a social norm by appealing instead to the beneficial consequences of equality; in other words, by claiming that efficiency in economic production would be maximized by egalitarian, democratic arrangements at the sites of production.[28] But such an argument still assumes a social norm of equality, since it is the resentment and unhappiness of workers or students trapped in unequal arrangements that the utilitarian believes impedes the

---

[28]Bowles and Gintis make such a utilitarian argument by claiming that "the reduction in enforcement costs" gained in the democratic workplace would "contribute to a more effective system of production" (1987 205).

maximal functioning of the economic and educational spheres. Only the prior existence of the norm can explain the resentment.

The third instance of power involves the violation of a particular sphere's autonomy. In pursuit of its particular end, each sphere develops the appropriate procedures; this process of "rationalization" by now (1990) encompasses a long, pragmatic (trial-and-error) historical development of means that function to accomplish the sphere's tasks. These techniques constitute the various spheres' specificity. Power manifests itself where and when a sphere's procedures and institutions become answerable to goals other than those internal to the sphere. Thus various prevalent practices on college campuses are clearly motivated by economic concerns, not by the pursuit and dissemination of knowledge. Similarly, advocates of a "free market" argue that political considerations (the government's need to keep voters happy, say) interfere with the pure pursuit of economic goals.

Postmodernism, of course, denies the possibility of autonomy and has continually demonstrated that various social spheres that pride themselves on or try to defend their autonomy are really (at best) the product of mixed motives. Furthermore, a suspicious, demystifying hermeneutic not only discredits any pure singularity of motive but also indicates that the most powerful motives are usually those least acknowledged. Thus the pursuit of advantage (be it economic, political, or social) is revealed as the true determinant of particular social institutions and techniques. The oddness of this position is the moral fervor with which it is put forward. If, as a matter of necessity, all social activities manifest an interested attempt to gain the upper hand, then it remains unclear what the source of outrage is. Perhaps some people are duped, and thus taken advantage of, by the rhetorical cover-up of naked interest. In that case, once all pretense of pure motives or autonomous procedures and ends is removed, all will be free to act in their own interest. But such a situation of enlightened (unclouded by false consciousness) pursuit of self-interest is the liberal ideal, surely not the implied goal of postmodernist demystification.

Power is clearly a negative term in postmodern polemics, connoting an illicit advantage of some agents over others at various social sites. The problem of dissolving all activities into instances of the will to power is that it collapses the very distinction between power and freedom that underlies the discussion from the start. A negative view of power can be maintained only where some positive notion of action not completely infected by power is advanced. Semiautonomy stands precisely for this positive notion of action, a notion willing to accept that power alters the procedures, institutions, and practices we might conceivably (or theoretically) expect from a pure pursuit of a sphere's goals if autonomy were ever possible, yet a notion that insists that other considerations apart from power do influence decisions and actions. The highly charged rhetoric surrounding the issue of power in postmodernist discourse indicates a desire to attain and protect some sort of semiautonomy, even while the monolithic logic of postmodern theory overwhelms that very possibility. A suspicious hermeneutic can always manage (in ways similar to the infuriating Freudian use of the labels "resistance" and "denial") to reinterpret each attempt to redraw the boundaries between power and knowledge (for example) as yet another instance of interest, but such recuperations cannot overcome the continual need to draw that very distinction if we are to talk about power at all and if we are to distinguish the specific procedures that inform our pursuit of knowledge. The uses to which those procedures are put will always be connected to agents' interests (derived from their existence in the lifeworld) and to pressures from other institutional spheres (the state, the economy), but that does not prevent all identification of the techniques and arrangements peculiar to educational institutions—an identification that allows agents to judge and to resist when their sphere's specificity is threatened.

Interference with a particular sphere's autonomy has to be seen as not only inevitable (semiautonomy, not autonomy, is the rule) but also ethically and politically ambiguous. The desirability of power's interference can be determined and negotiated only in specific instances between those who wish to interfere and those who want to resist interference. It is impossible to offer a general statement about state interference (for example) in the economy or in education. In a case such as state-enforced school integration, there are both benefits and costs; only a political decision about relative priorities and the desirability of risking certain consequences in order to reach certain goals can decide on interference or noninterference. Power's legitimacy in such cases will not depend—as pure, laissez-faire liberalism suggests—on its always and everywhere following a principle of noninterference, but on its interference being motivated by the relevant norms and on the decision to interfere having been reached by the agreed-upon democratic procedures.

The fourth instance of power involves the strong claim that, in Steven Lukes's words, "power may operate to shape and modify desires and beliefs in a manner contrary to people's interests" (1986a 10). I have already touched on some of the theoretical difficulties encountered by this notion of power in my discussion of Terry Eagleton's work. It presupposes an objective standard of interest that power violates and that can be known by the outside observer but not by the individual subject to power. The suspicious hermeneutic is necessary because power habitually obscures both its own workings and the disadvantages it imposes on subjects. *Ideology* and *false consciousness*, two closely linked terms, describe this successful mystification. Poststructural-ism's notion of a constituted subject strengthens the grasp power has on individuals, while Jameson's and Habermas's notion of a social totality that has become too complex for individuals to understand offers a new version of false consciousness, functioning now on a somewhat different level.[29]

One of the most satisfactory consequences of adopting Giddens's model of recursive reproduction is its reformulation of the usual understandings of ideology and false consciousness. As Giddens puts it, "the taken-for-granted cannot inevitably be equated with the accepted-as-legitimate. . . . Social life, in all societies, contains many types of practice or aspects of practices which are sustained in and through the knowledgeability [i.e., competence] of social actors but which they do not reproduce as a matter of normative commit-ment" (1981 65). Much of social life continues for no good reason—and no good reason is felt to be needed. Other portions of our daily routines may appear nonsensical or downright oppressive but inescapable because the very stuff of which daily life is made.[30] Thus, by going through the motions, agents may serve to reproduce social routines and institutions that they abhor. What is crucial here is that, in the absence of livable alternatives, agents are constrained to interact with others according to the available forms, and that such interactions do not imply intellectual consent. The emotional response to this situation appears to me a major point of differentiation between intellectuals and the populace (if I may be allowed this solecism; I generalize mostly from the attitudes expressed by my students, partly from the populist rhetoric found in various media). Intellectuals cheerfully disavow (or distance themselves from) their daily practices, offering instead allegiance to their theoretical principles, even though these principles exist only in thought and

---

[29]In his essay "Modern and Postmodern Architecture" (1985), Habermas identifies modern architecture with the will to understand, comment upon, and be involved in the social whole. "The spirit of modernism was to participate in the totality of social manifestations" (1985 322). The collapse of modernism is then seen as a reflection of a social reality that has become so complex that it can never be grasped in its totality by one viewer or in one place—an explanation of the transition from modern to postmodern architecture that is strikingly similar to Jameson's comments about the unrepresentable nature of late capitalism.

[30]See Abercrombie, Hill, and Turner (1980) for a full argument that the sheer facticity of the status quo, more than an ideologically manufactured consent to it, ensures the participation of social agents who understand perfectly well the system's inequities. Alain Touraine has wonder-fully sensible things to say about the nature of domination in contemporary societies and the points at which social conflict break out in *The Voice and the Eye* (1978 49–55). He has no patience for "the notion . . . of *dominant ideology*. This notion performs the function of a myth. Wherever practice does not match the image one wishes to impose upon it, the myth of the dominant ideology is cast into the chasm of the unintelligible: and are the dominated not reduced to the role inflicted upon them by the dominators? This is a theory that cannot be verified because it cannot be falsified, because it is truly mythical" (1978 51).

cannot (so far) be lived. Nonintellectuals defend everyday practices, even when admitting that such practices are far from perfect, on the ground that no demonstrably better, *concrete* alternative exists. The difference here is not between true and false consciousness; agents throughout the society generally appear perfectly capable of identifying inequality and other violations of justifying norms in the social institutions in which daily life takes place. The power vested in these institutions is not the mystification of agents but the much more direct (and perhaps even more unassailable) power of being the social reality in which life goes on.[31]

I want to reserve *ideology* as the term that designates the discourse of legitimation, a usage that follows Gouldner's and Ricoeur's writings on the subject.[32] The very need for such a discourse seems a defining characteristic of modernity. The existence of this need, and of the intellectual discourse devised to meet it, is hardly irrelevant to daily social life, since the gap between ideology and what actually goes on can serve as a focal point of resistance. But ideology understood this way cannot be used to explain the failure of resistance to occur. The ability of principles of legitimation to serve as acceptable social norms is a matter of social consent, and there is no reason to believe that parties to that consent make their decision from a position of false consciousness. (Some members of society may not be granted the ability to consent or dissent, but that is a matter of inegalitarian exclusion, not of

---

[31]I find persuasive Christopher Lasch's argument that the conservative victories in America in the 1980s did not reflect the people's inability to recognize the self-serving nature of Republican economic programs or the blatant contradiction between talking of fiscal responsibility while running up the largest peacetime deficits the nation has ever known. Lasch contends that voters choose the Republicans and their promise not to raise taxes out of a cynical despair that any new taxes, any new sacrifices, required of citizens will not be distributed equitably. The only defense of the relatively powerless against being made to carry more than their fair share of the burden is to support the party that transfers that burden onto the future. Lasch's analysis has the benefit of explaining two other conspicuous voter attitudes of the 1980s: the lack of any deep loyalty to either party and the conviction that whichever party wins, the little guy loses. Both of these attitudes explain the conjunction of the right's triumphs with unprecedented numbers deciding not to participate in elections at all. See Lasch (1988).

[32]For Gouldner, ideology is simply the speech of intellectuals, the way they try to explain (in theory), legitimate, and/or transform society. "Ideology premises it can transform society and surmount the tragic vision by the symbolic articulation and resonance of consciousness; by making it publicly accessible and visible through symbolic articulation. . . . Ideologies propose to change the world . . . through 'ideas' and through the rational appeal these may have to 'consciousness' " (1982a 82–83). Thus Gouldner abandons any attempt to differentiate between false ideologies and some kind of other, true discourse; the resolution of ideological conflicts occurs in the public space of social decision making, not on some epistemological grounds. Paul Ricoeur's *Lectures on Ideology and Utopia* (1986) has also influenced my thinking on both the topic of ideology and the issue of the fundamental attunement that lies at the basis of any social order. Ricoeur, among other things, offers a convincing refutation of Althusser's attempt to distinguish between ideology and science.

ideology or false consciousness.) Furthermore, there is no good reason to argue that certain agents are consistently unable to recognize the gap between accepted legitimating principles and the actualities of everyday practice. The evidence appears to favor just the opposite conclusion; agents are highly sensitive to and resentful of practices that violate their "rights" (to use the vocabulary in which such grievances are almost invariably expressed), and do whatever is possible to resist such violations. Power manifests itself not in ideology or false consciousness but in the more concrete limits it imposes on the possible forms of resistance. (To put it this way is to stress the "productive" side of power, its contribution to establishing the conditions under which we live. I hope it is clear, however, that I am far from presenting power as the sole productive agent of these social conditions. Traditions, norms, intersubjective ties geared toward the accomplishment of common purposes, the goals formulated by semiautonomous spheres and individuals, and the means adopted and actions undertaken to reach those goals are other contributing factors.)

Let me expand briefly on my objection to theories of "false consciousness." For starters, I think we should see that such theories are a prime instance of what Rorty calls the attempt to shift moral choices to matters of cognition. Individual action, I insist, is always based on relations to others to whom one feels answerable, and the choice among various possible courses of action is determined much less by knowledge than by the attempt to be the kind of person who is respected, admired, loved, or approved of by the others before whom and in relation to whom one acts. Let's take the concrete example of gender roles in contemporary America. Such roles are clearly in a state of flux; the lifeworld assumptions about gender are going through a historical and social process of transformation. Individuals, both women and men, who are negotiating their own relationships to spouses, friends, parents, children, employers, and various others during this transitional period will find such relationships more difficult, less easy to take for granted, than other social roles that are not currently being so extensively reexamined. We can identify as "ideologies" all the various possible models or images of gender roles that the society produces as it self-reflexively ponders this issue. And we can specify the various sites of that production (mass media, various popular oral forms such as jokes, academic discourse, among others). But I do not see how we can identify any particular individual's being influenced by any one of these images as "false consciousness" unless we have a predetermined sense of what the individual's interest must be and lay it down as a fixed rule that actions not furthering that interest could never be undertaken unless a cognitive mistake was involved. At best, we can perhaps talk about *incomplete* consciousness—that is, the fact that individuals probably never act upon knowledge of *all* the alternative images that have been produced at various sites in the culture. And I do think we can talk about how the inequities described in my discussion of the types of negative power will serve to give some members of the society less access to the totality of produced images than others. But unless we ascribe some kind of monolithic power to a culture industry that manages to make only one image available, I think we must see all individuals as having access to some range of models for action. Further, we must acknowledge that we fashion our own lived gender roles and own lived relation to others not according to some cognitive assessment of which role will best advance our interest (as if we know what that term might mean), but according to the daily give-and-take with the demands and expectations of the others with whom we live. In other words, social and gender roles are forged in the actual living of them, and a "false consciousness" theory is premised on an implausible model of choice as something made abstractly on cognitive grounds and on an implausible contention that individuals could, in their constant monitoring of their relation to others, fail to recognize (and thus fail to adjust), behavior that does not accomplish the purposes for which it was undertaken.

In the formation of new gender roles, power certainly plays a important part. The roles that will prove livable on a daily basis will have to respond to inequities that are lived every day. Thus, for me, the most significant factor in the current crisis of gender roles is the inescapable (for the majority of the population) economic fact of the late twentieth century that women must work. Women and men must now adjust their assumptions about (and their lived, daily experience of) gender roles to accommodate this new fact. The determination of what roles will prove possible is constrained by social arrangements in which power manifests itself as inequities that it also serves to maintain. Power's role explains why a full meditation on gender issues can open out into a much wider social critique. The question of where the gender crisis will eventually lead us is, to a large extent, a question about whether the adjustment of gender roles will remain confined to responding to changed economic conditions or will successfully bring about a realignment of economic realities.

Whether the more limited or the more drastic transformation occurs, however, is not a matter of false consciousness. At a time of crisis, we can expect the proliferation of culturally produced alternative images. Nothing precludes the critical appraisal of these images or arguments about their possibly desirous or disastrous consequences. But I do not see how any such critical appraisal can designate any particular image as, from the start, unlivable and only ever chosen by an individual because she has misunderstood the very terms of her social relation to others. Only the living out of various images will show us which ones work, and I think individuals have the ability (at least) to recognize what does or does not work in their own lives. Certainly it is the height of arrogance to think that we (no intellectual ever accuses himself of false consciousness) have this ability, but other members of the *polis* do not. Thus, whether gender issues lead to a restructuring of the economic depends, I believe, on whether the gender roles that become desirable to individuals who find them eminently livable (and satisfying) in personal relationships prove utterly contradictory with the current economic arrangements and there is widespread refusal to yield to the powerful facticity of what is lived as economic necessity. A daunting agenda, to say the least, and one that does not underestimate the blocking capacities of power but only refuses to think that individuals called upon to adjust to all kinds of conflicting claims and hopes in their daily lives are somehow blind to these conflicts and the compromises they are constrained to make all the time.

Let me add that my social theory would lead us to expect that the current rewriting of gender roles will result after a period of time in a set of assumptions (a range of livable roles) that will generally be taken for granted, become a settled part of the habitus, until some new transitional period opens up the issue again. Of course, as I have suggested, a crisis in one set of social relations might open up a wider crisis in the habitus and can, as certainly happens in some cases, lead to the dissolution of the whole formative social context. More usually, the general commitment to stability will have a conservative influence, so that the range of models that emerges from a crisis period will (as a radical would be quick to point out) likely be those that prove compatible with the larger social configuration. Certainly, this tendency toward compromise frustrates radical hopes; my only point is that, except when cherished social roles become unlivable, we really cannot expect there to be a mass impulse toward radicalism. Thus revolutionary change starts from daily, local practices that cannot find their way toward a livable continuation of ordinary life. For this reason, the current rewriting of gender roles is an extraordinary historic moment, one in which very large segments of the population are engaged in rethinking and rewriting the terms of a crucial segment of the habitus; this moment is fraught with difficulties, but also with heightened possibilities for dramatic change that fully justify the immense energy currently being devoted to this issue. Of course, radicals and conservatives alike are working hard either to widen or to limit the transformations that will attend the current rewriting. My point is that radicals have no right to accuse others of false consciousness who do not adopt the radical program;

these others have a different agenda, and they will lend support to radical calls for wide transformation insofar as current realities become unlivable. Outside of such moments of transformation, only small portions of the population are usually engaged in pondering images of action and of social being beyond the generally taken-for-granted range. (These radicals base their meditations on various radical traditions and the historical/textual record of alternatives imagined in earlier moments of transformation but then left behind by the lifeworld. As I have already suggested, radicals who do not live in times of transformation will often find it extremely difficult, if not impossible, to live out their imagined alternatives. It is this possibility of lived experimentation that makes times of transformation so fruitful.)

To return to the general discussion of power: all four instances of negative or constraining power that I have outlined might be said to point to *existing* constraints that inhibit the full working out of theoretically articulated possibilities. The first instance, the system's encroachment on the lifeworld, hampers achievement of the "ideal speech situation" so dear to Habermas. In the case of unequal social arrangements, our second instance, the specific theoretical norm of equality is never accomplished. The third instance, the exertion of various pressures on differentiated social spheres, renders the more general dream of autonomy inoperable. Finally, the fourth instance, which highlights the inertia of current arrangements, suggests an even more general explanation for the failure of accepted norms to find their way completely into practice. In other words, it is not surprising that intellectuals are so concerned with power in its negative sense, since such power stands for everything in the lived world that frustrates the rewriting of that world in the "absolute freedom" of thought. I must now consider if positive or situated freedom can describe effective political action less at odds with the concrete lifeworld and hence less continually frustrated by its inability to refashion that world totally.

POSITIVE FREEDOM AND THE RECOVERY OF THE POLITICAL

Our lived commitment to the lifeworld can, I believe, provide the terrain of political action under modernity's conditions, not the bounds of allegiance to the here and now that must be dissolved to gain a true, transcendent, negative freedom. Self-consciousness about norms and legitimation becomes political at the point where agreed-upon procedures of social decision making are utilized either to close the gap between everyday practices and those norms or to engage in the specific process of socially questioning and reforming the norms. This understanding of political action is utterly dependent on the notion of positive freedom because the political agent is dependent on the procedures for decision making already prevalent in the society (even when the goal is to change those procedures) and because the society's choice of actions and of legitimating principles (like an individual's choices) will derive from past choices. The political agent must engage that social past and those decision-making procedures, not only because they form the social grounds on which an enabling consensus could be reached, but also because they constitute the social grounds on which the individual can be recognized as a political agent in that society. The political reformer or revolutionary has only two choices if she wishes to bring about social change without any recourse to violence: either to appeal to existing norms that she convinces others are not being put into practice or to persuade others to adopt new norms, relying on the existing procedures of decision making to ratify the new norms. Thus she must use the existing norms to change the procedures or the existing procedures to change the norms, but she cannot expect to change both at the same time and also avoid violence.[33] Positive freedom names this embedding of agency within the social context that enables legitimate, purposive action. Power can be identified either as the inertia that makes society unresponsive to the political actions undertaken in positive freedom or as the violent attempt to impose new social norms or procedures without achieving a social consensus.

The dependence of political reform on social consensus underlines why negative freedom, even if it were possible, is so self-defeating a strategy for the would-be revolutionary. The "linguistic turn" in philosophy, sociology, and literary studies must be carried over into a politics that recognizes that the shared world of a language forms the basis for beginning to shape the kind of communal existence we wish to achieve. Habermas's crucial contribution has been to attempt to designate how that shared language both already provides us with certain norms and serves as the essential precondition (with its procedures for securing intersubjective understanding) for action of any sort. It is by pursuing the implications of this primary involvement in language and the social that we discover the ground and the means for political action, not by attempting to divorce ourselves from that involvement. We gain access to the political—the attempt to get the group to exercise its positive power (capacity) to achieve particular ends—only by virtue of participation in the

[33]See Altieri (1972) for a useful discussion of the would-be reformer's relation to the prevailing practices and norms of her society.

ethical (what Hegel calls *Sittlichkeit*), understood as the normative lifeworld consensus that grants us membership (the ability to participate) in the *polis*, the terms of appeal by which we urge fellow citizens to a particular end, and the procedures by which the group will make its decision about which proposed ends to pursue.

As both a summary and a final appeal, I want to indicate a last set of consequences of the postliberal social model that this chapter has presented, before ending with a consideration of the particular role intellectuals might play in that society.

First, the principle of democratic egalitarianism is not grounded in any transcendent sphere, but is culturally and historically specific, for which reason I would abjure all appeal to "rights." Civil liberties are the creation of specific historical communities in which the norms that underlie social and political arrangements guarantee those liberties. The problem of how to introduce such liberties and democratic egalitarianism into cultures in which they do not currently exist is the most tragic dilemma of our time. Western imperialism succeeded in utterly destroying the traditional social consensus in the areas of the globe it colonized without succeeding in laying the foundations of any new consensus (democratic or otherwise), which is why raw power prevails in so many postcolonial societies. Just how the West's democratic consensus was shaped has been a matter of devoted historical research and fierce theoretical debate, particularly around the issues of whether democracy and capitalism necessarily coexist and whether democracy is a luxury funded by the West's exploitation of the rest of the world. In any case, the social consensus is a fact the member of a society works from, and its ground is nothing firmer than its existence in this time and in this place.

Second, the historical and social specificity of the social consensus means that its continued existence is never secure, which is either a matter of concern or a reason for rejoicing, depending on one's position toward the desirability of radical change. It should be stressed, however, that, in spite of the fears of foundationalist theorists and the premature announcements of absolute freedom by the "God is dead, everything is possible" types, social order has proved remarkably durable in the absence of fundamental guarantees. Whether a society could endure with no ideological legitimation is questionable, but the sheer facticity of routine and "attunement" has proved a formidable barrier to anarchy. So formidable, in fact, that society's stasis and its seemingly effortless ability to reproduce itself have become the obsessions of postmodern theorists, who can cheerfully adopt positions so close to anarchism because the threat of chaos appears remote. Habermas's own anxieties about chaos—anxieties much stronger than those generally evidenced in France, America, and England—which make him temperamentally distant from postmodernism, probably reflect not some stereotypical German (Prussian) love of order but Germany's recent experience of how easily democratic norms and consensus can slip away.

Third, the existence of a consensual social norm is better demonstrated by the interpretation of concrete social activities and the evidence of a daily life fairly immune from irresolvable conflicts and violence than by the theoretical procedures of transcendental thought. At issue is how to convince the skeptic (i.e., one who insists that members of the same society have incommensurate viewpoints) that a social consensus does exist. Habermas's solution is to identify transcendentally the grounding conditions of all acts of social communication. (I should remind my readers that these conditions are, for Habermas, the counterfactual norms of the ideal speech situation, not positive conditions of production for utterances.) His transcendental work has the merit of attempting to articulate as fully as possible the implicit assumptions of a society's members. I think, however, that the skeptic is going to be more fully impressed by the more particular demonstration of what his own position shares with those with whom he is arguing. Transcendental limits have concrete manifestations in particular instances, and it is the ability to find these points of agreement in particular disputes that will convince someone that a social consensus exists. Thus interpretation or hermeneutics takes precedence over foundational or theoretical work; this shift toward interpretation explains why literary critics (more than philosophers, sociologists, and political theorists) in America and England have been particularly receptive to developments in France and Germany. Furthermore, this shift reflects an emphasis on meaning, understood as the result of an intersubjective process, in Habermas's work, as opposed to the traditional concern with knowledge, with its model of the knowing subject confronting the object to be known. Insofar as pragmatics and hermeneutics dominate postmodern theory, a similar shift from knowledge (theory) to meaning (interpretation) can be recognized.

Fourth, the existence of a social consensus by no means ends social conflicts. Alain Touraine is the great contemporary theorist of social conflict, insisting that conflicts "are not a sign of crisis or of tension in a social order; they are an outward sign of the production of society by itself" (1978 31). But Touraine also insists that "there can be no social relation unless the actors are operating in the same cultural field" (1978 32). Conflict is, for Touraine, the most crucial social relation, but it necessarily presupposes actors who share a basic "cultural orientation." Groups "fight each other . . . in order to give different social forms to the same cultural orientations" (1988 41). For this reason, the pursuit or celebration of difference makes no sense to Touraine, "for difference is nothing but the absence of relation" (1978 33). Only those who are related to one another within a social order will need to engage in the conflicts that Touraine believes are the stuff of social life and its essential historicity.

Thus the fact of a fundamental consensus does not rule out conflict but is precisely what makes conflict possible. An excellent example is modern economic practices. The liberal commitment to free contracts freely arrived at reflects the social consensus of egalitarian interchanges. A writer such as William Reddy can, on the basis of that consensus, protest that most economic exchanges are, in fact, asymmetrical, with one party enjoying a built-in systemic advantage over the other.[34] Even more grandly, Benjamin Barber can insist that the use of the word *free* to describe market procedures is a fiction.[35] Apologists for market capitalism, like Hayek and Friedman, do not counter such arguments by questioning the normative concepts of equality and freedom to which Reddy and Barber appeal. Rather, the argument takes place on the grounds of what concrete activities do promote those values. The foundationalist theorist might object that such a scenario makes Habermas's transcendentalism useless. Certainly, Habermas is at one with Rorty and other neopragmatists in trying to get philosophy out of the business of legislating solutions to issues that can only be decided in the give and take of political exchange, compromise, and decision making. But Habermas does insist that his transcendental philosophy helps to make explicit what counts as a fair, legitimate process of political decision making. Where Touraine emphasizes the conflicts, Habermas emphasizes how they are (at times and for a time) resolved. We can better identify abusive resolutions if we are clear about our norms for legitimate ones. The aim of transcendental philosophy in its contemporary modest form is not to decide specific disputes but to indicate the criteria that a process for reaching a decision must satisfy if it is to be accepted as democratic.

[34]Reddy (1987 64–73) introduces the concept of "asymmetrical exchange" to describe this built-in inequality in economic transactions and proposes that this concept, which focuses on individual moments of disadvantage, will prove more useful than notions of "interest" or "class conflict" to explain the sites of conflict and resistance within modern (i.e., capitalist) societies.

[35]Barber writes: "To pretend that the free market or the voluntary contract or the small firm have anything whatsoever to do with the activities of giant economic bureaucracies—which are aided and abetted (and regulated and controlled) by a still more giant political bureaucracy—is simply ludicrous. The elemental capitalism of entrepeneurial risk-taking, of saving and investment, and of gratification deferred in favor of long-term capital formation and enhanced productivity no longer exists (if it ever did). . . . And of course, in the absence of the elemental system, all the rhetoric about freedom, rights, markets, individuals, and equality—as well as the counterrhetoric about class, exploitation, surplus value, labor power, and economic parasites—is an archaic jargon employed in desperate invocation of a reality long since vanished" (1984 255).

Fifth, Barber has usefully emphasized that political decisions must be made in the absence of truth.[36] Decisions about what practices and procedures will serve to further egalitarianism and thwart negative power cannot be made on the basis of guaranteed knowledge of the exact consequences of the actions to be chosen. Rather than being legitimated by truth or certainty, political decisions are legitimated by having been made according to the procedures of decision making that currently embody the community's sense of how best to ensure its norms. In other words, the consenual grounds of the social are the conditions (identified by transcendental thought) of politics, and not politics itself. Furthermore, the transcendental naming of these conditions is not necessary to the activity of politics. Only their tacit acceptance by all who partake in politics is needed. These conditions *enable* politics, which is understood as the negotiations, compromises, arguments, and procedural steps taken to reach and to implement collective decisions. (This "enabling" is what makes it appropriate to talk of positive freedom and to think of the conditions—which do limit what is possible—as giving us capabilities, rather than as determining or suppressing us. The point is that there would be no politics, no communal decision making or action, at all apart from these conditions.) Where "truth" makes decision making obvious or easy, political processes are short-circuited or unnecessary. Where violence replaces negotiation, compromise, and the rest, then the consensual grounds that enable politics have been shattered and anarchy or civil war reigns until some new consensual social order is established. Any part of the consensual ground, of the lifeworld, can at one time or another become the subject of explicit political negotiation; this will occur whenever some hitherto-taken-for-granted truth no longer appears self-evident to some significant social group. And such negotiations over specifics of the consensual ground or even the specifics of particular issues always have the potential to become violent, to lead to civil war, if the contending parties are willing to risk the whole social order rather than accept a compromise or a loss on the particular issue at hand.

The similarity of this account to Bobbio's description of democracy's procedural consensus is clear; what Barber's point about politics occurring where truth is absent adds is that the consensus, as embodied in an institution, is provisional. This viewpoint opens up a theory of institutions quite different from that found in Foucault and Bourdieu. Institutions become the social site of exchange, conflict, compromise, and decision, sites that, in Hans Blumenberg's felicitous phrase, reflect "the principle of insufficient reason"

---

[36]According to Barber, "politics concerns itself only with those realms where truth is not—or is not *yet*—known" (1984 129).

(1987 447). Blumenberg contrasts "rhetoric" as the discourse of communal decision making in the absence of truth to "philosophy," the discourse of a discovered truth. He accepts that philosophy reigns in some fields of human endeavor; we do not use rhetorical discourse today about whether to use antibiotics to treat infections. "Rhetoric creates institutions where evident truths are lacking. . . . To put it differently: Philosophy's program [to find truths] succeeds or fails, but it does not yield any profit in installments. Everything that remains, this side of definitive evidence, is rhetoric; rhetoric is the vehicle of *morale par provision*. This statement means above all that rhetoric is an aggregate of legitimate means" (1987 435).

Institutions are the sites where the social interchange of rhetoric takes place, which is precisely why the repetition of institutional procedures is the crucial component in their reproduction. An institution exists in its practices alone—practices that are legitimated (ultimately) by appeals to norms. We may identify negative power as the current arrangement of the institution to promote inequities, but that very identification of power implies the need to formulate and carry out a program of action (a program of positive power) within the institution to move it toward more equitable procedures. Similarly, we may contest illegitimate appeals to truth on the part of certain social members, appeals they use to justify certain institutional arrangements. But in no case can we separate the institution from the practices of particular agents (or groups of agents) who sustain it or work to change it; social conflict is always within the context supplied by institutions and by the norms of legitimacy to which institutions are held answerable. The fact of conflict testifies to the insufficiencies of ideology and power. The difficulty monolithic theories from Adorno and Marcuse to Foucault have found in explaining the fact of resistance suggests that their portrait of reified institutions sheltered from all challenge or reform by social actors is vastly overstated.

Politics in the absence of truth offers no guarantee against the possibility of a tyrannical community that uses legitimate procedures to (in the case of postrevolutionary America, for example) legalize slavery. An antifoundationalist position has no way to define some possible human actions as absolutely wrong; my position can only refer to what actions will be deemed ethical or not, legitimate or not, in specific social contexts. I must admit that I do not see this failure to provide a guarantee as a major flaw. For one thing, philosophical or other absolutist guarantees (like religious ones) are not worth much if we are talking about the ability to prevent or to punish specific actions. That prevention or punishment can only be enacted by a specific group guided by its current set of convictions; they need no transcendent, superhuman justification of those convictions. The point is that tyranny is always possible; philosophy cannot make that mundane possibility disappear once and for all, just as no specific (utopian) social order can ensure unending justice. And the reason for these "failures" suggests to me that it is almost an unmitigated good that these attempts fail: the very meaning of the terms *tyranny* and *justice* will shift over time. These meanings cannot be fixed once and for all but will continually be shaped by the historical and social processes of norm and goal formation that Siebers calls "ethics" and "politics." In sum, failing to guarantee absolutely against tyranny (understood absolutely) stands as a necessary condition for the very possibility of politics at all—and for politics' essential seriousness. Our normative imperatives and the building of communities that will uphold them is a continual and unending task. Those who want absolute guarantees don't want politics.

Sixth, transcendental philosophy of the new sort, then, only indicates the necessary limits of reason's insufficiency (much like Kant's indication of knowledge's limits); the necessary establishment of legitimate procedures for making decisions in the absence of definitive truth; and the necessary involvement of the individual in the social processes by which meaning is created, social norms and institutions reproduced, and social and personal identities formed. This agenda is, no doubt, ambitious enough—and still too ambitious for many postmodern theorists. But we should note what contemporary transcendental philosophy gives up: any attempt to legislate a priori or from afar the actual establishment of the procedures by which institutions, norms, or identities are created and any privileged intervention in the daily functioning of those procedures once they are established. True, Habermas does use his account of democracy's implicit norms to suggest the kinds of procedures that would appropriately embody those norms. But that suggestion is in itself political, not theoretical, a proposal that must be submitted to the political processes by which a given society shapes its institutions. This submission of philosophy to the political is the only way to avoid tyranny. Thus Habermas insists "that the only utopian perspectives in social theory that we can straightforwardly maintain are of a procedural nature. For the utopian lineaments of any future emancipated society can be no more than the necessary general conditions of it. They cannot be in the nature of a design for a form of life" (1986 212).

Seventh, this notion of politics as collective decisions reached about the procedures needed to legitimate action returns us to positive power. In order to combat the threat of negative power, of the domination of decision making within the society by certain groups who possess a special advantage, the society must positively exercise its power to organize decision making in ways that protect the democratic norm. We should recall that the legitimacy of existing procedures is always provisional. Future events or arguments may convince the group that existing procedures do not in fact coincide with what they understand as democratic action. But the existence of some procedures, no matter how provisional, does allow for the distinction between legitimate and illegitimate decisions and between the legitimate authority that marshals resources to enact decisions and to protect procedures from the illegitimate power that attempts to use unrecognized (by the existing procedures) leverage to influence the decision reached. Reform of procedures still takes place within the norm; revolution names the social upheaval in which the fundamental norm is abandoned because the social consensus that upholds it has been shattered. I would venture to guess that revolutions are rarely, if ever, precipitated by an intellectual or theoretical dissent from the prevailing norm. Much more usual is the conviction that one (or more) group in the society is only paying the norm lip service, while actually using established procedures to further its own illegitimate advantage. When this group resists reforms meant to realign procedures so that they better approximate the norm, the reformers (in certain cases) become revolutionaries, and the fundamental charge (used to justify revolt) is that their adversaries do not uphold or consent to the prevailing norm. This group, of course, responds that the revolutionaries have stepped outside recognized, legitimate political procedures. The warring groups' mutual conviction that now they alone represent the full social consensus and full adherence to the society's norms explains the violence against erstwhile members of the society that a revolution unleashes. The reign of violence cannot be ended where the essential consensus has been lost. Positive power, then, directs itself toward the maintenance of that consensus, whereas positive freedom (at its most minimal) is the security enjoyed within a social order preserved from violence by consensus.

Eighth, beyond the freedom from violence that the social order grants the individual, the freedom of participation carries the full weight of my insistence on the necessity of positive freedom. If the political is understood as the realm of public decision making tied to the positive power (capacity) to enact those decisions, then positive freedom for the individual social actor is participation in that process and the concomitant power (capacity) to enact the identities implied and created in the interaction with others. This is not to say that everything is political; in fact, it is crucially important to retain the distinction between the political and other spheres of activity. The political refers only to those parts of social life that are answerable to the decisions made (on the basis of norms) by the collective as a whole. All kinds of decisions are, within democratic societies, left to smaller groups, without the collective as a whole taking any part. The point, rather, is that the process of political decision making and the kind of participation it calls for on the part of individuals is completely analogous to all the other social interactions in which the individual takes part. The intersubjective setting and the identity-constitutive nature of action hold true for political matters as for other sites of action; the political is distinguished only by the involvement of the whole society and by the primary orientation of its actions toward the production, preservation, revision, and enactment of the society's norms.

Ninth, the political's only special privilege comes from its claim to embody the social totality in a way that pulls the various semiautonomous spheres back into the whole. These spheres, pursuing their various independent logics and goals, are still answerable to the social consensus on norms and procedures. Thus, within democratic societies, the production and distribution of goods cannot justify itself solely by demonstrating its efficiency. The economic must, at the very least, show that it does not impede democratic processes or civil liberties or equality. In some cases, the economic might even be called upon to show that it positively fosters these normative goods. The same holds true for education, art, the family, and other spheres. The fundamental (in my opinion) split between leftists and liberals can be located in the former's insistence that the economic sphere generates inequalities that necessarily undermine the functioning of democratic institutions, whereas liberals (of every stripe, from activist liberals like Ted Kennedy to laissez-faire liberals like Hayek) refuse to recognize the market as a threat to the political freedom that is expressed in democratic participation in decision making. I assume that my phrasing of the contrast makes my own position obvious.

The impetus behind suggested reforms in current democratic practices in the West (by such advocates of a much fuller democratic participation as Bowles and Gintis, Macpherson, Barber, and countless others) almost always stems from the conviction that democracy by election leaves far too many social processes in the hands of subgroups (often elites); the reforms are directed toward placing these processes more firmly under the control of the collective as a whole. I would only add to such programs that an insistence on semiautonomy can yield a participatory democracy that is not connected to the enlarging of the state but that can take place at the social sites of various social activities. Of course, as I have tried to argue, such localized democracy depends on the embodiment of the collective democratic norm in a state that can enforce the primacy of democracy at each local site. But apart from this final appeal to the state's laws and power to enforce them, the appropriate procedures and decisions at each site would be left to the participants themselves. In this way, we achieve an intervention in the economic or the educa-

tional (or in other spheres) on the basis of the prevailing norm without an
administration of those spheres by an enlarged, bureaucratic state. The result
is a respect for semiautonomy, for the various separate spheres of activity
within a society, combined with an assertion of the relevance of democratic
norms to all activities.

Such a solution to the tendency of undemocratic practices to sprout up
throughout society will appear too weak to the theorists of power, but more
drastic solutions have invariably proved disastrous in this century. It is noteworthy that the new social movements, which embody the political hopes and
temper of our times, follow a strategy very close to the one I have just
suggested. These movements in the West, far from attacking the state directly
and dreaming of assuming its powers for themselves, studiously leave the
state intact and even appeal for its assistance (especially in the courts) while
concentrating on abuses within spheres that, within liberal society, claim an
exemption from political intervention. The goal is neither to overthrow nor to
enlarge the state; rather, the new social movements recognize the extent to
which the Western state does help to preserve democracy and focus instead
on particular instances of nondemocratic activities within society. (In some
cases, as in protests against American involvement in Nicaragua, the social
movements call attention to the way in which some of that state's activities
violate its own democratic principles; but even in these cases, there is little
evidence of a desire to overthrow the government.) We should also note that
the new social movements, in their use of nonballot expressions of opinion
such as demonstrations and sit-ins, do also suggest that the forms of democratic participation currently available in the West are not sufficiently rich or
diverse to allow for fully collective decision making. The range of methods
used, however, rarely extends to the extralegal (mass civil disobedience being
the one exception) and almost never to actions outside the prevailing norms of
what counts as democratic, while the use of the ballot and of the courts is not
spurned. In sum, the new social movements, unlike earlier revolutionary
groups, appear determined to retain the liberties that the Western democracies have managed to institute thus far and to respect the semiautonomy of
various spheres by recognizing that political action within those spheres is not
synonymous with state intervention or control. The aim, instead, is to make all
the various spheres, the state included, answerable to the democratic norm of
the collective.[37]

___

[37]By the "new social movements" is generally meant political groups who usually agitate about
a specific topic, make extensive use of nonballot forms (mass demonstrations, petitions, etc.) of
influencing government decisions, and evince no particular interest in overthrowing the government or in holding power themselves. These movements have been called "new" by theorists

Finally, we must question whether the democratic norm is really strong enough to stand up to the capitalist monolith that haunts so much postmodern theory. In many ways, this question can only be answered practically and empirically. The evidence of continued resistance to capitalism's destruction of uncommodified spheres and to capitalism's hierarchical, nonegalitarian procedures is poised against capitalism's apparently uncontrollable growth. Theoretically, as I try to show in this book, the logic of a whole that systematically constitutes and then holds in place its various components (including selves) carries a kind of elegance and conviction that puts models of diversity and plurality on the defensive, even though everyone claims to want to preserve and protect such plurality. Monolithic theories of late capitalism almost always imply some theory of a deformation of knowledge, an inability (because of ideology, or power, or whatever) on the part of agents to understand (and thus react to) the tyrannies to which they are subject. I have argued that such a deformation is hard to credit (given the continual resistance of various social groups), hard to justify (how does the theoretician escape that deformation himself?), and leads to political despair. I have also argued vehemently on the other hand that the opposite tack of giving up all reliance on notions of a social whole only generates a particularist anarchism that not only disregards the transcendent conditions of our social existence but also cannot lead to the political results for which it is introduced in the first place. Appeals to a pure other and dreams of negative freedom only contradict the very fact of social involvement that generates reformist and revolutionary aspirations in the first place.

Only in the context of a relationship to others within a social whole can political actions be desired or possible. And I have attempted to show that a social consensus about democratic norms underlies the recognition of and protest against the threat of global capitalism. I do not know if any merely theoretical discussion can convince my readers that such a norm can protect us from capitalism's encroachments; certainly, only the institutions and procedures in which the norm is embodied can do the actual work of protection. My discussion simply suggests that our societies do have values, daily interactions, and a shared outlook that continue to stand over and against the

---

who have been trained to think of revolutionary groups (especially the proletariat) as the "old" model of political action, but the consideration of a group such as the Chartists in nineteenth-century England might make us wonder just how new these forms of political appeal are. In any case, feminists, ecologists, antiabortion activists, and nuclear-freeze proponents are among the examples of new social movements offered by such theorists as Alain Touraine (the most important writer on the subject) and Chantal Mouffe. (See the bibliography.) I find Mouffe's work particularly compelling because she links my two major themes here—postmodernism and democracy—to the specific activities of the new social movements.

instrumental imperatives of capitalism and can serve as the skeletal frame upon which a fully democratic society can be fashioned by the political actions of the community. I also strongly believe that only if we will the institutional means by which such norms can be embodied in daily practices and brought to bear on economic, governmental, and other spheres of action do we stand any chance of making democracy even more of a reality than it currently is. When "the winds of winter blow," it might well prove that "we were crackpated when we dreamed" that the constitutive ties of our sociality afford any protection from the violences perpetuated by greed, intolerance, fear, and the desire to dominate.[38] But as long as intellectuals and others remain committed to the dream of a nonviolent social life, they must affirm and rely upon those instances of such communality that now exist and imagine future instances of communality that are even more satisfactory. And when, more specifically, we name that desired communality *democracy*, the strategies for its achievement must stress the capabilities *all* social agents currently possess that will enable them to participate in the communal political project of forging that democracy. To identify what makes the intellectual unique, what affords her a knowledge, a distance, or an *ethos* denied to other members of society, is to jeopardize the stated goal from the outset.

WHAT'S AN INTELLECTUAL TO DO?

Does the preceding vision of social interaction and democratic norms provide humanist intellectuals with a specific social and political role? Certainly not, if intellectuals expect either to have some privileged role to play in society's adoption of norms and making of decisions or to have their distinctive activities as intellectuals validated as, in themselves, politically efficacious and/or necessarily on the side of the angels. The conclusion, instead, would be that the activities that define intellectuals as a separate group (i.e., as participants in their own semiautonomous spheres) are less important to their political identities and impact than the capacities they share with all their fellow citizens by virtue of belonging to the same social whole. Intellectuals may, it is true, form a recognizable subgroup that pushes particular points of view in various social disputes, but nothing they do as intellectuals will differentiate their input practically from the input of other social groups. In fact, as we have seen, the intellectuals' attachment to negative freedom may

---

[38]The quoted lines are from Yeats's majestic poem of disillusionment, "Nineteen Hundred and Nineteen" (1983 206–10).

undermine any points of agreement they might share as a group, and certainly renders them peculiarly ineffective participants in any political negotiations based on group (not individual) interaction.

This last point can be summed up in the dictum that intellectual activities (theory, criticism, creative writing, painting, dancing, historical research, to name just a few) are not politics. This idea would be hardly worth stating, since it seems so obvious, except that the contrary is endlessly asserted. These activities are political only indirectly, insofar as communities gather around or are galvanized by the image and ideas found in the intellectuals' work. In many cases, however, it is not to the work's content but more to the social occasion of its presentation that communities thus formed can be specifically linked. (An obvious example is the community shaped by rock music in the 1960s; the vapid content of the Beatles' early love songs cannot explain the new awareness of themselves as a group that the young discovered in adopting this music as their own.) And it is notoriously difficult to translate from the impact cultural works have on an audience to any particular position taken in specific political negotiations in which that audience is subsequently involved. The intellectual (artist or theorist) is better understood as simultaneously pursuing the stringent exigencies/logic of his own craft/discipline, in dialogue with its past and present practitioners, *and* working to shape that craft or discipline so that it might better serve what the artist/intellectual deems are the actual needs (the lived goals and motives) of himself and the audience he hopes to win. Thus the intellectual is certainly aiming to shape and influence communal life; his work can be the occasion for forming new communities, although more usually it serves to gain the worker recognition from existing communities and/or provide a model for how some community might better align its commitments with its goals. In these terms, this book not only advances my own claims within my profession but also suggests what I believe is a better alignment of our (literary theorists first of all, but humanistic intellectuals generally) intellectual commitments (to nonfoundationalist thought and to the social creation of the self) to our primary values (pluralism and democracy). But this project becomes directly political only when those same goals and intellectual commitments motivate particular strategies of involvement on specific occasions of communal decision making.

The fallacy of intellectual work's direct political efficacy takes two forms: the foundationalist (ultimately platonic) notion that apprehension of the true will guide all action and the critique dream that knowing that some social form is invalid will cause it to topple. Postmodernism has thoroughly attacked the foundationalist belief in thought's capacities but at times retains critique's idealist assertion of thought's omnipotence. Placing the political outside the realm of truth and within the realm of social negotiation means that the thoughts of individual, isolated thinkers are neither here nor there until they have been brought to bear (as arguments, reasons, appeals, or claims) within public discussions aimed at defining or reforming particular actions within social institutions. Admittedly, most intellectuals would claim that their thoughts are meant as contributions to just such a public discussion and might very well complain that the ability to join the discussion is only partially in their power. We publish our books and teach our classes; if our thoughts are not taken up by anyone, are barely heard and rarely become the focus of purposive public debate, are we to blame? The sphere of public discussion may appear all too nebulous to the intellectual, who would like nothing better than to join the conversation if she could only find it and get its participants to listen to her.

On the other hand, we should not ignore how the institutional sites that intellectuals now inhabit (the universities and the media, primarily) conspire to insulate their work from political discussion. This fact is partly a holdover from the modernist pursuit of autonomy, partly the result of these institutions' internal development (and elaboration) over the past sixty years, partly the result of the liberal isolation of spheres from one another and from the political. In any case, the intellectual finds her audience and rewards and conversation within institutions that provide her with an identity and recognition even while insulating her work from the political. In other words, the institutional forms and contexts within which intellectuals work and publish serve to emphasize the autonomy of these institutions. As a result, the intellectuals' work is responded to, debated, and rewarded in ways that ensure that their work remains in the realm of thought, of the hypothetical, and is never addressed as the practically intended social program of a particular social group. The fate of academic Marxism in this country is the perfect example, and academic feminism is susceptible to the same danger. Again, the individual intellectual of socialist leanings may feel he is hardly to blame for such a state of affairs (and may even take recourse in the illusion that socialist thought alone, no matter where expressed, poses a threat to the status quo). But the suitability of these institutional arrangements to contemporary intellectuals' attachment to negative freedom makes them a comfortable, even if not fully deliberate, setup. Absolution from the political means not only that the intellectuals' hypothetical models never take up social existence but also that the intellectual himself achieves an identity by negation. The point here is not primarily hypocrisy (the charge that self-proclaimed radicals never live their radical views or do much politically to bring them about), but that the very form in which intellectual thought proposes its alternatives to current social life reinforces the image of freedom as distance and the belief that one's true identity is achieved in isolation from the restrictions of everyday concerns, relationships, and contingencies. Thought is separated from practice as a matter of both principle and institutional arrangement, and then we intellectuals agonize over why we are so politically ineffective.

The alternative, I believe, is a pragmatic politics that starts from particular issues at particular local sites, a position that has found its most influential expression in Foucault's description of the specific intellectual. Of course, intellectuals are already deeply involved in such politics in the various places where they work. But what needs to be overcome is the almost total separation of our intellectual work, of our thought, from our local political engagements. I am thinking here primarily of academic politics, in which academics feel much more of a stake, generally speaking, than they do in local community politics. To introduce academic politics as a site for political engagement will appear ridiculous to many, I imagine, since contempt for such politics and their triviality is the more acceptable attitude. But such contempt masks, I believe, three crucial flaws that afflict every attempt, no matter where, of intellectuals to bring their work to bear within specific social sites of decision making. First, the contempt suggests the continued desire to be above it all, to associate integrity with distance. Second, there is a strong tendency either to believe that politics is utterly unrelated to thought or, at the opposite extreme, to become impatient with every element in political negotiations that proves irresolvable by thought. (I return to this point below.) Third, there is a peculiar unwillingness to accept the responsibilities of power in local situations or the possibility that such power could actually be used to further the aims celebrated in our intellectual work. I have in mind, in particular, the manifestly unjust employment practices in English departments today: the reliance on part-time and/or nontenurable instructors to teach many of the lower-level courses. Various pronouncements against this practice have been made by professional organizations and by individual intellectuals, but as far as I know, no department has begun to convert such positions into tenurable lines; moreover, no department has even engaged its college's or university's administration in an open debate about the justification of such practices. The causes of such evasion are many and complex, but when academic politics includes such a fundamental and crucial issue as fair employment, the avoidance of such politics as trivial cannot be credited.

To return to my second point, the possible connection of intellectual work to local politics, we can identify two dangers that must be skirted: the undervaluation and the overvaluation of thought. The undervaluation of thought holds that the nitty-gritty of political negotiation is basically unprincipled, irrational, and ad hoc, a matter of merely appeasing (by whatever means) various raucous constituencies. Thought, it is believed, would be useless in such circumstances; only a besotted theorist could dream that it might apply, even when all the participants in this politics are theorists in their intellectual endeavors. The overvaluation of thought holds that only fully articulate, principled agents can recognize what is at stake in a particular dispute and determine judiciously what decisions are appropriate and legitimate. The most extreme version of this viewpoint yields the dream of the philosopher/king. The obvious flaw is that it introduces a principle that allows for the exclusion of some groups from full political participation, so that political negotiations often get stalled over the very basic issue of who has the right to participate.

A pragmatic politics tries to steer between the overvaluation and undervaluation of thought. Against overvaluation, such a politics insists that competent participation in politics, like competent participation in most social activities, depends on a blend of implicit and explicit knowledge and motives. Explicit knowledge, while helpful, serves as neither a necessary nor a sufficient condition of political action, which can also be based on the conviction—intuitive or not, fully articulated or not—that some basic norm must be enacted, protected, reasserted, or proposed. Thought can certainly be relevant to political action, but it is not its sole enabling condition. The terms of that relevance establish the possible contribution of theory and of intellectuals to politics, a contribution that guards against the undervaluation of thought.

In the pragmatic politics I am sketching, political action takes place at local sites as a specific response to specific ongoing societal practices and arrangements. This view suggests, among other things, that no one becomes a revolutionary by theory alone; some specific abuse must motivate the more systemic and global condemnation of society. Furthermore, as Gouldner's work argues, the appeal of theoretical arguments is most likely limited to a subset of the population, the subset called intellectuals. For most people, the focus of action is both more local and more concrete. Thus the origins of great social upheavals lie in specific crises: the rising cost of bread in 1789 France, the drafting of unwilling soldiers to fight in an endless and unnecessary war in 1968 America. It is, however, wrong to believe that considerations of legitimacy are irrelevant to such locally inspired disputes. The opposite exaggeration is much closer to the truth: there is no politics where no understanding of legitimate procedures and authority exists. The principle of legitimacy is the cornerstone of positive freedom, outlining the terms within which the agent understands her place and possible courses of action within society. Here is where my view differs fundamentally from those of Foucault and Rorty; thought and theory still play a role because the legitimation of protest and of political action is, finally, crucial to all social actors. These actors' identification with and by the social whole gives them the fundamental motive of being able to justify their actions through an appeal to the norms they understand as ratified by the social whole. Such appeals may be couched in the vaguest and most general of slogans (about liberty or rights or the general welfare), but the necessity of such legitimating principles should not be underestimated. Transcendental theory, as I have tried to sketch it in this chapter, strives for the fullest possible articulation of these legitimating principles and of the social conditions within modernity that make an appeal to them necessary. Intellectuals, as such writers as Gouldner and Chomsky among others have argued (sometimes in accusation, sometimes in praise), are primarily involved in the task of legitimation, of thinking through the principles by which particular actions are justified. Apart from those particular actions, theory can be, as I have argued, a vacuous exercise, but within the context of action, theory can play a crucial role and even have a galvanizing effect.

The legitimation crisis of the intellectuals, their current inability to articulate the way their work could serve the achievement of their stated goals, will end, I suggest, when intellectuals accept that not only do their own activities need to be legitimated, but so do those of all social actors. Postmodern theory has precipitated the legitimation crisis by (in Foucault's case) denying that any legitimation is possible, since all justifying principles are equally suspect; or by (in Rorty's case) insisting that mundane practice feels no need to legitimate itself according to the necessary conditions of social existence or to the norms of the social group in which the practice is undertaken; or by (in Derrida's case) suggesting that all action only "plays" (or oscillates) within a very limited set of already established possibilities. Intellectuals have been left to consider their legitimating discourses either as just one more example of the tragically inevitable alternations of domination or as a passé obsession with foundational principles.

Instead, the recognition of legitimation's heightened importance in the foundationless condition of modernity can turn the postmodern dual attack on universalist foundationalism and on the modernist search for autonomy into an invitation to bring theory into the give and take of the ongoing production of the social whole by social actors engaged in daily political decision making at local institutional sites. In the absence of foundations, principles of legitimation are going to have to come from within the social whole, not from some magical exterior. Furthermore, they will be articulated, ratified, and put into practice through political processes that involve social actors engaged in specific political negotiations. This essential political work cannot be done by a theoretical discourse that, by appeals to self-evident truths, deconstructive logic, or unspoken dreams of negative freedom, separates itself from the social whole and the mundane interactions through which it is reproduced and transformed. We recover the political as the domain of social making when we pay attention to norms of legitimation—both their existence and their possible transformation through processes of social construction—that define the site of possible political action.

Works Cited

Abercrombie, Nicholas, Stephen Hill, and Bryan S. Turner. 1980. *The Dominant Ideology Thesis*. London: George Allen & Unwin.

Adorno, Theodor. 1973. *Negative Dialectics*. Trans. E. B. Ashton. New York: Continuum.

——. 1978. *Minima Moralia*. Trans. E. F. N. Jephcott. London: Verso.

Ahmad, Aijaz. 1987. "Jameson's Rhetoric of Otherness and the 'National Allegory,'" *Social Text* 17: 3–25.

Althusser, Louis. 1970. *For Marx*. Trans. Ben Brewster. New York: Pantheon Books.

Altieri, Charles. 1972. "Northrop Frye and the Problem of Spiritual Authority," *PMLA* 87: 964–75.

——. 1981. *Act and Quality: A Theory of Literary Meaning and Humanistic Understanding*. Amherst: University of Massachusetts Press.

——. 1985. "*Ecce Homo*: Narcissism, Power, Pathos, and the Status of Autobiographical Representations." In O'Hara (1985): 389–413.

——. 1987. "From Expressivist Aesthetics to Expressivist Ethics." In Cascardi (1987): 132–66.

——. 1990. "The Powers and Limits of Oppositional Postmodernism," *American Literary History* 2: 443–81.

Anderson, Perry. 1988. "Modernity and Revolution." In Nelson and Grossberg (1988): 317–38.

Arac, Jonathan. 1986a. "Introduction." In Arac (1986b).

——, ed. 1986b. *Postmodernism and Politics*. Minneapolis: University of Minnesota Press.

Arblaster, Anthony. 1987. *Democracy*. Minneapolis: University of Minnesota Press.

Arnold, Matthew. 1962. "The Function of Criticism." In *The Complete Prose Works*. Ed. R. H. Super. Vol. 3: 258–85. Ann Arbor: University of Michigan Press.

Aronowitz, Stanley. 1987. "Postmodernism and Politics," *Social Text* 18: 99–115.

Barber, Benjamin. 1984. *Strong Democracy: Participatory Politics for a New Age*. Berkeley: University of California Press.

Baudrillard, Jean. 1983a. *In the Shadow of the Silent Majorities*. New York: Semiotext(e).

——. 1983b. *Simulations*. New York: Semiotext(e).

Baynes, Kenneth, James Bohman, and Thomas McCarthy, eds. 1987. *After Philosophy: End or Transformation?* Cambridge: MIT Press.

Berger, Peter L. 1986. *The Capitalist Revolution.* New York: Basic Books.

Berlin, Isaiah. 1969. *Four Essays on Liberty.* New York: Oxford University Press.

Berman, Marshall. 1982. *All That Is Solid Melts into Air.* New York: Simon & Schuster.

Bernstein, Richard J. 1983. *Beyond Objectivism and Relativism: Science, Hermeneutics, and Praxis.* Philadelphia: University of Pennsylvania Press.

———, ed. 1985. *Habermas and Modernity.* Cambridge: MIT Press.

Blumenberg, Hans. 1987. "An Anthropological Approach to the Contemporary Significance of Rhetoric." In Baynes, Bohman, and McCarthy (1987): 429–58.

Bobbio, Norberto. 1987a. *The Future of Democracy.* Trans. Roger Griffin. Minneapolis: University of Minnesota Press.

———. 1987b. *Which Socialism?* Trans. Roger Griffin. Minneapolis: University of Minnesota Press.

Bourdieu, Pierre. 1977. *Outline of a Theory of Practice.* Trans. Richard Nice. Cambridge: Cambridge University Press.

———. 1984. *Distinction: A Social Critique of the Judgement of Taste.* Trans. Richard Nice. Cambridge: Harvard University Press.

Bowles, Samuel, and Herbert Gintis. 1987. *Democracy and Capitalism.* New York: Basic Books.

Brecht, Bertolt. 1964. *Brecht on Theatre.* Trans. John Willett. New York: Hill & Wang.

Brown, Norman O. 1959. *Life Against Death.* Middletown, Conn.: Wesleyan University Press.

Bürger, Peter. 1984. *Theory of the Avant-Garde.* Trans. Michael Shaw. Minneapolis: University of Minnesota Press.

Burke, Kenneth. 1969. *A Grammar of Motives.* Berkeley: University of California Press.

Butler, Judith. 1990. *Gender Trouble: Feminism and the Subversion of Identity.* New York: Routledge.

Cascardi, Anthony J., ed. 1987. *Literature and the Question of Philosophy.* Baltimore: Johns Hopkins University Press.

Castoriadis, Cornelius. 1987. "The Movements of the Sixties," *Thesis Eleven* 18–19: 20–31.

———. 1988. "Intellectuals and History," *Salmagundi* 80: 161–71.

Cavell, Stanley. 1978. *Must We Mean What We Say?* Cambridge: Cambridge University Press.

———. 1979. *The Claim of Reason.* New York: Oxford University Press.

Certeau, Michel de. 1988. *The Practice of Everyday Life.* Trans. Steven Randall. Berkeley: University of California Press.

Collins, Randall. 1985. *Three Sociological Traditions.* New York: Oxford University Press.

Danto, Arthur. 1980. *Nietzsche as Philosopher.* New York: Columbia University Press.

Davidson, Donald. 1984. "Communication and Convention." In *Inquiries into Truth and Interpretation.* New York: Oxford University Press. 265–80.

Deleuze, Gilles. 1983. *Nietzsche and Philosophy.* Trans. Hugh Tomlinson. New York: Columbia University Press.

Deleuze, Gilles, and Felix Guattari. 1983. *Anti-Oedipus: Capitalism and Schizophrenia.* Minneapolis: University of Minnesota Press.

de Man, Paul. 1979. *Allegories of Reading.* New Haven: Yale University Press.

———. 1983. "The Rhetoric of Temporality." In *Blindness and Insight.* 2d ed. Minneapolis: University of Minnesota Press: 187–228.

Derrida, Jacques. 1967. *L'écriture et la différence.* Paris: Editions du Seuil.

———. 1970. "Structure, Sign, and Play in the Discourse of the Human Sciences." In Macksey and Donato (1970): 247–65.

———. 1976. *Of Grammatology.* Trans. Gayatri Chakravorty Spivak. Baltimore: Johns Hopkins University Press.

———. 1978. *Writing and Difference.* Trans. Alan Bass. Chicago: University of Chicago Press.

———. 1981. *Positions.* Trans. Alan Bass. Chicago: University of Chicago Press.

———. 1982. *Margins of Philosophy.* Trans. Alan Bass. Chicago: University of Chicago Press.

———. 1983. "The Principle of Reason: The University in the Eyes of Its Pupils," *Diacritics* 13: 3–20.

———. 1984. "Deconstruction and the Other." In Kearney (1984): 107–26.

———. 1986. *Glas.* Trans. John P. Leavey, Jr., and Richard Rand. Lincoln: University of Nebraska Press.

———. 1987. "Interview." In Salusinszky (1987): 9–24.

———. 1988a. "Afterword: Toward an Ethic of Discussion." In *Limited Inc.* Evanston, Ill.: Northwestern University Press: 111–60.

———. 1988b. "Like the Sound of the Sea Deep within a Shell: Paul de Man's War," *Critical Inquiry* 14: 590–652.

———. 1988c. "The Politics of Friendship," *Journal of Philosophy* 85:632–44.

Dews, Peter. 1987. *Logics of Disintegration.* London: Verso.

Donoghue, Denis. 1989. "The Political Turn in Criticism," *Salmagundi* 81: 105–22.

Dreyfus, Herbert L., and Paul Rabinow. 1983. *Michel Foucault: Beyond Structuralism and Hermeneutics.* 2d ed. Chicago: University of Chicago Press.

Dworkin, Ronald. 1978. *Taking Rights Seriously.* Cambridge: Harvard University Press.

Eagleton, Terry. 1981. *Walter Benjamin, or Towards a Revolutionary Criticism.* London: Verso.

———. 1983. *Literary Theory: An Introduction.* Minneapolis: University of Minnesota Press.

———. 1984. *The Function of Criticism.* London: Verso.

———. 1986. *Against the Grain.* London: Verso.

Feyerabend, Paul. 1987. *Farewell to Reason.* London: Verso.

Fiedler, Leslie. 1982. *What Was Literature? Class, Culture, and Mass Society.* New York: Simon & Schuster.

Fish, Stanley. 1985. "Consequences." In Mitchell (1985): 106–31.

Forester, John, ed. 1985. *Critical Theory and Public Life.* Cambridge: MIT Press.

Foster, Hal. 1985. *Recodings: Art, Spectacle, Cultural Politics.* Port Townsend, Wash.: Bay Press.

———, ed. 1983. *The Anti-Aesthetic.* Port Townsend, Wash.: Bay Press.

Foucault, Michel. 1965. *Madness and Civilization.* Trans. Richard Howard. New York: Pantheon Books.

———. 1973. *The Order of Things.* New York: Vintage Books.

———. 1976. *The Archaeology of Knowledge.* Trans. A. M. Sheridan Smith. New York: Harper & Row.

———. 1979. *Discipline and Punish.* Trans. Alan Sheridan. New York: Vintage Books.

———. 1980a. *The History of Sexuality,* vol. 1: *An Introduction.* Trans. Robert Hurley. New York: Vintage Books.

———. 1980b. *Power/Knowledge.* Ed. Colin Gordon. New York: Pantheon.

———. 1983. "The Subject and Power." In Dreyfus and Rabinow (1983): 208–226.

———. 1984. *The Foucault Reader.* Ed. Paul Rabinow. New York: Pantheon.

———. 1986. *The Care of the Self.* Trans. Robert Hurley. New York: Pantheon.

———. 1987. "The Ethic of Care for the Self as a Practice of Freedom," *Philosophy and Social Criticism* 12; 112–31.

———. 1988. *Politics, Philosophy, Culture.* Ed. Lawrence D. Kritzman. New York: Routledge.

——. 1989. *Foucault Live: Interviews, 1966–84.* Trans. John Johnston. New York: Semiotext(e).

Franco, Jean. 1987. "Gender, Death, and Resistance: Facing the Ethical Vacuum," *Chicago Review* 35: 59–79.

Fraser, Nancy. 1981. "Foucault on Modern Power: Empirical Insights and Normative Confusions," *Praxis International* 1: 272–87.

——. 1983. "Foucault's Body-Language: A Posthumanistic Political Rhetoric?" *Salmagundi* 61: 55–70.

Gallagher, Catherine. 1985. "Politics, the Profession, and the Critic," *Diacritics* 15: 37–43.

Gans, Herbert. 1974. *Popular Culture and High Culture.* New York: Basic Books.

Gasché, Rodolphe. 1986. *The Tain of the Mirror: Derrida and the Philosophy of Reflection.* Cambridge: Harvard University Press.

Gass, William H. 1985. "The Death of the Author." In *Habitations of the Word.* New York: Simon & Schuster.

——. 1988. "Vicissitudes of the Avant-Garde," *Harper's* 277: 64–70.

Geertz, Clifford. 1979. "From the Native's Point of View: On the Nature of Anthropological Understanding." In Rabinow and Sullivan (1979): 225–41.

Giddens, Anthony. 1971. *Capitalism and Modern Social Theory.* Cambridge: Cambridge University Press.

——. 1975. *The Class Structure of the Advanced Societies.* New York: Harper Torchbooks.

——. 1979. *Central Problems in Social Thought.* Berkeley: University of California Press.

——. 1981. *A Contemporary Critique of Historical Materialism.* Berkeley: University of California Press.

Giddens, Anthony, and Jonathan Turner, eds. 1987. *Social Theory Today.* Stanford: Stanford University Press.

Gouldner, Alvin W. 1982a. *The Dialectic of Ideology and Technology.* New York: Oxford University Press.

——. 1982b. *The Future of Intellectuals and the Rise of the New Class.* New York: Oxford University Press.

Graff, Gerald. 1979. *Literature against Itself.* Chicago: University of Chicago Press.

Habermas, Jürgen. 1975. *Legitimation Crisis.* Trans. Thomas McCarthy. Boston: Beacon Press.

——. 1983. "Modernity—An Incomplete Project." In Foster (1983): 3–15.

——. 1984. *The Theory of Communicative Action.* Vol. 1. Trans. Thomas McCarthy. Boston: Beacon Press.

——. 1985. "Modern and Postmodern Architecture." In Forester (1985): 317–29.

——. 1986. *Autonomy and Solidarity.* Ed. Peter Dews. London: Verso.

——. 1987a. *The Philosophical Discourse of Modernity.* Trans. Frederick Lawrence. Cambridge: MIT Press.

——. 1987b. "Philosophy as Stand-in and Interpreter." In Baynes, Bohman, and McCarthy (1987): 296–315.

——. 1987c. *The Theory of Communicative Action.* Vol. 2. Trans. Thomas McCarthy. Boston: Beacon Press.

Hall, Stuart. 1988. "The Toad in the Garden: Thatcherism among the Theorists." In Nelson and Grossberg (1988): 35–73.

Handelman, Susan A. 1982. *The Slayers of Moses.* Albany: SUNY Press.

Hegel, G. W. F. 1956. *The Philosophy of History.* Trans. J Sibree. New York: Dover Publications.

——. 1967a. *Hegel's Philosophy of Right.* Trans. T. M. Knox. Oxford: Oxford University Press.

——. 1967b. *The Phenomenology of Mind.* Trans. J. B. Baillie. New York: Harper & Row.

——. 1974. *Hegel: The Essential Writings.* Ed. Frederick G. Weiss. New York: Harper & Row.

——. 1975. *Hegel's Logic: Being Part One of the Encyclopedia of the Philosophical Sciences (1820).* Trans. William Wallace. Oxford: Clarendon Press.

Heritage, John C. 1987. "Ethnomethodology." In Giddens and Turner (1987): 224–72.

Horkheimer, Max, and Theodor W. Adorno. 1972. *Dialectic of Enlightenment.* Trans. John Cumming. New York: Seabury Press.

Hoy, David Couzens. 1986a. "Power, Repression, Progress: Foucault, Lukes, and the Frankfurt School." In Hoy (1986b): 123–47.

——, ed. 1986b. *Foucault: A Critical Reader.* Oxford: Basil Blackwell.

Huyssen, Andreas. 1986. *After the Great Divide.* Bloomington: Indiana University Press.

Inwood, Michael, ed. 1985. *Hegel.* Oxford: Oxford University Press.

Jameson, Fredric. 1972. *The Prison-House of Language.* Princeton: Princeton University Press.

——. 1981. *The Political Unconscious.* Ithaca: Cornell University Press.

——. 1983. "Postmodernism and Consumer Society." In Foster (1983): 111–25.

——. 1984a. "Foreword." In Lyotard (1984c): vii–xxi.

——. 1984b. "Postmodernism, or the Cultural Logic of Late Capitalism," *New Left Review* 146: 53–92.

——. 1986. "Third-World Literature in the Era of Multinational Capitalism," *Social Text* 15: 65–88.

——. 1987a. "A Brief Response," *Social Text* 17: 26–27.

——. 1987b. "Regarding Postmodernism—A Conversation with Fredric Jameson." Interview conducted by Anders Staphanson. *Social Text* 17: 29–54.

——. 1988a. "Cognitive Mapping." In Nelson and Grossberg (1988): 347–60.

——. 1988b. *The Ideologies of Theory,* vol. 2: *The Syntax of History.* Minneapolis: University of Minnesota Press.

——. 1989. "Marxism and Postmodernism," *New Left Review* 176: 31–45.

Jay, Martin. 1984. *Adorno.* Cambridge: Harvard University Press.

——. 1985. "Habermas and Modernism." In Bernstein (1985): 125–39.

——. 1988. *Fin-de-Siècle Socialism and Other Essays.* New York: Routledge.

Jencks, Charles. 1984. *The Language of Post-Modern Architecture.* 4th ed. New York: Rizzoli.

Joas, Hans. 1987. "Symbolic Interactionism." In Giddens and Turner (1987): 82–115.

Jones, Ann Rosalind. 1985. "Writing the Body: Toward an Understanding of l'écriture féminine." In Newton and Rosenfelt (1985): 86–101.

Kadvany, John. 1985. "Verso and Recto: An Essay on *Criticism and Social Change,*" *Cultural Critique* 1: 183–215.

Kant, Immanuel. 1949. *The Philosophy of Kant.* Ed. Carl J. Friedrich. New York: Modern Library.

——. 1950. *Prolegomena to Any Future Metaphysics.* Indianapolis: Bobbs-Merrill.

——. 1965. *Critique of Pure Reason.* Trans. Norman Kemp Smith. New York: St. Martin's Press.

——. 1970. *Kant's Political Writings.* Trans. H. B. Nisbet. Cambridge: Cambridge University Press.

Keane, John. 1987. "The Modern Democratic Revolution: Reflections on Jean-François Lyotard's *La condition postmoderne,*" *Chicago Review* 35: 4–19.

Kearney, Richard, ed. 1984. *Dialogues with Contemporary Continental Thinkers.* Manchester: Manchester University Press.

Kierkegaard, Søren. 1971. *The Concept of Irony*. Trans. Lee M. Capel. Bloomington: Indiana University Press.

Knapp, Steven, and Walter Benn Michaels. 1985a. "Against Theory." In Mitchell (1985): 11–30.

——. 1985b. "A Reply to Richard Rorty: What Is Pragmatism?" In Mitchell (1985): 139–46.

Kolb, David. 1986. *The Critique of Pure Modernity: Hegel, Heidegger, and After*. Chicago: University of Chicago Press.

Krauss, Rosalind. 1985. *The Originality of the Avant-Garde and Other Modernist Myths*. Cambridge: MIT Press.

Kucich, John. 1985. "Review of *Criticism and Social Change*," *Southern Humanities Review* 19: 171–72.

Kuhn, Thomas S. 1970. *The Structure of Scientific Revolutions*. 2d ed. Chicago: University of Chicago Press.

Laclau, Ernesto, and Chantal Mouffe. 1985. *Hegemony and Socialist Strategy: Towards a Radical Democratic Politics*. London: Verso.

Lasch, Christopher. 1979. *The Culture of Narcissism*. New York: Norton.

——. 1988. "Politics American Style," *Salmagundi* 78–79: 36–41.

Latimer, Dan. 1984. "Jameson and Post-Modernism," *New Left Review* 148: 116–28.

Lentricchia, Frank. 1980. *After the New Criticism*. Chicago: University of Chicago Press.

——. 1983. *Criticism and Social Change*. Chicago: University of Chicago Press.

——. 1988. *Ariel and the Police*. Madison: University of Wisconsin Press.

Lévi-Strauss, Claude. 1974. *Tristes Tropiques*. Trans. John and Doreen Weightman. New York: Atheneum.

Lukács, Georg. 1971. *History and Class Consciousness*. Trans. Rodney Livingston. Cambridge: MIT Press.

Lukes, Steven. 1986a. "Introduction." In Lukes (1986b): 1–18.

——, ed. 1986b. *Power*. New York: New York University Press.

Lyotard, Jean-François. 1974. *Economie libidinale*. Paris: Minuit.

——. 1982. "Presenting the Unpresentable: The Sublime." Trans. Lisa Liebmann. *Artforum* 20: 64–69.

——. 1983. "Presentations." Trans. Kathleen McLaughlin. In Montefiore (1983): 116–35.

——. 1984a. *Driftworks*. Ed. Roger McKeon. New York: Semiotext(e).

——. 1984b. "Interview: Jean-François Lyotard." Conducted by Georges Van Den Abbeele. *Diacritics* 14: 16–21.

——. 1984c. *The Postmodern Condition*. Trans. Geoff Bennington and Brian Massumi. Minneapolis: University of Minnesota Press.

——. 1984d. "The Sublime and the Avant-Garde." Trans. Lisa Liebmann. *Artforum* 22: 36–43.

——. 1985a. "Discussion entre Jean-François Lyotard et Richard Rorty," *Critique* 41: 581–84.

——. 1985b. "Histoire universelle et différences culturelles," *Critique* 41: 559–68.

——. 1985c. *Just Gaming*. With Jean-Loup Thébaud. Trans. Wlad Godzich. Minneapolis: University of Minnesota Press.

——. 1988a. *The Différend: Phrases in Dispute*. Trans. Georges Van Den Abbeele. Minneapolis: University of Minnesota Press.

——. 1988b. *Peregrinations: Law, Form, Event*. New York: Columbia University Press.

McCarthy, Thomas. 1988. "On the Margins of Politics," *The Journal of Philosophy* 85: 645–48.

———. 1989. "The Politics of the Ineffable: Derrida's Deconstructionism," *The Philosophical Forum* 21: 146–68.

McGowan, John. 1985. "Knowledge/Power and Jane Austen's Radicalism," *Mosaic* 18: 1–15.

———. 1987. "Postmodern Dilemmas," *Southwest Review* 72: 357–76.

———. 1989. "Can Marxism Survive?" *Southern Humanities Review* 23: 241–52.

———. 1990. "The New Tory Radicals," *Soundings* 72: 477–500.

McKeon, Michael. 1985. "Generic Transformation and Social Change: Rethinking the Rise of the Novel," *Cultural Critique* 1: 159–81.

Macksey, Richard, and Eugenio Donato, eds. 1970. *The Structuralist Controversy*. Baltimore: Johns Hopkins University Press.

Macpherson, C. B. 1987. *The Rise and Fall of Economic Justice and Other Essays*. New York: Oxford University Press.

Marcuse, Herbert. 1966. *One-Dimensional Man*. Boston: Beacon Press.

———. 1968. "The Affirmative Character of Culture." In *Negations*. Boston: Beacon Press, 88–133.

Marx, Karl, and Frederick Engels. 1970. *The German Ideology*. New York: International Publishers.

Miller, J. Hillis. 1985. "Dismembering and Disremembering in Nietzsche's 'On Truth and Lies in a Nonmoral Sense.'" In O'Hara (1985): 41–54.

Mitchell, W. J. T. 1987. "The Golden Age of Criticism," *London Review of Books*, 25 June 1987: 16–18.

———, ed. 1985. *Against Theory: Literary Studies and the New Pragmatism*. Chicago: University of Chicago Press.

Montefiore, Alan, ed. 1983. *Philosophy in France Today*. Cambridge: Cambridge University Press.

Mouffe, Chantal. 1988a. "Hegemony and New Political Subjects: Toward a New Concept of Democracy." In Nelson and Grossberg (1988): 89–104.

———. 1988b. "Radical Democracy: Modern or Postmodern?" In Ross (1988): 31–45.

Nehamas, Alexander. 1985. *Nietzsche: Life as Literature*. Cambridge: Harvard University Press.

Nelson, Cary, and Lawrence Grossberg, eds. 1988. *Marxism and the Interpretation of Culture*. Urbana: University of Illinois Press.

Newman, Charles. 1985. *The Post-Modern Aura*. Evanston, Ill.: Northwestern University Press.

Newton, Judith, and Deborah Rosenfelt, eds. 1985. *Feminist Criticism and Social Change*. New York: Methuen.

Nicholson, Linda J., ed. 1990. *Feminism/Postmodernism*. New York: Routledge.

Nietzsche, Friedrich. 1911. "On Truth and Falsity in Their Ultramoral Sense." In *Early Greek Philosophy and Other Essays*. Trans. Maximilian A. Mugge. London: T. N. Foulis.

———. 1967. *The Birth of Tragedy*. Trans. Walter Kaufmann. New York: Vintage Books.

———. 1968. *The Will to Power*. Trans. Walter Kaufmann and R. J. Hollingdale. New York: Vintage Books.

———. 1969. *On the Genealogy of Morals*. Trans. Walter Kaufmann. New York: Vintage Books.

———. 1973. *Beyond Good and Evil*. Trans. R. J. Hollingdale. Hammondsworth, Eng.: Penguin Books.

———. 1974. *The Gay Science*. Trans. Walter Kaufmann. New York: Vintage Books.

Norris, Christopher. 1987. *Derrida*. Cambridge: Harvard University Press.

O'Hara, Daniel T., ed. 1985. *Why Nietzsche Now?* Bloomington: Indiana University Press.

Ortega y Gasset, José. 1968. *The Dehumanization of Art*. Princeton: Princeton University Press.

Pinkard, Terry. 1985. "The Logic of Hegel's *Logic*." In Inwood (1985): 85–109.

Poggioli, Renato. 1968. *The Theory of the Avant-Garde*. Trans. Gerald Fitzgerald. Cambridge: Harvard University Press.

Poulantzas, Nicos. 1980. *State, Power, Socialism*. Trans. Patrick Camiller. London: Verso.

Putnam, Hilary. 1981. *Reason, Truth, and History*. Cambridge: Cambridge University Press.

Rabinow, Paul, and William M. Sullivan, eds. 1979. *Interpretive Social Science: A Reader*. Berkeley: University of California Press.

Rajchman, John. 1985. *Michel Foucault: The Freedom of Philosophy*. New York: Columbia University Press.

Reddy, William M. 1987. *Money and Liberty in Modern Europe: A Critique of Historical Understanding*. Cambridge: Cambridge University Press.

Ricoeur, Paul. 1970. *Freud and Philosophy*. Trans. Denis Savage. New Haven: Yale University Press.

——. 1986. *Lectures on Ideology and Utopia*. Ed. George H. Taylor. New York: Columbia University Press.

Robbins, Bruce. 1983. "Homelessness and Worldliness," *Diacritics* 13: 69–77.

——. 1986. "Deformed Professions, Empty Politics," *Diacritics* 16: 67–71.

——. 1987. "The Politics of Theory," *Social Text* 18: 3–18.

Rorty, Amélie Oskenberg, ed. 1976. *The Identities of Persons*. Berkeley: University of California Press.

Rorty, Richard. 1979. *Philosophy and the Mirror of Nature*. Princeton: Princeton University Press.

——. 1982. *Consequences of Pragmatism*. Minneapolis: University of Minnesota Press.

——. 1983. "Postmodern Bourgeois Liberalism," *Journal of Philosophy* 80: 583–89.

——. 1984. "Deconstruction and Circumvention," *Critical Inquiry* 11: 1–23.

——. 1985a. "Le Cosmopolitisme sans emancipation: En réponse à Jean-François Lyotard," *Critique* 41: 569–80.

——. 1985b. "Habermas and Lyotard on Postmodernity." In Bernstein (1985): 161–75.

——. 1985c. "Philosophy without Principles." In Mitchell (1985): 132–38.

——. 1989a. "Comments on Castoriadis," *Salmagundi* 82–83: 24–30.

——. 1989b. *Contingency, Irony, and Solidarity*. Cambridge: Cambridge University Press.

Rorty, Richard, J. B. Schneewind, and Quentin Skinner, eds. 1986. *Philosophy in History*. Cambridge: Cambridge University Press.

Ross, Andrew, ed. 1988. *Universal Abandon?: The Politics of Postmodernism*. Minneapolis: University of Minnesota Press.

Rousseau, Jean-Jacques. 1968. *The Social Contract*. Trans. Maurice Cranston. Harmondsworth, Eng.: Penguin Books.

Said, Edward. 1975. *Beginnings: Intention and Method*. New York: Basic Books.

——. 1976. "Interview: Edward W. Said," *Diacritics* 6: 30–47.

——. 1978. *Orientalism*. New York: Pantheon.

——. 1983. *The World, the Text, and the Critic*. Cambridge: Harvard University Press.

——. 1986a. "Foucault and the Imagination of Power." In Hoy (1986a): 149–55.

——. 1986b. "An Interview with Edward W. Said." Conducted by Gary Hentzi and Anne McClintock. *Critical Texts* 3: 6–13.

——. 1987a. "Edward Said: An Exile's Exile." Interview conducted by Matthew Stevenson. *Progressive* 51: 30–34.

——. 1987b. "Interpreting Palestine," *Harper's* 274: 19–22.

——. 1987c. "Interview." In Salusinszky (1987): 123–48.

——. 1988a. "American Intellectuals and Middle East Politics: An Interview with Edward W. Said." Conducted by Bruce Robbins. *Social Text* 19–20: 37–53.

——. 1988b. "Identity, Negation, and Violence," *New Left Review* 171: 46–60.

——. 1988c. "Introduction." In Said and Hitchens (1988): 1–19.

——. 1988d. "Michael Walzer's *Exodus and Revolution*: A Canaanite Reading." In Said and Hitchens (1988): 161–78.

——. 1989. "Representing the Colonized: Anthropology's Interlocutors," *Critical Inquiry* 15: 205–25.

Said, Edward W., and Christopher Hitchens. 1988. *Blaming the Victims: Spurious Scholarship and the Palestinian Question*. London: Verso.

Salusinszky, Imre. 1987. *Criticism in Society*. New York: Methuen.

Sandel, Michael J. 1982. *Liberalism and the Limits of Justice*. Cambridge: Cambridge University Press.

Schulte-Sasse, Jochen. 1984. "Foreword." In Burger (1984): vii–lv.

Sheridan, Alan. 1980. *Michel Foucault: The Will to Truth*. London: Tavistock Publications.

Siebers, Tobin. 1988. *The Ethics of Criticism*. Ithaca: Cornell University Press.

——. 1989. "Comparative Literature and Its Ethics," *Southern Humanities Review* 23: 217–28.

Silone, Ignazio. 1946. *Bread and Wine*. Trans. Gwenda David and Eric Mosbacher. New York: Penguin.

Skinner, Quentin. 1985a. "Introduction." In Skinner (1985b): 1–20.

——. 1986. "The Idea of Negative Liberty: Philosophical and Historical Perspectives." In Rorty, Schneewind, and Skinner (1986): 193–221.

——, ed. 1985b. *The Return of Grand Theory in the Human Sciences*. Cambridge: Cambridge University Press.

Spivak, Gayatri Chakravorty. 1988. *In Other Worlds: Essays in Cultural Politics*. New York: Routledge.

Stallybrass, Peter, and Allon White. 1986. *The Politics and Poetics of Transgression*. Ithaca: Cornell University Press.

Taylor, Charles. 1975. *Hegel*. Cambridge: Cambridge University Press.

——. 1976. "Responsibility for Self." In Amélie Oskenberg Rorty (1976): 281–99.

——. 1979. *Hegel and Modern Society*. Cambridge: Cambridge University Press.

——. 1985a. *Human Agency and Language: Philosophical Papers 1*. Cambridge: Cambridge University Press.

——. 1985b. *Philosophy and the Human Sciences: Philosophical Papers 2*. Cambridge: Cambridge University Press.

——. 1986. "Foucault on Freedom and Truth." In Hoy (1986a): 69–102.

Touraine, Alain. 1978. *The Voice and the Eye: An Analysis of Social Movements*. Trans. Alan Duff. Cambridge: Cambridge University Press.

——. 1988. *Return of the Actor: Social Theory in Postindustrial Society*. Trans. Myrna Godzich. Minneapolis: University of Minnesota Press.

Tucker, Robert C., ed. 1978. *The Marx-Engels Reader*. 2d edition. New York: Norton.

Unger, Roberto Mangabeira. 1986. *The Critical Legal Studies Movement*. Cambridge: Harvard University Press.

——. 1987. *Social Theory: Its Situation and Its Task*. Cambridge: Cambridge University Press.

Walzer, Michael. 1984. "Liberalism and the Art of Separation," *Political Theory* 12: 315–330.

———. 1986. "The Politics of Michel Foucault." In Hoy (1986a): 51–68.

———. 1989. "A Critique of Philosophical Conversation," *The Philosophical Forum* 21: 182–96.

Weber, Max. 1968. *The Theory of Social and Economic Organization.* Trans. A. M. Henderson and Talcott Parsons. New York: Free Press.

Wellmer, Albrecht. 1989. "Models of Freedom in the Modern World," *The Philosophical Forum* 21: 227–52.

West, Cornel. 1986. "Ethics and Action in Fredric Jameson's Marxist Hermeneutics." In Arac (1986b): 123–44.

———. 1988. "Marxist Theory and the Specificity of Afro-American Oppression." In Nelson and Grossberg (1988): 17–33.

Wilde, Oscar. 1973. "The Decay of Lying." In *De Profundis and Other Writings.* Harmondsworth, Eng.: Penguin Books, 55–87.

Williams, Raymond. 1981. *Culture.* London: Fontana Paperbacks.

Wolin, Richard. 1985. "Communism and the Avant-Garde," *Thesis Eleven* 12: 81–93.

Yeats, W. B. 1983. *W. B. Yeats: The Poems.* Ed. Richard J. Finneran. New York: Macmillan.

Young, Iris Marion. 1990. "The Ideal of Community and the Politics of Difference." In Nicholson (1990): 300–32.

Index

Abercrombie, Nicholas, 65, 257
Adorno, Theodor, 9, 12, 13, 14, 17–19, 20, 95–96, 111, 268
Affirmation: in Derrida, 97, 101, 108, 116, 119; in Jameson, 157, 159; in Lyotard, 184; in Nietzsche, 76–77, 79, 81–83; in postmodern thought, 88
Ahmad, Aijaz, 158
Althusser, Louis, 59, 63, 135, 145, 150, 152, 154, 214–15, 258
Altieri, Charles, 81, 232, 241, 263
Anarchism, 11, 15, 16, 28, 40, 52, 57, 128, 132, 134, 138, 172, 176, 191, 199, 203, 209, 228, 267, 273
Antifoundational thought. *See* Foundational and/or antifoundational thought
Apel, Karl-Otto, 205
Arac, Jonathan, 25, 26
Arblaster, Anthony, 213
Aristotle, 94, 212
Arnold, Matthew, 13, 160
Aronowitz, Stanley, 28
Artaud, Antonin, 93, 97, 98, 99, 116, 117, 118
Auden, W. H., 196
Austen, Jane, 248
Autonomy, 2, 4, 6–9, 12, 19–20, 25–26, 32, 102, 114, 127, 214, 247–49, 252, 255–56, 276; in Foucault, 141; Hegel's critique of, 43–44; in Jameson, 155, 158; in Kant, 34–40, 216; in Nietzsche, 83–85; in Rorty, 193, 197. *See also* Modernism

Avant-garde, 9–11, 28, 144, 184, 192

Babcock, Barbara, 122
Barber, Benjamin, 266, 267, 271
Barthes, Roland, 23, 84, 145
Bass, Alan, 24
Bataille, Georges, 84, 93, 98, 116–19, 122
Baudelaire, Charles, 54, 139
Baudrillard, Jean, 17–18, 62, 95
Baynes, Kenneth, 23
Beatles, 275
Beethoven, Ludwig van, 84
Bell, Daniel, 179
Benda, Julien, 166
Benhabib, Seyla, 218
Benjamin, Walter, 27, 163
Bentham, Jeremy, 7, 243
Berger, Peter L., 2, 61
Berlin, Isaiah, 37–38, 218
Bernstein, Richard, 23
Blake, William, 5, 6, 19, 21, 145
Blumenberg, Hans, 267–68
Bobbio, Norberto, 176, 234, 267
Bohman, James, 23
Borges, Jorge Luis, 31
Bourdieu, Pierre, 5, 13, 57, 206, 207, 236, 238, 239, 243, 248, 254, 267
Bowles, Samuel, 212, 225, 242, 244, 254, 271
Brecht, Bertolt, 12, 145
Brenkman, John, 163
Breton, André, 11, 145

Brooks, Cleanth, 146
Brown, Norman O., 179
Bürger, Peter, 9, 10
Burke, Edmund, 13, 242
Burke, Kenneth, 53–54
Butler, Judith, 223

Camus, Albert, 170, 176
Capitalism, 11, 13–18, 21, 50, 62, 126, 155–56, 185, 225–26, 229–30, 266, 271, 273–74
Castoriadis, Cornelius, 3, 144, 208
Cavell, Stanley, 218, 233, 239
Certeau, Michel de, 241
Chomsky, Noam, 279
Cicero, 227
Cixous, Hélène, 108
Coleridge, Samuel Taylor, 13, 54
Collins, Randall, 222
Comte, Auguste, 13
Consensus, 56, 199–201, 203, 222, 232, 234–38, 240, 249, 254, 263, 264–66, 267, 270, 271, 273
Contradiction, 240; in Derrida, 106; in Eagleton, 162–63; in Hegel, 45–47; in Jameson, 151–52, 155–56; in Lyotard, 203; in Nietzsche, 74; in postmodern thought, 49–50, 61
Criticism: in Eagleton, 160, 163–65; in Foucault, 123–24, 137–38; in Jameson, 148, 157; in Kant, 32–34; in leftist thought, 177–78; in Rorty, 197; in Said, 165–67, 171, 176
Culture, 2, 17–18, 21, 29–30, 140–41, 155, 160, 163, 165, 171, 197, 219, 224, 235, 248, 260. *See also* Social reproduction

Danto, Arthur, 71, 73, 101
Davidson, Donald, 188
Deconstruction of the self: in Deleuze, 81; in Derrida, 117–18, 120; in Foucault, 127, 129; in Lyotard, 190–91; in Nietzsche, 71, 75–76, 77, 83; in postmodern thought, 52, 156, 243
Deleuze, Gilles, 19, 42, 80–81, 86, 87, 90, 182, 191
De Man, Paul, 26, 54–55, 146–47
Democracy, 14, 15, 21, 28–30, 115, 163, 198–99, 201, 212–13, 217, 225–26, 229–35, 256, 264, 267, 269, 271–74
Derrida, Jacques, 2, 19, 23, 24, 25–26, 28, 43, 74, 75, 89–121, 122, 123, 124, 129, 131, 134, 143, 146, 150, 173, 174, 180, 182, 193, 194, 196, 205, 210, 214, 222, 234, 237, 238, 279

Descartes, René, 44, 204, 210
Dewey, John, 191
Dews, Peter, 19, 127, 136, 183, 217–18
Différance, 90, 92, 100–103, 105–10, 116, 120, 150, 173
Difference, 207, 211, 212, 215, 223–24, 244–45, 266; in Derrida, 91, 97–98, 106–7, 111, 120–21; in Hegel, 59–61, 93; in Jameson, 150, 154; in Kant, 34–36, 41, 120–21; in Nietzsche, 79, 81–82; in postmodern thought, 16–17, 43, 49–50, 60–61, 86–88; in Said, 176
Differential play, 28, 42–43, 69, 156, 191; in Derrida, 25–26, 90, 100–101, 102–9, 116, 119
Donoghue, Denis, 9
Dostoyevsky, Fyodor, 13, 178
Dreyfus, Herbert, 127
Durkheim, Emile, 13, 222
Dworkin, Ronald, 38

Eagleton, Terry, 2, 66, 147–48, 158–65, 174, 177, 180, 256
Eliot, George, 7, 13
Eliot, T. S., 4, 10
Engels, Frederick, 63, 64, 65, 68
Ethics, 15, 24, 28–29, 91–92, 109, 120, 128, 132, 212–13, 230–33, 236, 263–64, 268–69; in Foucault, 135–36, 139–41; in Lyotard, 201–3; in Rorty, 194–95; in Said, 168–73

Feminism, 20, 60, 108, 143, 146, 155–56, 174, 243, 259–62, 276
Feyerabend, Paul, 57, 195
Fiedler, Leslie, 30
Fish, Stanley, 180–81, 188, 196–97, 205, 209, 243
Flaubert, Gustave, 7
Foster, Hal, 11, 153, 155
Foucault, Michel, 2, 4, 23, 28, 42, 68–70, 74, 75, 77, 78, 79, 89, 92, 110, 121–45, 146–50 passim, 153, 157, 159, 161, 164, 167, 173, 174, 178, 180, 181, 182, 190, 194, 204, 205, 214, 219, 221, 223, 227, 237, 238, 239, 248, 250, 253, 254, 267, 268, 277, 278, 279
Foundational and/or antifoundational thought, 13–16, 23–24, 250, 265, 266–69, 275, 279; in Nietzsche, 71–75, 80, 87; in postmodern pragmatism, 180–81, 184, 192
Franco, Jean, 28
Fraser, Nancy, 92, 128
Freedom, 60, 67–69, 85–86, 165, 179, 203,

209, 216, 235, 247, 253, 255; in Derrida, 90–91, 101, 103–5, 110, 113–15, 120; in Foucault, 123–24, 128, 129–35, 137–38, 140, 145; in Hegel, 47, 51–53, 56–58; in Jameson, 151–52, 157–59; in Kant, 34–41; in Said, 176. *See also* Negative Freedom; Positive Freedom
Freud, Sigmund, 10, 16, 18, 48, 49, 104, 118, 151, 178–79, 219, 224, 244, 245
Friedman, Milton, 230, 266
Frye, Northrop, 146

Gallagher, Catherine, 170
Gans, Herbert, 30
Garfinkel, Harold, 13, 222
Gasché, Rodolphe, 97
Gass, William, 8
Geneaology, 95; in Foucault, 123–25, 128, 142–43; in Nietzsche, 77–79; in Said, 169–70
General will, 60, 234–35; in Kant, 38–39; in Rousseau, 56, 234
Giddens, Anthony, 13, 228, 239, 240, 242, 252, 257
Gintis, Herbert, 212, 225, 242, 244, 254, 271
Goethe, Johann W. von, 12, 76
Gouldner, Alvin, 1, 66, 251–52, 258, 278, 279
Graff, Gerald, 11, 111, 118
Greenberg, Clement, 9
Guattari, Felix, 19, 86, 90, 191

Habermas, Jürgen, 3, 4, 5, 7, 16, 57, 58, 73, 92, 113–14, 124, 128, 136, 181, 193, 203–5, 207–10, 218, 222, 223, 224, 231, 232, 233, 236, 239, 249–50, 253, 257, 263–66, 269
Hall, Stuart, 50, 214
Handelman, Susan, 99
Hayek, Frederick, 230, 266, 271
Hegel, G. W. F., 1, 4, 5, 6, 15, 19, 21, 22, 24, 27, 28, 31, 33, 35, 38, 43–61, 62, 63, 78, 80, 81, 82, 86–94 passim, 101, 102, 107, 109, 116, 118, 122, 150, 154, 169, 177, 181, 182, 191, 193, 194, 211, 215, 219, 220, 229, 230, 232–33, 247, 264
Heidegger, Martin, 94, 95–96, 117, 147, 191, 193, 243
Heraclitus, 82
Heritage, John, 222
Heterogeneity, 11–12, 15–17, 19–22, 24, 28–29, 49, 90, 97, 131, 135, 150, 156, 189, 203
Hill, Stephen, 65, 257

History, 235–36; in Hegel, 45–48; in Jameson, 150–53, 158–59; in Nietzsche, 77–79; in postmodern thought, 26–27
Hitler, Adolph, 12, 49
Holistic theory, 15, 22, 24–25, 27, 30, 43–45, 48, 52–53, 55, 57–58, 61, 62–64, 67, 135, 191–92, 194–95, 203, 216–17, 225, 229–30
Horkheimer, Max, 17–19, 20, 95–96
Hoy, David Couzzens, 127
Hume, David, 188, 208
Huyssen, Andreas, 10

Identity, 199–201, 211, 215–17, 219, 223, 235, 238, 241, 242–47, 253, 254, 259, 263, 269, 270–71, 276–77; in modernity, 248; in Rorty, 194
Ideology (and false consciousness), 49, 77, 167, 221–22, 237, 240, 242, 251, 256–62, 264, 268, 273; in Eagleton, 163–64; in Jameson, 148–49, 150–51; in Marx, 64–67
Incommensurability, 40, 73, 93, 182–83, 186, 187–91, 192, 195, 202–3, 209, 214, 216, 219, 250, 265
Individualism, 40–41, 177–80, 214, 216–17, 242–45, 248–52; in Eagleton, 159–65; in Foucault, 131–32, 139–44; Hegel's critique of, 50–51; in Nietzsche, 76, 83; in Rorty, 191–95; in Said, 165–66, 171, 173–76
Intellectuals, 1, 3, 5, 25, 87, 125–26, 128, 144–45, 160, 166, 186, 192, 205, 208, 210, 217, 220, 225, 233, 251–52, 257–58, 261, 262, 274–80
Interest and disinterestedness, 125, 129, 159–65, 166–68, 170, 173, 206, 242–43, 255, 256–57, 259
Interpretation: in Derrida, 90, 104, 111; in Foucault, 254; in Hegel, 33, 43–48, 53, 61; in Jameson, 151–52; in Nietzsche, 71, 77–78; in postmodern thought, 86, 265
Irigaray, Luce, 108
Irony, 23–24, 28–29, 42, 53–55, 81, 148, 151, 170, 176–80, 182, 184, 192–94, 245

Jackson, Jesse, 29
Jameson, Fredric, 2, 16, 22, 24, 89, 95, 145–59, 165, 168, 177, 180, 181, 183, 186, 190, 214–15, 224, 237, 246, 257
Jay, Martin, 9, 13, 62, 132, 150, 224, 232
Jencks, Charles, 29
Joas, Hans, 222
Johnson, Barbara, 146
Jones, Ann Rosalind, 108

Jordan, Michael, 241
Joyce, James, 8

Kadvany, John, 148
Kafka, Franz, 31, 238
Kandinsky, Wassily, 9
Kant, Immanuel, 1, 4, 23, 31–43, 44, 47, 61,
    79, 84, 89, 94, 120–21, 123–24, 128,
    137–38, 160, 183, 199, 204, 205–8 pas-
    sim, 214, 216, 250, 269
Keane, John, 199, 201
Kearney, Richard, 109, 110, 111
Kennedy, Ted, 271
Kierkegaard, Søren, 53–55, 99, 177–80 pas-
    sim, 245
Knapp, Steven, 180–81, 188, 196, 205, 209
Kojève, Alexandre, 217
Kolb, David, 95
Krauss, Rosalind, 10
Kucich, John, 148
Kuhn, Thomas, 120, 185, 195–96, 197, 221

Lacan, Jacques, 23, 114, 145, 150, 156, 179,
    217–18, 245
Lasch, Christopher, 179–80, 258
Le Corbusier, 10
Legitimation, 2, 3, 13–14, 24, 27, 28–29,
    56, 92, 112, 171–72, 183, 210, 213, 216,
    220, 222–23, 226–28, 233–35, 237, 241–
    42, 251, 254–59, 263, 264, 266–70, 278–
    80; in Foucault, 132–34; in Kant, 39, 41;
    in Lyotard, 190, 202–3; in Marx, 62, 64–
    65, 70; in Rorty, 192
Leibniz, G. W., 33
Lenin, V. I., 10, 125, 164
Lentricchia, Frank, 104, 126, 132, 146–48,
    159, 174
Levinas, Emmanuel, 91, 93, 98, 99, 100
Lévi-Strauss, Claude, 13, 151
Liberalism, 4, 6, 14, 15, 24, 32, 38, 40, 58,
    87, 132, 172–73, 192, 194, 198, 199, 203,
    212–14, 216, 219, 228–30, 242, 248, 255
Lifeworld, 4–5, 224, 236, 239–42, 249–51,
    259, 261–62, 264, 267
Lowenthal, Leo, 132
Lukács, Georg, 158
Lukes, Steven, 65, 67, 128, 256
Lyotard, Jean-François, 2, 27, 42, 93, 175,
    180–91, 195, 198–99, 201–4, 205, 209,
    214, 223, 250

McCarthy, Thomas, 23, 112, 113, 173, 218,
    241
McGowan, John, 11, 62, 248
Machiavelli, Niccolò, 227, 228
McKeon, Michael, 248

MacKinnon, Catherine, 24
Macpherson, C. B., 225, 226, 271
Mandel, Ernest, 155
Manilow, Barry, 29
Mannheim, Karl, 66
Man Ray, 11
Marcuse, Herbert, 9, 12, 57, 268
Marx, Karl, 1, 4, 27, 31, 49, 60, 61–70, 87,
    142, 145, 158, 160, 177, 228, 243, 246,
    251
Marxism, 10, 14, 17, 24, 28, 40, 47, 49, 62,
    148, 150, 183, 214, 220, 225, 227, 228,
    237, 254, 276
Matisse, Henri, 10
Mead, George Herbert, 222
Michaels, Walter Benn, 180–81, 188, 196,
    205, 209
Mill, John Stuart, 13
Miller, J. Hillis, 72, 146
Mitchell, W. J. T., 175
Modernism, 3, 6–12, 20, 22, 25, 29, 84–85,
    98, 102, 139, 155, 166, 180, 181, 184,
    186, 196–97, 210, 276
Modernity, 3–4, 6–7, 13, 16, 23, 32, 47, 63,
    124, 138–39, 184, 208, 234, 248–52, 258
Mondrian, Piet, 9, 10
Monolithic theories, 13, 16, 21, 24, 44, 48–
    49, 62, 70, 90, 95–96, 109, 119, 126, 135,
    148, 155, 161, 168, 173, 207, 217, 223,
    225, 244–45, 273
Morris, William, 13
Mouffe, Chantal, 273
Mozart, Wolfang Amadeus, 84
Mysticism, 46, 73, 92, 99, 101, 102, 115,
    117, 120, 184–85

Nabokov, Vladimir, 193
Naismith, James, 241
Napoleon, 49
Negative freedom, 2, 8, 15, 52, 54–56, 68,
    71, 79, 102, 159, 175, 177, 179, 198, 210,
    211, 218, 219, 228, 238, 240, 248, 251–
    52, 262–63, 273–77, 280; defined, 37–
    38, 40; in Derrida, 117–18, 120; in Ea-
    gleton, 165; in Foucault, 133, 134–35,
    138–39, 141–42, 144–45; in Lyotard,
    198; in Nietzsche, 82–87; in Rorty, 184,
    198. *See also* Freedom; Positive Freedom
Nehamas, Alexander, 75–76
New historicism, 146–47, 159
Newman, Charles, 9, 11
New social movements, 28, 143, 153, 158,
    272–73
Nietzsche, Friedrich, 1, 10, 16, 31, 47, 66,
    67, 68, 70–88, 90–91, 95, 97, 101, 107,

108, 118, 124, 128, 130, 148, 151, 170, 184, 188, 193, 194, 237
Norris, Christopher, 26, 106

Oakeshott, Michael, 200
Ortega y Gasset, José, 9
Other, the, 22, 240, 273; in Derrida, 90–96, 98–100, 102–4, 114–15, 121; in Foucault, 121–24; in leftist thought, 174–75, 221; in Lyotard, 182, 184–85

Parsons, Talcott, 222
Peirce, C. S., 222
Picasso, Pablo, 10
Pinkard, Terry, 44
Plato, 23, 51, 76, 89, 94, 204
Poggioli, Renato, 10
Politics, 7, 9–10, 15–16, 24, 28–29, 68, 87, 145, 178–80, 199, 211, 212, 217, 221–23, 241–42, 252, 261–64, 267–74, 276–79; conflict model of, 64, 67, 78, 130, 221–22, 237, 265–66; in Derrida, 110–15, 122; of difference, 53, 172–73; in Eagleton, 160; in Habermas, 207, 209–10; in Hegel, 49, 59–61; in Lyotard, 202; in Rorty, 194–95; in Said, 166, 172–73
Positive Freedom, 2, 15, 25, 29, 38, 68–70, 129–30, 141–42, 158, 180, 191, 217, 227–28, 236, 247, 262–64, 267, 270–71, 278; defined, 51–53. *See also* Freedom; Negative Freedom
Postmodernism: and ambivalence toward totality, 22–23, 49–50, 67; and commitment to negative freedom, 85–86, 210; and commitment to pluralism, 14–17, 19, 29, 172–73, 186, 202, 273; and consumerism, 118–19, 185–86; as critique of autonomy, 13, 16, 19–20, 25–27, 30, 255; as critique of modernism, 11, 21, 25, 85, 186; as critique of reason and humanism, 18–21, 42, 181–82, 225; and deconstruction, 20, 22; defined, 12–30, 52; and democracy, 28–30; and Derrida, 119–21; and Eagleton, 162–63; and Foucault, 121–22; and Habermas, 257; and Hegel, 49–51; and Jameson, 149–50, 155–59; and Kant, 42–43; and Lyotard, 182–84, 186; and Marx, 66–67; and Nietzsche, 85–88; and politics, 20–21, 24, 28, 211, 255–56, 273; and representation, 25–26, 95, 146, 157, 168; and Rorty, 181, 192, 197, 210
Poulantzas, Nicos, 225
Pound, Ezra, 147
Power, 28, 62–70, 219–21, 227, 237–38, 252–62, 263, 268, 269–70, 272–73; in Derrida, 76, 78–81; in Foucault, 68–70,

125–35, 140, 159; in leftist criticism, 147, 153, 157, 159, 161, 165; in Lyotard, 181–82, 203; in Marx, 63–65; in Nietzsche, 67, 76, 78–81; in Rorty, 198–99
Private language argument, 74, 81, 193, 195, 218
Public/private distinction, 40, 192–95, 203, 213–14, 253, 270–71
Putnam, Hilary, 31–32, 71, 195

Rabinow, Paul, 127, 132
Rajchman, John, 128
Ransom, John Crowe, 146
Realism, 6–8
Recognition, 15, 22, 59, 60, 102, 136, 207, 217–23, 224, 231–32, 235, 246–47, 248, 254; in Hegel, 51, 53; in Said, 169, 172
Reddy, William, 242, 243
Richardson, Samuel, 248
Ricoeur, Paul, 258
Robbins, Bruce, 166, 171
Robertson, Pat, 30
Robespierre, 56
Romanticism, 5–7, 48, 76–77, 110, 173
Rorty, Richard, 2, 21, 23, 27, 52, 75–76, 89, 96, 132, 180, 181, 184, 187, 188, 189, 191–201, 203, 208, 209, 210, 232, 233, 235, 259, 266, 279
Rousseau, Jean-Jacques, 52, 56–57, 233–34

Said, Edward W., 2, 124, 126, 127, 146, 147–48, 158, 159, 165–80, 184–85, 214, 221
Sandel, Michael, 35, 36, 242
Saussure, Ferdinand de, 43
Schönberg, Arnold, 10
Schulte-Sasse, Jochen, 10
Searle, John, 112
Sellars, Wilfrid, 194
Semiautonomy, 29, 135, 141, 154, 214–16, 217, 223, 226, 228–29, 231, 248, 252, 254, 255–56, 271–72
Shaw, G. B., 125
Shelley, P. B., 145, 148
Sheridan, Alan, 122, 123
Siebers, Tobin, 113, 212, 269
Silone, Ignazio, 241
Skinner, Quentin, 24, 227, 228
Smith, Adam, 20, 216, 243
Social constitution of the self, 51, 78, 86, 101, 113–14, 119, 147–48, 178–79, 190, 210, 211, 216–17, 218, 245–47, 252, 269; in Eagleton, 159, 161–64; in Foucault, 126–27, 128–30, 139–41; in Jameson, 156–57; in Said, 165. *See also* Identity

Social contract, 57, 216–19, 233–34; in
  Kant, 38–40
Social reproduction, 62, 236, 237–42, 252–
  53, 268; in Baudrillard, 18; in Habermas,
  249; in Jameson, 156
Socrates, 54, 91, 96
Spinoza, Benedict de, 94
Spivak, Gayatri Chakravorty, 23
Stallybrass, Peter, 121–22
State, the, 225–30, 271–72
Surrealism, 10–11, 118

Taylor, Charles, 52, 56–57, 92, 127, 128,
  132, 247
Thébaud, Jean-Loup, 184
Theory, 23, 204–10, 248, 250–52, 258, 269,
  277–78; and its consequences, 208, 275–
  76, 279; as critical and transcendental,
  32–33, 41–42, 61, 106, 125, 206–7, 269;
  in Derrida, 106–7, 110; in Foucault, 123–
  25, 128, 142–43; in Jameson, 148–49,
  152, 154; postmodernism's suspicion of,
  22–25, 42–43, 50, 148, 165; pragmatism's
  attack on, 180–83, 186, 204–5, 209; in
  Said, 165–68. *See also* Criticism
Thoreau, Henry David, 176, 228
Tocqueville, Alexis de, 13, 199, 249
Tolerance, 34, 199–201, 223, 228
Tolstoy, Leo, 7, 13
Tönnies, F., 249
Touraine, Alain, 257, 265–66, 273
Tragedy, 177, 237; in Derrida, 90–91, 98,

113, 115–16, 119; in Foucault, 128; in
  Jameson, 151; in Nietzsche, 75–77; in
  Said, 171, 175–76
Turner, Bryan S., 65, 257

Unger, Roberto Mangabeira, 24, 57, 222,
  223, 236–38, 239

Van Den Abbeele, Georges, 191
Violence, 91, 92, 96, 98, 102, 105, 109,
  110–18, 202, 221, 222–23, 234–35, 263,
  267, 270, 274

Wagner, Richard, 84
Walzer, Michael, 170–71, 214, 235
Weber, Max, 13, 212, 223, 224
Wellmer, Albrecht, 52, 59
West, Cornel, 16, 59, 60, 80, 149
White, Allon, 121–22
White, Hayden, 27
Wilde, Oscar, 9, 196
Williams, Raymond, 2, 28, 214
Wimsatt, W. K., 146
Wittgenstein, Ludwig, 13, 57, 74, 118, 126,
  188, 192–95 passim, 198, 205, 218, 233
Wolin, Richard, 9

Yeats, W. B., 23, 126, 274
Young, Iris Marion, 53

Zola, Emile, 7

Library of Congress Cataloging-in-Publication Data

McGowan, John, 1953–
    Postmodernism and its critics / John McGowan.
      p. cm.
    Includes bibliographical references and index.
    ISBN 0-8014-2494-1 (alk. paper).—ISBN 0-8014-9738-8 (pbk. alk. paper)
    1. Postmodernism (Literature)   I. Title.
  PN98.P67M37 1991
  149—dc20   90-55758